The Secret of Chabad

Inside the World's Most Successful Jewish Movement

Toby

David Eliezrie

THE SECRET OF
CHABAD

**INSIDE THE WORLD'S MOST
SUCCESSFUL JEWISH MOVEMENT**

The Toby Press

The Secret of Chabad
Inside the World's Most Successful Jewish Movement

First Edition, 2015

The Toby Press LLC
POB 8531, New Milford, CT 06776–8531, USA
& POB 2455, London WIA 5WY, England
www.tobypress.com

© David Eliezrie 2015

Photos 2, 3, 9, photo of the Rebbe ©
by, and used with permission of, Jewish Educational
Media, Inc., The Living Archive

ISBN 978-1-59264-370-7, *hardcover*

A CIP catalogue record for this title is
available from the British Library

Printed and bound in the United States

Contents

Introduction

An Encounter in Brooklyn

It was a wintry New York night in January of 1966. Some high-school and college-age rabbinical students from Montreal[1] were spending their last evening in Brooklyn. They had come as part of a spiritual pilgrimage to what is known, simply, as 770. The name was taken from the address of the three-story red brick building located at 770 Eastern Parkway in the Crown Heights section of Brooklyn, New York, the center of the Chabad-Lubavitch[2] Movement. At the time, this Chassidic community was still small, but it held on to the historic Jewish neighborhood, even as white flight lured many Jews to the green lawns of Long Island. It had been fifteen years since Rabbi Menachem Mendel Schneerson had become the Seventh Lubavitcher Rebbe.

The group had made the journey from Montreal to Brooklyn to mark the yartziet (Yiddish for "anniversary of the passing") of the Sixth Rebbe, Yosef Yitzchak Schneersohn. Over the few days of their visit, the students had attended a farbrengen (a Chassidic gathering), and the fifteen high-school students had enjoyed a private group meeting with the Rebbe. Now, the night before returning to

Montreal, they – and guests from other communities, clustered in the small synagogue just off the main entrance waiting for the evening service, Maariv, to begin. They wanted to see the Rebbe for the last time before their early morning departure.

One of the teens, who was only fourteen at the time, had just begun attending the Lubavitcher High School in Montreal that year. He arrived at 770 a few minutes before the service was to begin. He tried to squeeze into the sanctuary, but that was impossible, since it was full to capacity. The overflowing crowd blocked the second entrance at the end of the hallway, so he stationed himself in the lobby that straddled the synagogue and small foyer that led into the Rebbe's office. At the very least, he thought, he would see the Rebbe as he walked across the fifteen-foot-wide lobby. Suddenly, there was a hush. The Rebbe opened the door of the foyer and strode across the lobby. Holding the synagogue door open, standing like a sentry, was the Rebbe's secretary, Rabbi Chaim Mordechai Aizik Hodakov.[3] Caught up in the emotion of the moment, the teen suddenly turned and followed closely behind the Rebbe. The Rebbe entered the synagogue, and Rabbi Hodakov started to close the door. The teen suddenly found himself halfway in and halfway out with the door closing on him. Since the Rebbe was always the last one to enter, those inside, surprised that the young boy had broken the protocol, made motions with their hands for him to back out. The boy was confused. Like someone stuck on a road with headlights glaring at him, he did not know exactly what to do.

The Rebbe turned to see what the commotion was. He noticed the high-school student (without the classic black hat), whose face reflected bewilderment. The Rebbe motioned to Rabbi Hodakov to open the door and for the teen to stand next to him during the service. Standing at the Rebbe's side, the young boy watched as the Rebbe opened the pages of a worn prayer book and intently prayed.

The next morning, the group boarded the buses. The trip organizers had chartered a regular school bus in an effort to save a few dollars, but by the time they reached Saratoga Springs, four hours north of New York, the wisdom of that decision seemed doubtful. The bus broke down, and it would take hours to repair. The students found refuge in a local Conservative synagogue, Congregation Shaarei Tefillah, just a mile off the highway. Later that afternoon, the pupils of the synagogue's Hebrew School began to arrive. One of the more outgoing rabbinical students on the broken-down bus, twenty-year-old Moshe Yosef Engel, had befriended the Hebrew-School director. Within a short time, Engel stood at the front of the room dazzling the children in this small Jewish community with stories and song.

I was that fourteen-year-old high-school student. Earlier that year, my family had moved to Montreal, and I had enrolled in the Chabad-Lubavitch Yeshiva just down the block. It was a bit more religiously intense than the Modern-Orthodox day school I had attended in California. I had joined the New York trip with a sense of adventure, but I had not expected the two events on the trip to set the tone for my life. The Rebbe saw a confused teenager, not wearing Chassidic garb, ill at ease, and out of place. Instinctively, he reached out to me, breaking the protocol, taking away the angst I felt at that moment. Then the next day, I witnessed the power of the Rebbe's teachings and how his students view their lives as a series of opportunities to inspire others: Moshe Engel, instead of complaining about being stuck in upstate New York, seized the moment to touch another soul.

In the second half of the twentieth century, the Seventh Lubavitcher Rebbe, Rabbi Menachem Mendel Schneerson, would open the doors of Judaism for millions. He would do it Jew by Jew. It would be slow, painstaking work. He would have to overcome skepticism from his own Chassidim, from Orthodox Jews, and from the broader Jewish community. Few envisioned that in the process, the Rebbe would redefine Judaism in the modern age as a balance of tradition and compassion, observance and responsibility. He would inspire thousands of his disciples to become his shluchim (emissaries), to take up the mantle of Jewish leadership in over eighty countries, as well as countless others who did not consider themselves followers. A small Chassidic group, hammered by the Holocaust and the harsh hand of Communism in Russia, would become the largest Jewish organization in the world[4] and the fastest-growing in the United States.[5]

It would be a daunting task. There were many challenges, both internal and external. A Chassidic community whose historic focus was on spirituality and scholarship would be redirected toward activism and responsibility for Jewish destiny. A Jewish community whose level of Jewish scholarship and observance had weakened[6] would learn to appreciate the timeless teachings of the Torah and traditions of their ancestors. In the US, Orthodoxy had retreated to the sidelines as communal leadership marginalized tradition. Change could not happen from within, so there would be no choice but to create a totally new community infrastructure, costing billions. In Europe, Australia, South America, and South Africa, more open to observance,[7] Chabad would have to overcome local opposition as it slowly became an essential part of the communal leadership. During Communist times, while millions were trapped in the Soviet Union, the Rebbe's underground operatives preserved the community. With the fall of the Soviet Union, Judaism would emerge from the shadows. Chabad would take the lead in rebuilding from the bottom up. Schools, synagogues, and communities would have to be recreated after seventy years of Communist rule. In Israel, where politics and religion split the country, Chabad would take the role of a unifier, straddling the societal divide. In smaller remote countries, such as the Congo, Thailand, Tunisia, and the Caribbean Islands, Chabad would provide vital leadership and new strategies to preserve Jewish life in shrinking communities.

Creating this Jewish renaissance would entail a paradigm shift. Since Jews began to wander the globe after the destruction of the Temple in Jerusalem in 70 CE, the position of Jews in many countries has been precarious. Religious and human rights were subject to the whims of kings and despots. Anti-Semitism, culminating with the Holocaust, shaped a communal culture of defensiveness. The Rebbe instilled in his followers a bold new self-confidence. As Dennis Prager[8] says: "Chabad changed the outlook of Judaism that had been prevalent for two thousand years."

An army of rabbis and rebbitzens would have to be trained and encouraged to move to the four corners of the earth. They would live far from friends and family, dedicating their lives to Jewish destiny and the welfare of others. They would need to learn to remain true to their ideals and raise their own families outside the classical religious community, and, at the same time, create environments of openness to Jews of all backgrounds, and a culture of welcoming.

Never before in history[9] did a single Jewish leader undertake the task of Jewish renaissance on a global scale, attempting to reach every Jew in the world. As Great Britain's former chief rabbi, Jonathan Sacks, said, "The Nazis hunted down every Jew with hate and the Rebbe hunted every Jew with love."

Few understood the immense scope of the Rebbe's vision. Those who did thought the goal difficult, if not impossible, to attain.

The historian Dr. Jack Wertheimer, remarked to me some time ago, "We are all wondering about the mystery of Chabad." Hopefully this book will unveil that secret.

Chapter One

Gabi and Rivkie

I t was a crisp fall morning in Kathmandu, perched in the mountains of Nepal. Chani[1] Lifshitz was starting her morning on the day before Thanksgiving, Wednesday, November 26, 2008. As is often the case for young mothers, things were hectic for Chani as she went about getting the four kids up, dressed, and ready for their day. When things calmed down a bit, she lifted the phone to call her BFF, Rivkie Holtzberg, who was not around the corner in a suburban housing track. Rivkie was a thousand miles away, across in the Himalayas in the bustling city of Mumbai. Chani and Rivkie, two Chabad rebbitzens, shared the responsibility of Jewish leadership in remote communities with their husbands. They had met accidentally in Bangkok five years earlier. Chani was waiting for her visa to return to Nepal. Rivkie was teaching in the local Jewish school, but was about to leave for Mumbai to launch a Chabad Center. Both were Israelis. Chani was raised in the hustle of Rechovot, part of the Tel Aviv urban sprawl. Rivkie grew up in Afula, the dusty agricultural town at the center of the hot Yizre'el Valley in Israel's north.

Both women came from Chabad families, but had never met before Bangkok, where, as Chani[2] put it, "We clicked." Both lived in exotic, but similar worlds: young religious women, raising families in Nepal and India, far from friends and family. "There was no one religious like us," says Chani. Nepal was one of the only countries in the world without an indigenous Jewish community. In Mumbai, Rivkie and her husband, Gabi, were among only a few religious Jews, and Gabi was the only rabbi in the city. Thirty-five hundred Jews lived among twenty million Indians in Mumbai with no anti-Semitism. The local Jewish population was aging, but far from observant. By the time Rivkie arrived with her husband, Chani had been in Kathmandu for six years, and she offered to mentor Rivkie. "I was a relatively veteran emissary in this neck of the woods," Chani explains. "Rivkie was searching for knowledge, and she wanted to do everything in the best possible way."

In Nepal, the mission of Chani and her husband Chezki were the thousands of Israeli backpackers[3] trekking this mountainous region. Many young Israelis take a "shnat chofesh" (a year-long break after their army service or after university). They are looking for adventure and an escape from the pressure cooker of Israeli society. Gabi described these wandering Israelis: "They come here to do everything the army didn't allow them to do. Their shoes had to be polished and tied – here they wear sandals. They had to cut their hair – here they grow their hair long."

A string of Chabad Centers[4] popped up as outposts[5] of hospitality for these wanderers. Most secular Israelis feel comfortable in Chabad, whose Judaism is non-judgmental. The Shabbat dinners and the Hebrew-speaking rabbis and rebbitzens remind them of home. Passover in Kathmandu has become legend for young Israelis. Trekkers often plan their journeys to reach the Chabad House in Nepal for the holiday celebration. In Mumbai, the mission of Rivkie and her husband Gabi was more diverse. They split their attention among the local community, business people coming to Mumbai who needed kosher food, and the Israeli travelers.

That pre-Thanksgiving morning's conversation between Chani and Rivkie was foreboding. "I had a sense of unease," Chani says.

"The conversation was unusual, almost fatalistic. Rivkie had been different for the last month, she had always been very optimistic, but now, something was troubling her. Later on, her mother told me she sensed it also."

Rivkie was under strain. Her second child was sick in Israel, where the hospitals were equipped to handle his disease, so Rivkie and her husband were commuting from Mumbai to Israel to take care of him. The newest baby, Moshie, was not sleeping well; there were financial pressures involved in a new building they had purchased.

Rivkie carried her challenges on the inside; Chani was one of her few outlets. Erin Beser,[6] an American intern for the JDC,[7] the American Jewish organization, was a regular at the Chabad Center. Beser says, "There was always a smile on Rivkie's face; she acted like she had no problems. We didn't know she had a sick child, she never mentioned it; finally someone else in the community told us."

Chani tried to lift her spirits. "We talked about plans for the building dedication. I would come there for a week, and then she would come to Nepal to help me in a few months when I was due to give birth." Rivkie wanted to take a break that day. "I suggested that she go to the Taj Hotel[8] to sit in the lobby and relax a bit."

Mumbai is one of the world's largest cities – sprawling, dirty, children begging on every street corner, some just hundreds of yards from luxury hotels. Polytheism is still prevalent. Rivkie was far away from her family and friends. But despite the unease these elements of her life in India aroused in her, Rivkie was deeply committed to her shlichus, her mission. Her cousin Penina Glitzenstein,[9] a Chabad emissary in the Ukraine, says, "She always told me how great and interesting life is helping others." Rivkie hosted people nightly, and looked effervescent on a video shot by a visitor.[10] "It's wonderful," she said. "In Israel you don't host people every day." Beser says, "She was always full of ideas to do more for the community. She had a sense of mission. To Rivkie, her first concern was everyone else."

Off and on that day, Chani and Rivkie spoke. The last time was just after 7:00 p.m. "She told me what she was preparing for each guest for dinner. This was typical Rivkie, catering to the individual needs of each guest." The rainbow of the Jewish world was at her table, Rabbi Leibish Teitelbaum, age thirty-seven, from Jerusalem and Rabbi Ben Zion Croman, age twenty-eight, from Brooklyn, in India to certify kosher food production. Yocheved Orpaz, sixty-two, who came to thank the Holtzbergs for their help. Norma Rabinovich-Shvarzblat, forty-nine, from Mexico, planning to fulfill her lifelong dream of immigrating to Israel the next day. David Bialka, an Israeli diamond dealer.

Just before dinner, Chani received an e-mail. Rivkie was wondering, "What color should I paint the bedrooms in our apartment on the sixth floor of the Chabad House?" Chani had some ideas and tried contacting her again, but it was too late.

As Rivkie was preparing dinner, a fishing trawler[11] hovered a few miles off the coast of Mumbai. The five sailors on board had been killed when it was hijacked three days earlier near Jakhau, thirty miles south of Pakistan, seized by the Islamic terror group Lashkar-e-Taiba (LeT),[12] literally, "Army of the Pure," based in Pakistan with links to both Pakistani intelligence and Al Qaida.

The trawler headed south five hundred miles toward Mumbai, India's window to the West. During the journey, the group was in constant contact by satellite phone with their handlers in Pakistan. The ten terrorists on board had undergone rigorous training for months in Pakistan. They made up five lethal teams, each with a different target in the city. In a phone conversation picked up by Indian intelligence, the handler in Pakistan told his men before they began their attacks: "This is a struggle between Islam and the unbelievers."

The ship arrived off the coast of Mumbai around 2:00 p.m. The terrorists waited onboard until darkness engulfed the ocean. They hugged each other and prayed together, then boarded a raft that moved silently in the water for the last five miles toward the beach on the southern tip of Mumbai. Fishing boats dotted the water, masking their incursion. Not far away were the five prominent targets: the posh Taj and Oberoi hotels, the railway station, the popular Leopold Café, and the Chabad House.

The attack was meticulously planned. David Headley,[13] an American-born Pakistani, later arrested by the FBI and tried in Chicago,[14] was LeT's spy. Headley's US passport allowed him to travel to India eight times to survey different targets. The Chabad House was added only after his last visit in August 2008. The terrorists thought the Chabad House was a base for the Mossad, the Israeli intelligence service – probably because the place was almost always full of Israelis. Erin Beser says, "The guys from EL Al, the members of the consulate staff were all welcome on Shabbat." And Israeli backpackers were coming and going all the time. Rabbi Yosef Chaim Kantor[15] of Bangkok says, "We are a religious organization[16] providing hospitality and educational and religious programs, and are not involved in any government activity." Headley later testified,[17] "[LeT] considers the Jewish people a number one target." The handler in Pakistan told the terrorists by phone, "Every person you kill there (Chabad House) is worth fifty killed in the hotels."[18] Headley did extensive surveillance, "I did not go inside; it was a very small establishment and would serve the purpose of the stronghold."

The boat reached the shore around 8:30 p.m. The terrorists split up into five groups. One continued in the raft to the oceanfront Oberoi Hotel in Nariman Point. Three other groups, of two terrorists each, hailed taxis to the Taj Hotel, the train station and the Leopold Café. Each team left a bomb in its taxi, set to go off a half hour later, in order to add confusion to the attacks. Two gunmen, Abu Amar and Babar Imran, headed out by foot toward the Chabad House just five hundred yards away.

In the Chabad House, things had settled down after dinner. David Bialka[19] from the Israeli beach town of Netanya was getting ready for bed in a fourth-floor guest room. Sandra Samuel, Rivkie's Indian assistant and nanny to young Moshie, was with Jacky the cook in the ground-floor storage area putting leftovers in the fridge. In the third-floor synagogue, Rabbis Ben Zion Croman and Leibish Teitelbaum were studying. Gabi and Rivkie were nearby. The two other women, Yocheved and Norma, were about to leave after dinner.

After making their way through the darkened alleyways, Amar and Imran arrived at the Chabad House around 9:00 p.m. There was a guard on duty every day, but, strangely, that night he had disappeared. Sandra, who was on the ground floor, heard some noise outside. Thinking it was some kids shooting off fireworks, she opened the door and the two terrorists pushed their way inside, shooting toward her and Jacky. The nanny and cook ran down the hallway into a storage room and closed the door. Sandra phoned Rivkie on the third floor to warn her of the attackers. On the phone she heard the voices of Gabi, Rivkie, and others all talking at once.

When the terrorists entered the third floor, they spotted Rabbis Teitelbaum and Croman studying. Teitelbaum was killed instantly, Croman put up a fight, but, hit by bullets, he succumbed. Their books remained open and covered with blood. Hearing the attack, Gabi called the security officer at the Israeli Consul General telling him quickly, "The situation is not good – terrorists…" The phone was cut off. Gabi was wounded in the leg; later that night he tied a tourniquet in an attempt to stymie the bleeding. The terrorists started taking shots from the windows. Neighbors heard Rivkie's voice screaming from the Chabad House later that night, "Save us, save us!" and yelling out her husband's name, "Gabi, Gabi!" The terrorists seized the two other women, Norma and Yocheved, and moved them up to the fourth floor.

Upstairs, Bialka was reading when he heard the shooting. He realized that the only escape was though a bathroom window. He climbed down the pipes that ran along the outside of the building. Later, he told the story to Israeli TV.[20] "I went down to the ground and hoped they would not notice me. Glass was breaking from every direction. When I reached the ground, the local Indians were sure I was a terrorist and knocked me down." The police arrested him, then released him the next day. Traumatized from the experience, Bialka fled India and arrived home in Netanya, Israel, before the Sabbath.

Sandra passed the night behind the jammed door of the service kitchen on the second floor together with Jacky. "I got down low between the wall and the fridge." She was surprised the terrorists never came back for them, later telling an interviewer,[21] "Maybe they thought we had run away through the back door."

The news began to dribble out of Mumbai. On Wednesday morning, a reporter contacted Rabbi Motti Seligson, director of Media Relations at Lubavitch headquarters on Eastern Parkway in Brooklyn. "Something is going on in Mumbai; check up on your people on the ground." Seligson started to reach out, but there was little information. He called both sets of parents to verify that Gabi and Rivkie were in Mumbai. No one was answering any of the numbers in the Chabad House or the cell phones.

In Afula, Rivkie's mother, Yehudit Rosenberg, got a call around 8:00 p.m. Israel time from Israel's Cheder Matzav, the government's emergency control center, asking if they could verify her phone number but gave her no information. As the rumors intensified, Yehudit[22] called the control center back. "They told me there was an attack in India but they did not give me any details, nor that the Chabad House was a target." The family was on edge. "We were worried. At 2:30 a.m. (5:00 a.m. in Mumbai), we got a call from Gabi's cousin in New York telling us the terrorists had entered the Chabad House; things were confusing." In the morning, the news became tragically clearer. The Israeli media arrived and encamped outside the Rosenbergs' home.

Gabi's father, Rabbi Nachman Holtzberg,[23] was home that Wednesday in the Crown Heights section of Brooklyn. "Late in the afternoon, my wife called. Her sister had seen a media report that there was an attack in Mumbai, and terrorists had entered the Chabad House." Holtzberg tried to reach his son but no one answered. "I realized the situation wasn't good." Holtzberg headed to Chabad's main synagogue on Eastern Parkway in Brooklyn, New York. Together with others who had flocked there, they prayed through the night.

As the news turned bleaker, a crisis-management team was assembled. Seligson[24] filled a dozen of the workstations in Chabad. org, on the fourth floor of the office building adjacent to 770, with a team of young rabbis. They set up communications with India and began monitoring the media and government sources of information. They decided to call the local hospitals, but they didn't speak the language. An e-mail[25] was dispatched on the internal Chabad mailing list read by thousands of rabbis around the world. Cryptically worded, not wanting to reveal exactly the reason a translator was needed, it asked for someone who spoke the native language of India. Professor P. V. Viswanath[26] of Pace University volunteered and headed from his home in New Jersey to Brooklyn.

The two senior executives of Chabad were each dealing with personal adversity. Rabbi Yehuda Krinsky, the Rebbe's secretary for over forty years, and chairman of Merkos, the Chabad educational arm that operates Centers in over eighty counties, was sitting Shivah (the week of mourning) for his brother. Rabbi Moshe Kotlarsky, the vice-chairman, who travels extensively and is intimately involved with the network of Centers around the world, was at the hospital, his father on the edge of life. Seligson, along with Rabbi Mendy Sharfstein,[27] director of the security office in New York, was constantly updating Rabbis Krinsky and Kotlarsky.

That evening in California, I got a call from the team in New York asking me to join the Crisis Management Team. For the next thirty-some hours, we had an open conference call, and we needed someone on the ground in Mumbai. Late that night, Seligson[28] contacted the CNN International News desk in Atlanta. An acquaintance was on duty and she gave him the cell number of Raksha Shetty,[29] a CNN-IBN reporter in India who was broadcasting live outside the Chabad House. During the coming hours and days, we spoke to her during the breaks in her live updates. She provided crucial details and background to the team in New York.

After midnight, FBI agents arrived at Chabad headquarters. The agents were deeply impressed with the professionalism of the operation mounted in Brooklyn, telling Seligson, "You have better information than we do at the FBI office."

CNN's Shetty was helpful, but we still needed our own representative on the ground. Rabbi Dov Goldberg[30] was at the Chabad House in Goa, an hour away from Mumbai. He had spoken to Gabi at 7:00 p.m., and sent him a text message later, but did not get a reply. Around 3:00 a.m., the phone rang waking up Goldberg in Goa; it was Chabad headquarters in New York. "They told me that the terrorists were in the Chabad House and I should fly out on the first plane in the morning."

In Washington, Rabbi Levi Shemtov, who directs Chabad's American Friends of Lubavitch DC office, tried calling Gabi's cell phone. Someone answered speaking a foreign language. Realizing it must have been the terrorists, he needed a translator.[31] Viswanath, the Indian translator who was now in Brooklyn, got on the phone. Shemtov called Gabi's cell phone again. I monitored the call from

California. Viswanath had some trouble with the dialect of Urdu that originated in Pakistan. The caller said his name was Imran; he claimed no one had been hurt. "Put us in touch with the Indian government and we will let the hostages go," he said. Shemtov[32] called the Indian embassy in Washington and tried to reach someone of authority in India, Viswanath said later in a newspaper interview. "When we tried to call the Indian authorities, we were bounced from one office to another. The calls continued on and off till around 5:00 a.m. New York time, and ultimately they failed to connect the terrorist in Mumbai with officials in India."

The Crisis Management Team in the US feared that the terrorists could be following the media reports. Later it was revealed that there were 181[33] calls between the controllers in Pakistan and the terrorists in Mumbai. Independent community blogs[34] were asked to suspend any reporting. The spokesman of Chabad in Israel was being interviewed on Israeli TV. I called his associate and told him to pull him off the air. We feared any detail emanating from Chabad sources could be used by the terrorists in Mumbai. We began issuing reports on Chabad.org, the movement's official site. Each piece of information[35] was carefully vetted to ensure that no one in the Chabad House would be put at risk.

An assault was needed to free the hostages, but the Indian authorities seemed paralyzed. A commando unit had been mobilized in Israel and was preparing for the six-hour flight to Mumbai. Two Israeli consular officials were on the ground not far from the Chabad House, observing the situation. In the middle of the night, the crisis team in Brooklyn received a notification[36] from a senior Israeli government official: the Indian government rejected Israeli assistance. Only the Indian military could save those alive in the Chabad House.

The terrorists were holed up on the fourth floor with the two female hostages during the phone calls with us in the US.[37] Sandra Samuel, the Indian nanny, was still hiding in the second-floor kitchen. Around 11:00 a.m. India time, she heard a baby cry. "Suddenly I hear the baby calling me, 'Sandra, Sandra, Sandra.'"[38] Moshie was a few days shy of his second birthday. Opening the door of the kitchen, Sandra saw that the staircase leading up to the second floor had been blown up by the terrorists. Climbing over the rubble, Sandra moved up to the third floor where the baby was crying. A few hours later, she told Israeli reporter, Aimee Ginsburg,[39] "The baby was standing next to his mother, who was lying on her side. His father was lying next to her on his stomach. Their eyes were closed, unconscious. Next to them, I saw the legs of another man sticking out from under the table, with blood. Baby's pants also had a big circle of blood. The terrorists must have been upstairs. I grabbed the baby and ran out." Five hours later, sitting in the Israeli Consulate, Sandra was full of misgiving, regretting not going back into the Chabad House a second time. "I should have tried to help Rabbi and Rivkie. I should have checked to see how they were. What kind of person am I just to have run out?"

In Afula, the report that a woman ran out of the Chabad House with a baby gave Yehudit Rosenberg[40] great hope. "Suddenly we heard that a European-looking woman and child had escaped from the Chabad House. I was so happy, I thought it must be Rivkie and Moshie. They were saved, but what about Gabi, I wondered." In a short time, the news changed. Yehudit heard the woman was not European, and realized that her daughter was still in the Chabad House. She thought, "At least Moshie was saved." The Rosenbergs decided to head to Mumbai, and they finally arrived early Friday morning.

Not far from another of the targets, the train station, where dozens lay dead and wounded, police captured a member of the terrorist team, Abu Jujahid. The Pakistani handlers[41] ordered the terrorists in the Chabad House to open negotiations with the Israelis and use the two female hostages to free Jujahid. Discovering the number of the Israeli Consulate on Gabi's phone, they made the call. One of the Pakistani controllers even spoke to one of the hostages in the Chabad House, urging her to help with the negotiations. "You will be home for your Sabbath," he promised. When this failed, the Pakistani voice on the telephone ordered the terrorists in Mumbai to kill the hostages.

By Friday morning, the terrorists had been subdued in the two hotels and in the train station, but the Chabad House remained under their control. A close friend of Gabi and Rivkie, Dr. Aron Abraham, and some Jewish volunteers, began moving toward the Chabad House on foot. Late Friday afternoon, they crouched in the narrow street outside the Chabad House waiting for the final assault to begin. For hours, there had been shooting. Indian soldiers were firing into the Chabad House from nearby buildings.[42] Just before sunset, the Indian commandos began their final attack. Soldiers dropped from helicopters and another group assaulted the building from below. As the Sabbath began in Mumbai, the shooting stopped. After sunset, Dr. Abraham entered the building. Tear gas lingered in the air; hand grenades littered the floor. Confirmation[43] was passed on to Chabad in New York that there were no survivors.

It was Friday morning in California. Sitting in my office, I heard the news. The last few days had been a roller coaster of emotions. There were moments when we had much hope and others when we secretly feared the worst. Still, we did not want to believe that the end would be so heartbreakingly catastrophic. The reality sank in, the anguish intense. I just slumped down and began to cry.

Dr. Abraham[44] had been studying for conversion to Judaism, and the conversion process would be completed some months later in Israel. Later Friday night,[45] he accompanied the remains of those slain in the Chabad House as they were transferred to JJ hospital, where all the bodies of those killed in the attack were being placed. Prior to leaving the Chabad House, he covered each of the bodies with a talit (prayer shawl). In the hospital, he asked that Jewish tradition be respected regarding any unnecessary autopsies.[46]

As Shabbat began at sunset in Mumbai, the Rosenbergs, Moshie, Sandra, and others found refuge in homes of the Israeli consular officials. At that point, the battle at the Chabad House was still grinding on, the final outcome unclear. There was a sense that the news was bad; still a feeling of hope lingered. Yehudit, Rivkie's mother,[47] says, "We did not want to give up, we were filled with faith."

Yehudit remembers those moments: "We lit the candles. With tears and prayers, we entered into Shabbat." She prayed that women around the world would light candles for Rivkie's sake. "Our hosts already knew late Friday night the bad news. At eleven the next morning, they shared the information with us. Afterward, my husband began to pray the Sabbath morning prayers. I will never forget the Av Harachamim." This is the prayer said every Shabbat and on holidays during the Yizkor Memorial Service. Composed in the wake of eleventh-century crusades, the prayer recalls the death and destruction that European Jewry suffered as armies driven by religious zealotry marched across Europe on their way to the Holy Land. Its poignant message, reaching through the centuries, is: "May the all-merciful Father remember with mercy the pious, the upright, and the perfect ones and the holy communities who gave their lives for the sanctification of the Divine name." As her husband, Shimon, uttered these words, Yehudit says, "He was full of tears." Her voice drops off as she tells me of those terrible moments. Finally there are no words; we sit in her home in Afula, in absolute silence.

In New York, Shabbat would not begin for a few hours. The press converged on Lubavitch World headquarters. Rabbi Yehuda Krinsky had completed his observance of Shivah the previous day. Now he was faced with the task of consoling others. The world paused, focused on Brooklyn, where CNN and other networks were broadcasting live. In a voice laced with deep emotion, Rabbi Krinsky[48] said, "With profound sadness and deep sorrow, we received the definitive news, just a short while ago, confirming the brutal murder of two of our finest, Rabbi Gavriel Noach, twenty-nine, and Rivkah Holtzberg, twenty-eight, our dear representatives in Mumbai, India, who served their community with love and devotion. We express deeply heartfelt condolences to the parents and family of this beautiful young couple, and to the families and loved ones of each of those who have been brutally murdered in this senseless, barbaric attack. In the traditional Jewish blessing to mourners: May G-d Almighty comfort you among all the mourners of Zion and Jerusalem."

Rabbi Krinsky seemed to sense Rivkie's mother's private prayer as she lit the candles in Mumbai. He added a special request, asking Jews around the world to do a mitzvah (a good deed, a personal act of goodness) in their memory. "As the Shabbat approaches, we call upon Jewish women and girls to brighten the profound darkness the world is witnessing, and usher in the Shabbat by lighting the traditional Shabbat candles, eighteen minutes before sunset. I am certain that this would be Gabi's and Rivkie's wish."

The tragedy in Mumbai cut a deep wound; Chabad Rabbis and Rebbitzens around the world were stunned. Their brother and sister had been killed. Absolute evil had encountered absolute goodness, and this time, evil had prevailed. Across the globe, hundreds of thousands, seeing the deep pain and anguish, shared the despair of their community leaders. A chord had been touched. The loss in Mumbai revealed the intrinsic link that connects Jews and humanity from all over.

In our Chabad Center in Yorba Linda, California, we were numb with sadness. We sent out an e-mail with Rabbi Krinsky's request. As the sun began setting in Yorba Linda, dozens of women – soccer moms and seniors, religious and secular, many who rarely frequent a synagogue – converged on our Center. They welcomed the Shabbat together with the traditional ceremony of lighting the Shabbat candles. Singing songs, and sharing words of inspiration, they were a microcosm of communities around the globe. The Jewish people mourned, but in a unique way, by lighting up the world with one more mitzvah.

As the sun set Saturday evening in Mumbai, and Shabbat ended, Israel's Ambassador to India, Mark Sofer, who had arrived Friday from Delhi, told Rabbi Goldberg that the Indian government wanted to use the bodies for their investigation. But Jewish tradition mandates that funerals be done swiftly, out of respect for the deceased. An investigation would delay the funerals unnecessarily, possibly for weeks. Finally, the ambassador reached the Indian prime minister[49] and told him, "Mr. Prime Minister, if the government does not release the bodies, it will become an international incident. Tomorrow there will be demonstrations in New York, Paris, and Tel Aviv, and I cannot stop it." Fearing public pressure, the prime minister relented, permitting the remains to be flown to Israel. The Israel Air Force dispatched a plane to Mumbai to bring the families and bodies home.

On Monday morning in Mumbai, some Jewish volunteers were given a four-hour window by Indian authorities to re-enter the

Chabad House. The building still reeked from the battle that had ended on Friday evening. Bullet holes peppered the walls. Death and destruction were everywhere. The volunteers went from floor to floor, collecting many personal items. As they finished the task, they all gathered in the synagogue on the third floor. They planned to take the Torah scrolls back to Israel, fearing they could be vandalized where they were. Before removing the scrolls, they began singing Jewish melodies.

On Monday before the families of the slain left India to return to Israel, Mumbai's Jewish community gathered for a memorial prayer. The historic Knesset Eliyahoo synagogue was full.[50] Rabbi Shimon Rosenberg, the Israeli ambassador, and others spoke. Prayers and psalms were said. Two-year-old Moshie shattered the hearts of all. Not understanding the events that were surrounding him, he clutched a red ball, crying out time and again, his voice echoing throughout the large sanctuary, the Hebrew word for Mommy: "Ima, Ima, Ima, Ima."[51]

As the Israeli plane left Mumbai Monday evening, the cargo hold was filled with the bodies of those who had lost their lives simply for being Jews. On board, the families, friends, volunteers, and Israeli officials sat mostly in silence, trying to make sense of the senseless evil. Mati Goldstein[52] sat with Rabbi Shimon Rosenberg and told him of the Torah scroll they had discovered earlier that day with the words "after the death of the two sons of Aaron" torn by a bullet.

When Gabi left home to take up his new post in Mumbai, he eerily told his father (referring to the classical Jewish belief in the coming of the Messiah),[53] "I will come back with Moshiach or in a casket." Chabad shluchim accept a posting for life. No one had dreamed that the Holtzbergs' return would be so quick and so brutal.

The road to Mumbai had started for both of them decades earlier. Both grew up in Chabad homes, where idealism and caring for others were instilled from childhood. In the early seventies, inspired by the Rebbe to move to a small city without a strong religious tradition, Rivkie's parents moved to Afula in Israel's north. When they arrived, a young Chabad couple in an immigrant agricultural town with few friends and no family, they were much like Gabi and Rivkie, who arrived in Mumbai thirty-five years later – an anomaly. At the time, the Chabad community was centered in Kfar Chabad, Jerusalem, and Tel Aviv. The national network of institutions that reaches today to every community in the country was just beginning to evolve.

They both became Jewish educators. Every Shabbat, Shimon would visit a different synagogue, getting to know the residents, sharing a few words of Torah from the pulpit. Yehudit taught in the government-sponsored Chabad school in Taanach, a small agricultural village a few miles south of Afula.[54] The classrooms were filled with immigrant children whose parents were farmers. Most were not religious, but they chose the Chabad school to give their kids a foundation in Jewish tradition.

The Rosenbergs raised a big family; Rivkie was number six out of eleven children. The Rosenbergs' home was open to the community; it was an environment of kindness and hospitality for guests and Jews from all backgrounds. When Russian Jews began immigrating to Israel in large numbers, Yehudit designated a room that she filled with donated clothing. Daily, the newly arrived families would come to find things for their children. "Every Shabbat, a few of those families would join us for meals," Yehudit said, "and years later, when I would run into them, their first question was always, 'How is Rivkie?' She was the dynamic one; she was the child they always remembered."

Rivkie and her good friend, Chani Goldstein, were the only two Chabad kids in the class in the school in the village of Taanach where her mother taught. The other children were from varied backgrounds, somewhat traditional with a mix of secular and a few Orthodox. Chani Goldstein[55] remembers, "Rivkie began acting like a shliach from childhood. She had the character, and was very outgoing. She was best friends with everyone but she did not compromise her standards."

For high school, she commuted to the Chabad girls' school in nearby Haifa. One of her classmates tells of the first day in school. "We are sitting in class and she comes in with smiles and self-confidence: 'Hi, I'm Rivkie Rosenberg from Afula.'" She was a natural leader. Rivkie was fifteen when a troubled girl, from outside the Chabad community, joined the school. Her parents were divorced, and she was disheveled, distraught, her face disfigured. It was Rivkie who befriended her. "One day," Chani[56] says, "the girl revealed her secret. She told us that her father was beating her." The girls feared getting involved, but Rivkie took action. She marched off to the school counselor and arranged an intervention. Her mother was proud of her taking responsibility. "Others would not befriend this girl, but Rivkie took her home, bought her clothes; she uplifted her." Rivkie nurtured the girl to a point where she could function normally.

Rivkie attended seminary, a post-high-school, college-level program in Kfar Chabad. She and her cousin, Penina Glitzenstein, joined her older sister and another cousin. Four grandchildren – two sets of sisters – lived for three years with their elderly grandmother in Lod. Their grandfather had passed away a few years earlier. Rivkie's grandmother, Itta Kaylah, came from Poland. At sixteen, she was in a Soviet work camp in Siberia. After the war, she moved to Israel. She lived in a simple apartment in the Chabad neighborhood in working-class Lod, spending much of her time in Torah study. Penina[57] says, "She had a profound impact on us." Deeply pious, she would share Chassidic lore with her granddaughters, one of whom recalls that she recited the whole book of Psalms every day. The gregarious girls enjoyed the intergenerational mix – the way their grandmother connected them to the richness of European Jewish culture, tradition, and scholarship, as well as the good times they had. "Four granddaughters together was lively," recalls Penina.

At twenty, Rivkie was off to Riga in Latvia with her cousin Penina to teach. Rivkie insisted they stay for the summer and organize a camp.

Gabi was number six of an Israeli family of eight. When Gabi was eight, the family moved to the US where his father, Rabbi Nachman, had landed a job as a schochet (ritual slaughterer of kosher meat). Yisroel Hahn,[58] today a shliach in Spokane, Washington, was another Israeli kid in Brooklyn, and they became buddies. Gabi, he said, was studious. "He could be rowdy if he wanted to, but he was very focused. He never got into sports like the American kids." Hahn said Gabi had drive and ambition. "He was stubborn. If he wanted to get something done, it got done." At eleven, Gabi had mastered the six orders of the Mishnah by heart. Hahn said this surprised his teachers. "No one had ever done that before. Gabi would look for a challenge and overcome it."

At fourteen, Gabi encountered Islamic terror for the first time. His father's job had brought them to Argentina for a short stint. Hezbollah terrorists bombed the local Jewish Community Center killing eighty-seven, and injuring over one hundred. Gabi's yeshiva was down the block. After the massive explosion, Gabi[59] ran to the burning building and started pulling out the wounded.

Gabi's classmate, Menachem Heller,[60] recalls, "At fifteen, we decided to finish the Talmud[61] (sixty-three tractates, over five thousand pages). Every night we would stay late, till after 11 o'clock." They studied for a year. After that, Heller had other things he wanted to accomplish. He told Gabi, "Maybe we can continue this at a later date." Gabi, however, completed this monumental task. As Heller puts it, "He wanted to finish, so he finished it."

In the Chabad community, young people begin to think about settling down and getting married in their early twenties. They date with the intent of marriage.[62] Family, friends, and at times a shadchan (matchmaker), suggest ideas. Most young people seek the advice of their parents, who help screen prospective candidates. Still, the choice is theirs, and, as the Rebbe advised a young woman, "There must be Hamshachas Halev, an attraction of the heart." The goal is marriage; if it clicks, they pursue the relationship. With Gabi and Rivkie, it seemed like destiny from day one. Her childhood friend Chani[63] says, "When they became engaged, she was radiant. She was on a high, two souls connected."

They married in Tel Aviv in 2002; he was twenty-three, she twenty-two. For the first year, they lived in Migdal Ha'Emek, not far from Afula. Gabi studied in kolel (an advanced rabbinic program for married men) and Rivkie taught in school, as well as aerobics. After marriage, most couples spend a year near family, the husband still studying. This gives the young couple time to adjust to marriage before being propelled into the hustle of regular life. Later, some choose shlichus – joining the Chabad network, either opening a new location or finding a position in an existing institution. Others pursue careers in business or they may choose to pursue additional education to provide them with job skills. A few outstanding students remain studying for additional years.

India was slated for expansion. The idea had been batted about between the headquarters in New York and Rabbi Yosef Chaim Kantor, the regional director in Thailand. Mendy Glitzenstein,[64] married to Rivkie's cousin Penina, had heard the rumors about India and thought it was a good idea for Gabi and Rivkie. "He wanted a place where he could realize his true potential. He was a schochet,[65] and he knew Hebrew and English." Gabi was intrigued; India was one of the few countries without a permanent Chabad presence, and the idea excited him. Gabi had spent a year in Bangkok with five rabbinical students, and he became good friends with Rabbi Kantor,[66] who says, "The year in Thailand inspired Gabi and he wanted to go to a similar kind of place." During a visit to New York, Gabi spotted Rabbi Kantor on the corner of Crown Street and Brooklyn Avenue in Crown Heights. Kantor recalls the encounter: "Gabi walked by and said to me, 'I heard you guys are looking for someone to go to India, what about us?'" India had special challenges: it was remote, a totally different culture, a local community in decline. To Kantor it seemed like a natural fit. "You would be the perfect people," he said. Shortly afterward, Gabi and Rivkie met with Rabbi Moshe Kotlarsky when he was visiting Israel. He formally offered them the position and they accepted.

Now the question was funding. They applied for a Rohr Grant to underwrite the initial startup costs for the first few years. George Rohr is a venture capitalist in New York. Together with his father, Sami, he has fueled the expansion of Chabad around the world. With the help of Rabbi Moshe Kotlarsky at Lubavitch World head-quarters in Brooklyn, the grant was approved. Gabi and Rivkie started to plan the move.

Gabi's father felt deeply honored. "Our son would head Chabad in a country," a rare privilege in a time when most such positions had been filled. Rivkie's mother, Yehudit, said, "We were proud that our children were chosen to fulfill the Rebbe's mission in such a difficult place." She asked her daughter about the security. "Rivkie did not have any concern; they did not feel there was risk."

After a while, they visited Mumbai for the first time. Yehudit says, "Only after going there did we understand how tough this mission was."

Just before Chanukah in 2003, Gabi and Rivkie arrived[67] in Mumbai with one-year-old Menachem Mendel. There had not been a permanent rabbi in town in years; local synagogues were run by chazzanim. There were beautiful edifices populated by aging Jews. For centuries, there was a small Jewish community in Mumbai. In the early nineteenth century, the population boomed with large numbers of Baghdadi Jews fleeing anti-Semitism and seeking economic opportunity. The immigration of David Sassoon in 1832 propelled the community to a new plateau. His philanthropy fueled the growth of Jewish life. Numerous synagogues and Jewish schools were erected. In the late 1940s, over thirty thousand Jews lived in Mumbai. In the postwar years, the great majority of Jews immigrated to Israel. Today, the Jewish community in Mumbai numbers some 3,500.

Gabi and Rivkie set up shop in the three-star Shelleys Hotel in Mumbai's tourist district. The place was cramped; there wasn't a proper kitchen. They would host Shabbat meals on the roof overlooking the sprawl of Mumbai. Kantor says, "Gabi was gung ho." Gabi and Rivkie found a community whose glory had faded. He began attending services in the beautiful Knesset Eliyahoo Synagogue built by the Sassoons a century ago. The members took a liking to Rabbi Gabi. He began to speak at the services and became accepted as the rabbi of the synagogue. On Sundays, Gabi would provide educational programs for the descendants of the Bene Israel in the Tiferet Israel Synagogue. Dr. Aron Abraham says, "Forty to fifty young people would come every Sunday to Rabbi Gabi's classes."

The hotel was untenable; they needed more space. Renting proved impossible. Gabi found the Nariman House, a relatively new building six stories high. Kantor says, "It was perfect." It was tucked away in a small street and was considered a minimal security risk. Gabi was fortunate when George Rohr visited on Chanukah for a business meeting. They lit the menorah together at the Star of India. Kantor says, "Mr. Rohr admired the self-sacrifice of this young couple." The Rohrs made a major grant that enabled the purchase.

The new building changed everything. It was six stories high, air-conditioned, in a good location, and near the main hotels. The days of the cramped Shelleys Hotel were gone. Gabi had dreams of making major improvements: a restaurant, guest rooms, place for classes and programs. Gabi and Rivkie moved into the sixth floor. Meals were served daily to travelers. On Shabbat, the Chabad House was full with Israeli trekkers, businessmen, and locals. Erin Beser, the JDC staffer, says, "Chabad was our haven." In his relaxed, informal way, Gabi drew his disparate, ever-changing congregation together each week. Beser says, "Everyone had to either tell a story, sing a song, or say a thought of Torah."

The programs were growing, but a major personal crisis erupted that would forever alter their lives and complicate their mission in Mumbai. Young Menachem Mendel was sick with Tay-Sachs, a genetic disease found among Eastern European Jews. The doctors said there was no cure; almost all children with the disease pass away by the time they reach age five. The couple cared for the child in Mumbai as long as possible. Finally, they moved him to an Israeli hospital where the medical standards were higher and the doctors had experience with the sickness.

Rivkie, the outgoing girl, dealt with this crisis inwardly. When visitors to the Chabad House asked about children, she withdrew to a side room and burst out in tears. Together with Gabi, they shouldered the problem on their own. Visitors to the Chabad House had no idea that they had a sick child. Rivkie confided to one of her close friends,[68] "If someone can help me, good." She didn't need everyone's sympathy. A classmate of Gabi says, "He did not want to be a burden on anyone."

In Israel, little Menachem Mendel was placed in a special medical facility for children with Tay-Sachs. The doctors there told them the same thing they had heard in India: "There is nothing you can do. It's just a matter of time."

Now the couple wrestled with a bigger question: should they leave their post? Rabbi Kantor says, "The Holtzbergs could not easily be replaced, but ultimately, it was their decision." A close friend of Rivkie's explained: "Medically, there was no hope. They saw shlichus, the mission in Mumbai, as a source of spiritual blessing." They shuttled back and forth between the child's bedside in Israel and Mumbai, but the sickness was so destructive, the young child barely knew his parents were there. Their second son Dov Ber, born in December 2006, tragically had the same disease. In September 2007, three-year-old Menachem Mendel succumbed and was buried in Israel. A close friend, a shliach[69] in another country, had long conversations with Gabi about his crisis of conscience. "It hit them very hard. One child had passed away; the other was in the hospital in Israel. He was alone in India, his wife in Israel taking care of Dov Ber." Crying on the phone, he asked me, "Should I leave?" They spoke for a long time; Gabi said he was very torn. He felt that he was needed in Mumbai. "Ultimately he decided to stay." Sadly, Dov Ber, the second son, passed away a few weeks after the terror attack on the Chabad House.

The funeral for Gabi and Rivkie was slated for Tuesday afternoon in Kfar Chabad,[70] the movement's hub in Israel, located just ten miles from Tel Aviv. In Brooklyn, Gabi's close friend, rabbi, and mentor Moshe Kotlarsky,[71] was facing his own crisis. As the tragic events unfolded in Mumbai, he had been at the bedside of his father in New York, ninety-one-year-old Rabbi Tzvi Kotlarsky. The situation was critical; the father had only a few more hours to live. Rabbi Kotlarsky wondered how he could leave for Israel, even for just one day.

Kotlarsky had helped Gabi get the Chabad House off the ground in Mumbai. Globe-trotting Kotlarsky is known for his profound commitment to the shluchim, whether it involved attending a bar mitzvah in Kinshasa or sitting at the bedside of a sick child in California. Saturday night, twenty-four hours after the attack, we spoke. It was late, after midnight New York time, and he was sitting at his father's bedside. He told me about his special kinship with Gabi, the moments they shared, the joy that Gabi felt when Moshie was born, how minutes after the birth, he called Rabbi Kotlarsky with the wonderful news of a healthy child. With a voice full of tears, Rabbi Kotlarsky said, "We were dear friends."

Kotlarsky[72] headed to the Ohel,[73] the resting place in Queens of the Lubavitcher Rebbe. Jewish tradition teaches that prayer at the grave of a tzadik (a righteous person) has unique spiritual power. Kotlarsky prayed for the ability to go to the funeral. He raced back to the hospital and was told by the doctors about a sudden improvement. "He is doing better, you can take the flight." A week later, Tzvi Kotlarsky passed away.

In Israel, the whole country had plunged into mourning. Israeli writer Yossi Klein Halevi realized the depth of the despair felt throughout Israel when he arrived at work that day and discovered coworkers, far from religious, sitting and crying. A few days later, he penned an article for *The New Republic*[74] titled: "Why Israelis Love Chabad." An excerpt follows:

> It is doubtful the country would have reacted with the same emotional intensity had the Holtzbergs been ordinary ultra-Orthodox Jews rather than Chabadniks.[75] Mainstream Israelis resent ultra-Orthodox Jews for separating from the state. Chabad neither separates nor demands, but gives. When our young people just out of the army travel the most remote corners of the world (because military service doesn't provide enough dangers and thrills), they invariably encounter a Chabad House. Israelis also love Chabadniks for their courage. Chabad activists rush to the front lines during war. One friend told me about her sister who was serving in a border post so sensitive that a visitor required special permission from the general in command of the front: "And then who shows up on Hanukah with jelly donuts? Chabadniks."

It was a tearful sight.[76] Tens of thousands gathered in front of the 770 Building in Kfar Chabad, the red brick replica of the Rebbe's synagogue in Brooklyn. In front of the red-bricked building, Israel's political and religious leaders stood near the bodies of Rabbi Gavriel and Rivkie Holtzberg wrapped with a talit,[77] lying on simple wooden benches. Rabbis Krinsky, Kotlarsky, and Shemtov, and shluchim from all over the world flew in. This wasn't just a Chabad funeral but a loss for all of the Jewish people. Israel's president, Shimon Peres, said the Holtzbergs were the "emissaries of all of the Jewish People." Chief

Rabbi Shlomo Amar, who, as a young man, attended Chabad schools in Morocco, recognized "the holiness of their sacrifice." Political leaders Binyamin Netanyahu, Ehud Barak, Eli Yishai, and others participated. Rabbis Krinsky and Shemtov each eloquently eulogized the Holtzbergs' sacrifice. Tens of thousands of regular Israelis, from the most secular to religious, Ashkenazi and Sephardi, all converged on Kfar Chabad. Israeli TV interrupted regular programming to broadcast the funeral live.

Rabbi Shalom White stood among the crowd. He is the shliach in the growing town of Perth on Australia's western coast, the most distant outpost on the global network from Chabad headquarters in Brooklyn. White had arrived home from the grueling thirty-hour trip from Brooklyn after attending Chabad's Kinus Hashluchim, the annual conference of Chabad emissaries. After landing in Australia, he heard about the attack in Mumbai, and he said, "I have to be at the funeral in Israel." He headed back to the airport for another exhausting thirty-hour trip, this time to Tel Aviv. He arrived on Tuesday morning and went directly to Kfar Chabad. Standing next to him in the crowd was a young Israeli Chabad businessman, Rafi Goldmitz. They had been classmates years earlier at the Yeshiva in Kiryat Gat, Israel. Goldmitz knew that his old friend lived in distant Perth, Australia. Goldmitz wondered why he came so far. "Were you a good friend of Gabi?" he asked White. "No, we never met; he was a fellow shliach – I had to come. We were both shluchim, we were brothers." That night, a few hours after the funeral, White headed back on the long flight to Perth, spending less than half a day in Israel.

But it was Rabbi Kotlarsky whose words penetrated everyone's heart. Arriving straight from the airport, he spoke in Hebrew and English with passion and tears. He described Gabi and Rivkie as a couple of deep faith and purity of spirit, people who would always do for others.

Turning to the shluchim around the world he said, "This is the time to take strength, this is the time to do, we will answer the terrorists, we will not fight them with AK-47s, we will not fight with tanks, we will not fight them with grenades. The Rebbe taught us that a little candle in a room lights up the whole room. Such brutal darkness can be fought only by torches of goodness and kindness and light." He called on Chabad rabbis around the world to reach out to more Jews, to strengthen their work as an everlasting memorial to the Holtzbergs.

He told the massive crowd that Chabad would not retreat, and was committed to rebuilding the Chabad House in Mumbai.

Rabbi Kotlarsky raised the question all were pondering. "To Moshie, what do I say? You do not have a mother and father who will hold you, say with you the daily prayers, a mother who will kiss you and hug you." His voice breaking, impassioned, he answered his own question: "Today you have become the child of the Jewish people, you are the child of four thousand shluchim and four thousand shluchos around the world. We are adopting you, you are our child, you are and will remain a shliach of the Rebbe." With tears, he concluded with words directed to Gabi and Rivkie, "I say goodbye, you were good friends; you were shluchim par excellence. I have no idea why G-d has done this. You are prime examples of shluchim of the Rebbe. You did the mission to its fullest."

Rabbi Rafi Goldmitz[78] came home from the funeral in a different state of mind. The encounter with his old friend Shalom White from Perth caused him to start rethinking his life. He told his wife, Leah, "There is such a love and unity among the shluchim. We need to go on shlichus. Together with his four children (including triplets, age four) they were living in what he calls, "the cocoon of the Chabad neighborhood in Kiryat Malachi." Leah's parents and uncles and aunts were just around the corner. Daily, he had been commuting to a teaching job in B'nai Brak, the bastion of traditional Judaism in Israel.

A few days later, Rafi Goldmitz headed to Chabad headquarters in Israel, located a few hundred feet from the site of the funeral in Kfar Chabad. Meeting with Rabbi Naftoli Lipsker, coordinator of the network of Chabad Centers, he said, "I want to find a place to move immediately and become a shliach." Within a week, he and Leah were looking for a home in Merkaz Shapira, a small community of five hundred families in the Negev. Rafi says, "We started programs there a week later." Goldmitz put a focus on the youth in the community. "I work with the soldiers in the local training base." He started classes and today has a synagogue with over one hundred attending every Shabbat.

In 2012, Goldmitz attended the annual shluchim convention in New York. Everyone was bused from Brooklyn to the Hilton in Manhattan for the banquet to conclude the five-day conference. Goldmitz sat next to Rabbi Moshe Lieblich[79] from North Carolina. They had never met; he told Lieblich he was from Israel, never revealing his name. Hearing he was Israeli, Lieblich decided to tell him a story he had heard that weekend at the conference. "The rabbi in Perth was flying back from the New York convention as the terror attack was underway in Mumbai. During the long trip he was not aware of the assault on the Chabad House. When he landed in Perth, he heard the tragic news. A few hours later he headed straight to the Holtzberg funeral in Israel. At the funeral he met an old friend of his from yeshiva. That friend was so deeply moved by this act of brotherhood that he was inspired to become a shliach." As Goldmitz listened, it became clear he was hearing about himself. He turned to Lieblich and surprised him: "That's my story!"

Chapter Two

"America Iz Nisht Anderish" – America Is Not Different

Thirteen-year-old Risia Kazarnovsky[1] woke early on the morning of March 19, 1940, too excited to sleep anymore. Before sunrise, she dressed in a special outfit for the balmy day, a camel-colored coat with brown buttons and a broad-brimmed hat to match. By dawn, she had arrived at the Fifty-Seventh-Street Pier in New York harbor, waiting for the arrival of the Lubavitcher Rebbe, Rabbi Yosef Yitzchak Schneersohn. The Rebbe[2] was leader of Chabad (Lubavitch) Chassidim, a scholar greatly respected among Jews around the world, legendary for his courage in defying Communism. The Rebbe personified Jewish ideals of sanctity, learning, and devotion to others. He was the sixth in a dynasty of great rabbinical leaders who stood at the helm of Russian Jewry since the late eighteenth century. Until the outbreak of World War II, the spiritual epicenter of Jewish life had been in Europe. The Rebbe's arrival in America represented a shift in focus of Jewish spiritual life from the old world to the new.

Risia's oldest sister, Sara, stood nearby. Her younger sibling Rivka,[3] eleven, was kept home – despite her protests – because the organizing committee had requested that younger children not attend. Instead, she was sent to her school, PS 247, and she missed this momentous day.

Risia's father, Rabbi Shlomo Aaron Kazarnovsky, was one of the leaders of the small Lubavitch community in the US. "You could count the actual Chassidic families on two hands," Risia said in an interview with author Sue Fishkoff many years later. Across the country, Jews filled some eighty Nusach Ari synagogues,[4] congregations with a historic connection to Chabad, filled with members who did not follow the Chassidic lifestyle.[5] While many Jews were swiftly assimilating into American society, a small group of Chassidim maintained their vibrant religious lifestyle. To them America was a haven, a place where they could live Judaism to the fullest without the oppression that dominated Europe. The Chassidic Movement had evolved two centuries earlier in Europe. It empowered Jews to focus inward on their personal spiritual development, imbuing their lives with joy and purpose. One of the largest Chassidic groups was Chabad (Lubavitch). Its comprehensive system of intellectual thought synergized the profound concepts of Jewish mysticism with applications in daily life.

Risia's family lived in Bensonhurst, where her father served as a congregational rabbi. There were no Jewish schools in the area, so Risia and her siblings attended public schools. At the time, Risia was the only Orthodox Jewish girl in her school, but a few times a week, she attended Cheder, afternoon Hebrew school.

For Risia and her sister, that early morning in March of 1940 at the New York dock would mark a major change in their lives. At the time, they thought they were just celebrating the Rebbe's miraculous escape from war-torn Europe. They never imagined that the Rebbe carried with him a far-reaching vision that would revive and remold American Jewish life. More than a thousand people gathered that early morning. *Time* magazine reported that the crowd included five hundred rabbis and seventy-five cantors. They were singing Chassidic songs. Before this day, Risia had heard these tunes only in her home, around the Shabbat table, and suddenly she felt empowered.

"On the dock, I heard the melodies that my father had sung. Now I felt that we were home; they were singing our songs," she said. "There were other Jewish groups in Bensonhurst, but they were not mine. This was mine."

The Rebbe's ship had pulled into New York Harbor the night before. On the ship with the Rebbe were his mother, wife, eldest daughter, son-in-law, and a handful of his close followers. His two other daughters, their husbands, and thousands of his Chassidim remained trapped in Europe. A year later, his second daughter, Chaya Mushka, and her husband, Rabbi Menachem Mendel Schneerson would manage to escape the Nazis and join him in America. Unable to obtain a visa, his youngest daughter Shaina and her husband Mendel Horenstein, would meet their fate in the Nazi death camp, Treblinka.

Before the war, the Rebbe had been living in Poland for six years, most of the time in Otvotsk, a suburb of Warsaw. There, he reestablished the center of the Chabad Movement after escaping from Russia's Communist regime. More than three hundred studied in his famed Yeshiva Tomchei Temimim.[6]

Avraham Hecht[7] stood on the pier to welcome the Rebbe to America. He had been one of the American yeshiva students who had arrived in Otvotsk[8] seventeen days before the war broke out. When the fighting began, the Rebbe advised the American students to flee to Latvia and contact Mordechai Dubin,[9] an influential member of the Latvian Parliament and follower of the Rebbe. Twelve years earlier, Dubin had helped save the Rebbe from a Russian death sentence.[10] The Rebbe hoped Dubin would be successful in helping him again.

The Nazi invasion of Poland began on a Friday. A few days later, the Latvian Embassy – on the orders of the Rebbe's Chassid, Dubin – sent a diplomatic car to transport the Rebbe to Warsaw. The Rebbe took refuge in the home of one his Chassidim, Rabbi Zalman Shmotkin. Ten days later, a few hours before Rosh Hashanah, the Nazi bombing started again. Rabbi Yosef Wineberg[11] documented those harrowing days in his diary.[12] "Firebombs fell on the Shmotkin house and it burst into flames. The Rebbe found some protection under an arch of a nearby building." There he whispered prayers, pausing to ask Wineberg about the yeshiva students and a pregnant woman whom the Rebbe feared had not escaped the house. The intensity of the bombing continued, and the fires almost reached the Rebbe.

That night, there was not even a minyan (quorum) for Rosh Hashanah services, as nearby Chassidim could not reach the Rebbe due to the bombardment. The following morning, a small group joined the Rebbe for services. The German onslaught continued throughout the High Holidays, and the Rebbe's entourage was forced from one refuge to another. On Sukkot, the holiday when Jews build sukkot (temporary outdoor dwellings) to recall the Exodus, the Rebbe wanted to erect the Sukkah. When the shelling subsided around 4:00 a.m. the night before the holiday, the Sukkah went up. The next night, the Rebbe ate a brief meal in the Sukkah. Shortly afterward, Nazi soldiers marched victoriously down the streets of Poland's capital.

As the Rebbe endured the siege of Warsaw, his supporters in America and Latvia launched a campaign to free him from the clutches of the Nazis. Asher Rabinowitz, an attorney from Boston who came from a distinguished Lubavitcher family, rushed to Washington DC. A decade earlier, he had arranged meetings for the Rebbe with Justice Louis Brandeis and President Herbert Hoover. Brandeis agreed to meet with him and recalled his visit with the Rebbe in 1929.[13]

Now at the zenith of his career, Justice Brandeis was arguably the most influential Jew in America. He used his clout to open doors in the White House and the State Department. Secretary of State Cordell Hull agreed to help the Rebbe.

Still neutral at that point, America retained a diplomatic presence in Nazi Germany. Hull instructed Raymond Geist, his consul general in Berlin, to enlist the help of a German official, Helmut Wohlthat.[14] He had been a student in the US before the war and was friendly with Americans. Geist and Wohlthat had developed a personal rapport during the Evian Conference held in July of 1938, and they tried to find ways to save European Jews, an effort doomed to failure due to immigration restrictions of the US and other countries.

At the conference, Wohlthat confided to Geist that, in the future, he would be willing to be a backdoor conduit, should the need arise.

Wohlthat thought the plan to smuggle out the Rebbe had little chance of success, but he decided to try. He hoped that efforts to help the Rebbe would endear the US government to Germany and maybe even cause it to help negotiate an end to the war.

Wohlthat enlisted the help of Admiral Wilhelm Canaris,[15] head of the Abwehr (the German military intelligence service). Canaris had been deeply disturbed by Hitler's plans against the Jews. (Later in the war, he would be executed for plotting to assassinate Hitler.) He agreed to lead the clandestine effort to find the Rebbe in war-torn Warsaw. It was feared that the SS Einsatzgruppen were searching for the Rebbe.

Canaris dispatched three officers of Jewish descent to Warsaw. Lt. Colonel Ernst Bloch, whose father was Jewish, led the group. This decorated veteran officer had been deemed German by Hitler himself.[16]

The officers scoured Warsaw in search of the Rebbe, fearing he had been killed in the bombing. Finally, they uncovered what they thought was the Rebbe's hideout. Family members hiding the Rebbe denied he was there. In a postwar interview, one observer recalled that when the Rebbe heard that the Germans were looking for him, he said, "I have never hidden and I will not hide now." He emerged to meet his captors.

Bloch told the Rebbe about his plan to help them escape. The Rebbe and his entourage "would have to act like prisoners; I will be forced to speak harshly to you." As an SS unit walked by, Bloch addressed the group of Jews callously, hurriedly loading them on the vehicles and heading to a railroad station on the outskirts of Warsaw. Along the way, SS officers repeatedly challenged Bloch, asking why and where they were taking these Jews. At one checkpoint, Bloch threatened to inform Canaris himself that the soldier was an obstacle to an important investigation. After a few tense moments, the SS officer lifted the barrier and let the group pass.

From Warsaw, the group traveled first class on a train to Berlin. At the station, one army officer asked Bloch, "Why is a group of Orthodox Jews traveling first class?" After staying overnight in Berlin, the group departed, heading to Latvia by train, still escorted by Bloch's unit and a delegation from the Latvian embassy. The next day, when the Rebbe arrived in Riga, the Chassidim celebrated the miraculous escape. In New York, a telegram arrived telling the Chabad community that the Rebbe had been saved. Rabbi Israel Jacobson was so overjoyed he went out in front of the Lubavitch synagogue in Brownsville and did somersaults on the street.

For two and a half months, the Rebbe and his entourage waited in Riga for the State Department to issue visas. Finally in March, they boarded the *ss Drottningholm* to the United States. The trip across the Atlantic was terrifying. Twice, German submarines stopped the ship searching for military cargo. A British warship also detained the ship. After thirteen days on the Atlantic, the ship pulled into New York harbor.

The first Chabad (or Lubavitch) Rebbe, Rabbi Schneur Zalman of Liadi,[17] known in the Jewish world as the Alter Rebbe – the old Rebbe – was born in 1745 in the town of Liozna in Belorussia. A prolific scholar, at age twenty, he stood at a spiritual crossroads. One path led to Vilna, the center of classic Jewish scholarship and the seat of the great Gaon, Rabbi Eliyahu.[18] The other led to Mezeritch, the home of Rabbi Dov Ber,[19] the Maggid (Preacher) of Mezeritch,[20] prime disciple of Rabbi Israel Baal Shem Tov, founder of Chassidism. The Alter Rebbe recalled this crucial moment: "I knew that in Vilna they were proficient in talmudic scholarship; in Mezeritch, the focus was on praying. In learning, I had some ability, but in the sphere of prayer, I knew little, so I went to Mezeritch." Years later, he commented, "In Vilna they taught you how to master the Torah, and in Mezeritch, they taught how the Torah could master you." There, he found an approach to life that focused not just on intellectual achievement, but also on the service of G-d. The Maggid himself had been an adherent of the great sage, Rabbi Israel Baal Shem Tov (literally, Israel, the Master of the Good Name).

The Baal Shem Tov, founder of the Chassidic Movement, was born in 1698. His parents passed away at a young age leaving him an orphan. He became a protégé of mystical teachers, initiated into Machne Israel, the Society of Hidden Tzadikim (righteous Jews). Its leader, Rabbi Adam Baal Shem, arranged his instruction in the esoteric teachings of Torah. In 1734, at the age of thirty-six, Rabbi Israel Baal Shem Tov began to publicly reveal his teachings. He focused on the deeper mystical knowledge of Torah that had lain hidden for centuries to all but a few great scholars of the Kabbalah (Jewish mysticism).

Jews had reached a spiritual nadir with centuries of vicious anti-Semitism, culminating with the brutal attacks of the Cossacks. Starting in 1648, Bogdan Chmielnicki led a peasant rebellion that devastated close to a thousand Jewish communities in Poland. The Catholic Church fanned the flames of hatred with blood libels and pogroms. False hope arose with the claim of Shabbetai Tzvi (1626-1676)[21] as the much-awaited Messiah, with promises of an era of peace and spiritual renewal. Jews believing in the news sold their homes and began preparing to move to the Holy Land, only to discover his promises were empty when, in 1666, he converted to Islam.

Rabbi Israel Baal Shem Tov touched a deep chord in Jewry. He preached the unique value of the simple Jew's service of the Almighty, that every Jew could pursue a life enriched with purpose and sanctity. Writer Yitzchak Buxbaum[22] explains the paradigm shift the Baal Shem Tov created:

> "Many Jews lived in fear of their gentile neighbors. Their world was dark around them. These fears produced a morbid ascetic piety that was based on an exaggerated fear of G-d. The Baal Shem Tov broke out of this trap. He taught a piety based on the love of G-d. By overcoming the often-irrational fears that depressed the people, he opened the gate before them to a path of joy in the service of G-d."

Rabbi Israel revealed the inner teachings of Judaism, reserved in the past for a small group of mystics. The Baal Shem was renowned for his compassion for the common man, his teachings of love for one's fellow and numerous stories of wonders. His popularity spread across Europe, uplifting Jews. Classical Jewish scholars opposed his innovations, however, and attempted to stifle his growing influence. The Baal Shem emboldened the common man with a sense of spiritual dignity and purpose. He shattered the intellectual monopoly of Jewish scholars who remained disconnected from the common folk. In 1760, the Baal Shem passed away in Mezibuz[23] in western Ukraine.

His successor, Rabbi Dov Ber, the Maggid (preacher) of Mezeritch carried on this legacy. Born around 1700, he met the Baal Shem Tov in 1753. Building inward, he surrounded himself with a remarkable group of gifted scholars. Rabbis Levi Yitzchak of Berditchev, Menachem Mendel of Vitebsk, Yaakov Yosef of Polonya, the Maggid's son, Reb Avrohom Der Malach (the angel, after his saintly character) and others. The Maggid instructed his students in the deep secrets of Kabbalah, Jewish mysticism. His students would become a new generation of leaders that would propel Chassidism to a movement touching the majority of European Jews.

The Maggid dispatched his disciples across Eastern Europe. Rabbi Schneur Zalman was sent to Lithuania, the stronghold of the Misnagdim (those opposed to Chassidic teachings). The scholars of Vilna felt that this revolutionary approach to Judaism reached beyond the boundaries of classical Jewish norms. Chassidic leaders meticulously followed Jewish law, believing that the teachings of Chassidism provided deeper meaning to lives of the Jews of their times. They showed how the esoteric concepts they were teaching to the masses had existed in the teachings of Judaism for millennia and they were making them accessible.

Rabbi Schneur Zalman was a great scholar, thinker, and theologian. Upon the direction of the Maggid, he composed an updated edition of the Code of Jewish Law,[24] which became a Jewish legal classic. His greatest work was the Tanya,[25] which articulated his philosophy that synergized the mystical and the practical. Rabbi Schneur Zalman was active in communal affairs in Russia, helping to expand the Pale of Settlement to provide economic opportunity to Jews in Czarist Russia. He founded Colel Chabad in 1788[26] to support the growing Chassidic community in the Land of Israel.

The Misnagdim[27] failed to stifle the growth of Chassidism. In a desperate attempt to destroy the fledging movement, they orchestrated a series of false charges against Rabbi Schneur Zalman. In 1798, he was accused of subversive activity against Russia for supporting Jews in the Land of Israel, then part of the Ottoman Empire, which was in the midst of a conflict with Russia. The infamous "Black Carriage" reserved for the most serious crimes transported him from his home in Liadi to the capital, Saint Petersburg. Imprisoned in the Peter and Paul Fortress[28] on the banks of the Neva River in Saint Petersburg, the Rebbe was visited in jail by the Czar.[29] Over seven weeks later, he was vindicated and freed on the nineteenth day of the Jewish month of Kislev, in 1798, celebrated still today as a Chassidic holiday. He passed away, avoiding Napoleon's[30] invasion of Russia, in 1812.

His son and successor, Rabbi DovBer, continued the line of Chassidic Rebbes of Chabad. He moved the center of the growing movement to the small town of Lubavitch, and the rebbes became known as the Lubavitcher Rebbes. Lubavitch,[31] not far from the city of Smolensk, and some eighteen miles from the nearest train station in Rudniya, had a population of two thousand. Tucked away behind country roads, it was an oasis of Torah and spirituality for over a century. Four of the seven Rebbes of Chabad lived there. Chabad's founder, Rabbi Schneur Zalman, spent some of the early part of his life there, and lived in nearby Liadi.

Yosef Yitzchak, destined to become the Sixth Rebbe, was born in Lubavitch in 1880. At the young age of fifteen, Yosef Yitzchak began to assist his father, Rabbi Sholom DovBer, who was the Fifth Rebbe, in communal activities, attending major rabbinical conferences in Kovno in 1895, and a year later, in Vilna, Lithuania. In 1901, he arranged financing to open a textile factory in Dubrovna that created jobs for two thousand Jews. Three years later, during the Russo-Japanese war, he led the campaign to provide matza for the Jewish soldiers on the frontlines at Passover. In 1906, he traveled to Germany and Holland to enlist the help of Jewish bankers to pressure the Russian government to curtail the pogroms.

At a young age, Yosef Yitzchak showed fearlessness, for which he would become famous, and was arrested numerous times for standing up to authorities. During the Czar's rule his father sent him to the Russian capital of Saint Petersburg to prevent the enactment of a detrimental government regulation. Young Rabbi Yosef Yitzchak's lobbying efforts failed. With no options left, he quietly entered the government building during the lunch hour and secretly made his way into the minister's private office. There, he found the documents, took out the minister's personal stamp and stamped "rejected" on the paper and placed it in the out-box.

When the Germans invaded during World War 1, Rabbi Sholom DovBer fled the ancestral home of Lubavitch in Byelorussia to Rostov-on-Don, six hundred miles south of Moscow. There, he reestablished the spiritual center of the Chabad Movement. He passed away just before Passover in 1920, leaving bereft a Jewish community facing an assault from the forces of Communism. His son, Rabbi Yosef Yitzchak Schneersohn, known by Chassidim as either the Frierdiker (Yiddish for previous) Rebbe or the Rebbe Rayatz (the letters of his name) succeeded him.

It was a fateful hour; the Communists were consolidating their power in the wake of the Russian Revolution. Communists wanted to create a new society, and religion was viewed as a part of the bourgeoisie, a past that must be cleansed. Many Jews embraced Communism, seeing it as an opportunity for freedom after the despotic Czarist regime. Young Jewish Communists stood at the helm of the battle against their own religion, establishing the Yevsektsia[32] and Yevkom.[33] These groups attempted to control the Jewish community, eliminating any vestige of religious observance. Semyon Dimanstein, a former student of the Chabad Yeshiva, headed the Yevsektsia. One of its leaders, Maria Frumkin,[34] a granddaughter of a rabbi, said, "It rests with the Jewish Communists to be more ruthless than others in shutting down Judaism."

The Yevsektsia harassed rabbis, instituted a ban on ritual slaughter and circumcision, and closed ritual baths and synagogues. They abolished the Kehillah, the system that guided Jewish community life, providing rabbinical leadership, education, and social and religious services. Authorities declared yeshivas and Chadorim (Jewish elementary schools) illegal. They banned Jewish publishing. The last religious book printed in the Soviet Union was a commentary on Maimonides in 1926; the last Jewish calendar was printed in 1928.

The group's greatest obstacle was the new Rebbe. In the summer of 1920, just a few months after his father's passing, the Rebbe was confronted in his synagogue by three Communist agents with pistols drawn. They ordered him to curtail his activities. Unafraid, the Rebbe faced his tormentors and told them that "many a man with but one world and two G-ds has been intimidated by toys like these, but I have one G-d and two worlds and do not fear them."

The new Rebbe shifted Jewish life underground. Many rabbinical scholars left Russia[35] and relocated their institutions of Jewish learning to Poland and Lithuania. Orthodox Jewish historian, Rabbi Berel Wein, says that the yeshivas' deans, such as Rabbi Baruch Ber Leibowitz, were "persecuted and hounded by the Communists."

The Rebbe refused to abandon Russian Jewry. Instead, he established a clandestine Jewish communal and educational network. Wein[36] notes that "Lubavitch alone among all Jewish religious organizations was able to maintain underground Jewish religious life for the entire seventy-five-year period until the collapse of the Communist system."

This secret system of synagogues, schools, yeshivas, and mikvahs sustained Jews against the Communist onslaught on Judaism. Throughout Russia, the Rebbe appointed representatives to lead the Jewish underground. He turned to Jews around the world to help keep Judaism alive in Russia. He used the diplomatic mail of Latvia, Estonia, and Poland to communicate abroad. American Jewish organizations like the Joint Distribution Committee[37] funneled funds to the Rebbe's projects via the diplomatic pouch. Children would secretly gather, one would stand lookout and the others would learn with the teacher. At the slightest suspicion, the kids would quickly disperse. When Communists closed underground Jewish schools in one location, the Rebbe moved them to another locale.[38]

In 1924,[39] the Rebbe invited a select group of his students to a clandestine meeting in Moscow. He established a secret covenant with them. Years later, the Rebbe recalled this historic moment:

"I chose nine students with intelligence and feeling for the Yeshiva Tomchei Temimim and invited them to a meeting in Moscow.

Together we made an oath: whatever will be, together we will give up our lives for Torah to our last drop of blood."

The Rebbe divided Russia's expanse among these nine students. They established hundreds of schools and Chadorim. Their identities remained secret. The Rebbe instructed them not to reveal their participation in the secret covenant to anyone.[40] Some survived and moved, years later, to the West; others lost their lives in the Soviet Gulag.

One of those who is believed to have been a member of the secret pact was Rabbi Elchonon Morozov. He had been the Rebbe's secretary and close confidant. Wanted by the police, he successfully hid for years under the false name of Berke Pewsner, spending almost a decade in the Raskin family home in Saint Petersburg. In 1938, the Secret Police, the NKVD, caught up with him and his son, Shmuel. Needing verification of Morozov's identity, they tortured Shmuel in front of his father.

"Is he Elchonon Morozov?" they demanded. The young man refused to answer, understanding the father's fate if his true identity was revealed. Seeing his son near death from the blows of his tormentors, Morozov cried out, "Shmuel, tell them I am your father!" Shortly afterward, Shmuel took his last breath. Then the interrogators turned to Rabbi Elchonon and told him that now, they would carry out his death sentence.

"Your crime:" the police told him, "the Lubavitcher Rebbe is G-d's representative in Russia and you are his representative."

Morozov was murdered by a firing squad.[41]

Shortly after convening the Chassidim to take the secret covenant, the Rebbe traveled back home to Rostov, only to be accosted by Communist authorities. They searched his home and interrogated him. After six weeks, they decided not to imprison him if he left Rostov. The Rebbe moved to Saint Petersburg.

Until 1927, the Communists and the Rebbe battled each other from a distance. The Rebbe operated surreptitiously, but the authorities knew that he was the architect of the Jewish underground. He would open a school; they would close it. He would position a rabbi in a city; they would imprison him. The Rebbe argued time and again that Russian law allowed for religious practice and what he was doing was legal. In 1927, the Yevsektsia decided to organize a rabbinical conference in newly named Leningrad (formerly Saint Petersburg), planning to use it as a forum for intimidating the rabbis into adopting their agenda. The Rebbe thwarted their plans, spearheading a successful boycott. After the Rebbe's success, the Communists decided to end the shadowboxing.

On June 14, 1927, they pounded on the Rebbe's door at midnight, calling out, "Schneersohn!" The police brusquely pushed the door open, headed by Soviet Agent Nachmanson, who had come from the Chassidic community of Nevel. His father had been a Chassid who would visit Lubavitch.

Nachmanson challenged the Rebbe's youngest daughter, Shaina. "Which party do you belong to?" Shaina retorted, "We belong to our father's party, we are nonpartisan daughters of Israel." He threatened her: "You should take into account our power and our opinions." He went on describing their ability to make everyone testify with "their methods," insinuating force, or even torture would be used to impose their view. Shaina stood her ground, saying, "People want to take everything by brute force – what a repulsive and unjustifiable thing it is to take hold of men with minds and opinions by the might of the fist and threat of the revolver."

As this confrontation was playing out in the front room of the apartment, the Rebbe's middle daughter, the future Rebbitzen Chaya Mushka, called out to her husband-to-be, warning, "Schneerson guests have come to visit us." Quickly Rabbi Menachem Mendel Schneerson, the Rebbe's future son-in-law, went to work hiding and destroying incriminating papers of the secret Jewish educational system.

That night, they took the Rebbe to the notorious Spalerka prison, a six-story fortress filled with small cells. Among the arresting officers was Lulav, whose father had been a Lubavitcher Chassid. He told the Rebbe, "My grandfather carried the bags of your grandfather. Let me carry yours." The Rebbe refused, telling him, "Your grandfather was a Chassid, so he had the good fortune to carry my grandfather's parcels wherever my grandfather went; you want to carry this parcel so that I should go, G-d forbid, where you want me to go. No, that cannot be! I'm not going to go your way." The Rebbe then seized his belongings from Lulav and gave them to one of the other guards.

It was the Rebbe's seventh arrest. Five times he had been detained during the Czar's rule, the first time in his hometown of Lubavitch in 1891. Just eleven years old at the time, he intervened when a policeman viciously attacked the local kosher butcher, accusing him of stealing. The young Yosef Yitzchak was hauled off to jail. Later, authorities found the policeman guilty of the crime. Subsequent arrests came from accusations made by Jewish groups in conflict with traditional Judaism, such as leaders of the Haskalah.[42] Each time, the Rebbe stood up for Jewish principles and in the end was freed.

This time, the situation was grave. The Rebbe was held in subhuman conditions.[43] He was denied the use of his talit and tefilin,[44] used in daily prayer. He launched a hunger strike until his religious items were provided. Two nights later, at 10:00 p.m., after two days of fasting, the first interrogation began. Lulav led the interrogators threatening the Rebbe. At the end of the questioning, Lulav told the Rebbe, "In twenty-four hours, you will be killed by a firing squad."

The arrest alarmed the Chassidim. Immediately, they began to reach out to government officials in Russia. The pressure from higher authorities prevented the death sentence from being carried out that day, but the Rebbe's life still hung in the balance.

The Rebbe's hunger strike succeeded; his talit and tefilin were returned. Still, he refused to acknowledge the authority of his jailers. When they entered his cell on the Sabbath to photograph him, he continued to pray with the talit on his head as if they were not there. Despite their pleas, he ignored them. Frustrated by their inability to shake the Rebbe, they left and returned, only after the Shabbat ended, to get his picture.

A fast was declared for Jews in Russia, and prayers were offered in all synagogues. As the news moved beyond Russia's borders, an international campaign to save the Rebbe began in Europe and the US. In Latvia, a close follower of the Rebbe, Mordechai Dubin, used his influence as a member of the Latvian Parliament.

In the United States, Agudas Chassidei Chabad (Association of Chabad Chassidim) mobilized. This same group would help the Rebbe escape from the Nazis thirteen years later. The small organization lacked any kind of political clout. Peretz and Asher Rabinowitz,[45] sons of prominent Boston Chabad Rabbi, Dovid Rabinowitz, were dispatched by their father to Washington. One was an attorney, the second an IRS employee. They tried to enlist the help of the most prominent Jew in the US, Supreme Court Justice Louis Brandeis. Failing to get an appointment, they stalked the hallways of the court, accosting Brandeis. He knew of the Rebbe and responded, "The prince of Israel is in trouble." Brandeis enlisted the support of high officials in the United States, including Senator William Borah, chairman of the Foreign Relations Committee. Borah brought the issue to President Herbert Hoover, who expressed his concern to Russia about the Rebbe's fate.

Jewish community leaders and others flooded Russian President Mikhail Ivanovitch Kalinin and Premier Alexei Rykov with telegrams. Madame Ekaterina Peskova, a human rights activist in Russia, used all her contacts to mitigate the sentence.

The worldwide pressure worked. The death sentence was reduced to ten years of hard labor in the distant Solovki Islands of Siberia. Instead of shipping the Rebbe to Siberia, however, the authorities interrogated him further. Again the Rebbe refused to answer his tormentors. A day later, the sentence was changed yet again. He was to be sent for three years of exile to the town of Kostroma. The journey by train would take some twenty-four hours. The Rebbe feared that he might be forced to arrive Friday after sunset, causing him to transgress the Sabbath. He chose to remain in prison over the weekend.

On Sunday, the Rebbe stood at the Leningrad train station waiting to depart to Kostroma. Thousands of Chassidim had gathered to say farewell to the Rebbe. Rabbi Mendel Meises told his grandson Avraham Zajac[46] decades later, "None spoke of their plans to go to the station since we all feared arrest, but thousands came, out of their concern for the Rebbe." So many Chassidim wanted to travel with the Rebbe that the Russians stopped ticket sales. Surrounded by Communist guards, the Rebbe ignored their presence and rose to address the large crowd. "We must proclaim openly to all that the Jewish religion, Torah, and its commandments are not subject to the coercion of others. No one can impose his belief on us, or force us to conduct ourselves contrary to our beliefs. We must remember that imprisonment and hard labor are only of this physical world, and of a brief duration, while Torah, mitzvahs, and the Jewish people are eternal."

Less than two weeks later, the Rebbe came for his weekly appearance at the police station in Kostroma and was informed of his release. Three days later, he arrived back home in Leningrad.

The Rebbe had been freed, but he still was in great danger. Shortly after his return, the Yevsektsia paper, *Der Emes*,[47] called for the Rebbe to be arrested again and sent into exile. There was no choice for him but to leave Russia and continue the battle from abroad. In Latvia, Dubin used all his diplomatic connections to force the Russians to release him. He held up the signing of a treaty that would have benefited Russia until the Rebbe was permitted to leave the country. In the end, it was the formal invitation by the Latvian government for the Rebbe to become the chief rabbi of Riga that gave him the diplomatic cover to escape Russia.

The Rebbe left Russia for Latvia with his family, a few of his closest Chassidim, and his library. From his new home in Riga, and later in Poland, he continued to direct and support the covert effort in Russia to keep Judaism alive.

In 1929, the Rebbe spent close to a year in America galvanizing support for Russian Jewry. Electrified by his courage against Communism, American Jews gave the Rebbe a hero's welcome and money to support the cause. He toured major Jewish population centers, including Boston, Baltimore, Detroit, and as far west as Saint Louis. Thousands greeted him when he arrived in Chicago and Detroit.[48] Throughout the visit, he gained a keen understanding of the challenges facing American Jewry. He witnessed the early stages of assimilation, and understood that this was an existential threat to the Jewish people. His visit set the stage for the revolution that he would launch just a decade later after his escape from Nazi Europe.

During the visit, he strengthened Agudas Chassidei Chabad. It had been started by Morris Kramer in 1924. There were some eighty Nusach Ari synagogues that followed Chabad custom, the members mostly immigrants from Russia who had an ancestral connection to Chabad. Rabbi Israel Jacobson, who arrived in the us in 1925, spearheaded Agudas Chassidei Chabad's efforts to raise funds for the Rebbe's projects in Russia, Europe, and British Palestine.

The Rebbe met with Jewish community leaders such as Louis Brandeis. Reform Rabbi Stephen S. Wise, who helped raise money for the Rebbe, came to visit him in his temporary residence in Brooklyn, remarking later to his students that they should go see the chacham (the wise leader of the Jewish people). One rabbi called him the "Lion of Russian Jewry" and the label struck a chord with the public.

Just before returning to Europe, the Rebbe went to Washington and met President Hoover, thanking him for his help in saving him from the Russian death sentence. Even after his return to Europe, he kept in communication with American Jewry, sending a series of emissaries to continue disseminating Chassidic doctrines and expand support for his ongoing work for Jews the world over.

A decade later at the Fifty-Seventh-Street Pier, the American Chassidim celebrated the Rebbe's escape from war-torn Europe. On that March morning in 1940, a harbor boat carried a delegation of important Chassidic leaders to the ship to welcome the Rebbe. Among them were the Kramer family and Rabbis Shmuel Levitin, Shlomo Aaron Kazarnovsky, and Israel Jacobson. Jacobson had come to the United States fifteen years earlier with his wife, two daughters, and one dollar in his pocket, infusing Agudas Chassidei Chabad with energy and Chassidic spirit.

Levitin, or Reb Shmuel as he was known, was a scholar who had studied in the original Yeshiva in Lubavitch and was sent to the us before the war as a "Shadar" (Shlucha Derabanan[49] – a private emissary of the Rebbe). Levitin had also been sent by the Fifth Rebbe, Rabbi Sholom DovBer, to revitalize Jewish education in remote Russian Georgia. Later he was arrested by the Communists and sentenced to three years in prison. Reb Shmuel's wife and some of his family members remained trapped in Poland and lost their lives in the Holocaust. After the Rebbe's arrival in the US, Shmuel would become the mashpiah (spiritual mentor) of a generation of students in the yeshiva in Brooklyn.

Rabbi Shlomo Aaron Kazarnovsky arrived in the US in 1924. He would evolve as a key figure in the Rebbe's efforts, even arranging the purchase of the Rebbe's home in Crown Heights. He had a knack for fundraising, and played a leadership role in Chabad's development.

On the ship, the Rebbe received the delegation individually in his stateroom. When Israel Jacobson entered, the Rebbe told him, "The sufferings I endured in prison in Russia do not compare to the torments of twelve weeks under their rule.[50] Now we will take care of the formalities quickly and get to our work immediately. Our work is Torah and Yiddishkeit.[51] As for the contention that we are weak physically, that we have no strength, the Almighty is, after all, He who gives strength to the weary."

At 11:00 a.m., the Rebbe appeared on the gangway adorned in his fur hat,[52] usually worn only on Shabbos, holidays, and special festive occasions. For him, his arrival in the United States was a joyous moment. He did not walk off the ship as he had done eleven years earlier. Transported in a wheelchair, his face, while radiant, reflected the tribulations he had suffered. No one on the dock knew that the Rebbe had been inflicted with multiple sclerosis seven years before.

The crowds cheered at the sight of the Rebbe.[53] Rabbi Avraham Hecht,[54] a member of the welcoming committee, said, "The Rebbe was the leader of the Jewish people. He was spiritual royalty." The police struggled to control the crowd's enthusiasm. Dockside, the Rebbe called for activism to save Polish Jewry and the students of the yeshivas stranded under Nazi rule. A few hours later at a reception for the Rebbe in the Greystone Hotel in Manhattan, the Rebbe wanted an intensification of Jewish education. "The Jewish people must strengthen Jewish education by establishing schools and yeshivas." He called on American Jews to focus inward on their spiritual and intellectual advancement, saying, "American Jews have exemplified the Jewish principle of compassion for others, now it is the time for American Jewry to take its proper role in Jewish scholarship and Avodah (service to the Almighty)."

In Riga, the Rebbe had prepared for this day by inviting Rabbi Chaim Hodakov to come with him to America to help organize a Jewish school system. At first, he refused the Rebbe's request, but when told it was now or never,[55] Hodakov joined him on the ship to America with the intention of returning to Europe after a short while.

Hodakov was born in White Russia; his family relocated to Riga when he was a toddler. As a young man, he was active in Jewish affairs, serving as a Jewish representative on the Riga City Council and heading the Jewish school system, a department of the Latvian government. On the ship while they crossed the Atlantic, the Rebbe instructed Hodakov[56] to draw up a plan for starting a Jewish school system in the US.

That day, the Rebbe called a meeting of his key supporters and Chassidim. He wanted immediate action. He asked them to reopen the next day the Lubavitcher Yeshiva that had existed in Poland and earlier in Russia. He wanted what seemed the impossible, to recreate in the US a yeshiva with the values and academic rigor that existed in Europe, championing his theme that "America is not different." Later that evening, two of the Rebbe's closest supporters came to him. They each advised against such a strident course of action.

At four o'clock the following morning, the Rebbe wrote in his diary about this private meeting with "devoted friends" recalling their words: "We heard what you suggested at the meeting earlier about establishing a yeshiva. We are saddened to tell you that the spiritual situation in America is depressing. We must save you from a catastrophic mistake. America is a country that consumes many great and good people. It's a country of momentary excitement and coldness. Many great rabbis have been welcomed with enthusiasm only to see the enthusiasm cool off and forgotten."

The Rebbe wrote that as he recited the evening prayers, tears came to his eyes his first night in America.

In a poignant entry in his diary a week later, the Rebbe reminisced about Chassidic life in his birthplace of Lubavitch – how Chassidim would come on pilgrimages to immerse themselves even for a few days in Torah study and spiritual reflection. He lamented the tremendous disparity between Chassidic life in Europe and what he saw in New York, writing that "Lubavitch in New York is too painful to write about." The Rebbe contemplated the challenge that lay ahead of him. He did not feel that his miraculous escape was a random event. Rather, Divine Providence had brought him to these shores for a purpose.[57] He was determined to remake Jewish life in the United States. His physical handicaps, confinement to a wheelchair, and fragile health, did not deter him; nor did the lack of financial resources. He saw American Jews adrift in a sea of assimilation, losing connection to their heritage. He was determined to change that destiny. He told one of his close Chassidim, "I shed tears that could fill a bathtub to remove the coldness and insensitivity of American Jewry."

The yeshiva (rabbinical school) wouldn't open the next day, but in less than a week, studies began in Congregation Oneg Shabbos in Brooklyn.

Still tearing at his heart, however, was the plight of European Jewry. Decades later, in a speech in Sydney, Rabbi Yitzchak Groner recalled Purim celebrated a few days later in New York: "Thousands came and the Rebbe wished everyone good Yom Tov (literally, good day; colloquially, good holiday), saying 'But is it a Yom Tov? My ears and my eyes still see the catastrophe of Polish Jews. I will never forget the cries of Shema Yisroel from the Jews who were in the cellar with me during the bombing.'"

A few months after the Rebbe's arrival in New York, the address that has become synonymous with Lubavitch – 770 Eastern Parkway – was purchased. A committee of Chassidim, headed by the attorney Sam Kramer and Rabbi Shlomo Aaron Kazarnovsky, organized the campaign to raise the funds. The three-story building was located on the central artery of Eastern Parkway in upscale Crown Heights with its mansions, draped in leafy walkways. The Rebbe moved into the second floor. The yeshiva found a permanent home in the Beth Medrash (study hall) on the ground floor. Chassidim began to call the new center of Lubavitch "770" after the street number of the address on Eastern Parkway, Brooklyn.

The decision to locate in Crown Heights was indicative of the Rebbe's vision to change American Jewry. The logical choice for the

Rebbe's residence was Brownsville, the center of Orthodox Judaism in the US, called, at the time, the Jerusalem of America. Instead, the Rebbe settled in a neighborhood that represented Jews making their first steps away from observance. He was making his first beachhead in his campaign to change Jewish life in the United States.

A block away from the Rebbe's new home towered the Brooklyn Jewish Center,[58] one of the most prestigious Conservative temples in the country. With more than two thousand members, it cast great influence over the neighborhood. Built in the early 1920s, the center pioneered the concept of bringing religious, cultural, educational, and even recreation activities, into one facility, earning the nickname, the Shul with the Pool. The Conservative rabbi, Isaac Leventhal, did not want the Rebbe down the block. Avraham Hecht says Leventhal contacted Borough President, John Cashmore, claiming "property values would go down and anti-Semitism would rise if the Rebbe moves in." Around the corner was the Farband (the Workmen's Circle), the center of the Yiddish secular Movement. President Street, just two blocks from the Rebbe's new home, was full of mansions and affluent Jews on the road to the American dream. Israeli writer, M. Nirberger, wrote that "the Rebbe's move into one of the most affluent and secular neighborhoods was intentional."

The Yeshiva was the first initiative and would always remain the crown jewel of the Rebbe's efforts. Eventually, it would spawn the largest network of college-level rabbinical colleges (yeshivas) in North America.[59] He was not satisfied with creating a small institution with a limited student body, however. The whole continent was in his sights.

This vision was beyond the scope of others in the small American Orthodox community. Other prominent roshei yeshiva (rabbinical scholars) had fled Europe and arrived in the United States. They, too, were advocating the establishment of centers of Jewish learning, but their philosophy was different. They created small fortresses of Torah that included little engagement with the wider community. These were enclaves similar to those in Europe where life as it had been known across the Atlantic could be reconstructed. Through encouraging an elite group of scholars in citadels of Torah,[60] they hoped to ensure the survival[61] of Judaism in the United States. They were in a defensive mode of protecting the small nucleus of observant Jews from greater attrition. They called themselves the She'airis Haplaitah, the surviving remnant.

It was a replay of the strategies two decades earlier in Russia. With the rise of Communism, most of the great yeshiva scholars abandoned Russia, relocating their institutions of Jewish learning and students to nearby Poland and Lithuania. On American soil, some of these same scholars[62] advocated a retreat into insular communities. As in Europe, their prime agenda was the preservation of Jewish scholarship and their small group of students.

In Russia, the Rebbe remained and defied the Communists, moving Jewish life underground. He was concerned for the welfare of all Jews, not just the scholarly elite,[63] when he set up a network of secret schools. He left the Soviet Union only when there was no choice. Now on American soil, the Rebbe again took the offensive.

The Rebbe's vision included all Jews. Jewish education was essential for Jewish survival. Every Jewish child must be placed in a Jewish school. The Rebbe did not want to wait for a generation of scholars that might create a trickledown effect on the broader community. He wanted immediate action directed toward every Jew, practicing or not, in America. As he told Avraham Hecht, one of the first students in the yeshiva, "When you are at war and the general loses his life, then the private rises in rank swiftly. It's time for you to become a general and start teaching others."

At the time, Rabbi Hershel Fogelman[64] was a student in Yeshiva Torah Vodaath[65] in Brooklyn. Later, he would become one of the Rebbe's early shluchim, moving to Worcester, Massachusetts to run the day school there. He explained that the Rebbe wanted to change the whole mindset of religious Jews. "We, the few students in one of the few New York yeshivas, felt like we were on a wagon train on the prairie, isolated, surrounded by Indians, and holding on for dear life," he said. "The Rebbe arrived like the US Cavalry. He was not satisfied in fending off the Indians, protecting the wagons, and saving the settlers. He wanted to conquer the whole continent."

The desire to withdraw from the broader society was under-standable.[66] Starting in the mid-nineteenth century, the yeshiva system had been under attack in Europe. First, there was the Haskalah (the effort to secularize the Jewish community that started in Germany and then moved eastward). It drew many students away from the study of Torah to secular subjects.

A wide spectrum of new ideologies emerged promising varied solutions to anti-Semitism in Europe and the lack of human rights. Zionism offered a secular homeland; Communism, equality for all; and Socialism, workers' rights. These ideologies drew Jews away from yeshivas and observance. When Jews arrived in the US, many discarded religious ritual in the quest for the American dream.

The Rebbe's strident new strategy for America received little support from the secular Jewish establishment. The Reform and Conservative Movements had emerged as the major forces in Jewish life in the US. During the latter part of the nineteenth century, Reform had blossomed under the strong leadership of Isaac Mayer Wise,[67] who emigrated from Bohemia in 1846, moving to Cincinnati where he founded the Reform seminary, the Hebrew Union College, and other institutions. The first wave of European immigration of Jews from Germany, the birthplace of Reform in the early nineteenth century, provided Wise a strong base.

The Eastern European immigrants who came to America toward the end of the nineteenth century had stronger roots in tradition, but were fast becoming more American. They looked for a balance between the radical changes of Reform and what some viewed as the rigidity of Orthodoxy. This quest for the middle road by large numbers of immigrants empowered the growth of the Conservative Movement. By the time the Rebbe arrived on American shores, these groups dominated Jewish life.

Both the Reform and the Conservative viewed with disdain the Rebbe's strategy of remolding communities by building yeshivas and day schools. They espoused what one rabbi called the eleventh commandment of Jewish life of that era: "Thou Shalt Melt," or integrate, into the society. For most American Jews, the public schools were the ticket to advancement in the new society. Jewish schools were viewed as archaic and a handicap to getting ahead in America.[68] In 1940, there were only seven thousand children, a bit more than one percent of Jewish school-age children, in the US and Canada who were enrolled in Jewish day schools and yeshivas. Some children attended supplementary schools known as Hebrew Schools or Chadarim. Avraham Hecht says, "The majority of the teachers were personally not religious and were poorly trained. Teaching was a way to supplement their meager income."

Jewish social scientist, Charles Silberman,[69] wrote that the principle of Jewish identity in the fifties and sixties was "Shah," or "Don't be too Jewish in public." Judaism was a source of anxiety and discomfort. Prominent Jews tried their best to keep their Jewish identity hidden. Famous Jews such as columnist Walter Lippmann, and Robert Moses, the great builder of New York, denied their Jewish background. Lippmann worried that Jews were too conspicuous in America.[70] Moses told people he was not a Jew, a hard thing to deny with a name like that. The Jewish moguls of Hollywood bent over backward to be more American than most Americans, as did the Sulzberger family, owners of *The New York Times*, who published few stories on the Holocaust, fearing too much coverage might turn the war into a "Jewish issue."

Anti-Semitism was still strong in the United States. Jewish immigrants discovered that when they changed their names from Cohen to Colton, Levine to Levitt, they suddenly received job interviews and their children were accepted to prestigious colleges.

Progress had been made in the early decades of the twentieth century to strengthen Orthodoxy. The Orthodox Union[71] united many of the Orthodox synagogues in the US. Young Israel,[72] Agudath[73] Israel of America, Yeshiva University,[74] and the Mizrachi[75] made valiant efforts. Yeshivas such as Torah Vodaath in Brooklyn created centers of classical Jewish learning. Yeshiva University produced young American rabbis who were meeting with success. The approach of the Orthodox was defensive and parochial – the deck was stacked against them. The push for Americanization was causing many Orthodox synagogues to drop the traditional separation of the genders and affiliate with the mushrooming Conservative Movement. As the older generation passed on, many smaller congregations closed. The Depression had brought great economic difficulties; many observant Jews, out of desperation for jobs, ceased to be Sabbath-observant.

The Rebbe's theme was "America Iz Nisht Anderish – America Is Not Different." Time and again he stated, "Just as Yiddishkeit (Judaism) flourished in Europe, so too it could in America." He challenged the status quo of both the Orthodox and broader community. He started by drafting his Chassidim and students to seize the initiative. In that first year, no more than fifty people were present at the farbrengens that the Rebbe led. After one of these celebrations, his small group of American yeshiva students convened on Saturday night to decide how to implement the Rebbe's goals. They sat around the table in the small dining room in the basement of 770.

Avraham Hecht stood on a table and told his friends that he had a speech that each could deliver to synagogues about the need for enrolling children in Jewish schools. Shy, and scared of crowds, Hecht had refrained from making a bar mitzvah speech. Now he stood in front of the ten or so students in the tiny Lubavitch Yeshiva and suggested that they take to the podiums of local synagogues with the Rebbe's message.

The next day, Rabbi Avraham Pariz, a Lubavitcher Chassid living in Israel, stranded in the US because of the war, called a local synagogue. The congregational rabbis shared the Rebbe's concern for Jewish education but lacked tools to implement a plan of action. They agreed that a yeshiva student could come over. Hecht and Pariz made a strange pair. Nearing fifty, Pariz originated from the Russian city of Babrouisk, had studied in Lubavitch, and fled Russia for Palestine before the war. Pariz was short and slight, spoke no English, and lived in the small Chassidic enclave of 770 with little understanding of America. Hecht was an American boy; he towered over Pariz and spoke in Brooklyn-infused English.

They came to the shul, and Hecht[76] went up to the podium for his first public address. "A parent is obligated to circumcise his child, to teach him Torah, train him in a profession, find him a wife, and – some say – how to swim." Hecht asked why it was important to instruct a child how to swim if he lives far from the ocean. And he answered with the classic commentary of Rashi: "Maybe the person will be on a ship that sinks and swimming will be essential." He drove home the point that this is really an allegory for life. "We need to teach our children to swim in the society, this can be done only with Jewish education."

Hecht's speech was so well received that he started visiting shuls throughout Brooklyn, and his fellow students used his speech in their visits to congregations.

The Rebbe challenged other Orthodox groups, asking the National Council of Young Israel to set a goal of opening a few hundred new synagogues in the near term. The Rebbe's demands were beyond their wildest dreams. Nevertheless, the Rebbe lost no time. While making every effort to save his students and Chassidim in war-torn Europe, he began infusing new life into American Jewry. Within two years, he opened fourteen yeshivas, primarily as day schools, and appointed his eldest son-in-law, Rabbi Shemaryahu Gurary, as the director of these yeshivas. The Rashag, as Rabbi Shemaryahu Gurary was known among the Chassidim, worked tirelessly, raising money and organizing.

In 1943, the Rebbe established the organizations that would have the deepest impact on Jewish life in the United States: Merkos L'inyonei Chinuch (Central Organization for Jewish Education) and Machne Israel. The mandate of Merkos was Jewish education. Machne focused inwardly on the needs of the observant community. Named to head these institutions was the Rebbe's second son-in-law and eventual successor, Rabbi Menachem Mendel Schneerson. Known at the time as the Ramash, which was a Hebrew abbreviation of his name, Schneerson had escaped the horrors of Nazi-controlled France via Vichy France and Portugal, arriving in America in the spring of 1941.

Merkos was the first national Jewish organization dedicated to the development of Jewish education in the United States. Under the leadership of Rabbi Menachem Mendel, it quickly blossomed. Within four years, it had eighteen schools operating in the US. Merkos launched a network of youth clubs known as Mesibos Shabbos, where children would gather on Shabbos afternoon in a Torah atmosphere. Its division, Shalah (the National Committee for the Furtherance of Jewish Education), pioneered Released Time at public schools throughout New York and other cities. State law permitted children to be released for an hour a week of religious instruction. The Rebbe stood up to the Jewish establishment that opposed the program on grounds that it lowered the barriers between church and state. Merkos launched a publication division, Kehot Publication Society. In 1943, Merkos initiated a summer outreach program that sent yeshiva students to visit Jewish communities outside of the New York area.

Rabbi Hershel Fogelman recalled a Chassidic gathering in the early 1940s. The Ramash told the small crowd of students, "My father-in-law is starting with clubs for children but he intends to transform all Judaism in America."

The initial steps to open the first yeshiva outside the New York area began on a wintry Saturday night in December of 1941. The Rebbe called in one of his students from the yeshiva, Rabbi Mordechai Altein.[77] The Rebbe told him that he had just received a letter from the Nusach Ari Synagogue in Pittsburgh with a request for a rabbi.

"Tomorrow," the Rebbe instructed, "you are to go to Pittsburgh to assume the position." The young student asked the Rebbe for permission to stay for two days until the Chassidic holiday of Yud Tes Kislev[78] so he could celebrate with the Rebbe. "No," the Rebbe replied, "you must go tomorrow. I will send a telegram that you are coming." The next morning, Altein, with a sense of excitement, took the train to Pittsburgh. As the train rolled east, news arrived about the Japanese attack on Hawaii. Arriving at the local synagogue in Pittsburgh, Altein was given a crash course in politics. The synagogue's president had moved to the new neighborhood in the city. His goal was to Americanize the shul, which meant to do away with the old-style Orthodoxy.

Altein took the trolley across town to the president, who hadn't imagined that his letter to New York would produce a young rabbi adorned with a beard and hat. At first, he mistook the yeshiva student for a schnorrer (fundraiser). Realizing that his mission was not to collect funds, the president showed little enthusiasm for his synagogue's new leader. However, the hostility of the president and the apathy of the community couldn't withstand the energy of the

Rebbe's student. A few weeks later, on Chanukah, the Rebbe wrote Altein to start organizing a yeshiva. That winter, operations began.

A year later, Rabbi Altein was sent by the Rebbe to the Bronx where he established another yeshiva. In his place, Rabbi Shalom Posner came to Pittsburgh from Chicago.[79] One of the members of his congregation in Chicago told him that hair would grow on his palm before he would succeed in Pittsburgh. Posner galvanized a small group of students, but it would take years of hard work before the yeshiva flourished. In 1999, however, the yeshiva earned a Presidential Blue Ribbon Award as one of the most outstanding elementary schools in the United States, the only Jewish school to receive the award that year. Pittsburgh was among the many communities that the Rebbe's pioneering vision transformed.

The yeshiva day school in Worcester started when the duo of Pariz and Hecht – feeling success in their visits to New York synagogues – were asked by the Rebbe to go to Worcester. There, they found Yiddish-speaking European rabbis, overwhelmed by the challenges of America. There were many old-time shul-goers, but the younger generation was becoming much less observant. So when Hecht and Pariz proposed opening a school, the rabbis agreed. The next day, without books or curriculum, and with only one student, the yeshiva opened.

Rabbi Hershel Fogelman, fresh out of yeshiva and still single, came in 1944 to Worcester to direct the school. Fundraising was tough, but he found those willing to help. "Many of the grandparents feared their families would be gone from Judaism, so they supported it." At times, it was very rough, Fogelman recalls. "We worked hard to get local support; little money came from New York." Rachel Fogelman,[80] who joined her new husband in Worcester in 1947, said, "We had more guts than money."

The story repeated itself in city after city. A student of the Rebbe would arrive, start off in the local synagogue with a handful of students, then a school would blossom. Rabbi Pinchus Weiler,[81] a Russian Jew from Riga, served as an advance man for the Rebbe. In one city, he discovered a Jewish milkman and joined his morning route. At each house, the milkman would fill him in on the family.

"Oh, the Levines in this house have three kids…" Rabbi Weiler marked down the information and returned later in the day to ask the family to place their kids in the school.

The Rebbe was the pacesetter, and other Orthodox groups followed. By 1944, there were already seven thousand students in yeshivas in the New York area. The Rebbe had proved to all that Torah education could succeed in the US. In 1944, one of his Chassidim brought him news that a coalition of yeshiva scholars had started a similar organization called Torah Umesorah, whose plan was to develop Jewish schools. Expecting the Rebbe to be upset by the competition, the Chassid was surprised to hear of the Rebbe's joy. "That's what I hoped they would do," the Rebbe remarked. The impetus for Torah Umesorah had come from Rabbi Shraga Feivel Mendlowitz, one of the visionary founders of America's pioneering yeshiva, Yeshiva Torah Vodaath.

As the war ended in 1945, a host of new challenges and opportunities emerged. Chassidim who had succeeded in escaping from behind the Iron Curtain congregated in Europe. The Rebbe set up a refugee office in Paris headed by Rabbi Binyomin Gorodetsky to help the families. The Rebbe suggested that some should move to Australia, others to Canada, the US, South America, and Europe. Instead of concentrating all his followers in one location, the Rebbe was setting the stage for the next step in his agenda – seeding the international growth of Jewish life that he was anticipating in the postwar era. These Russian Chassidim would evolve into the nucleus that would create vibrant Jewish life in their new countries.

One of the major priorities of the Rebbe was the strengthening of the Chabad community in pre-State Palestine, where many Russian refugees were advised to move. He founded a Chabad town near Tel Aviv called Kfar Chabad. With time, this would become the epicenter of Chabad in Israel.

The Rebbe's extensive correspondence[82] from the last decade of his life reveals a remarkable breadth of interest. A mikvah in Washington Heights, a shul in Chicago, the need for Torah study for young and old. No aspect of Jewish life in the United States was untouched by the Rebbe's reach. When Yeshiva Torah Vodaath faced a financial crisis, he quietly provided a large sum of money to quell the emergency. From his home in Brooklyn, still in a wheelchair, suffering serious illness and, in the last five years, debilitated by a stroke that left his speech difficult to understand, he was connected to all sections of the Jewish community. News of illness of a Chassid would bring him to tears, and information of the success of one of his shluchim enrolling a few more children in a yeshiva would cause his spirits to soar.

In 1949, the Rebbe began sending young rabbinical students to college campuses. He told one group, "The time has come for us to start working with college students."

Still, the Rebbe saw himself first and foremost as a teacher of Torah and Chassidic philosophy. Rabbi Leibel Schapiro,[83] dean of the Rabbinical College of Greater Miami, placed the Rebbe's initiatives in historical perspective: "The Rebbe's foray into the battle against assimilation was because no one else was leading the charge. First and foremost, Chabad is a Chassidic way of life, focusing on service of G-d, not a movement or organization." The Rebbe was a great Talmid Chochom (prolific writer and teacher of Torah). More than fifty volumes of his deep insights into Torah have been published.

Within ten years of the Rebbe's arrival in America, the number of children in Jewish day schools in the US and Canada grew by three and a half times to 23,100. But the Rebbe's vision was to reach Jews everywhere. In the period prior to his passing, with the help of the Ramash, he began to investigate the situation of Jews in Morocco, Tunisia, and Libya. He instructed his representative in Paris, Rabbi Binyomin Gorodetsky, to review the status of Jewish education in those countries. A week before his passing, he asked his son-in-law, the Ramash, to arrange to send a shliach to North Africa to revitalize Jewish education.

On the last Thursday evening of the month of January in 1950, the Rebbe received visitors for yechidus (private audiences) until late in the evening. The visitors that night had included Rabbi Yitzchak Dubov, a prominent Chabad rabbi from Manchester, England. When he asked the Rebbe how he felt, he answered, "We have to be satisfied and with G-d's help we will hear good news about the Jewish people."

That evening, a bride-to-be, nineteen-year-old Terry Wertheim[84] from Washington Heights, saw the Rebbe with her parents. She was planning a formal engagement that coming Saturday night. After the visit, around midnight, the Rebbe's secretary, Rabbi Moshe Rodshtein, called her parents. He explained that the Rebbe was concerned that the family was offended since he had not formally wished them Mazel Tov during the meeting. He went on to explain in the Rebbe's name that Mazel Tov is wished only after the formal engagement, which was not happening until Saturday evening.

Late the following Friday night, a loud noise woke up seventy-four-year-old Moshe Feiglin. He lived some ten thousand miles from Brooklyn in the agricultural community of Shepparton, Australia, a hundred miles north of Melbourne. Startled, he jumped out of bed, waking his grandson, twelve-year-old Uri.[85] Together, they investigated the source of the strange noise. Moshe Feiglin had been the first Chabad follower to move to Australia, arriving in 1912 from Turkish-ruled Palestine. Feiglin had established his farm in Shepparton, as the first beachhead for Chabad down under.

Grandson and grandfather hurried to the dining room to explore the cause of the noise. The framed picture of the Rebbe, featured prominently in the room for years, had fallen, its frame broken on the floor. "Something has happened," Feiglin told his grandson. Uri attempted to calm his grandfather, who was deeply disturbed, suggesting, "It was just a wind that blew through the window, or a tremor, that knocked the picture off the wall."

Feiglin could not be consoled, convinced the shattered picture was a foreboding sign. Throughout the Sabbath, Feiglin was deeply troubled by the ominous event. The next day, a telegram arrived with two simple words "Histalkut Admor." The Rebbe had passed away during the Sabbath in New York.

The news shocked the Chassidim in New York. The Rebbe had suffered from illness, but none thought his situation critical. The heart attack was fatal, taking the soul of the sixty-nine-year-old

Rebbe on January 28, 1950, corresponding with the tenth day of the Jewish month of Shvat.

The next day, thousands gathered to pay their last respects to the Rebbe. The aron (coffin) had been hastily constructed from wood of the prayer-stand and tables the Rebbe had used for Torah study. Prior to the funeral, Chassidim walked by the coffin paying their last respects, asking forgiveness. At 12:30 p.m., the coffin was taken through the front door of 770 and draped with the Rebbe's long Shabbat coat. The funeral continued down Eastern Parkway and finally to Montefiore Cemetery in Queens.

On that Sunday, Chassidim around the world gathered for memorial services. In Tel Aviv, hundreds of Chassidim convened that evening for a special service in the Chabad Synagogue on Nachalat Binyamin Street. Jewish law requires that when a great Jewish leader passes away, every Jew should sit Shivah (period of mourning) for a brief time. Together they tore their clothes and sat on the ground, as is customary.

The somber mood was shattered by Rabbi Avraham Pariz.[86] He had traveled to New York before the outbreak of war and was stranded there during the 1940s. He stood up proclaiming, "Jews, we have a Rebbe!" referring to the Ramash, the departed leader's son-in-law. No one thought, at this moment of mourning, about a successor. His audacity shattered the somber feeling in the synagogue. Many of the Chassidim were disturbed about his outburst. Despite the consternation, he continued: "I had the honor to get to know him. He tries to hide his greatness. He is fooling us. I worked with him in the same room for ten years."

Pariz asked the Chassidim in Tel Aviv to send a letter requesting the Ramash to become the Seventh Lubavitcher Rebbe. Focused on their terrible loss, the Chassidim did not heed Pariz's call that night, but the seeds that would blossom in the months to come had been planted.

Chapter Three

Even a Needle Could Not Fit Between the Crowds

No official invitations had been sent. No dignitaries were invited. It wasn't a formal event. Sensing history, Chassidim and many other Jews had flocked to the synagogue on the main floor of Chabad's headquarters at 770 Eastern Parkway in Crown Heights, Brooklyn, New York. Along the hallway, the wall between two rooms had been removed and the larger space converted into a place of worship and study. Tudor-style windows graced the side wall. The simple sanctuary was a humble setting to start a new era in Chabad leadership. The room itself was not very large, measuring some six hundred square feet. Simple wooden tables and benches ran down its length. The people were packed from wall to wall, standing on the benches and tables. One witness said that "even a needle could not fit between the crowds." The crowd spilled into the hallways, adjacent rooms, lobby, courtyard, and out to the street. Some peeked in from the windows on the building's side. Others stood in the adjoining office, straining to see over the partition that partially blocked the view into the shul.

All of these people had come hopeful that forty-nine-year-old Rabbi Menachem Mendel Schneerson, known as the Ramash, would accept the position of the Seventh Lubavitcher Rebbe, although, officially, the gathering was just a farbrengen (a Chassidic gathering), to mark the first yartziet of the Previous Rebbe, Rabbi Yosef Yitzchak Schneersohn. The event was slated for January 17, 1951, the tenth day of the Jewish month of Shevat. In the twelve months since the Rebbe's passing, Chassidim had been lobbying his son-in-law, Rabbi Menachem Mendel, to assume the position of Rebbe. Time and again he had refused, but as the memorial day approached, efforts had intensified. In previous generations, Chassidim would petition the most appropriate descendant of the earlier Rebbe to carry on the legacy. Rabbi Yosef Yitzchak Schneersohn, the Sixth Rebbe, had three daughters. The oldest was married to Rabbi Shemaryahu Gurary. The second, Chaya Mushka, to the Ramash. The youngest, Shaina, perished with her husband in the Holocaust.

The grassroots movement from the Chassidim had started almost as soon as Rabbi Menachem Mendel Schneerson's father-in-law had passed away. Rabbi Yitzchak Dubov, an elder Chassid from Manchester, had already approached Rabbi Menachem Mendel during the Shivah of his father-in-law, the Sixth Rebbe. As his friend, Avraham Pariz, did in Tel Aviv, Rabbi Bentzion Shemtov, the leader of the Chabad community in London, sent a letter to the Ramash declaring him Rebbe, as did Chassidim in other parts of the world.

In New York, some began to treat the Ramash with the deference usually reserved for a Rebbe: refusing to sit in his presence, not taking his hand, or addressing the Ramash in the formal third party in Yiddish. When a Chassid, who had long been close to the Ramash, refused to shake his hand in a meeting, the Ramash remarked, "You, too?!" They turned to him for advice on personal and communal issues. A knock on his door – and he would find time for anyone. Just a few months after the Previous Rebbe's passing, Rabbi Shmuel Levitin told a group of students, "The fact that the Ramash answers questions about issues of spiritual service is not proof he is a Rebbe. That, he could have learned from Jewish classics. The fact that he is willing to give advice on worldly issues, questions of health – that is a sign he is accepting the position of Rebbe."

A few Chassidim felt that the eldest son-in-law of the Previous Rebbe, Rabbi Shemaryahu Gurary,[1] known as the Rashag, would be the right choice. This effort did not garner much popular support, and dissipated.

A few weeks before the first yartziet, a group of senior Chassidim met with the Ramash. They had been followers of the Previous Rebbe and even his father, the Fifth Rebbe, Rabbi Sholom DovBer. Thirty of them, headed by the community elders, entered the Ramash's office. Emotion filled the air as they presented him with a Ksav Hiskashruth, or Pledge of Loyalty, from the US community. Hundreds of Chassidim had signed, asking the Ramash to accept the leadership and pledging their loyalty to him.

When they entered the office, he asked, "What do you want?"

Reading the first line, the Ramash closed the letter and began to cry. Sobbing, he asked them to leave, saying, "This has no connection to me." Time and again through the year the Ramash had rebuffed the requests of the Chassidim. Chassidic historian Rabbi Yosef Greenberg[2] explains: "Throughout Chassidic history, it had taken the urging of others for potential leaders to accept the position of Rebbe." The founder of Chassidism, Rabbi Israel Baal Shem Tov, was reluctant to assume communal leadership. For six years, Rabbi Adam Baal Shem, leader of the secret fellowship of Jewish mystics, implored Rabbi Israel Baal Shem Tov to begin spreading the principles of Chassidism before he finally began teaching publicly.

According to Greenberg, "Until this point, the Ramash was able to dedicate himself to scholarship and personal spiritual development; now he would have to be immersed in the mundane aspects of leading the community." Chassidic theologian, Rabbi Yoel Kahn,[3] explains: "The Rebbe was very reserved, a private person. Public leadership was the opposite of his character."

Later that week, Jewish newspapers reported[4] that the Chassidim presented a petition accepting the Ramash as the new Lubavitcher Rebbe. The Ramash directed his assistant, Rabbi Hodakov, to notify the papers that this was an incorrect report. Before calling the media, recognizing how fateful the moment was, Hodakov informed the Chassidic elders, Rabbis Shlomo Aaron Kazarnovsky, Shmuel Levitin and Israel Jacobson. He told them he could wait a few hours until he actually called the press, but he urged them to intervene with the Ramash. The three rushed to the Ramash's office, imploring him not to make a public retraction. They discovered that he had prepared a formal public statement that he was not accepting the position. Levitin argued the paper did not say the Ramash had accepted the leadership, only that the Chassidim had presented him with a letter. Kazarnovsky begged the Ramash to, at the least, not place a retraction in the paper. They told the Rebbe, "All the statement said was that the Chassidim are accepting the Rebbe as their leader. And that, they are doing." Reluctantly, the Ramash agreed.

In anticipation of the yartziet, the Ramash had issued a letter to the Chassidic community encouraging everyone to learn specific teachings of the Rebbe, visit his grave in prayer, light a yartziet candle, and perform other observances common in a Jewish memorial.

As is customary on a yartziet, the Ramash would lead a Chassidic farbrengen. For Chassidim, a farbrengen is an event of great joy and celebration. The structure was simple; the Rebbe would give a series of talks ranging from fifteen to forty-five minutes. The topics could vary from a deep explanation of a concept in Torah, Talmud, or mysticism to a comment on contemporary issues. Between the talks, the Chassidim would sing melodies and toast the Rebbe, saying, "L'Chaim – To life!" At the directive of his father-in-law, the Ramash had begun occasionally leading farbrengens shortly after his marriage in 1928. When he arrived from Europe in 1941, he started doing this monthly, as requested by the Sixth Rebbe. Until this public exposure, he had been quite unknown to many in the Chassidic community.

Rabbi Tzvi Kotlarsky was a student in the Chabad Yeshiva in pre-war Poland. He saw the Ramash during his visits to his father-in-law. "He wore a light hat and suit." He described him as reserved and as someone who shunned the limelight. "It was hard to imagine that in the future he would emerge as such a strong leader."

Rabbi Yitzchak Groner recalled the Ramash's arrival in New York[5] in spring of 1941. The Rebbe had asked Rabbi Jacobson to lead a delegation of prominent Chassidic elders and the students to welcome his son-in-law. Describing him, the Rebbe said, "My son-in-law knows the entire Shas (the sixty volumes of Talmud), the commentaries, Chassidic works, and the codes, all by heart." Groner recalled his first encounter at the pier. "All the students of the yeshiva went to greet him. Down came a youngish man, his beard tied under. He came over to every boy, and he projected much warmth." A few days later, the Chassidic community organized a formal welcome. Rabbi Leibel Groner attended with his father, and he observed: "For two hours, the Ramash explored the obligation of giving thanks according to the Talmud. For another two hours, he explained the Chassidic perspective of the same theme. Finally, he connected it all, showing how to apply these ideas to one's personal service of G-d. The Chassidic elders were in awe of the depth of scholarship, his ability to integrate various dimensions of Jewish learning, and their application to daily life."

Earlier on the day of the yartziet, delegations of Chassidim from various communities met the Ramash, presenting him yet again with requests for him to become Rebbe.

The Ramash entered the synagogue at 9:45 p.m. The room was packed; there was barely place for him, and he sat on a simple chair on the small podium in the front of the room. The Chassidic elders with long white beards positioned themselves around the small head table, waiting like palace guards. Two tables stretched down the middle of the room, and hundreds of people stood around on the floor and on benches, straining to get a glimpse. Despite the winter cold outside, Rabbi Shlomo Zalman Hecht of Chicago passed out from the heat. It was so full, one observer later said that "the sweat seemed to roll down the walls." Sensing history, Chassidim had arranged for the event to be recorded on audiotape.

Chassidim have no formal ceremony to appoint a new leader. The farbrengen would be the venue. A farbrengen led by the Rebbe was unique. It would be highlighted by a Maamar (Chassidic discourse). A Maamar explores the philosophical depths of Chassidic philosophy and is delivered only by a Rebbe. Traditionally, Chassidim stand when a Maamar is presented, and sing a special melody, the Maamar nigun, before a Rebbe's utterance of the Maamar. Everyone wondered, would there be a Maamar? If yes, it would mean that he had finally assumed the position of Rebbe.

In his first talk, the Ramash spoke of the need to strengthen the connection to the Previous Rebbe: "Each one of us must continue the task the Rebbe entrusted us with." This represented a deeper theme. He, himself, was carrying on a sacred mission entrusted to him by his father-in-law, the Previous Rebbe.

As the second talk began, it seemed a change was happening. The tone was different. "It's customary," he said in Yiddish, "that in America, when you begin something new, you issue a statement." He used English for the word "statement." This caused a ripple in the crowd; many thought he was alluding to his acceptance of the leadership. Then he explained, "Three loves are intertwined: the love of G-d, the love of Torah, and the love of our fellow Jews. If you have only the love of G-d and not the love of your fellow, that is a sign that the service of G-d is deficient. The love of your fellow will bring you to the love of G-d and the love of Torah." The Ramash concluded the talk asking that this statement be publicized.

The crowd remained very restless. Statements were not Maamarim. The Chassidim waited, singing during a break between talks. About an hour after the farbrengen began, Rabbi Sender Nemtzov, past eighty years, stood up. A distinguished rabbi in Manchester, England, decades earlier, he was one of the early students of the yeshiva in the town of Lubavitch in Russia. He surprised the crowd when in the middle of the farbrengen he stood up and faced the Rebbe proclaiming in Yiddish, "The crowd wants the Rebbe to say Chassidus – a Maamar. The talks are wonderful, but we are asking the Rebbe to say a Maamar, a Chassidic discourse."

Absolute silence filled the room; the crowd held its breath, the hearts of the Chassidim pulsating, waiting to see how the Ramash would respond. The quiet was shattered as the new Rebbe began his first Chassidic discourse,[6] starting by quoting the verse from the Song of Songs, "Basi Legani Achosi Kallah" ("I have come into My garden, My sister, My bride"). The verse refers to the time of the construction of the Mishkan (sanctuary built by the People of Israel during their forty years of wandering in the desert) by Moses, when the Shechinah (Divine Presence), came into its "garden," for it was then that the Divine Presence, distant for a time, was again revealed in this world.

Realizing what was happening, the crowd rose to its feet and surged forward. As Chassidim, they wanted to be closer to their new Rebbe, much like a child who wants to be near his father. When the Rebbe finished the first section of the Maamar, he paused and asked the crowd to say "L'Chaim," a toast.

Nemtzov surprised everyone a second time. Despite his age, he jumped on a table and proclaimed, "Chassidim, we have a Rebbe! Say, 'Shehecheyanu (the blessing for good tidings)!'"[7] Loudly, he said the blessing and everyone answered, "Amen."

Seen in a historical context, the Maamar and statement were the Rebbe's sweeping new vision for Jewish life. The Rebbe called upon each person to recognize his responsibility to uncover the holiness latent within himself, to reveal the inherent holiness of the world and to take responsibility to similarly inspire others. Doing so, the Rebbe explained, not only helps a person realize his or her own spiritual potential but also plays a pivotal role in achieving the long-yearned-for ultimate global revelation of G-dliness, achieving a world perfected, with the arrival of the Moshiach (Jewish Messiah). Each act is completely transformative.[8]

The Rebbe's first talk of the evening would set the tone for decades to come. "The three loves are an eternal chain and will not be weakened. Just as the Diaspora of the Jews[9] was caused by the lack of love for one's fellow, so the redemption would come with increased love for one another." The Rebbe was calling for a Judaism of compassion and inclusion, where all have a place with dignity.

The Rebbe was challenging the emerging strategy of the small post-World War II Orthodox community in America, referring to themselves as the She'airis Haplaitah, the surviving remnant. Religious Jewry at the time was a combination of second-generation immigrants clinging to observance and refugees from the Holocaust. They hoped to preserve Judaism by turning inward, holding on to a committed core, recreating old-world enclaves, and keeping assimilation at bay. A small group of scholars had found refuge in the US, where they established Lithuanian-style yeshivas in Lakewood, New Jersey; Baltimore; Cleveland; and New York.

Other Chassidic Rebbes who had found refuge in the US were attempting to rebuild their communities. The response to the opportunity of America was to create havens, small clusters of Chassidim in Brownsville, Williamsburg, and later in Boro Park, reflections of the spiritual grandeur of a world destroyed in Europe.

The new Chabad Rebbe viewed scholarship without responsibility for Jewish destiny as imperfect, Jewish observance, without compassion and caring for others outside the Orthodox orbit, as inconsistent with Torah. The new Rebbe advocated principled engagement with a society where observant Jews could make a contribution to modern life, while enjoying its bounty of freedom and opportunity. No question it would be easier to withdraw from engagement with the rest of the world, but he encouraged his followers to strike this balance of articulating Jewish values to the broader society, contributing to its welfare, and rejecting those elements that were inimical to Jewish ideals.

Few present that night in the packed synagogue realized the scope of the Rebbe's ambitions. The Rebbe's broad vision would in time transform both the Chassidic community and world Jewry. His goal was to reach every Jew, regardless of level of observance, background, and affiliation, and to transform Jewish life in every community in the world. Throughout, the Rebbe saw himself as a shliach carrying out the mandate from the Previous Rebbe.

Rabbi Menachem Mendel Schneerson was the seventh in a line of Lubavitcher Rebbes. Born in 1902, the eldest of three brothers, in Nikolayev, Ukraine, his family moved seven years later to Dnepropetrovsk, where his father served as the chief rabbi of the third-largest Jewish community in Ukraine. His youngest brother, Dov Ber, perished in the Holocaust. His middle brother, Yisroel Aryeh Leib, escaped Russia on a fake passport in 1930, reuniting with his brother in Berlin. Yisroel Aryeh Leib moved to then-Palestine and married. After the war, he immigrated to England. He passed away at a young age in Liverpool, England, where he studied mathematics in a local university.[10]

Young Menachem Mendel was a child protégé, receiving private tutoring and dedicating himself to intense Torah study. In 1928, he became engaged to his distant cousin, Chaya Mushka, the second daughter of the Sixth Rebbe, Rabbi Yosef Yitzchak. When the Previous Rebbe escaped the Soviet Union in that year, Menachem Mendel joined the family entourage and was finally married in November of 1928 in Warsaw. His parents, stranded in Soviet Russia, could not attend his wedding.

Shortly after their marriage, the Ramash and his new wife moved to Berlin where he attended university and continued to assist his father-in-law in communal affairs. His classmate in Berlin, the renowned scholar Rabbi Joseph Soloveitchik, who later would head Yeshiva University, recalled that the Rebbe would sit in the back of the class with a Talmud on his desk. When a professor said, "Schneerson, what are you reading?" the Ramash expertly recounted the lecture that had been given, despite also being immersed in the talmudic volume. One Purim, the Ramash gave a speech standing on a soapbox and lectured on campus about the importance of the holiday. He was promptly arrested for not having a permit to preach. Rabbi Soloveitchik bailed him out, telling him that "all the Rebbes of Lubavitch were arrested. Now you have been put in jail, your destiny is to become a Rebbe."[11]

With the rise of Hitler, the Ramash moved to Paris in 1933. He studied engineering in the Sorbonne and other colleges. He and his wife lived modestly in Paris, preferring to remain out of the limelight.

During the decade that the Ramash was in Europe, he spent much time assisting his father-in-law in Europe and editing his works for publication. At times he accompanied the Rebbe on his travels. He met with many leading rabbinic figures on behalf of his father-in-law. In 1937,[12] he was dispatched to Vilna, Lithuania, the great center of Jewish learning, to secure the signature of Rabbi Chaim Ozer Grodzinski, Chief Rabbi of Vilna, for a public letter the Previous Rebbe was publishing.[13] As the Ramash waited in the study hall, some students realized that he was a Chassid. Vilna was the center of the Misnagdim, those opposed to Chassidim, the animus reaching back to the eighteenth century. Challenging the Chassid might be good sport. Not knowing who he was, the students decided to test his acumen in Talmud, badgering him with questions. The Ramash remained silent, not entering their game. Rabbi Chaim Ozer opened the door and overheard the conversation, then invited the Ramash into his office. With him was Rabbi Baruch Ber Leibowitz, head of the great yeshiva in Kaminetz in Poland. Once inside the office, he promptly began to review the questions he had been asked, systematically answering them with clarity. Rabbi Chaim Ozer, taken aback by the Ramash's talmudic erudition, asked, "Why the sudden change?"

The Ramash answered, "I did not come here for debates. I was afraid it might have a derogatory effect on my mission from the Rebbe," referring to his father-in-law. "I felt compelled to clear the air."

As Rabbi Chaim Ozer reviewed the letter, Rabbi Baruch Ber engaged the Ramash in a deep scholarly discussion. Highly impressed, he invited the Ramash, "Come study with me and I promise you will be the Gadol Hador (the leading scholar of the next generation)." The Rebbe refused, causing Rabbi Baruch Ber to break out in tears.[14]

When the Nazis seized Paris, the Ramash and his wife managed to escape to Vichy, France.[15] From France, they made their way to Lisbon, and finally, in late June of 1941, to the US. In America, the Ramash moved to a more public role, appointed by his father-in-law to head the newly established educational arm of Chabad, Merkos L'inyonei Chinuch and Machne Israel. During the war years, he also spent time working for the US Navy at the Brooklyn Naval Yards.

To the Jewish establishment at the time, Chabad was a sideshow in Brooklyn. Writer Jonathan Mark in *The Jewish Week* describes the mood at mid-century: "In 1950 all American Jews heard of was Liberal Judaism but almost no one heard of Chabad. Chabad seemed a relic of history. Liberal Judaism was ascendant, inevitable."

The Rebbe's vision was vast, but the resources at his disposal were severely limited. Chabad was small, hammered by the twin disasters of the Holocaust and Communism – a battle that was still underway in the Soviet Union. There were a few hundred Chassidic families in the United States, and others scattered in Europe,

Australia, and Israel. Many were still locked behind the Iron Curtain. The community was not affluent; most were immigrants with few skills or resources. The financial support the Rebbe would require for such a sweeping vision did not exist within Chabad. In the yeshiva at 770, there were just some thirty college-age students – many whose first language had been Yiddish or Russian. The students were mostly children of the refugees, newly emigrated from Europe or who had escaped the Soviet Union after the war.

Jews at mid-century were moving away from tradition. Returning war veterans were a catalyst for the flight to the suburbs. Orthodox synagogues in urban areas, which had sustained at least minimal Jewish observance in the United States, were declining. The new generation was choosing to affiliate with the Conservative and the Reform Movements. As Jewish historian Dr. Jack Wertheimer explains, the new spirit of American individualism caused Jews to define Judaism according to their own whims instead of learning from the past. The postwar generation was the product of a limited exposure to Jewish education. They had a sense of nostalgia and a warmth for tradition, but they lacked any serious knowledge of Judaism.

In a study on the status of the American rabbi[16] at the time, Jerome Carlin recounts the frustration of the Orthodox European rabbi in modern America. "The authority and respect of the old country was gone – viewed as old-fashioned, no longer respected by the community." A new brand of liberal rabbis had introduced significant changes[17] to Jewish belief and conduct. Most had attended college before entering rabbinical school. They were urbane and educated – a marked contrast from the bearded, Yiddish-speaking rabbi in the small shul of their grandparents.

Orthodox synagogues were closing; others were dropping their Orthodox customs, such as separate seating, and swiftly shifting their affiliation to the burgeoning Conservative Movement. A sense of pessimism was reflected in a study[18] of the Orthodox community published in 1958. Only 21 percent of Orthodox members felt that their synagogues would remain Orthodox; the majority believed that their congregations would become Conservative with time. Noted Jewish sociologist Marshall Sklare[19] wrote in 1957 about the weakening of the Orthodox community, claiming "they were a case study in institutional decay."

After the war, while Orthodoxy was shrinking, more than 450[20] new Conservative congregations started, and Reform doubled in size to more than six hundred temples. Some new Orthodox synagogues opened, but they were, as a rule, much smaller than the liberal congregations. The Conservative Movement launched the "Jewish Centers" concept. They had swimming pools, gyms, youth clubs, and halls for social events. The new synagogues created not just religious centers, but also social ones. Given the choice of the old-world rabbi who spoke English with a Yiddish accent, and a polished American whose building had a swimming pool and mixed seating, Jews were choosing the latter.

Youth activities fueled the growth of the Reform and Conservative Movements. Families chose the synagogue Hebrew School for Jewish education. Most schools were under Liberal auspices; by the early sixties, 600,000 children were enrolled. Synagogue membership was mandatory to celebrate the milestones of bar and bat mitzvah.

This trend had a trickle-down effect on the family's observance. In the older traditional synagogues, the rabbi reminded congregants to follow tradition. Rabbis in the newer Liberal congregations not only tolerated change, but also, in many cases, endorsed dramatic steps away from the historic norms of Judaism. If the rabbi would attend a bar mitzvah that was not kosher, why not discard observance of kashrut (dietary laws)? The Conservative Movement made a radical departure from ritual in 1950 when its Committee on Law and Standard endorsed driving to synagogue on the Sabbath.[21] The decision opened the door to Jews choosing to move farther afield from synagogues, weakening strong Jewish neighborhoods.

The Jewish Federation Movement was also growing dramatically. The pillars of identity building were supporting Israel, remembering the Holocaust, and fighting for equality in postwar society. Judaism rooted in spirituality, Torah, and tradition was considered an anachronism.

The postwar era brought in a new sense of optimism for American Jews. Hank Greenberg helped the Detroit Tigers clinch the World Series. Bess Myerson was crowned Miss America. Jews were beginning to feel fully accepted in America. However, acceptance came with a price: the holdovers of the past, religious trappings, had to be discarded.

The existing communal infrastructure in the United States would not facilitate the new Rebbe's goals. The Liberal Movement and communal structures, like federations, did not see spirituality as a central component of Jewish identity, and the Orthodox didn't have the self-confidence that would enable them to affect the broader community. To achieve his goals, the Rebbe would have to create a totally new institutional model. The Rebbe needed foot soldiers. The first challenge was to inspire a new generation of leaders with a sense of responsibility to all Jews, who would be willing to dedicate their lives to the Rebbe's shlichus mission. This group would be essential to realizing the Rebbe's intention of creating a renaissance of Jewish learning and observance.

The Sixth Rebbe, Rabbi Yosef Yitzchak, had laid the groundwork; the new Rebbe had a more comprehensive strategy. The Previous Rebbe had sent rabbis and their wives to communities with specific tasks. Congregations and schools would request the Rebbe's assistance, and he would dispatch someone to be the rabbi of a community, another to teach, a third to provide kosher meat.

The new Rebbe would take this to a new level. The shluchim were sent to communities simply as shluchim, emissaries of the Rebbe. Their mandate was to engage every Jew and foster all aspects of Jewish life. Everything was on the agenda – a school, youth program, summer camp, mikvah, synagogue, or campus center. Whatever was the need, they were supposed to meet it.

Creating a corps of young men and women who would have the confidence to leave the confines of the secure religious community to live in cities that lacked religious resources would be a daunting challenge. Rabbi Yitzchak Groner, head of Chabad in Australia until his passing in 2008, described the mood at the time when he was sent to Australia.

"It was unprecedented to take a Groner with six kids in 1958 and send him to Australia," he told an audience years later in Sydney. "The self-sacrifice in Russia was greater, but to take a chocalada (Yiddish slang for an American kid who loves chocolate), a Yankee, and send him to a faraway country had never been done in Jewish history."

The future shluchim were incubating in the Chabad educational system – the yeshivas and the Beth Rivkah girls' schools. The system was still small during the first decade of the Rebbe's leadership, with schools in Brooklyn, Newark, Montreal, Melbourne, Paris, and Israel. The students numbered just a few hundred worldwide with some thirty senior students studying in the yeshiva at Chabad's Brooklyn headquarters. It was from this diminutive group that the new generation of shluchim would be born. Most of the students were the children of Russian Chassidim who had lived for decades under the harsh rule of Communism. After the war, they had escaped Russia in the hope of freedom. Others were the children of Polish yeshiva students, who had reached American shores, some spending the war years in the Chabad Yeshiva in Shanghai. A few of the students were American-born. They would be the first soldiers in the Rebbe's army.

Chapter Four

The Great Escape

The first shliach of the soon-to-be Rebbe would be Rabbi Michoel Lipsker,[1] a forty-two-year-old Russian refugee living in Paris. Just ten days after the passing of the Sixth Rebbe, Rabbi Yosef Yitzchak Schneersohn, the Ramash (Rabbi Menachem Mendel Schneerson) dispatched a letter to Lipsker asking him to travel to North Africa to establish a Jewish educational network, saying that Rabbi Yosef Yitzchak had been gravely concerned about "our brethren, the Sephardi Jews," and wanted to launch an effort to provide Jewish education for them in their homelands.[2] In the letter, the Ramash added that the Joint[3] would assist the project and he should coordinate with Rabbi Binyomin Gorodetsky,[4] the Rebbe's representative in Paris. With his wife's approval, Rabbi Lipsker accepted the mission. His daughter Sara[5] Chaikin says he was a very devoted Chassid. "Whatever the Rebbe would request, he would do."

Lipsker was one of the first who had fled Russia on a false Polish passport in the wake of World War II in the Great Escape. A thousand Chassidim would cross the border seeking freedom. They would become the vanguard of soldiers of the army that the Rebbe would field in the coming decades.

Michoel Lipsker was raised in the Ukrainian town of Poltava. His father, Rabbi Chaim Tzvi Lipsker, the local rabbi, was not a Chassidic Jew, but he realized that the only segment of the Jewish community preserving its identity under Communism were the Lubavitcher Chassidim. He sent his sons to the underground Chabad yeshivas.

Michoel studied first in his hometown of Poltava, then Samarkand and Kremenchug. He was married in 1935 in Vitebsk. It was a difficult time to build a Jewish family; Communists had destroyed almost all religious observance. Work permits obligated labor on the Sabbath, and Soviet education was mandatory.

Michoel was maintaining a secret Jewish school in Kremenchug in central Ukraine. But danger lurked everywhere, even in the synagogue. One day he noticed a new face at services. Bearded, the stranger had the appearance of a religious Jew. Still, he seemed suspicious. Sensing danger, Lipsker warned his fellow Chassidim to beware. "Let's get out of here," he said. "This guy might be a smechker[6] (a spy) sent by the Soviet Secret Police. Fearing arrest, he fled from the synagogue. Minutes later, the police arrived and ensnared the other Chassidim.

When World War II began, Lipsker was living in Leningrad in the small Chassidic community there. The Nazis marched into Russia, surrounded Leningrad, and cut it off from the rest of Russia. Lipsker's daughter, Sara, was almost five years old when the war broke out. "Food was rationed, the hunger was terrible," she remembered years later in her comfortable apartment in Crown Heights, Brooklyn. And then there was the German shelling. "I was thrown on the snow and my mother laid over me, the bombs were all over." Lipsker would pull a sled through the streets, picking up the bodies of dead Jews and burying them.

After two years, in January of 1943, the Soviets succeeded in creating a land bridge to Leningrad. Lipsker volunteered to work in a small factory town in Siberia. As Sara recalled, "This was a ticket out of siege. At least there was food in Siberia."

As the war ended, Lipsker made the journey thousands of miles south to Soviet Georgia. During the war, his brothers had fled to the Georgian city of Kutaisi, a hundred miles north of Turkey. Rabbi Azriel Chaikin[7] was fifteen at the war's end, studying[8] there in an underground yeshiva. He recalls the atmosphere: "To a certain extent, it was easier to observe Judaism." Georgian Jews have always remained a bit independent and more traditional. Thousands of miles from Moscow, the Communist rule was more benevolent. The Fifth Rebbe, Rabbi Sholom DovBer, had sent rabbis there at the turn of the century. They had established Jewish schools that helped the Georgians[9] remain devoted to Jewish tradition. One of those emissaries had been Chaikin's grandfather.

Lipsker's journey was similar to that of many other Russian Chassidim and Polish Jews escaping the Nazis. With the Nazi onslaught, they headed east. Some went to Georgia, larger numbers to even more remote Uzbekistan, almost two thousand miles east of Moscow. In Tashkent, Uzbekistan's capital city, and in Samarkand, 180 miles away, they found a haven.

Fourteen-year-old Moshe Levertov came on the train to Samarkand from Moscow just before the High Holidays in 1943. Years later, he wrote in his memoir:[10] "A new world unfolded before my eyes, observant Jews walking in the streets without fear of arrest or anti-Semitic attacks. Unlike Moscow, where Jews were afraid to come to synagogue, here, the shuls were full of Chassidim." Levertov was amazed to find young boys his age well advanced in their talmudic studies.

Rachel Raskin[11] also reached Samarkand at the end of the war. In 1938, the secret police invaded her parents' house in Leningrad at midnight arresting her father and eventually murdering him. Rachel recalled, "We were educated that we would go in fire and water for Judaism. As children, we were told stories about the Marranos, the secret Jews during the Spanish Inquisition."[12] As the Nazi siege first began, she, her mother and siblings fled Leningrad to distant Kazakhstan. There, her mother passed away, leaving four orphan girls. After the war, in Samarkand, Rachel married a young rabbinical student, Nissan Pinson.

Rachel and her new husband, Nissan, heard rumors circulating that there was a rare opportunity to escape from Russia. Many Polish Jews had found refuge in the Soviet Union during the war. The Polish and Russian governments had reached an agreement that Polish citizens could return to their homeland. If a Pole married a Russian, they, too, would be permitted to return with their new family members to Poland.

Azriel Chaikin described the confusion: "Some were trying to marry Poles, there were rumors you could buy papers." Failure would have catastrophic consequences; Russian citizens attempting to escape would face imprisonment or even death. The mood was tense. Chaikin recalled that people began speculating whether to take the risk.

Michoel Lipsker was one of the first to take the chance. Chaikin says, "He was a man of action. He took his family and went." The journey to the western Russian border could take up to a month. During the first leg of the trip, they used their regular Russian identity cards, riding the train thousands of miles to the Polish border town of Lemberg (Lvov). At the border, they received forged Polish documents. Sara was given a new passport. "I had a different name that I don't remember now," she said. They crossed the border in cattle cars. Afterward, the Lipskers traveled to Paris, finding sanctuary with Rabbi Zalman Schneerson, a prominent Lubavitcher rabbi whose home became the gateway for the refugees from Russia.

The successful escape of Lipsker and a few others sparked an intense debate in the Chassidic community in Russia. With the war ending, Soviet oppression returned even to remote Georgia and Uzbekistan. Yechezkel Brod, who later would operate a kosher meat market in Brooklyn, recalled the fierce dispute.[13] Attempting to leave Russia was a crime punishable by death, and many questioned whether Jewish law permitted exposing oneself to such risk. Others asked if it was morally permissible to leave Russia and other Jews behind. Lubavitchers were the key Jewish activists responsible for preserving the flame of Judaism in the Soviet Union. Abandoning their leadership role would place many Jews at the mercy of the oppressive regime. On the other hand, many thought it was worth the risk to escape Russia and give the next generation an opportunity to live in freedom.

The slight hope of freedom was enough to prompt many to travel to the border town of Lemberg on the Polish frontier. There, the Chassidim decided to convene a rabbinical court to examine the question of life or death.[14] Jewish Law, or Halacha, would be the basis for the court's decision. Moshe Levertov described the court in his memoir: "It was composed of twenty-three judges – like the Minor Sanhedrin[15] in the time of the Holy Temple, which determined issues of life and death. Renowned scholars like Rabbis Nachum Sassonkin, Schneur Gorelick, Shmuel Notik, and Avrohom Glazman were joined by notable Chassidim such as Reb Mendel Futerfas and Reb Shlomo Chaim Kesselman."

The court ruled that whoever wanted to escape could try. In addition, Levertov explained, "All were obligated to give up any money and jewelry they had to a communal fund that provided expenses for food, accommodations, tickets, passports, and bribes. Everyone complied without hesitation."

With the court's sanction, the Great Escape began. It would require money, logistics, and organization. Time was of the essence; the Russians would permit Polish citizens to leave for only a short period. Large amounts of money were essential for false passports, travel, and safe houses. The logistics of moving over a thousand Chassidim across Russia to the Polish border were daunting. The largest concentration of Chassidim was in distant Soviet Georgia and Uzbekistan, thousands of miles from the Polish border. Once they arrived in Lemberg, families had to be housed while they waited for their chance to leave. Secrecy was crucial. If the Russians got wind of the audacious plan, all the Chassidim would end up in prison or even face the death penalty.

Rachel Pinson and her husband masqueraded as siblings. They had secured false papers of a brother and sister. Fortunately, they flew from Samarkand in Uzbekistan to Lemberg. On the thirteen-hour flight, they encountered a traveler who described Lemberg to them. Rachel recalled, "It was a miracle – he told us about the city and the university." This sparse knowledge was just enough to help them bluff their way through. "We acted as brother and sister and said we were planning on attending the university."

For a month, they camped out in an apartment. Rachel's husband could not venture outside. His beard and religious appearance would have drawn attention. Moshe Levertov described the predicament of the growing numbers of Chassidim arriving in Lemberg: "It was a much smaller city than Moscow or Leningrad. Several hundred new faces were immediately noticeable. Most were bearded, making them especially conspicuous."

Levertov recalled, however, that "it was impossible to stop them from coming. After all the persecution and suffering over a quarter of a century, everyone was desperate to leave."

Chabad women took the lead, acting as couriers. Unlike the men, they were not conspicuous because of religious appearance. The women did much of the legwork by moving people from safe houses, and transporting food, money, and papers. Yocheved Zalmanov[16] described their experience: "We went on the streets like young students, like we had no fear."

For months, the Chassidim waited in Lemberg for the right moment. Soviet police patrolled the streets. Passports had to be provided, and border guards had to be paid off. Travel arrangements had to be made to move the refugees beyond Poland to other countries quickly, due to the risks of Polish anti-Semitism. It was impossible to bring in money from the West. Everything had to be done in Russia. Money could be collected only within the Chassidic community, as secrecy was paramount.

The most terrifying moments were the last ones spent in Russia on the train ride from Lemberg to Poland. Moshe Levertov's train was loaded with a group of Chassidim ready to depart Poland. A Soviet soldier gave an ominous speech. "How can you leave this paradise? Our motherland is the best on earth; the Party is creating a new world." Levertov described the tense moments: "The group sat stone-faced during the tirade."

The train ride took twenty-four hours to reach Poland. Levertov recalled, "As the train approached the border, the organizer drilled us with our new identities, names, birthdates, and siblings." At the border, the Russians took a man off the train whom they suspected of having some money. Levertov says the wait on the train was terrifying. "During these anxious moments, we felt our lives hung in the balance. This was our only possibility to reach freedom and leave the Soviet hell. If that unfortunate man would buckle under questioning and give any hint about our illegal exodus, we could all lose our lives." After what he called "an eternity" the passenger returned safely and the train left.

"Slowly, our train pulled out of the station, picking up speed. Soon, to our indescribable relief, we crossed into Poland. Bottles of vodka instantly appeared as everyone toasted each other 'L'Chaim – To life!' thanking G–d for our miraculous escape."

The last successful escape was on New Year's Day in 1947. Notice was never given by the Soviets in advance; usually they announced the departures hours or even minutes before the trains would leave. Quickly, messengers fanned out in the city to notify the Chassidim that they needed to run to the station. A soldier told one of the organizers, Laibel Mochkin, that the train would be leaving in minutes. But time was needed to round up the Chassidim, so Mochkin ran to the station and grabbed the official. Bluffing, he said, "I have already arranged with Yehiavov [the local NKVD commander] that the train would wait two hours." He sent the soldier to the station's restaurant with money to buy dinner, and then he bribed the train's engineer to wait. Within two hours, two hundred Lubavitcher Chassidim were on the train.

After the train left, Mochkin realized that, in the rush, some passports were left behind. As the border got closer, he hastily added names of family members to each passport. Quickly, he informed each of the families of their new identities. At the border, tension filled the cars as the Russian police inspected the hurriedly forged papers. Still fearing the long arm of the Soviets might reach into Poland, Mochkin gave the conductor more cash to make an unscheduled stop in Krakow. Within minutes, the Chassidim abandoned the train.

In Poland, Chabad activists reached out to Bricha[17] (Hebrew for escape), the clandestine Zionist organization that smuggled Jews from Europe to British-controlled Palestine. Zvi Netzer,[18] Bricha commander in Poland, recalled his first encounter with Chabad.

"A Jew with a nice-looking beard walked in, telling me that I was the commander of the Bricha. He asked for documents to smuggle the Chassidim from Poland into Czechoslovakia." Netzer says the Chassid was elusive. "He asked me many questions but evaded mine." Finally, the Chassid decided to confide in Netzer, telling him, "Our Rebbe has sent word to us to go to Palestine." Netzer was amazed by their organizational abilities. "We could not get over their ingenuity and secrecy."

Ephraim Dekel, Bricha's European commander, said, "Bricha workers had high regard for them. Unlike other refugee groups, these Chassidim were thoroughly disciplined and never lost hope that G-d would let them live to see better days. They worshipped G-d with song and gladness; one of their outstanding traits was Ahavat Yisrael – sincere love and concern for all Jews, regardless of degree of religious observance."

The final train was organized to leave via Romania in early 1947. This time, hope turned to despair. Police boarded the train arresting all those with false passports. The secret police scooped up Chassidim. One of the activists, Reb Mendel Futerfas[19] was arrested by the secret police just before he crossed over the Russian border, sending him off to prison for nearly a decade.

Many Chassidic women were heroes in the Great Escape. One of the main organizers was the Muma Sara (Yiddish for Aunt Sara) Katzenelenbogen, as she was known by Chassidim. After the last train was stopped, she was the target of a national manhunt. Wanted posters hung throughout the country. Born in 1891, she lived in the town of Lubavitch after she married. Later, in 1937, her husband was arrested and never heard from again. A successful businesswoman, she supported the underground yeshiva network, moving funds from town to town as a courier. Her niece, Luba Zarchi,[20] recalls that "she was a very smart woman."

In 1946, Aunt Sara escorted Rebbitzen Chana Schneerson,[21] the Rebbe's mother, on a harrowing trip from Moscow to Lemberg, telling police that the woman she was accompanying "was an old, sickly lady and not to bother her." Discovery of a Schneerson family member could have been fatal. In a remarkable act of self-sacrifice, she gave Rebbitzen Chana her false Polish passport, and she remained behind in Russia.

Finally in 1951, Sara Katzenelenbogen was arrested[22] and stood trial with five other Chassidim, including her son, Moshe,[23] who was just seventeen when detained. The Muma Sara was sentenced to death,[24] her son Moshe to ten years. Just before Passover in 1952, she was permitted to see her son in jail.[25] The jailers hoped the sight of her son would prompt a confession. On death row, she had hoarded some sugar. As her son says, "When they plan on killing you, they wanted to make sure you ate well." She gave her son the sugar but was horrified by his appearance. Returning to her cell, she suffered a heart attack and passed away the next day at the age of sixty-one, just six days before Passover.

Moshe Levertov's father, Dov Ber, was arrested in the summer of 1947. He was accused of collecting money to support yeshivas and helping Jews escape Russia. Levertov was sentenced to ten years in Siberia for being a member of an "anti-Soviet organization." Before he passed away in prison in 1949, he mocked his jailers: "I have nothing to fear from you now that my children have escaped Russia."

More than one thousand Chassidim fled Russia during the Great Escape that began in 1946 and extended to the winter of 1947. None envisioned that this exodus would set the stage for an upcoming revolution in Jewish life that the new Rebbe was planning. Some of them, and more important, their children, became the nucleus of the Rebbe's army.

The self-sacrifice of these Chassidim forged in the bitter Soviet system would give them the tools to build Judaism in an open society. They had passion, resilience, and determination. The elder Chassidim would become the first generation of leaders in the communities being set up in the postwar era. Many of them studied in the Great Yeshiva in Lubavitch before the Soviet regime. They were the bridge between the historic homeland of Chassidism and the Western world. They were symbols of self-sacrifice, role models for the next generation.

After the Great Escape, the Sixth Rebbe, Rabbi Yosef Yitzchak, orchestrated the seeding of new communities throughout the world, encouraging some to stay in Europe, but most to move to the US,

Canada, Australia, South America, and then-Palestine. He planted in each country a core of committed Chassidim – a strategy that would blossom in time under the leadership of his son-in-law, the new Rebbe.

Micheol Lipsker had met the Ramash in Paris after the war. In 1947, after the dangerous escape of his mother, Rebbitzen Chana Schneerson, the Ramash traveled to France to meet her and facilitate her immigration to America. Lipsker assisted the Ramash during that visit, which lasted a few months. This strong personal bond served as the basis for the devotion he would have in the years to come in Morocco and later in the United States.

Jews had been living in Morocco for at least two thousand years. One tradition holds that in the time of King Solomon, Jews immigrated there and built a synagogue. After the destruction of the Second Temple in 70 CE, greater numbers of Jews moved to the area, which had become a Roman province three decades earlier. The Spanish expulsion in 1492 brought an influx of Spanish Jews, many of whom were scholars.

By the twentieth century, the Jews in Morocco were divided between the sophisticated urban residents living primarily in the coastal towns, and the great majority who lived in cities and villages across the country in mellahs (the Moroccan brand of ghetto), where the gates closed each night. There were also Berbers, or mountain Jews, who lived in very primitive conditions.

In 1912, Morocco became a French Protectorate, and French Jews took a strong interest in the country, establishing a network of schools under the auspices of the Alliance Israelite Universelle.[26] The goal of these schools was to integrate Jewish children into French culture. There was a smattering of Judaism. The schools closed on Jewish holidays, for instance, and served kosher food.

Traditionally children in Morocco attended a yeshiva or Cheder. Faced with the choice of an old rabbi sitting in the back of a synagogue teaching a few students, and a new modern government-supported French school, most Moroccan Jews chose the latter. A new generation was growing up in the country with a greater appreciation for French culture than for its own traditions.

Lipsker's first obstacle was getting to Morocco. He was refused a visa. After repeated requests, he was told that if he had an invitation from someone in Morocco, French authorities would reconsider. He was in a kosher restaurant in Nice describing his difficulties when the proprietor overheard him and said, "Morocco – wait a moment." He opened his drawer and removed a card with the address of Rabbi Baruch Toledano, chief rabbi of Meknes, Morocco. The rabbi and grandson had visited the restaurant and left the card.

Sensing Divine Providence, Lipsker wrote Rabbi Toledano, telling him of his mission to invigorate Jewish education in Morocco. Lipsker's letter arrived as Toledano was fighting his own battle in Meknes. The secularly oriented Alliance Universelle School was drawing children away from observance. Toledano sent back a warm invitation, and Lipsker promptly applied for a visa, only to be denied again. Frustrated, he hired a lawyer in Paris whose intervention with the French authorities proved unsuccessful. Official channels weren't working, so the attorney took a new approach. Secretly, he met in a Paris park with a government official, and after an exchange of cash, the first shliach of the soon-to-be Lubavitcher Rebbe received his visa and was on his way to Morocco.

Lipsker flew to Fez and then took the bus thirty-five miles to Meknes. Meknes had a Jewish community dating back more than a thousand years. When Lipsker got off the bus, he headed to the local synagogue. In a courtyard, he discovered an old rabbi teaching a few students. A few blocks away was the beautiful Alliance school with 1,200 pupils.

Lipsker had a serious challenge in this city of about fifteen thousand Jews. The Alliance had been established in Paris in 1860. Its goal was to assist Jews around the world in fighting anti-Semitism. Eventually, it began to take a role in education with the goal of "cultural and moral elevation," with some leadership advocating assimilation. More than twenty-eight thousand students were enrolled in Alliance schools in 1952.

Rabbi Toledano hoped to curb the French influence with the help of Chabad. Toledano was a distinguished scholar, descending from a long line of rabbis who originally reached Morocco after escaping the Inquisition in Spain. The majority of Jews were not scholars, even though they observed the basic traditions of Shabbat and kashrut. Lipsker hoped to change that by creating schools that would empower Jewish children with the skills and knowledge of Judaism.

His first task was to transform the small, primitive yeshiva housed in the ancient synagogue into a modern school. Lipsker found the students sitting on wooden slats, their feet folded underneath and listening to the teacher explain the Talmud. Lipsker recalled later, "I ordered desks from a carpenter, and benches; they were installed, and it took on the personality of a school."

Lipsker was not aware that his innovations were creating a political controversy. Meir Amar, a member of the Jewish community council, confided to Lipsker, "There is a fire behind you." He explained that there had been a long-simmering feud between Chief Rabbi Toledano and Yosef Bardugo, chairman of the community. The split was centuries old. Meknes was comprised both of Jews originally from Morocco and descendants of Spanish immigrants. The Toledano family came from the Spanish city of Toledo. The Bardugo family had been in Morocco centuries earlier. Over time, a power-sharing arrangement emerged. The rabbi would come from the Spanish Jews and the community leader from the Moroccans.

Lipsker met with Bardugo, who thought Lipsker's activities were part of a plan of Rabbi Toledano to expand his influence. He grilled Lipsker, "Why have you made a yeshiva? Why does Rabbi Toledano claim it as his school?" Lipsker responded saying he had been sent by the Rebbe to educate Jewish children and did not want to be part of the local politics. Bardugo was willing to let him continue, but he demanded one condition: "Rabbi Toledano cannot set foot in the yeshiva," he said.

Lipsker refused, saying, "He is chief rabbi of the community. This is not possible." Lipsker told Bardugo that his mission did not include taking sides in local politics. Finally, Bardugo softened, and over the years, strongly supported Rabbi Lipsker's work in Meknes.

When summer rolled around, Rabbi Lipsker discovered an avenue to broaden his program. The Alliance school had no summer program, so he offered one. Hundreds of children flocked to the Jewish summer school. The administration of the Alliance school complained that the summer should be used for vacation, not study. Once this failed, they decided to create their own program the following year.

The next winter Lipsker was summoned to a meeting of the Jewish Community Council. Bardugo asked him, "What are your plans for this year?"

Lipsker explained, "The same as last year: six days a week with classes from 9:00 a.m. to 1:00 p.m. with scholarships for those in need."

The next year, the Alliance school also decided to offer a summer program, but just for a few days a week. Bardugo called a vote, and Chabad's program won the community's support. This did not sit well with the leaders of the Alliance, so they approached the JDC (the Joint Distribution Committee), Chabad's prime funder in Casablanca, to complain about the Chabad inroads into what they felt was "their turf."

Lipsker received calls from Casablanca, asking him not to make dramatic moves that "shifted the control of Jewish education to Chabad hands." Then the JDC representatives made a surprise visit to Meknes to curb Lipsker's streak of independence. Lipsker refused to budge. The Chabad summer program remained and thrived.

Another Great Escape refugee was soon recruited to join the Rebbe's Moroccan army. At thirty-three, Shlomo Matusof[27] was preparing to marry. He was born in the Russian town of Vitebsk, and attended underground yeshivas. He was arrested and sentenced to ten years in a labor camp for being part of "an organization of counterrevolutionaries."[28]

Shlomo Matusof ended up in the same camp as Rabbi Lazer Nanes, a Chassid a few years his senior. Both stood on principle and refused to work on the Shabbat. They were thrown into solitary. Matusof was forced to stand in the middle of the camp with a sign proclaiming "Subbota," Sabbath observer. One Passover, he existed on beets for more than a week because he refused to eat leavened products. In 1943, his sentence was commuted as part of a plan to draft prisoners into the Russian Army. He was sent to a military camp in Kazakhstan, where he was able to obtain the papers of a Polish citizen who had passed away.

With a new identity, Matusof found his way to Tashkent, where he joined the faculty of the secret yeshiva in Tashkent led by Rabbi Nissan Nemanov. Matusof had been passing as a Pole for a few years, and left Russia without incident. Later, in France, Nemanov asked Matusof to help him in reconstituting the yeshiva in Brunoy, a suburb of Paris, but in the years after the war, Matusof spent most of his time in intense Jewish learning.

When the Rebbe's request came asking him to move to Casablanca, Matusof was engaged and dreaming of moving to Israel. "Sitting in a Russian prison, the dream that kept him alive was that of going to the Eretz Hakodesh – the Holy Land," said his son, Eli. He had lost most of his family in Russia and wanted to be reunited with his brothers who had immigrated there.

Matusof's bride, Pessia, was brought up in the city of Nevel, renowned for its Chassidim fiercely loyal to the Lubavitcher Rebbes. She didn't object to the Moroccan mission.[29] She said, "My father had instilled the principle in us, that when the Rebbe made a request, you listened." In the summer of 1950, Matusof wrote one letter, and another one a week later, to the Rebbe sharing his reservations about accepting the request to move to the Arab country.

The Rebbe responded[30] that "we are not just private individuals, we are to be beacons of light to illuminate the lives of others; they will affect others that will touch all corners of the globe." The letter swayed Matusof, and he headed to Morocco shortly after his wedding.

Matusof set up schools in Casablanca and expanded the network to smaller communities where there had been no proper educational system. Working in cooperation with the local chacham (literally, the wise one, the title used by Sephardi Jews for rabbi), he would hire teachers and organize schools in remote areas. Eventually the network reached seventy communities in Morocco.[31]

Years later, one of Matusof's students, Rabbi Shlomo Amar, was elected chief rabbi of Israel. He visited the teacher of his youth in Brooklyn, where Rabbi Matusof had relocated for medical treatment after forty years in Morocco. In the modest apartment on Crown Street, Rabbi Matusof was greatly honored to welcome his former student. The chief rabbi waited for his host to be seated, saying, "It is not proper respect for me to sit before my teacher."

Other escapees and their wives were also dispatched to Morocco – Rabbis Zalman Teibel, Leibel Raskin, and Sholom Eidelman. And the couple who had masqueraded as brother and sister to escape Russia, Rabbi Nissan and Rachel Pinson, also went to Morocco. Rachel had been very wary of moving to Morocco but her resistance melted after receiving a personal letter in Yiddish from the Rebbe. The Pinsons joined the school in Casablanca; seven years later they set out for Tunisia, pioneering Chabad's Jewish education there.

There were twenty-six thousand Jews in Tunis when the Pinsons arrived. Rachel relates[32] that the Tunisian Jews "had no strong Torah education, and the chief rabbi of Tunisia was happy we had come to lend a hand." First they established a girls' school, later a yeshiva for boys, and then branches in the island of Djerba[33] and other locations. Life was not easy in Tunisia. The government would have preferred they leave. However, Rachel recalled, "I told them I liked Tunisia and did not want to leave."

With time, Morocco and Tunisia[34] would witness massive demographic changes. Jews moved to Israel and Europe, as well as other countries. In 1969, Rabbi Lipsker came to visit New York for the High Holidays. In a private audience, the Rebbe told him, "The mission has been fulfilled." Lipsker moved to New York from Meknes; in Casablanca and Tunis, Jews remained, and the Chabad shluchim stayed at their posts.

Rabbi Raskin of Morocco passed away in 2004 and Rabbi Pinson of Tunisia in 2007. Their wives, Rebbitzens Reizel Raskin in Morocco and Rachel Pinson in Tunis are still doing the Rebbe's work. Mrs. Raskin heads Chabad operations in Morocco and Mrs. Pinson in Tunisia.

In Morocco 2,500 Jews remain, and Reizel Raskin soldiers on. She coordinates activities in Casablanca. She covers the budget, teaches weekly classes, and organizes community events.

Rachel Pinson,[35] in her mid-eighties, commutes every six to eight weeks from her son's home in Nice, France, to Tunisia, where two thousand Jews remain. She flies on a stateless UN passport, never having received citizenship after fleeing Russia. She oversees the school in Tunis, directs the staff, and covers the budget. "Our alumni support our programs with grants from the JDC and Lubavitch in New York." Full of energy and dedication, she says about her travels and fundraising, "Yes, it's tiring but we have to stay on top of things." Invariably when she arrives in Tunisia, immigration officers detain her for an hour or two. "I always get a touch of anxiety when I come into the country."

Fifty-eight years after Rachel moved to Morocco, and then to Tunisia, we met at her relatives' home on Eastern Parkway in Brooklyn on a wintry night. She was in New York for a family wedding. Spry, optimistic, sharp as a whistle. I asked her how she felt having lived so many years in a remote country far from friends and relatives.

Upbeat, full of energy, she responded, "What greater zechus – honor – could I ask for than dedicating my life to the Rebbe's shlichus (mission)?"

Chapter Five

The Front Row

The sky was overcast, the crisp air biting into the November Brooklyn morning. Rows of temporary wooden bleachers towered in front of 770, the headquarters of Chabad on Eastern Parkway. Hundreds of children wrapped in warm jackets were waiting in the cold. When they got the word from their counselors, six hundred children marched in straight lines and climbed onto the temporary wooden bleachers. They had come from across the globe, joining their fathers at the annual Kinus[1] Hashluchim, the International Conference of Chabad Emissaries. Speaking a dozen languages, and ranging from age six to bar mitzvah, they enjoyed a three-day, summer-camp-style conference while their fathers were busy attending workshops and sessions. Here, they belong. At home, these Chassidic kids live in communities with few or no religious friends. Here, they see their fellow classmates in person instead of interacting online in the virtual school for those who live in smaller communities with no proper Jewish education. The program is designed to make the kids feel special as tze'irei hashluchim[2] (young shluchim).

Crowded onto sidewalks and overflowing into the blocked street were two thousand rabbis observing their children. The rabbis were up next for the annual convention photo. In 1983, a few dozen filled the benches inside the synagogue for the first group picture. Soon afterward, though, thousands would jostle for a place, hoping to be identifiable in the sea of black hats, coats, and beards, when they showed the picture to family and friends back home.

The kids were finally all lined up on the bleachers. The head counselor instructed them to quickly shed their jackets in order to show off their long-sleeved camp shirt emblazoned with the emblem of Tze'irei Hashluchim. Just as the photographer was ready to shoot, Rabbis Krinsky, Kotlarsky, and Brennan, the conference leadership, squeezed onto a bench in the middle of the picture. The photographer turned on his microphone, his voice bellowing over the PA system, cajoling the rabbis to move to the side so he could take the picture. A song arose from the crowd; again the photographer bellowed into a megaphone for everyone to settle down. The rhythm picked up as the parents clapped in cadence, led by the counselors. Finally the photographer gave the all clear. The kids donned their jackets and filed off the bleachers.

Disorder followed as thousands of rabbis rushed to fill the places where six hundred kids had stood. When the bleachers were filled, more benches appeared from the side, adding more rows in front of the bleachers. After almost everyone was settled, a final row of benches was placed for the senior shluchim. They were not rushed. They each headed large organizations[3] with budgets of tens of millions – collectively, over a billion: Shlomo Cunin from California, Avrohom Shemtov from Philadelphia, Gershon Mendel Gorelick from Milan, Moshe Feller from the Twin Cities, Avrohom Korf from Miami, and Moshe Herson from New Jersey. Then the younger shluchim who head major operations abroad – such as Russia's Chief Rabbi Berel Lazar and Yosef Yitzchak Aharonov in Israel took their places. A few senior rabbinical scholars were escorted to reserved seats. And finally, the heads of the Kinus, Rabbi Yehuda Krinsky, Rabbi Moshe Kotlarsky, and Rabbi Lipa Brennan again sat in the middle three seats.

Those in the front row had been the first to answer the Rebbe's call over half a century ago. Then, they were young idealistic men full of dreams and ambitions. Today, they are adorned with distinguished-looking beards, most of which are turning white, although the beard of Rabbi Avrohom Shemtov from Philadelphia retains its red hue. When he was young, he was nicknamed in Yiddish, "Der Roite Illui," the Red Genius, due to his exceptional scholarship. They were dispersed around the globe in the late 1950s and '60s, but in this picture, they are all linked by the building in the background, the legendary 770 Eastern Parkway, Brooklyn.

In the 1940s, the first generation of shluchim had been dispatched by the Previous Rebbe with specific tasks: open a school, become a rabbi of a synagogue, or a teacher. This second generation that started leaving New York a decade later under the leadership of the new Rebbe had a broader mandate. In most cases, they were not sent to direct a specific institution, but rather, to identify the needs of the community and build Judaism from the ground up. As Rabbi Hodakov, the Rebbe's chief of staff, would brief them before they left: "You are responsible for the welfare of every Jew in your city, state, or country."

Some of these shluchim were born in Russia. Their families practiced Judaism secretly; almost all had relatives who were arrested and imprisoned in Siberia for their loyalty to Judaism, and many of these did not survive. The Russians had left during the Great Escape. As teens, they had converged on Brooklyn in the 1950s and '60s to study at 770, enticed by the dynamic personality of the new young Rebbe.

Not all the second-generation shluchim were Russian. Rabbi Yehuda Krinsky, who would become a member of the Rebbe's secretariat and later chairman of Chabad's education arm, Merkos, and social arm, Machne, began his education in Boston as the first student in the Maimonides Academy. When he was too old for the fledgling school, he attended the elite Latin School, finally coming to New York as a teenager. Shlomo Cunin was born and raised in the Bronx. His father was one of the early lay leaders of Chabad in the 1930s. Moshe Feller from Saint Paul began his circuitous route to Chabad in 1952 when he met some Chabad yeshiva students visiting his hometown. Yisroel Shmotkin was from an old-time Lubavitch family – his father emigrated from Poland to pre-State Palestine before the war. Moshe Herson, head of Chabad in New Jersey, dreamed of being a doctor. He was sent by his mother from Buenos Aires to attend yeshiva high school in Brooklyn. Yitzchak Groner, who would lead Chabad in Australia, was a descendant of the Alter Rebbe, Chabad's founder. His parents had immigrated to the US from Palestine in 1929.

This small group had close personal contact with the Rebbe and would eventually become the generals in his army of shluchim. Like Lewis and Clark, they would chart unknown territory. They were sent to communities with a broad mandate to do whatever was required to build Judaism.

Some European scholars criticized the Rebbe's plan. They claimed that by leaving the Orthodox world in New York, young rabbis would be placing their own observance at risk. They questioned how the young couples[4] could raise children in an environment that did not reinforce tradition.

In America, Liberal Jews controlled the levers of power and the financial resources. Jewish education, spirituality, and tradition, the core of the Chabad agenda, were not communal priorities. Eventually, the shluchim, lacking acceptance by the communal structure, would have no choice but to build a new network of institutions from the bottom up. This would take decades and require vast sums, easily exceeding several billion dollars.

European cities had structured communities, centuries old, supported in many cases by government funding.[5] A new element, independent, not under local control, was not warmly welcomed. In these communities, there was a détente between the congregants and their Orthodox rabbinical leadership: "We will come to shul, but don't be too demanding." The rabbis did not want to rock the boat. The newly arriving shluchim would have to overcome a lack of self-confidence that pervaded most of the rabbinical leadership.

In the US, the new rabbis with beards and hats were viewed as an irrelevant anachronism, a quaint leftover from a European Jewish culture on its last breath. In many cities, there were few fully observant

Jewish families. As one Conservative rabbi told me, "They looked like they belonged in another century, they spoke good English, and they made for an interesting evening." They would get invited to a local temple to put on a program: "An Evening with Chabad," a bit of nostalgia for Jews drifting from tradition. It was a cultural curiosity, like "Fiddler on the Roof."

In the fifties and sixties, the incubator for the new generation was the yeshiva in 770. That single, three-story brick building was Chabad's foothold in Crown Heights, which, at the time, was a neighborhood overflowing with Jews. Chabad's beachhead was sandwiched between the prestigious homes that lined Eastern Parkway and an apartment building at the end of the block, kids playing handball in the alley in the back. Inside, thirty students spent their days and nights in intense study. Yiddish was the mother tongue for most. They learned on the main floor in 770 in the study hall just to the right of the main entrance. It would be some time before the large sanctuary would be built extending from the basement below.

Across the small lobby, some fifteen feet away, was the Rebbe's office. He was involved intimately with each of the students as they evolved from teenagers to young men. In 1950, shortly after the Previous Rebbe passed away, the Rebbe met individually with the students. Yehuda Krinsky,[6] at sixteen, was one of the youngest students to receive this personal attention. "For the students, the Rebbe was like a father." Rabbi Nachman Sudak,[7] who would go to London in 1959, describes the close relationship between the Rebbe and the students: "I felt the Rebbe held my hand." They would pray every day with him and be together at his farbrengens. Some were part of the editorial team that transcribed his talks and prepared them for publication. Three times a week, the Rebbe would receive visitors for private audiences. The meetings, known as yechidus[8] (to be alone) began at around 9:00 p.m. and would go on until early morning. The Rebbe's door was open to all: rabbis, Chassidim, community leaders, politicians,[9] and people in need. After their meetings, the yeshiva students would debrief the visitors, gaining interesting insights into the Rebbe's perspective on a wide variety of issues.

The new Rebbe was optimistic about the Jewish future in the US, telling social scientist Dr. Gershon Kranzler[10] in 1951, "As the Jewish sun set in one land, it had already begun to rise in another. Now that the great centers of Eastern Europe have been destroyed by Fascism and Communism, America has become the focus and fountainhead of Jewish survival." The Rebbe told historian Charles Raddock,[11] "We should take the offensive." The Rebbe needed foot soldiers and they were being nurtured in the yeshiva in Brooklyn. Krinsky says, "The Rebbe had started the process of developing the shluchim."

There were those who did not answer the Rebbe's call, but stayed behind in Crown Heights and entered business or other professions. Others did not have the leadership abilities or the drive to succeed in a venture into the unknown. Some parents did not want their children to move far away. The Rebbe's plan was still not detailed, just a broad vision, unproven. Success was still years away. Rabbi Krinsky explains the mentality of students at the time: "In the fifties and the sixties, no one had a dream that this would develop into a network in over eighty countries."

Rabbi Moshe Feller[12] says, "The yeshiva students were fired up, but many of the parents did not want their kids to leave home." The idea of leaving the cocoon of the religious world in Brooklyn for a faraway city was unthinkable to some. The Russian Chassidim had suffered under decades of Communism. For the first time in their lives, they had found freedom and opportunity. They wanted their kids nearby, not living in some far-off country.

Some Chassidim were skeptical of the new Rebbe's ideas. One of the prominent Chassidic elders told one of the students, "Our job is to learn Torah, not to go live in some far-off country and build Judaism." Rabbi Manis Friedman,[13] whose class heralded the wave[14] of shluchim in the 1970s, says, "They were used to someone being sent to a community to be a rabbi, schochet,[15] or teacher. His prime involvement was with the Orthodox community. Now the agenda was to draw Jews distant from observance to Judaism. This was revolutionary; not all were ready to accept this idea."

Feller witnessed the tensions simmering in the community up close one night. "There was a line of those waiting to enter the Rebbe's office. One Chassid who did not have an appointment pushed his way in. He told the Rebbe that he and his wife did not want their son to leave Brooklyn. He asked the Rebbe to withdraw his request, and left the office only after the Rebbe agreed." Others gave shlichus a try, but lacked the stamina to persevere and ended up returning to New York. A series of shluchim was sent to Baltimore, San Francisco, and other cities, only to return after a year or so.

Rabbi Berel Shemtov was the first to open a Chabad regional office in the US under Merkos[16] L'inyonei Chinuch, (the Central Organization for Jewish Education). In 1958, he was dispatched to Detroit. On the train, a Jewish man asked Shemtov where he was going. "To Detroit as a shliach of the Lubavitcher Rebbe," he answered. The man told him to stay on the train all the way to Chicago. "It has a larger community; you can raise more money there." Shemtov's mission was not to send money to Brooklyn, but to build Judaism in Detroit. The community leaders were not very welcoming; one gave him an offer: "I'll pay your way back to Brooklyn."

A terrorist attack in Israel in 1956 proved to be a turning point for many of the future shluchim. The terror attack[17] took the lives of five students and their teacher in the Chassidic community of Kfar Chabad near Tel Aviv. The community was demoralized; its future was in doubt. As reporter Menachem Barash[18] wrote in the Israeli daily, *Yediot*: "These Chassidim, who had survived the pogroms in Czar Nikolai's Russia, and whom the Red Army could not intimidate, who had been banished to the frozen plains of Siberia, whose backs decades in Stalin's prisons and camps could not bow, now stood stooped and despairing – now, that the blow had hit home in the heart of the Jewish state."

After the attack, the Rebbe sent a telegram, telling the residents, "You will find consolation by rebuilding." The message infused the community with a sense of direction. The wounds were still fresh, so to console the community, the Rebbe sent a delegation of twelve senior rabbinical students, ten from the US and two from Europe.

The students' mission brought new hope. Thousands waited for their arrival in Lod Airport. For close to a month, they visited rabbinical leaders, and spoke in communities and synagogues across the country. Twelve eloquent, intelligent American rabbinical students who were imbued with Chassidic values – it made a deep impression. The Gerer Rebbe, Rabbi Yisroel Alter,[19] known as the Beis Yisroel, received the delegation, telling his Chassidim, "Halevai (please G-d) everyone would come and see such outstanding Chassidishe bachurim (Chassidic scholars) the Lubavitcher Rebbe sent."

In New York, these scholars had been students, but on the mission to Israel, they were transformed. Krinsky, a member of the delegation, recalls that the Chassidic elders would listen to their talks. The Rebbe had empowered them, showing them their potential to become leaders.

For Avrohom Korf, the mission to Israel was the tipping point. He recalls,[20] "When we returned, I wrote the Rebbe saying that I want to become a shliach." Many of the twelve would become part of the first vanguard of shluchim. They included Berel Shemtov to Detroit, Avrohom Korf to Miami, Dovid Schochet to Toronto, Shalom Adelman to Casablanca, Zushe Posner to Israel, Yossel Rosenfeld to head Chabad's largest yeshiva in New York, and Yehuda Krinsky, who would join the Rebbe's secretariat in New York.

For Rabbi Avrohom Korf, Miami was a world away from Tashkent in Uzbekistan and a DP camp in Europe. When he arrived in Miami in 1960 with his young bride, Rivka, he did not speak English. Once he reported to the Rebbe that he made a speech at the University of the Miami. The Rebbe asked, "You don't speak English, how did you do it?" He responded, "It's a long ride from Miami Beach. Along the way, my wife helped me prepare my talk."

Jews were flocking to Miami, but the religious community was very small. Rabbi Alexander Gross[21] had made a major pioneering effort establishing the Hebrew Academy, a community day school. Some families wanted a more intense Judaic program. Gross helped Korf by providing classrooms to open a yeshiva-style school inside the Hebrew Academy. Rabbi Berel Wein, then leader of the Orthodox synagogue, Beth Israel, was much more skeptical, telling Korf, "Hair will grow in my palm before you succeed." Quickly, Korf outgrew the space in the Hebrew Academy, the school took off, and Wein lent his support. Today the Lubavitch Educational Center has a thousand students between preschool and rabbinical college.

Rabbi Avrohom Shemtov moved to Philadelphia a few months after Korf came to Miami. His purpose was to establish the third regional office of Merkos, but his influence would reach farther than Philadelphia. In Washington DC, he nurtured relationships with presidents and government leaders. The fourth regional office was opened by Moshe Feller in 1962. He had dreamed of being a shliach, but never in his hometown of Saint Paul in Minnesota. His family was one of only a few Shabbat-observant ones in the Twin Cities. But his widowed father, tired of life in a city with very few religious Jews, wanted to move to New York. Just before his son's wedding in December of 1961, he met with the Rebbe to discuss the idea. The Rebbe had other plans:[22] "You should not move, we have to send Moshe on a shlichus, and we are sending him back to Minnesota."

Moshe Feller first encountered Lubavitch as a teenager back in Minnesota when two yeshiva students, Mendel Shemtov and Yehuda Krinsky, visited the area in the summer of 1952. They met young Feller at Ahavas Achim Congregation in Minneapolis, and when he was also at the next synagogue they visited, they realized he was following them around.

At fourteen, Moshe went to Yeshiva Torah Vodaath in Williamsburg, Brooklyn. He loved the learning and the comradery among the students from all segments of the Orthodox community. Chassidic and non-Chassidic, right-wing and more moderate Orthodox. Many of the students slipped away in the evening to attend college, but Moshe was intrigued by the more spiritual side of Judaism, and he would visit the Chassidic Rebbes who had emigrated from Europe and lived in Williamsburg. At the Friday-night tishes, or Shabbat gatherings led by these Rebbes, Feller could catch a glimmer of the grandeur of Jewish life that existed in Europe before the war. He made a visit to Crown Heights a few miles from Williamsburg, and on the steps of 770, he encountered Yehuda Krinsky again. Their friendship blossomed and they began studying Chassidic philosophy together on Saturday nights. Moshe was gaining a greater appreciation of the intellectual depths of Chassidic ideas and found himself drawn to the unique approach of Lubavitch.

Feller began to notice the differences between Yeshiva Torah Vodaath and the ideals taught in Lubavitch. "In Torah Vodaath it was 'us' and 'them.' The small yeshiva world was 'us,' and the rest of the community was 'them.' In Lubavitch, all Jews were 'us.'" Krinsky suggested that Moshe meet the Rebbe, "But first you must attend a farbrengen."

Feller came to his first farbrengen in July of 1955. The Rebbe touched on many issues that evening, but the topic that seized Moshe's attention was the summer Merkos shlichus, when rabbinical students would visit Jewish communities for outreach. "The students would be soon setting out on their trips. The Rebbe was giving them a pep talk," said Moshe. The Rebbe recalled that two students had traveled to a small town a year or two before and were disappointed with their marginal success. "What they didn't realize," said the Rebbe, "was the young girl sitting by the window [in that small town] who turned to her grandfather and said, 'Look at those strange-looking fellows on the street.' When the older Jew saw the two young yeshiva students, he was reminded of his roots back in Europe and the life that he had left behind. That feeling of spiritual awakening," explained the Rebbe, "was worth the whole effort of the trip."

Moshe wanted to join the summer project, but realized that it was impossible. Students at Torah Vodaath went home or to camp. A week later, he entered the Rebbe's room for his first yechidus. The Rebbe surprised Moshe when he asked him, "How would it be if you go along with the fellows that are traveling in your area?" The Rebbe paused, his face lit up, and he added, "You want to go, don't you?"

Leibel Raskin and Yossel Rosenfeld met up with Moshe in Saint Paul. Raskin was from Russia via Israel, Rosenfeld was from Brooklyn. Up to Winnipeg and down to Saint Louis they traveled in that summer of 1955. The group was a strange mix. Two Lubavitch yeshiva students, one who barely spoke English, another with a Brooklyn accent, and a Midwestern American boy who was a student of Torah

Vodaath. They met Jews, sold Jewish books not available locally, and planted spiritual seeds together on their three-week journey.

"I should have switched yeshivas right away after that summer," said Moshe. Three years later, he finally made the move to 770, living in a small apartment on Saint Johns Place with Avrohom Shemtov. As they walked home late at night, they would talk of the future. Moshe says, "We dreamed of changing the Jewish world." Not knowing the mechanics of exactly how, they did know they wanted to be the Rebbe's shluchim, and the rest would follow.

In 1962, Moshe married and moved to Minnesota to open the fourth regional Merkos office in the US. Before leaving, the couple met with the Rebbe, who asked, "Do you have a copy of the Shulchan Aruch, Mishnah Brurah, and She'arim Metzuyanim Behalachah (classic works on Jewish Law)?" When Moshe answered, "Yes," the Rebbe added that he was not going to give specific directives. "Zolst du zein flexible (You should be flexible)," using the English word to end the Yiddish sentence, to Feller's surprise. What was unsaid but understood, according to Moshe, "You got a head – use it." Keep the rules, but push the edge of the creative envelope, maintain a strong fidelity to Jewish tradition, yet at the same time be innovative. Moshe's new wife, Mindy, was a Phi Beta Kappa graduate of Hunter College with a degree in mathematics. The Rebbe encouraged her to use her knowledge of mathematics to strengthen Jewish identity in the academic community. She took a position at the University of Minnesota.

With no formal position in the community, no local support other than a few friends that Moshe knew from childhood, the young Fellers headed off to Minnesota. There wasn't a synagogue for Moshe to be a rabbi, or a school to teach in. They had been given a broad mandate and a small starting salary from New York of seventy-five dollars a week. When they purchased a car, the salary was raised to a total of one hundred dollars.

The Twin Cities were among the most highly organized Jewish communities in the United States. There were synagogues, community centers, and a wealth of activities. The small Orthodox remnant, mostly older, coalesced around a few synagogues. In Saint Paul where

Moshe and Mindy settled, there were just three Shabbat-observant families. Finding that niche was tough.

Rabbi Hodakov suggested that Moshe sell Chabad publications. So Moshe prepared a book fair in his father's house and placed ads in the local Jewish paper. "It was far from successful," he said. Clearly, he needed to be "more *flexible*." The Fellers started a Shabbat afternoon program for boys approaching bar mitzvah. Moshe traveled out to smaller towns making Sunday Schools for the children in these remote communities that had no Jewish educational opportunities. In 1965, Moshe purchased ten acres of land with a twelve-bedroom house near a lake on the outskirts of Saint Paul as a retreat center. Youth groups began coming for Shabbat, and Feller's program would enhance theirs with stronger Jewish content. He was upbeat and American, and his wife was highly educated. Groups began coming for the weekends, and it slowly became the "in thing" to spend a weekend with Lubavitch. Feller had discovered his niche.

Nachman Sudak[23] became engaged to the daughter of Rabbi Bentzion Shemtov in the winter of 1958. Shemtov had been one of the ten Chassidim who had taken the secret oath to keep Judaism alive in Russia in 1924. After the war, he escaped Russia and became the Rebbe's emissary in England. Sudak met with the Rebbe and discussed the date and place of the wedding. The Rebbe told him, "We will see, maybe in the summer month of Tammuz."[24] Later it would emerge that the Rebbe had another plan; he was setting the stage to send young Sudak to London as his shliach, but the Rebbe had not yet revealed his intentions to Sudak. During those winter months of his engagement Sudak met with Rabbi Hodakov[25] a few times to discuss different ideas about where he could go. Sudak told Hodakov, "It makes no difference to me where I go, I want to be a shliach." While he did not understand it at the time, years later he told me, "The Rebbe was testing me."[26]

As the summer drew near, Sudak met with the Rebbe again and suggested the wedding take place in New York since the bride was there. The Rebbe rejected the idea. "It's an ancient Jewish tradition that the wedding is done in the hometown of the bride – do it in London," he said. The Rebbe instructed him that he should remain there after the wedding and begin to work with the community. "Work with the local Anash, the Chassidic community,[27] but the long-term goal is that you should take over the operation." There was a small Lubavitch community there made up of a few older Chassidim, schochtim, and others. The Rebbe wanted Sudak to be the infusion of young blood that would propel Lubavitch in London in a new direction. Changing the mindset of the Chabad community would not be easy.

Sudak didn't understand exactly what he was expected to do in London. But the Rebbe told him "there were thousands of things to do." Decades later, he told me, "In the summer we went out to visit communities as part of the Merkos shlichus; I thought it would be something like that." He didn't foresee the challenges of developing a financial base, negotiating the communal politics, building institutions and communities, not to mention the unique challenge of London: convincing the local Lubavitch community to shed its insular identity and shift its focus outward.

Sudak recalls, "A few months after I got there, I decided to organize a Lag B'omer parade for the children of the Jewish schools." Lag B'omer, celebrated in the spring, is a minor holiday linked to the great sages of old, Rabbi Akivah and Rabbi Shimon Bar Yochai. The local Chassidim asked Sudak, "Why do we need this?" They were used to Chassidic communities whose priorities were focused inward toward scholarship and observance.

One prominent rabbi publicly directed the Orthodox yeshivas not to participate. Sudak went to meet him and was told, "For years I dreamed of such of a parade, and we the rabbis would walk in the head." Sudak had stolen his dream, so he had retaliated by boycotting. Despite the difficulties, close to a thousand children participated in the first Jewish parade in London history. The parade had a broader message: Judaism in England had been sedate, reserved, and proper. By taking the children to the streets, Sudak was heralding a new era of self-confident Jewish identity. Sudak continued to direct his attention to children through the development of Lubavitch schools in London. Still, he needed the financial support for these and other projects.

As a generation of shluchim would learn, with time, help would come from the most unexpected places. Rabbi Koppel Rosen was head of Carmel College, one of England's most prestigious centers of Jewish learning with connections to the upper echelons of English society, places that Sudak could only dream of reaching. Unfortunately Rosen was a well-known critic of Chabad. However, Rosen had a fatal illness, and this personal crisis sparked a desire to meet with the Rebbe. Together, Rosen, Sudak, and Shemtov traveled to New York. After meeting with the Rebbe, Rosen told Sudak and Rabbi Shemtov, "I was wrong to have criticized Lubavitch all these years, the Rebbe is a true Jewish leader." Afterward, although his health was weakening, Rosen used his influence to help. Sudak recalled, "He brought us to Sir Isaac Wolfson," one of the richest Jews in the country. "Every Jewish organization wanted to enlist Wolfson's help, but no one could get to him. Koppel Rosen knew him well and convinced him to help us build a new building for Lubavitch." That facility, erected in the mid-sixties, was one of the first large Chabad buildings in the world, and it set the stage for the growth of Chabad in Britain.

Leibel Raskin was a charismatic young man, optimistic, outgoing, an outstanding scholar. He spoke Yiddish, but his English was non-existent. He was engaged to be married when he met with Rabbi Hodakov in 1958, passionately telling him[28] that he wanted a shlichus. He wanted to be assigned a mission from the Rebbe "to any city or any country." Hodakov pushed him off: "Just wait a few months and we will see." Meantime, the growing yeshiva in Newark was trying to entice Raskin there. They had even written the Rebbe about offering him a position. There were other job possibilities, too, but Raskin would have none of it. No offers from anyone. He wanted to be sent somewhere, anywhere, by the Rebbe.

Raskin's parents had escaped the Nazi invasion of Russia by fleeing to remote Kazakhstan, not far from the Chinese border. There, his father had cared for the Rebbe's father, Rabbi Levi Yitzchak Schneerson, who had been arrested and exiled by the Communists in 1939. At that time, Leibel was not yet bar mitzvah, yet he had been at Rabbi Levi Yitzchak Schneerson's bedside when he died in 1944, and helped bury him afterward.[29] Following the war, Raskin's family was smuggled out of Russia on false passports as part of the Great Escape, and they immigrated to Israel.

In 1953, Raskin was studying in Chabad's main yeshiva in Israel. What he really wanted was to learn at 770, near the Rebbe, but such a dream was almost impossible. Israeli yeshiva students received army deferments while studying full time, but foreign travel was prohibited prior to completion of military service. His repeated requests to the army to allow him to travel abroad had been rejected. So he composed three letters, one to Prime Minister David Ben Gurion, the second to President Yitzchak Ben Tzvi, and the third, yet again to the army draft board, writing, "I was brought up in Russia under the cruel hand of the Communists. They persecuted us; still we remained Jews, proud and loyal to our traditions. As Chabad Chassidim, we stood up to the oppression. I have a physical father and a spiritual father. I need to visit my spiritual father, the Rebbe, in New York."

The draft board sent him yet another rejection, and President Ben Tzvi didn't answer. Surprisingly, however, a few weeks later, he received a note from the prime minister's office inviting him to meet with Ben Gurion next Wednesday at noon. The leaders of the Chabad community were astounded and urged him to cancel the meeting with the prime minister, fearful that the brash student might not represent the community properly.

Raskin was not deterred. That Wednesday at noon, he presented himself at the entrance to the prime minister's office. Quickly, he was ushered upstairs into the office of Ben Gurion's military advisor, Nehemia Argov, who told Raskin that the prime minister was meeting with an official from the United States and could not be interrupted. However, Argov told Raskin, "Ben Gurion is very interested in your letter. He wants to know how you grew up as a religious Jew in Russia under Communism."

Raskin told Argov his story. "In 1897, the Fifth Lubavitcher Rebbe, Rabbi Sholom DovBer, established a yeshiva in the town of Lubavitch that my father attended. The students were like brothers and the Rebbe like a father. The central pillar of the educational philosophy of the yeshiva was Mesiras Nefesh (self-sacrifice for Judaism).

That principle was ingrained in us. My father was imprisoned by the Russians; my brother refused to cut his beard and when he walked in public he covered it with a kerchief."

"Did you attend Russian schools?" Argov asked. Raskin explained that his parents did everything to keep the children away, hiding them from authorities and eventually fleeing to remote Kazakhstan to evade the heavy hand of the Communists.

Argov explained to Raskin that his story had touched a chord with the prime minister. "Ben Gurion has instructed the Army to allow you to leave to study near the Rebbe. We want you to be a positive voice for us there; we are making you an emissary on behalf of the government." Then he added, "Many of the Chassidic Rebbes opposed Zionism, but we have a special sympathy for Chabad." In 1947, Zalman Shazar[30] asked the blessing of the Rebbe, Rabbi Yosef Yitzchak, who assured him that Israel would prevail in the UN. Later, Chabad established a town in Israel.

In New York, Raskin joined the small group that studied under the Rebbe's personal guidance. The turning point in Raskin's life was a farbrengen in the winter of 1955. The Rebbe asked the students to volunteer[31] to follow his guidance. "Whoever wants to make a commitment should send me a note with their name." Half of the thirty students in 770 signed up. Those students who volunteered received special personal direction from the Rebbe in the years to come.

After months of waiting, Raskin was finally invited for another meeting with Rabbi Hodakov. "Are you willing to go on a mission?" he asked Raskin. "Whatever the Rebbe wants, yes," Raskin replied. Finally Rabbi Hodakov disclosed his assignment. "We want you to go to Casablanca." Hodakov lifted the intercom and told the Rebbe, "He is willing to go." Later, in a private meeting, the Rebbe[32] told Leibel, "Make the wedding in Paris. The bride is from there, and you should leave from there to Morocco."

A few days later, Raskin was walking on Eastern Parkway with a family acquaintance. Unbeknownst to him, the Rebbe was walking home a few steps behind. Raskin's friend asked him, "How could you go to Morocco, it's so far away and an Arab country?" He responded, "If the Rebbe sends, it will be good." Later, Rabbi Hodakov told Leibel the Rebbe had overheard the conversation and was very gratified to hear his determination.

Years later, Raskin told me it was clear to him that this long wait was a test. He could have accepted an easier job in the US. The Rebbe wanted him to make the choice on his own for what would be a demanding mission that would last a lifetime.

Even though Morocco was remote, in one way it was easier. Raskin did not have to find a niche like the other young shluchim in American cities. Chabad had a school system in the country. Nor would he have the financial challenges of many of his friends because the JDC (the Joint) would underwrite most of the expenses.

Decades later, in 1995, we spent two days together in Washington DC as part of the celebration when the Rebbe was post-humously honored by Congress with the Congressional Gold Medal. It was an exuberant event: a reception in Congress, events in the State Department and Library of Congress, and a celebratory banquet in the evening. We were whizzed around Washington in buses with police escorts, sirens and lights blazing. At the concluding concert at the Kennedy Center, I said to Raskin in Yiddish, "Nu Leibel, what do you think of us traveling from the State Department to the Congress and now the Kennedy Center with police escorts?" He turned to me and said in Yiddish, "Dos iz gornisht (it's nothing). You should have seen when I walked the streets of Fez[33] to the home of Maimonides, surrounded by police provided by the King of Morocco himself."

The major Jewish community where, arguably, Chabad would make the greatest inroads was located the most distant from New York: Australia. Eight Jews were on the First Fleet, the original prison ships that arrived in 1788 from England, including Esther Abrahams, sentenced for stealing a bolt of silk. She eventually married the colonial governor of New South Wales. Voluntary Jewish immigration began with Barnett Levey, who arrived in 1821. Eastern Europeans began to cross the vast ocean in the 1880s. After World War I, there was a large influx.

The first Chabad follower, Moshe Feiglin,[34] came to Australia before World War I to find refuge and opportunity in the far-off land. His father, a long-time Lubavitch Chassid, had immigrated to the Jewish homeland, then under Turkish rule. Moshe was born in Gorky, Russia, in 1875 and got married in 1911 in Palestine. The Turkish Army, desperate for recruits for World War I, raided his home in Metula. Fearing for his life, Feiglin fled, first to Port Said in Egypt and then east to remote Australia. The voyage to Australia was a grueling ordeal concluding with the ship's boiler bursting, setting the ship adrift not far from the coast of western Australia. Passengers and crew were rescued, but the rescue mission landed them at the port city of Fremantle. Local Jews, surprised at seeing a young religious man, asked him, "What are you doing in this treif [non-kosher] country? This is no place for you."

Feiglin made his way to Melbourne by ship, praying in his cabin for the spiritual fortitude to raise his children as observant Jews in this remote land. Feiglin's wife and children followed, and the family staked their claim in the agricultural community of Shepparton, just over a hundred miles north of Melbourne. They were able to create an oasis of religiosity in the small farming community with a synagogue, school, and even a mikvah.

The first generation of Australian Jews was almost all English. Author Uri Kaploun, Feiglin's grandson, called them "Mayflower Jews." They were somewhat traditional; they attended synagogue from time to time. After World War II, Polish immigrants gravitated to Melbourne, and they brought a vibrant Jewish culture to Australia. Among them were five Lubavitcher families[35] whom Feiglin helped with visas. These Chassidim, Rabbi Elisha Greenbaum writes, "jump-started the expansion of Chabad in Australia."

In 1947, Rabbi Shemaryahu Gurary, son-in-law of the Sixth Rebbe, Rabbi Yosef Yitzchak, asked the then-young Rabbi Yitzchak Groner to travel to far-off Australia to fundraise for the yeshiva. But there was another agenda, too: uplifting Jewish life in Australia. Before he departed, the Sixth Rebbe wrote to Groner that this was the true intention of his mission. Groner was born in Brooklyn in 1925. He came from a long, distinguished Chabad line, a fifth-generation descendant of the famed Rebbitzen Menucha Rochel,[36] granddaughter of Chabad's founder. She passed away in Hebron in 1888.

When Groner departed for Australia, he left his wife, Devorah, behind,[37] though they had been married for only eleven months. Devorah's father had been a student in the town of Lubavitch. She was three years old in 1927 when her mother lifted her up at the train station to see the Sixth Rebbe, Rabbi Yosef Yitzchak, as he was departing from Russia. "I remember it like today, the angelic red-tinged beard of the Rebbe," Devorah told me eight decades later in an interview in Melbourne. In 1930, pursued by the NKVD (the Russian secret police), the Sixth Rebbe fled Russia to New York. Devorah grew up attending public school until she was eight, then a small yeshiva for girls. The Ramash, the future Rebbe, officiated at her wedding to Yitzchak Groner.

The journey across the Pacific took some fifty-five hours for twenty-two-year-old Rabbi Yitzchak Groner. The Pan Am Clipper hopped from island to island. Devorah says, "It was an adventure for him." Groner reflected years later, "I was the first Jew to daven (pray) with talit and tefilin on layover in Fiji." Rabbi Chaim Gutnick, a handsome young man, waited to greet him in Sydney. His father had been a well-known Lubavitch rabbi in England. When the war engulfed Europe, including Telz, Lithuania, where he was studying at the yeshiva, he found a haven in Australia with a group of other yeshiva students. Nevertheless, he wished to immigrate to America, and he wrote to the then-Rebbe, Rabbi Yosef Yitzchak, seeking sponsorship for a visa to the US. But the Rebbe told him to remain in Australia and build a life there. "Man's steps are ordained by G-d, and since Providence has guided you to Australia, this is your place," wrote the Rebbe. "Prepare the ground for the arrival of Jewish refugees so that it will be a place of Torah, where G-d can be found." He had received a letter from the Rebbe asking him to assist young Rabbi Groner with his mission to Australia. Gutnick said, "It is quite possible that the Rebbe's intention behind this mission was to have Rabbi Groner look around and get a feel for the place. This was the far-reaching look of a Gadol, a great Jewish leader."

Gutnick and Groner formed a friendship and partnership that served as one of the foundations of Jewish life in Australia. Together they celebrated the Chassidic holiday of Yud Tes Kislev with the first-ever farbrengen in Sydney. It was just the two of them, plus Gutnick's oldest daughter, Penina, who crawled around on the floor of the small apartment. They did not imagine that, as the decades unfolded, they and their children[38] would play a crucial role in molding Jewish destiny in Australia.

In Melbourne, Rabbi Groner discovered a community in the early stages of assimilation. The fully observant were few and aging. Most of the young were eager to be part of the postwar boom and leave their Jewish roots behind. Jewish education was primarily in Jewish supplementary afternoon schools. Yeshivas were nonexistent. With Moshe Feiglin's support, Groner gained access to some of the more affluent members of the community.

But Rabbi Groner did not neglect the second part of his mission. He started classes, spoke in synagogues, and participated in communal events. Mendel New,[39] a young man from one of the religiously observant families in Melbourne, recalls Groner's arrival: "There were a few religious Jews with beards who spoke Yiddish. Suddenly Groner came and shattered all the stereotypes. He was young, spoke English, knew baseball, and went to the mikvah. He electrified the young Jews of Melbourne." Nevertheless, Groner wanted to return to the US, and as Passover was nearing one year, he sent a telegram to the Rebbe in New York, saying he wanted to come back. Hearing nothing in return, he headed home to his wife and child. Devorah says, "The Rebbe never gave him permission to leave." She explains that the fact that the Rebbe did not answer caused a sense of unease and lingering doubt. Maybe, after all, Australia was his destiny. It would take years before the Groner's would move for good.

Groner made such an impact during his first visit to Australia that the Jewish Newspaper in Melbourne lamented his return to the US. "When he finally leaves, none will be so grieved as the flock of young people whose close friendship he has captured and into whose hearts he has brought a wider understanding of Judaism."

Soon after arriving in the US, the Groner family went to Buffalo to teach in the Chabad yeshiva. In 1953, Groner returned for a second visit to Australia. The local community leaders and the

Rebbe encouraged him to stay, but Groner declined, finding a host of reasons. Instead he returned to Buffalo.

Some years later, Rabbi Gurary asked Groner to come to New York to fundraise for the growing network of Chabad yeshivas. Groner asked the Rebbe for advice, and the Rebbe told him, "You don't want to be in Buffalo, or go to Australia, but you have to support your family, so you might as well take the job in New York." The Rebbe's answer caused Devorah a sense of angst. "I saw the Rebbe was not happy we were coming to New York," she said. "We were escaping from a shlichus, a mission." Devorah felt that they weren't in the right place; she realized that the Rebbe was waiting for volunteers. "He wasn't going to send anybody," she said.

A few months later, on his birthday, Groner met with the Rebbe again.[40] They discussed fundraising projects and he told the Rebbe he was traveling to Chicago to test the students in the Chabad yeshiva there. As the meeting concluded, the Rebbe said, "Yitzchak, we are dealing with small things – kleinekeiten." He used the Yiddish word, which stressed that what Groner was doing was not significant. As the Rebbe finished his sentence, he gave a big sigh. Groner told his wife, Devorah, about the Rebbe's final words and the anguish the Rebbe seemed to be feeling.

Devorah was very distressed. "I couldn't sleep for a whole week," she said. "I began to realize we needed to go to Australia." Groner was also troubled after the meeting. He said to his wife, "If the Rebbe wants me to go to Australia, why doesn't he tell me?" Devorah explained that the Previous Rebbe had not given him permission to leave Australia. Shortly afterward, Nosson Werdiger, one of the community leaders from Melbourne, came for a visit to New York and asked the Rebbe to send Groner. Werdiger's request was the tipping point. The Rebbe asked him to go, and Groner finally agreed. His life's destiny finally caught up with him. Yitzchak Groner headed to Melbourne. His wife and six children came five months later by boat.

Yitzchak Groner was a blunt, charismatic American. The local institutions were being run by Russian Lubavitch refugees a generation older than he was. He was full of ideas, but he was relegated to fundraising. Devorah said, "Sometimes he would get a few guineas

[Australian currency at the time]." The pioneering families that had brought Chabad to Australia had settled the beachhead. With the leadership of Rabbi Serebryanski, the educational institutions had been established. Rabbi Groner, brimming with enthusiasm, wanted to push forward, but the old generation and the new, the Russians and brash American, had different visions. Tensions lingered below the surface.

Devorah said, "He was depressed; he wanted to go to New York to visit the Rebbe." One of the local Chassidim told him, "It will take you ten years to save the money to go to New York." Groner had led High Holiday services in Bogota, Columbia, a few years earlier, so he wrote them and they invited him back. Bogota was his ticket to New York. He led the services for the High Holidays in Bogota in 1960, and then he was able to the visit the Rebbe for the holiday of Sukkot that comes a few days after Yom Kippur.

While Groner was in New York, a fire damaged one of the buildings of the yeshiva in Melbourne. It dampened the community's mood, and one of the locals who sensed the Groners' unease told Devorah, "The ship is sinking and the rats are the first to leave." His insinuation was that the Groners were planning to abandon their mission in Melbourne.

Sometime earlier, the Rebbe had asked Devorah to write him "everything that was going on." Regularly, Devorah wrote to him describing the details of life in Melbourne, and the Rebbe would respond, usually briefly, to her letters. After the fire, Devorah composed a long letter to the Rebbe describing the situation, the isolation, and lack of appreciation by some in Melbourne. Deep down she wondered about the very purpose of being in Melbourne, and she asked the Rebbe, "Whose ship is this?" In a long, personal letter written in English, the Rebbe replied to Devorah Groner: "The ship was that of my father-in-law, the Previous Rebbe of saintly memory." The Rebbe continued, writing that the Zohar, the great classic of Jewish mysticism, teaches that tzadikim, the righteous, continue to be linked to events in the physical world after their passing. Devorah said, "The Rebbe poured out his heart in the letter." The Rebbe compared the role Yitzchak had had in Buffalo to that of a clerk with specific hours and responsibilities. In Melbourne, by contrast, her husband was like an executive "upon whom the full responsibility rests, all the more so being at a great distance and having to make decisions." The Rebbe explained that some have only the capacity to be clerks, while others have greater abilities. He noted that if Groner "would confine himself within the framework of a clerk's job, it would be a gross injustice to himself, not to mention to the cause." He wrote of the nobility of their mission of educating children, calling it "of vital interest to themselves and also to posterity for all generations."

Ultimately, the Rebbe left the choice in Devorah's hands. "You have the freedom to decide whether you wish to continue your work in Australia or return to an easier job in this country," he wrote, adding that the mission in Australia "must be carried out willingly." The Rebbe told her that it was not just about Yitzchak Groner's position; Devorah, herself, shared fully in the responsibility of strengthening Jewish life in Melbourne, and the mission "applies to your work," he wrote. The Rebbe shared the content of the letter with her husband, who was in New York at that time.

"It was a turning point," Devorah Groner said. Groner returned again to Australia. For over a decade, he had struggled with his destiny, but now the doubts were resolved. Finally, Groner was ready to emerge as a leader who would mold the destiny of Australia. He realized that being a shliach helped him reach his own potential, telling an interviewer years later, "It's not only to help the other people who are there, it's to help the individual emissary to reach his fulfillment and a certain sense of accomplishment."

In the years to come, Groner's impact would be felt throughout Australia. He poured his energy first into building Jewish education in Melbourne. The European immigrants were open to a traditional education that reminded them of their roots. The schools grew, creating a new generation of committed Jews. His leadership propelled the growth of traditional Jewish education in Melbourne and later in other cities.[41] Chabad's influence grew in other directions. Chabad Houses were opened around the country. Even though Groner was wary of creating these smaller, local community centers, in time he began to see their value. Yeshivas and a kolel (advanced Torah study institute) infused the community with young scholars. Chabad rabbis entered many of the community pulpits. Today some 85 percent of the synagogues in Australia have Chabad rabbis. Rabbi Yanki Barber, a member of the rabbinical court in Melbourne, says that "the reason for the growth of Judaism in Melbourne was Rabbi Groner." After his passing in 2008, six decades after his arrival in Australia by Pan Am Clipper, Isi Leibler, leader of the Executive Council of Australian Jewry for close to twenty years, said, "History will record that Rabbi Yitzchak Groner was, beyond a doubt, the greatest Australian Jewish leader of the past century."

Shlomo Cunin never had any doubts about his life's direction. He was brought up in the Bronx, a third-generation American. His father was one of the founders of Chabad in the US. Cunin attended public school, but at age eleven, he went to the Lubavitch yeshiva in Brooklyn. At sixteen, he received his first personal mission for the Rebbe. It was Passover eve, and the Rebbe gave the teenage Cunin[42] an extra matza and asked him to give it to a family in the Bronx. Close to sunset, young Shlomo reached the address. A burly man with tattoos answered the door; there was a loaf of bread on the table. "The Rebbe sent me," Shlomo told the family. Looking around, it was clear they were far from observant. Still Cunin suggested, "Let's make a Seder."

Cunin says the man called his wife, who was pregnant, to join in, and then they were joined by two adorable little girls, five or six years old. Both girls were blind. "We cleaned the table, I placed my hat on his head, and I invited him to start the Seder. I tried to remember the correct order of the Seder, but it was difficult without a Hagadah (booklets containing the narrative of the Exodus of the Hebrews from Egypt)."

We ate the matza, and used water and paper cups to represent the Four Cups drunk at the Seder. I was trying to figure out what the Rebbe would do if he were here. I started to tell them things that I had heard from the Rebbe. I told them to strengthen their faith, that this is the night that Hashem (literally, "the name," used to refer to G-d) freed our forefathers from slavery, and He frees us tonight as well. The husband and wife drank in every word, as if their lives depended on this.

At 1:00 a.m., the mother put the girls to sleep; it was time to leave. Cunin asked the husband how he knew the Rebbe. He said he worked in a meat factory with a rabbi who worked in another department. His wife became pregnant, and since the doctors feared that this baby would be born blind, they suggested that she terminate the pregnancy. The husband was very depressed and consulted with this rabbi, who suggested that he write to the Rebbe, who replied that they should have faith in Hashem. That night Cunin learned to appreciate the Rebbe's great love for others.

Eight years later, now married, Cunin headed for Los Angeles with his wife, Miriam. California was not going to be easy. Traditional Judaism was very weak, Cunin[43] says. "Some Holocaust survivors and a few religious Jews."

His first major project put him head-to-head with the local Jewish establishment. The battleground was Laurel Elementary School in LA's Fairfax district. Since the early forties, Chabad had run Released Time in New York public schools, under the leadership of Rabbi Jacob J. Hecht.[44] Released Time is a program in which children are released from the public school classroom for an hour a week for religious instruction. In Los Angeles, Protestant and Catholic groups had created large programs with eighty thousand attending weekly. Cunin decided to implement the project in Los Angeles for Jewish children. He applied to the Los Angeles Interreligious Commission, which administrated the program in the public schools. The Board of Rabbis,[45] a group backed by the Jewish Federation of Los Angeles, and made up primarily of Reform and Conservative rabbis, blocked his membership. They claimed to speak on behalf of the Jewish community. Cunin rallied a group of Orthodox rabbis and, finally, he was accepted as a member of the LA Commission. Once he was a member, he encountered opposition from the only other Jewish member of the commission, a public-school employee with ties to the Jewish Federation. She tried to scuttle Cunin's efforts, but she failed. Finally, with the proper authorizations, Cunin opened a program in Laurel Elementary in the Fairfax district, the heart of LA's Jewish community.

Soon enough, however, Cunin was summoned to the offices of the Jewish Federation of Los Angeles, where three members of the Community Relations Committee informed him of the rules in town. "We run the Jewish community.[46] There will be no Released Time." Even though the Supreme Court had ruled that the program was not a breach of the separation of church and state,[47] Federation leaders believed that it was more important to maintain that strict separation, even more than the law required, than to educate Jewish children. But Cunin felt that any opportunity to educate Jewish children should be seized.

Deep down, this conflict reflected a more profound debate. Federation leaders feared the influence of religion in the public sphere, recalling the European Jewish experience. They were concerned with outside threats to the Jewish community. Cunin felt confident in his identity as a Jew in America. He understood that the US was not Europe and the greatest threat to a Jewish future was the lack of Jewish education, not anti-Semitism.

Cunin was twenty-four, young, brash, and fearless. He stood up and said, "This meeting is over. I am the train coming down the track; either get on board or get out the way," and he stormed out.

For the next few years, they battled. The Jewish Federation claimed they represented the "Jewish community"[48] and their policy was against Released Time, but the small group of local Orthodox rabbis continued to support Cunin. They protested the Federation's heavy-handed approach, even staging a public march. The Federation[49] worked behind the scenes to scuttle Cunin's program. They pressured the school administration with claims of technical violations of school-board policy, forcing the closing of the Released Time at Laurel Elementary.[50] Cunin fought back, attacking the Federation in the press, organizing public demonstrations, and demanding an investigation from the state government. Finally the State Department of Education[51] issued a report stating that LA school officials had become embroiled in an internal Jewish issue, and the closing of the program at Laurel Elementary was a mistake. After almost five years of conflict, the Federation[52] realized that Cunin was an unstoppable train and they threw in the towel.

This was a battle that Chabad would fight in community after community. At the time, Jewish communities were dominated by Liberal Jewish leaders. Orthodoxy was small and its influence marginal. Most Orthodox leaders were in a defensive mode. The arrival of shluchim who were not willing to toe the line in American Jewish communities marked a shift of philosophy to a more strident, self-confident Orthodoxy. Cunin was one of the first to face down the establishment.

The Released Time battle was one of the first ideas that Cunin had in order to jump-start Jewish education and outreach in California. He would bring his suggestions to the Rebbe who would guide him. At about this time, a rabbi was retiring in Israel and wanted to give Cunin his storefront synagogue of a few aging members, but the Rebbe rejected the idea. Then Cunin wanted to buy a swim school and create a combination Hebrew School-swimming school in order to draw in kids. Again, the Rebbe nixed it. Along the way, Cunin says, "The Rebbe was sending me on a path."

It would take five years before Cunin finally came upon the idea that would revolutionize the Jewish world: the Chabad House. It all began when a group of parents who were worrying about the direction of their kids asked him for help. Cunin decided to open a center at the University of California, Los Angeles (UCLA). What to call it was the dilemma.

Mrs. Greg Davidson was helping Cunin navigate the upper crust of Jewish LA. They had met in LA's only kosher bakery, Schwartz's on Fairfax, when her ten-year-old daughter had asked if she could touch Cunin's beard. A young rabbi in a beard was a rare sight in Los Angeles then. Davidson told her daughter that the rabbi probably did not understand English. She was surprised when he responded in a brash Bronx accent, "I am third-generation American." The encounter in the bakery led Davidson to become Cunin's executive assistant.

Davidson told Cunin,[53] "We can't call it Lubavitch House, that's the name of a town in Russia." She said a different name was needed, something with a message. "Let's call it Chabad House, it represents the central ideas of Chabad: wisdom, understanding, and knowledge." Cunin suggested Davidson's idea to the Rebbe, who responded enthusiastically. Later, the Rebbe told Cunin and some supporters: "Chabad Houses will spread from the north to the south, the west to the east, like Gimbels (a department store chain at the time) in every community."

In California, Cunin had broken the ice of the American Jewish community. Cunin had overcome community opposition with determination. He was an innovator who did not become intimidated by anyone or anything. The Liberal Jewish establishment tried to shut him down, and he emerged triumphant from the confrontation. But most important, he had established Chabad's independence. The creation of the first Chabad House produced an organizational structure that propelled Chabad forward. He also moved outside the traditional Orthodox community of Fairfax and put down roots in trendy Westwood, making the statement that Chabad was reaching out.

When a fire devastated the Chabad House at UCLA in 1980, Cunin created a telethon. Dancing rabbis and Hollywood stars raised millions and boosted Chabad in the state. Not only did he raise money, he changed attitudes. The telethon brought the Chabad message, unfiltered, directly into the homes of hundreds of thousands of Jews. Cunin had bypassed the communal structure with his message, earning respect and financial support. Chabad was not anymore an anachronism, but a modern dynamic group on the cutting edge. The telethon set the stage for even more growth, and as the years went by, Chabad would become a fixture throughout the state. Today, Chabad is the largest Jewish organization in California.

Cunin was the pacesetter, the shliach who translated the Rebbe's vision into reality in the American Jewish community. He created the institutional modality that facilitated Chabad's growth; he pushed the edge of the envelope, proving that Chabad could succeed in a big way. His influence transcended California. In the seventies, as younger shluchim began to move to new communities, they all looked to California, asking, "What is Cunin doing?" He showed everyone, and most important, his fellow shluchim, that the sky is the limit.

Chapter Six

The Birthday Present

As the end of March 1972 approached, there was excitement and optimism in the air. Despite the devastating losses of the Holocaust and Communism, Chabad was experiencing a miraculous rebirth. Around the world, Chabad was expanding, and young people filled its schools. Twenty-one years earlier, the Rebbe had accepted the leadership of Chabad. Now, the entire community was coming together to celebrate his seventieth birthday.

No one dreamed of giving him a gold watch or a vacation. The bond between the Chassidim and the Rebbe was spiritual. In Jewish tradition, a birthday is considered a moment for personal reflection and spiritual resolutions, so a grassroots effort had emerged to prepare gifts of a sacred nature. In Israel, this development had caught the interest of reporters. The leading Israeli daily, *Yediot*, carried a headline: "Chassidim Study Another Page of Talmud as a Birthday Present." Yeshiva students in the US organized initiatives to increase their studies. In London, the community decided to print a special edition of the Chassidic classic, *The Tanya*. Zalmon Jaffe, a community activist from Manchester, led the English delegation that gave

The Tanya to the Rebbe. And the Rebbe asked him to present it to his wife, the Rebbitzen,[1] Chaya Mushka.

The farbrengen twenty-one years earlier when the Rebbe had accepted his position was in the small synagogue on the ground floor of 770. This time, crowds would fill the greatly expanded sanctuary. The building now incorporated the original three-story building of 770, and a new sanctuary reached under the adjacent apartment buildings that had been purchased. The sanctuary's most distinctive quality was its unpretentiousness: linoleum floors, wood paneling, and rows of simple wooden benches. The only indulgence was a row of chandeliers that dotted the ceiling, incongruent with the architectural minimalism of the cavernous room. Chabad had always put the focus on the internal, the spiritual core of each person. The architecture was reflective of this philosophy. The important thing was not the façade, but the essence.

The sanctuary was full in anticipation of the Rebbe's arrival. Hundreds had made the pilgrimage from around the world to be at the farbrengen. A charter flight had brought seventy Chassidim a few days earlier from Israel; another charter had arrived from London. Buses brought groups from Montreal, Toronto, Detroit, and other cities. In the middle of the room, Chassidim clustered on stark, simple wooden benches that extended from the stage. Bleachers rose from the sanctuary floor filled with young rabbinical students who would stand during the farbrengen, which could last up to six hours. Women, young and old, filled the balcony that stretched along the second floor of the synagogue.

While most American Jewish leaders were bemoaning the inroads of assimilation, 770 was full of energized young Jews. The college-age rabbinical students who clustered close together on the bleachers, and the young women who filled the balcony, were fostering their identity based on Jewish scholarship and spirituality. They were excited about their Judaism, enthusiastic about a Jewish future. They were the prospective soldiers in the Rebbe's fledgling army.

Why were young people so drawn to Chabad, and why were they willing to move far from Brooklyn and dedicate their lives to serve the Jewish community? How did the Rebbe succeed in instilling in them a sense of mission and purpose? How were they able to sustain this passion and commitment for a lifetime?

Rivkah Slonim, a shlucha in Binghamton, New York, was a young teen on the day of that birthday farbrengen. She explains how the Rebbe succeeded in instilling idealism: "The Rebbe told young people, 'You can change the world, you can do something that has cosmic implications.'" Chabad philosophy teaches that every individual has a transcendent purpose for being on earth. Rabbi Yehoshua Binyomin Rosenfeld learned that lesson during his first years in Colombia. Writing to the Rebbe of a talk given by Israeli Finance Minister, Yitzchak Modai, while visiting Bogota, Colombia's capital, he said, "I wish the Israeli diplomatic corps had the same level of commitment as Chabad shluchim." The Rebbe wrote back to Rosenfeld that every person should view his role as the deciding factor in human destiny, [quoting Maimonides] that each person would see the world as half meritorious and half guilty, and his role can tilt the scales of justice for the entire world.

According to Rabbi Manis Friedman, the Rebbe's message to the young was: "You can affect the whole world, including its Creator. Youth love to be challenged, particularly if it's global and in particular if it's cosmic." Rabbi Yossi Jacobson, a Chabad scholar, says the Rebbe invested in the young. Recalling how he felt growing up in Brooklyn, Jacobson said of the Rebbe: "He touched our souls in the deepest way. One of those major elements of inspiration was seeing the Rebbe's personal unwavering passion." He recalls that when the Rebbe was in his eighties, he was afflicted with sciatica and could barely walk. Jacobson remembers the Rebbe presented a siyum (a scholarly summing-up analysis) of the conclusion of Maimonides' Code of Jewish Law. "It was one of his deepest farbrengens. For an hour and a half, as he explained Maimonides, there was no sciatica; there was a man of ideas, a man of holiness." Rabbi Manis Friedman argues that this young generation was not inspired only by the Rebbe's charisma. According to Friedman, the Rebbe taught the shluchim to understand that the responsibility they have undertaken for Jewish destiny is based in truth as taught in the Torah.

Dennis Prager, columnist and talk show host, argues that, in the Chabad community, young people are empowered with meaning. "Chabad rabbis and their wives have an acute sense of transcendent purpose, probably on a near-daily basis. How else can one leave the Chabad and Orthodox cocoons of Brooklyn for a lifetime in Cambodia, the Congo, or Bolivia, to live?"

The Rebbe's approach was one of personal empowerment, to foster the creativity and abilities inherent in each person. Rabbi Jonathan Sacks describes the Rebbe's approach to building Jewish leaders: "He could find in each individual the unique contribution that the individual could make to the totality of the Jewish people."

Rabbi Mendel Gluckowsky, leader of the Chabad community in Rechovot, Israel, received the lesson of personal empowerment first-hand at the young age of twenty-nine. He had been one of the fifty foreign shluchim sent by the Rebbe to Israel starting in the mid-seventies to bolster Chabad in Israel. He began to assist one of the senior Chabad leaders in Israel, the legendary Reb[2] Zushe, the Partisan, and they visited Chabad institutions throughout the country.

On the long flight to New York, Mendel composed an eight-page report detailing problems they had discovered, and he submitted it to the Rebbe when he arrived. He says, "For over a week, there was no reply." But as he was about to leave for his return flight to Israel, he received a call that there was a response. Rushing to his flight, he stopped at 770 to see the response. On the side of the report, the Rebbe had written in Hebrew, "The majority of things you have written are general issues in Israel that need improvement. What are you going to do about it?!" Gluckowsky read the reply, and he said, "I was floored." On the plane, he looked at the answer again and again. "Finally, I realized the point." The Rebbe had not sent him to Israel "to be a spectator or a news reporter. You were sent to Israel to make a difference. You are one of the players, so get moving." Until then, Gluckowsky says, he saw himself as just one small person in a big country. "I'm a little American guy who walks into this gigantic State of Israel, wondering, 'Can I make a difference?'" Finally he understood the Rebbe's point. "Yes, I am asking you to make a difference. Not only that, I'm empowering you to make a difference."

Gluckowsky says that until then, "I didn't have enough confidence in myself. I didn't really believe I could make a difference. The Rebbe's question: 'What will you do about it?' was my turning point."

Rabbi Yisroel Deren of Stamford, Connecticut explains there is a deep spiritual bond between Rebbe and Chassid. "For a Chassid, the essence of his or her life is to become one with G-d, in effect to have his existence sublimated to G-d Himself. For a human, that would seem to be an impossible task, but in the Rebbe, the Chassid finds a human being who has accomplished that."

By 1972, the foundations had been established. The first group of couples, rabbis and their wives, had been dispatched in the fifties and early sixties. By the early seventies, a network was bubbling up across the world. In the US, regional offices had been established in eight cities. In South America, Europe, South Africa, and Australia, Chabad was developing infrastructure, which included schools, community centers, and social programs. In Israel, the central institutions of Chabad were firmly established in Kfar Chabad and other cities.

Many of the shluchim had made the trip to be at the birthday farbrengen. The crowd had been congregating in the synagogue and jostling for space for hours. At exactly 8:30 p.m., there was a hush in the room. In the sea of Chassidim, a path miraculously appeared in the sanctuary, which was filled to the rafters. The Rebbe, followed by his secretaries, led by Rabbi Chaim Hodakov, walked briskly into the room. The Rebbe took his seat on the stage at the middle of a long wooden table decked out with a white tablecloth. Rabbi Mordechai Mentlik, dean of the yeshiva at 770, stood at his side and, from time to time, he poured wine into the Rebbe's silver Kiddush cup. The Rebbe sat at a large podium on a regal red chair, a gift of the students of a vocational school in Israel. He sat on the southern side of the room so his back would not face the Holy Ark. Behind him, benches filled with distinguished, white-bearded rabbis who sat facing the audience. As the Rebbe was seated, the community burst out in song. Zalmon Jaffe from Manchester, England, describes the moment in his diary: "The Rebbe was in an uplifted mood, smiling to all, in particular, to the group of young students who had just left Russia and were living in Israel."

That night, politicians, prominent rabbis, and community leaders had come to pay tribute. Earlier in the evening, Pulitzer Prize-winning author, Herman Wouk, had delivered a personal greeting from US President Richard Nixon. Israeli Ambassador to the United States, Yitzchak Rabin,[3] had a private meeting with the Rebbe to express congratulations on behalf of the country. As the farbrengen started in Brooklyn, Chassidim in a dozen countries listened. From a control room above the synagogue, phone lines reached around the world carrying the farbrengen live. In the middle of the night in Israel, they clustered to listen in the yeshiva in Kfar Chabad and synagogues around the country. In Australia, it was mid-morning in the sanctuary of the Yeshiva College, where they sat with their ears perked to the loudspeakers carrying the audio from Brooklyn. One community, across the globe, connected.

It was nearing midnight, some four hours after the farbrengen started, an evening filled with richness of Torah, when, surprisingly, the Rebbe reflected upon the occasion, his seventieth birthday. The Rebbe explained that he had received suggestions from some that the time had come to slow down and rest a bit, saying that "we shouldn't look at the passport but rather how we feel." The Rebbe then repeated the talmudic saying that had become a common theme in many of his talks. "A person with one hundred desires two hundred and the person with two hundred desires four hundred." The Talmud is referring to the human quest for money and fortune. The Rebbe would say that this has a deeper meaning, that whatever you have accomplished in the spiritual realm should be doubled and tripled.

The Rebbe's next statement surprised those in the synagogue and around the globe. He said that every positive effort needed to be connected to a specific goal, "otherwise a person has no idea how to measure the achievements. Therefore since we are going from seventy to eighty, we should open in the coming year at least seventy-one new institutions. "He noted that the expansion would entail significant expense and that he would participate in 10 percent of the first-year budget. Rabbi Shmuel Lew, one of the first shluchim to London, summed up the feeling. "It was a bold and unprecedented move; the financial and human resources were very limited – it sounded almost unrealistic." It was totally out of character. "The Rebbe almost never spoke about himself." Rabbi Lew said, "In the tens of thousands of pages of the Rebbe's writings and talks, there are just a few occasions of brief autobiographical references, otherwise he never referred to himself."

The farbrengen ended close to 2:00 a.m. Afterward, the shluchim clustered on the wooden benches in the synagogue for an impromptu meeting to debate the Rebbe's newest challenge. It was the Rebbe's classic style of leadership: throw down the gauntlet, set a broad goal, and expect the creativity and ingenuity of the Chassidim to find a way to reach it.

Late into the night, the shluchim debated how to meet the Rebbe's challenge. According to Rabbi Manis Friedman, the arguments reflected two schools of thought, as represented by the older versus the newer generation. Some argued, "Let's raise the money, give it to the Rebbe, and he will open the institutions." Rabbi Shlomo Cunin of California led the other side of the debate, declaring that what is necessary is action, and not talk. "We need to open the institutions, and I will undertake 10 percent of the seventy-one the Rebbe is requesting." Those advocating raising the money and presenting it to the Rebbe were harking back in Chassidic history to a time when a person's spiritual achievements were intrinsically linked to the Rebbe. Those supporting opening the institutions themselves were part of the new generation. Of this new generation, Friedman says, "They had internalized the concept of personal empowerment and responsibility that the Rebbe had strived to implant in his Chassidim."

The next day, the two Chabad leaders from Israel, Rabbi Ephraim Wolf and Rabbi Shlomo Maidanchik, met with the Rebbe before flying back. Wolf was the administrator of Chabad's central educational institutions. Maidanchik was mayor of Kfar Chabad, earning his living as a railroad engineer, and was well-connected to Israel's political and military[4] establishments. The Rebbe instructed them to create a committee to spearhead efforts in Israel. He stressed that new activists should be enlisted in this effort, thus creating a new cadre of leaders. He also told them that the institutions could be big or small "as long as the agenda would be spreading Judaism and teaching Torah." The Rebbe asked Wolf and Maidanchik to make a special effort to create schools that would meet the needs of the Jews who had recently immigrated to Israel from the Soviet province of Georgia.[5]

The Chassidim returned to Israel energized and excited. In Israel, front-page news told of Chassidim seizing a flight to Israel, and according to the *Jewish Telegraphic Agency*, an El Al jet was "hijacked" over the Atlantic by a group of Israeli Chabad Chassidim, euphoric over their meeting with the Lubavitcher Rebbe in New York. The "takeover" was actually limited to the plane's public address system, which was used to broadcast Chassidic songs and a detailed account of the meeting.

A group of Chassidim led by Rabbi Baruch Gopin and Reb Zushe, the Partisan, began crisscrossing Israel, encouraging Chabad communities to open new institutions. Within a year, 147 new institutions were started in Israel.[6] They included a major expansion of Chabad women's colleges in Israel, new classrooms and dorms for the vocational schools in Kfar Chabad, and a second vocational program in Kiryat Malachi. Youth clubs, yeshiva programs, and libraries were also initiated, as were new elementary schools in Netanya, Or Yehuda, Lod, and Nazareth. There were new senior centers, synagogues, and schools for Georgian immigrants, a Jerusalem Chabad House for foreign college students, preschools, and loan funds. A multi-million-dollar housing development was initiated for immigrants and young couples and, in addition, there was a host of social-service projects. It is safe to say that an equal number of institutions or more were opened outside of Israel during the year.

A few months after the Rebbe's seventieth birthday farbrengen, Rabbi Aron Dov Sufrin, a distinguished Chabad educator from London, met with the Rebbe. It was his forty-second birthday and he was questioning his accomplishments in life. The Rebbe told him, "I am seventy, and I have undertaken to open seventy-one new institutions. You should take upon yourself to start forty-three new projects in the coming year." The Rebbe's suggestion jolted Sufrin from his melancholy mood. In the next year, he initiated forty-three new efforts to touch the lives of others, keeping detailed records of each accomplishment.

In California, Rabbi Baruch Shlomo Cunin hit the road. During
the next twelve months, ten new institutions would be launched,
including new Chabad Centers in Santa Monica, the Fairfax District,
and the Encino neighborhood of Los Angeles; campus Chabad Houses
in Berkeley and San Diego; a summer camp opened in Long Beach, as
well as smaller programs, like libraries and an adult education institute.
Racing from city to city, Cunin looked for local supporters of this dramatic expansion. In a year, Chabad in California was transformed into
a statewide organization with branches in the major cities.

Rabbi Moshe Kotlarsky started his position in Chabad World Headquarters a few months before the Rebbe's birthday farbrengen. Moshe
and his wife, Rivkah, wanted to be shluchim. Rabbi Hodakov had
suggested a few options to Kotlarsky. The Rebbe made the choice,
telling young Moshe and Rivkah in a private meeting: "Here lived
my father-in-law, the Rebbe, for the last ten years of his life on this
earth, and from here he spread the teachings of Torah and Chassidus
to all corners of the world. You should stay here and from here you
will spread out over the whole world."[7]

Kotlarsky was brought up in Crown Heights. His father, Rabbi
Tzvi Yosef, had studied in the Chabad yeshiva in Poland. He escaped
from the Nazis and spent the war years in the Chabad yeshiva in
Shanghai. After the war, he immigrated to the US where he married
and was a member of the administration of Chabad's main yeshiva in
Brooklyn. Moshe Kotlarsky was educated in Brooklyn and Montreal.
In 1971, he married Rivkah Kazen from Cleveland. Her father was
a prominent Chabad rabbi in Europe and moved to Cleveland
after the war. Her grandmother was the Muma Sara (Aunt Sara)
Katzenelenbogen, organizer of the Great Escape.

At the beginning, Kotlarsky's responsibilities were visiting
Jewish communities and raising money. His first trip was in the
fall of 1973 just after the High Holidays. Kotlarsky says, "I was told
to make a route and travel." He started in Tulsa, Oklahoma. Louie
Kahn, a successful oilman who came from a Chassidic background,
was his very first appointment. Kotlarsky made his pitch and at the
end of the conversation, he asked about Kahn's family. Kahn told

him about his son, Danny, and Kotlarsky went to visit him. Rabbi Yehuda Weg, who later became the shliach in Tulsa, says, "This surprised Kahn. Every other fundraiser came to town and got a check; Moshe Kotlarsky took a real interest in his family." Kahn was so touched he gave a thousand dollars. Kotlarsky was in seventh heaven; he had a home run in this first at bat. When he crossed the street and visited another businessman, he got just ten dollars, and reality set in. At twenty-two, Kotlarsky was beginning to understand that fundraising was not so easy. Still, he did very well in his first visit to Tulsa, leaving town with almost $5,000. From there, he headed to other southern towns: Little Rock, Jackson, Yazoo City, New Orleans, Atlanta, and Memphis.

In Little Rock, he met Rabbi Shaya Kilimnick, who had come fresh out of rabbinical school at age twenty-three. Full of idealism, he came to town as Orthodox synagogues were closing. The immigrant generation was passing on; younger Jews were drifting from tradition. Kilimnick says, "The only education was a Hebrew School." They connected. Kilimnick says, "We bonded. It was uplifting to have another young rabbi visiting who shared a passion to spread Judaism." This ability to connect to others deeply would become the keystone for Kotlarsky. Kilimnick says that "the connection that started decades ago in Little Rock stayed for life." Rabbi Kilimnick left Little Rock a few years later. It would be twenty years before Chabad opened in Little Rock.

As his visits increased, Kotlarsky got to know the local leaders. Invariably, the conversations would turn to the idea of bringing a Chabad shliach to the community. Community leaders were beginning to recognize the unique contribution that Chabad was making. In Atlanta, Kotlarsky met with local rabbis from all backgrounds, as well as the Federation director, Emanuel Gettinger. Starting with Atlanta, Chabad slowly began to open new regional offices.

In 1979, Kotlarsky was in New Orleans. "Rabbi Hodakov called me and told me to return to New York immediately." The next morning, a Thursday, he was back in New York. Rabbi Hodakov gave him instructions on behalf of the Rebbe to take responsibility for South America. He was told to head to Bogota, Colombia, first, and then to begin expanding Chabad in South America. There was already a presence in Buenos Aires, San Paulo, and Caracas. The rest of Central and South America had no shluchim. A few years earlier, the Rebbe had given Rabbi Kotlarsky guidelines for Chabad expansion in foreign countries. At the time, Kotlarsky had been perplexed, since he had been working only in the US and Canada. But soon, he realized that this was the Rebbe's vision for the future. He knew that when the right time arrived, the Rebbe would instruct him to begin a new phase of expansion outside North America. The directive to travel to Bogota was the beginning of that new era.

The guidelines given to Rabbi Kotlarsky had four conditions: the expansion should not create local communal conflict, there should be a solid financial foundation for the first year, there should be a mikvah, and there should be a stable political situation without a chance of revolution.

Kotlarsky asked for more detailed guidance for the mission to Bogota. The instructions from the Rebbe were relayed via Rabbi Hodakov: he should try to leave today, the latest on Sunday. When he asked whom he should meet and what he should do, he received yet another cryptic directive from the Rebbe: "He will meet whom he needs to meet, and, with time, he will understand."

It would take decades before Rabbi Kotlarsky would comprehend the full implications of the enigmatic instructions. He said, "Only after Gimmel Tammuz [the third of the Jewish month of Tammuz, the day the Rebbe passed away] did I begin to understand what the Rebbe told me."

Puzzled by the instructions, but committed to his mission, Kotlarsky flew to Bogota on Sunday. When he arrived in town, he met the community's Ashkenazi chief rabbi, Alfredo Goldschmidt, who told him, "Tomorrow evening, there is a going-away party for the rabbi who has been an educator in the community. Come there and you can meet the leaders of the community." Kotlarsky thought maybe the whole reason he was told to be in Bogota no later than Sunday was to be at this event. Kotlarsky asked who would be replacing the rabbi. Rabbi Goldschmidt told him the decision is up to Sami Rohr, who had sponsored the rabbi in Bogota. "Where can

I call him?" asked Kotlarsky. Goldschmidt replied, "You can't, you need to send a telegram to this address and he will call you." It was a tumultuous time in Bogota; affluent Jews feared being kidnapped and were taking major precautions to protect themselves.

Rabbi Goldschmidt sent Sami Rohr a telegram telling him that Kotlarsky wanted to speak with him and would be back in Brooklyn in two weeks, after touring countries in the region. As he walked into his home on Thursday, the phone rang. On the line was Sami Rohr. He, like many other South American Jews, had an apartment in Miami. He asked, "Rabbi Kotlarsky, when will you be in Miami?" Realizing that the moment should be seized, Kotlarsky responded, "On Sunday." Rohr then told him, "We'll meet for lunch Monday at the Embassy Kosher Steakhouse."

Rohr had come to Colombia after the war. His family fled Germany to Switzerland where he spent the war years. Many refugees found a haven in Colombia after the Holocaust. Rohr had remarkable success as a developer, building in the rapidly expanding city. His was one of the few fully observant Jewish families in the community.

Bogota had been a city renowned for its charitable giving. Years later, Rohr said in a speech at the shluchim convention that when rabbis came from abroad to raise money, there was a krekhtz (sigh) in the community. "Better there should come a hundred rabbis than once a tax inspector," he said. At that same convention, he told of his first impressions of Chabad. "There was something different about the Chabad fundraisers. They were not just interested in getting the check; they asked about your family and were concerned with your spiritual welfare." Rohr continued, "Whenever a Lubavitcher came, I would give a bigger contribution." This Chabad fundraising attitude that reached beyond money had piqued Rohr's interest in Chabad, setting the stage for him to hear Kotlarsky's suggestions.

Kotlarsky and Rohr struck up a friendship. In the decades to come, the bond between them would transform Jewish communities the world over. The first fruits were modest, however. Rabbi Yehoshua Binyomin Rosenfeld, along with his young bride, Rivka, and their month-old baby, moved to Bogota. Rohr undertook to underwrite all the expenses. Rosenfeld says, "He wanted that all we should do was to give to the community." There were some nine thousand Jews in Colombia, most concentrated in Bogota. It was a well-organized community, with synagogues, schools, and a vibrant communal spirit. Still, the level of Jewish observance was low. Rosenfeld knew he had a daunting task to refocus the community toward observance and Jewish learning. He also understood the best approach would be to create a strong partnership with local institutions and integrate his activities as much as possible into the existing communal structure.

Rosenfeld created a strong bond with the community rabbi, Alfredo Goldschmidt. Rosenfeld developed youth programs and adult education, and built a new community mikvah. Today there are five shluchim couples in between Bogota and Barranquilla, about 150 miles north of Bogota, including the Rosenfeld's son, Moti, and his wife, Shaina.

In Bogota, all the synagogues were Orthodox and Chabad was welcomed. In the US, by contrast, Chabad had to strike out on its own. The Liberal Jewish groups, focused on issues such as anti-Semitism, civil rights, support of Israel, that dominated Jewish life at the time, were unwilling to permit Chabad to play a meaningful role. Chabad had to create its own structure.

In the next decade, Kotlarsky would crisscross South and Central America meeting community leaders and slowly building a network of centers. The Rebbe expected him to take full responsibility for all the Jews of the area. One day Rabbi Hodakov called him. The Rebbe had received a letter from the tiny Jewish community of Cochabamba, Bolivia. A few hundred Jews had found refuge there during the Holocaust. Rabbi Hodakov asked Kotlarsky what he intended to do about this. Kotlarsky replied that he was not aware of this community. The Rebbe was on the line and said, "He is responsible; if he is not aware, how can this be?"

In 1986, the Rebbe launched a new initiative: "A Shliach Creates Another Shliach." The network of regional centers had reached most states and countries by then, and each regional center had a head shliach who was responsible for Chabad activities in his region. The Rebbe was encouraging all of them to open more branches and expand existing institutions with additional rabbis and rebbitzens in their regions. By 1986, a new shliach was being appointed each week. In the three years between 1986 and 1989, 183 new shluchim were added to the Chabad system. Some went to new neighborhoods to start new centers from the ground up, others joined existing centers, creating new programs.

This new focus on growth by the Rebbe caused Rabbi Kotlarsky to consider expanding to states with fewer than ten thousand Jews. Some felt that with such a limited demographic base, the chances of success would be marginal. However, with a green light from the Rebbe, five states were selected: Oklahoma, Maine, Nebraska, Hawaii, and Delaware.

In 1987, Rabbi Yehuda Weg and his wife settled in Tulsa, Oklahoma. The challenges were much different from those of the larger Jewish communities with a variety of organizations and synagogues. In Tulsa, there were two congregations: the Conservative, known as "the Synagogue," and the Reform, referred to as "the Temple." Both had histories reaching back to the beginning of the twentieth century. The last Orthodox synagogue in Tulsa had ceased to exist decades earlier.

While many in the town welcomed Rabbi Weg and his wife, the rabbi of "the Synagogue" was not very hospitable. As shluchim were experiencing at the time, some non-Orthodox rabbis were quite hostile to Chabad's emerging role. Chabad represented a new independent spirit and a return to tradition, which was opposed by many Liberal Jewish leaders. In larger towns, this resistance could be overcome, since there were usually enough Jews sympathetic to Chabad. Strong opposition in a small town like Tulsa from one of the two local rabbis made it difficult.

Weg says, "The rabbi launched a campaign against us. First, he told everyone we were sinister." This strategy failed when people began to get to know the Wegs. "Then he started a new tactic. He told the community we deal only with people who are troubled," which sent a message that something must be wrong with you if you go to Chabad. Weg says that the beginning was very tough, but some community leaders refused to be swayed by this rabbi's animosity and proved instrumental in helping the Wegs. For example, the local Federation director, David Bernstein, opened many doors for the young couple. "As Jews began to see that the assertions of the rabbi were not based on facts, they began to make their own decisions about being involved with Chabad."

The opposition in Tulsa was not an anomaly, and the antagonism emanated mostly from non-Orthodox rabbis. It almost became a nationwide issue. In 1984, at its national convention, the Reform Movement considered a resolution condemning Chabad. Some Reform leaders were angered that college students were becoming more involved with the growing network of Chabad Houses on campus. Others did not like the fact that some of their members had begun supporting Chabad Centers. The proposed resolution created a public debate, reaching even the pages of *The New York Times*. In the end, it was voted down.[8]

With the Jewish New Year of 5748[9] (1988-89), the Rebbe launched another campaign to expand Chabad. He declared it "Shnat Habinyan – the Year of Building." Week after week he spoke about expanding, purchasing, or building new facilities. In addition, he was encouraging individuals to purchase homes, too. He participated with a hundred-dollar symbolic contribution with any Jewish family who would acquire a home that year. It prompted many shluchim to purchase homes and facilities, putting down deeper roots in their communities.

In Omaha, Rabbi Mendel Katzman had been operating out of his house since his arrival three years earlier as part of the expansion to smaller states. Until he heard the Rebbe's new campaign, he says, "I was thinking small. Some of our supporters pointed to the demographics and thought there was limited potential for growth. We were thinking of what we needed for our existing programs." The Rebbe's initiative prompted him to start "thinking big." Katzman rented a storefront that gave him more public exposure and larger space. "The Rebbe's new campaign raised our horizons to greater heights. The move to the storefront set the stage for us to grow and eventually to purchase a larger commercial building that met our long-term needs."

The new campaign prodded not only those who were dreaming of expansion. It pushed some who felt, before, that it was totally unrealistic to take a leap of faith. That happened in Orlando to Rabbi Sholom Dubov, who said, "We were struggling to pay the monthly budget." He had been in Orlando since late 1984, operating out of his house. "After I heard the Rebbe speak, the first week I thought to myself, 'He is encouraging those who have a strong financial position,' but I was barely covering our rent." At each Shabbat farbrengen, the Rebbe repeated his message of building, saying that even those who have challenging financial situations should consider new building projects. That gave Dubov the push. "I decided to find a facility even though I did not know where the funds would come from," he said. He approached a local developer, Robert Mandell, today the US ambassador in Luxemburg. Mandell found property at a very low rent. Dubov recalls, "In a miraculous series of events, we moved from my living room to a proper facility. We could have stayed in our home with a small mindset, but this new campaign gave us the impetus that led to the growth of Chabad in Central Florida." Today, Dubov has a beautiful synagogue in Orlando, and has opened three other Chabad branches in Orlando.

In Montevideo, Uruguay, one of the branches opened by Rabbi Kotlarsky, Rabbi Eliezer Shemtov was renting a facility and dreaming of buying a building. He had been in Uruguay for just a few years, and it had been a tough challenge for Chabad. Uruguay is still known as the most secular country in South America. In the synagogue at the holiday resort of Punta del Este, he met Perez Friedberg, a philanthropist from Toronto who was originally from Uruguay. Shemtov then went to see him in his hotel. "What do you want?" he asked the young rabbi. Shemtov thought he should go for broke and share all his dreams. "We need a new rabbi, a mikvah, and a building for a Chabad Center." On the spot, Friedberg agreed to cover half the cost of the rabbi and a mikvah. Then he started to cry, telling Shemtov, "I remember what Jewish life was like here many years ago, and I see what it's like now and how important and courageous your work is." The next day, he called Shemtov. "We need to talk again about what I promised yesterday," he said. Shemtov feared he had regrets, but at the second meeting, Friedberg told him, "What you really need is a building. Find it, and I will underwrite the complete cost." Shemtov was able to complete the deal before the end of the "Year of Building."

Around the globe, Chabad expanded. In Israel, Australia, Europe, and other countries, new projects were inaugurated. The Rebbe's constant push for growth created a unique culture: "One cannot be satisfied with existing accomplishments; one must always reach new heights." It was ingrained by the Rebbe that every living thing must grow and that a person cannot remain static; a person should aspire for more. "In spiritual matters, we dare not be satisfied with our lot. We cannot be content with what we have accomplished. As good as the achievements of yesterday were, a person must strive to achieve more." When the chairman of the building committee in the Chabad House in Hartford was introduced to the Rebbe, he remarked, "He should not be satisfied with building just one Chabad House." When a shliach presented the Rebbe with a key to a new school, he remarked, "You should have to build an addition."

The Rebbe, time and again, pointed out that each person has distinctive Divine gifts that should be used to reach his unique potential and fulfill his mission. "If an individual has the ability to raise two million dollars for Jewish education and he raises only one million, he has not fulfilled his mission." The same, he argued, for a person who has the gift of writing. "He should try to use that creative ability to teach Judaism."

Rabbi Yisroel Deren, whose grandfather, Rabbi Shalom Posner, was the pioneering shliach in Pittsburgh in the early forties, has witnessed how average people were propelled to remarkable accomplishments. "The Rebbe took otherwise ordinary people and made them extraordinary, and at times, giants. People who, under other circumstances, would never have taken the risks, or the challenges, in expanding their communities, would be successful. Due to the Rebbe's encouragement, they believed they would be successful."

Chapter Seven

The Menorah Wars

An exercise in showmanship." That's what a rankled Rabbi Joseph Asher of Temple Emanu-El in San Francisco[1] labeled the twenty-two foot Chanukah menorah that had been placed in Union Square by the local Chabad Center in December of 1975.

Over a thousand Jews, beaming with pride, crowded into Union Square on the blustery first night of Chanukah to attend the lighting – not far from the park's Christmas tree. But Asher thought the event was pretentious, saying it threatened the Jewish community with "the forces of vulgar sensationalism and crass parochialism." Besides, he argued, a menorah in the public square violated the principle of separation of church and state and represented "the newest challenge to the Bill of Rights."

It was a curious argument. The Reform rabbi never protested against the Christmas trees displayed in Union Square. But a menorah was somehow different. He asked whether "a giant menorah really intensifies Jewish values," and claimed that Chabad "really wanted to secularize Chanukah, as Christmas has become secularized."

Rabbi Asher[2] came from a distinguished line of Orthodox rabbis in Germany. He fled Nazi Germany just before World War II to England where he gravitated from his Orthodox roots. He attended the Reform rabbinical seminary, Hebrew Union College in Cincinnati, after the war's end. As a young rabbi in Greensboro, South Carolina, he championed civil rights, joining Jesse Jackson in sit-ins in the local Woolworth cafeteria. In San Francisco, social justice remained the centerpiece of his rabbinate. But his most contentious public controversy during his almost two decades in the City by the Bay was his battle against Chabad's menorah.

Some of the local Orthodox and Conservative rabbis were made uneasy by his public attacks, but the Reform rabbis stood strongly behind him. Established in 1849, Temple Emanu-El had the largest congregation in the city, and its members included the Jewish elite. Asher was, without question, the most influential rabbi in the Bay Area.

The target of Asher's ire was a young Chabad rabbi, Chaim Itche Drizin, who came to San Francisco in 1971, first as a synagogue youth director and then head of Chabad in Northern California, based at the Chabad House in Berkeley. San Francisco was not an easy nut to crack. Traditional Judaism had never sunk deep roots. There were some historic Orthodox[3] synagogues in San Francisco, beautiful edifices of an immigrant generation built decades before and populated by a few elderly Jews holding on to the traditions of their ancestors.

The German Jews who had arrived in the nineteenth century with the Gold Rush had put their stamp on the city. Germany had been the birthplace of the Reform Movement, and its descendants dominated San Francisco's Jewish community.

After four years in the community, Drizin was looking for ways to promote Jewish identity and pride. At first he thought about having a public blowing of the shofar in Union Square on Rosh Hashanah, the Jewish New Year. Rabbi Chaim Mordechai Hodakov, the Rebbe's chief of staff, was concerned that it might be misunderstood, telling Drizin, "Jews will think they don't have to attend services on High Holidays." So Drizin brainstormed with his friend, Zev Putterman, an executive at the local public TV station. The year before, the Rebbe had called for a campaign to promote Chanukah observance. "Why not a menorah in Union Square?" Drizin asked. "Chanukah is a holiday when we are supposed to publicize the miracle that happened thousands of years ago. It fits."

Putterman agreed and suggested they propose the idea to his old friend and rock impresario, Bill Graham,[4] promoter of concerts for Bob Dylan, the Rolling Stones, The Who, and the Grateful Dead. Graham was raised in a Jewish family in Brooklyn, but didn't join the Jewish community when he moved to San Francisco in the 1960s. Still, he had strong Jewish feelings and was very influential. Sitting in Graham's Mission-District office, Drizin and Putterman pitched the idea. Graham fell in love with the concept. He had the political connections, the financial resources, and craftsmen who built sets for shows and who could construct the menorah.

San Francisco would not be the first menorah in a public square; a year earlier, Rabbi Avrohom Shemtov, the senior shliach in Philadelphia,[5] lit a menorah near the Liberty Bell in Philadelphia. Drizin was unaware of the lighting in Philadelphia; he was forging new ground by erecting the first giant menorah in a public venue.

Drizin worried what the local Jewish establishment would say. He called Brian Lurie, a Reform rabbi who was the executive director of the Jewish Federation[6] of San Francisco. In most American cities, federations are the central communal bodies. They raise funds for local needs and help Jews overseas and in Israel. In the seventies, the federations' primary goals were social welfare and supporting Israel. It would be decades before Jewish education and Jewish continuity would become prime issues on their agenda.

The Federation had an aggressive fundraising arm, and the involvement of key community leaders made it a powerhouse in San Francisco. Historically, across the country, federations had limited interaction with the Orthodox communities. At the time, even in cities with a larger Orthodox presence, such as Chicago or New York, the secular-oriented federations and the Orthodox communities lived side by side with little engagement and very different agendas and goals.

Drizin invited Lurie to bring the Federation president, Franny Green, a few days before Chanukah, to the official installation of the menorah, wanting them to share the spotlight. He figured that it would keep them from mounting a campaign to stop his project.

In Drizin's mind, attendance of even a hundred at the ceremony would have been a great success. The first night, over a thousand attended the menorah lighting. The media covered the story. Chanukah, for the first time, was big news in San Francisco.

Then Asher launched his public campaign denouncing Chabad's newest project. On the pages of the *San Francisco Examiner*, he chastised the menorah lighting. He lambasted the Jewish Federation for supporting Drizin. He contended that they had shattered one of the sacred principles of modern Jewish life by "eroding the separation of church and state."

The so-called "wall of separation"[7] had been championed by Jewish defense organizations in the United States for decades, largely to keep Christianity from being the de facto state religion. They lobbied to ban prayer in school, government support of parochial schools, and religious symbols on public property. In Europe, governments under the guise of religion had oppressed generations of Jews, so the defense organizations believed Jews would be secure in the United States only if there were no government involvement in religion. By the seventies, they had made significant strides in thickening the wall of separation.

Orthodox groups in the United States, such as the Orthodox Union, Young Israel, and the Agudath Israel, did not subscribe to this view of absolute separation, but, at the time, they were small and less influential. They did not have offices[8] in Washington, and their efforts to lobby for government support of parochial schools had little effect. It would be years before they would have enough clout to influence the public debate.

The menorah debate in San Francisco climbed onto the national Jewish stage. Rabbi Marc Tanenbaum,[9] who spearheaded interfaith initiatives for the American Jewish Committee,[10] condemned the menorah in Union Square on national radio. The controversy became the talk of the Jewish community across the country, and few came out in support of Chabad's effort.

Nothing could be done that year in San Francisco to take down the menorah, which was already up and lit in the city center. After the holiday, Jewish Federation leaders summoned Drizin to a meeting. Stung by Asher's criticism, they told Drizin, "We should never have supported you. The menorah was on public property and inappropriate. Next year, it should not be at Union Square."

Years later, Drizin reflected on the real cause of the backlash. "The leadership was asking, 'Who are you to put up a menorah and speak in the name of the community? We are the community leaders; we set the agenda. Who is Chabad to capture the spotlight?'" It was simply unacceptable for a Brooklyn outsider from a tiny segment of the Jewish community to take center stage. It was not how things were done. Drizin represented a threat to the status quo of San Francisco's Jewish community, one that danced to a different drummer and was not under their control.

Drizin was taken aback. His great success was being turned on its head, and now he – a young Chabad rabbi with a newly opened Chabad House and a shaky base of local support – was up against the leader of one of the nation's largest Reform temples. But the Jewish leaders did not want a major communal confrontation. After much debate, a compromise was floated. The Federation leaders suggested that the menorah be placed next year in the Stonestown Shopping Mall in San Francisco's Sunset District. It was private property so there would be no constitutional issues. They even agreed to help him if he would just move it off public property.

"What happens if no one comes?" Drizin asked. "Union Square is unique; it's in the center of downtown." They promised that if the new venue proved unsuccessful they would not oppose his return to Union Square the following year.

Young Drizin was perplexed. Shaped by years of battle against the Soviets, Chabad policy was not to retreat when faced with pressure. But he also knew the Rebbe did not want to alienate the Jewish leadership, instead attracting them to the value of Jewish education. He also hoped that the local leadership would begin to support Chabad's programs in the Bay Area. Yet he feared that the great success with the menorah would not be repeated in a mall far from the center of town. He asked the Rebbe for guidance. The Rebbe advised him to seek counsel from someone there with a good understanding of the situation in San Francisco.

At the time, Rabbi Mendel Futerfas was visiting the Bay Area on one of his annual fundraising trips. Reb Mendel was one of the Chassidic elders. He had been imprisoned in the Soviet Union for close to a decade for directing the Jewish religious underground. After finishing his prison sentence, intercession from overseas secured permission for him to leave for the West in 1962. Once a year, he would come to California to raise money in order to secretly ship food packages behind the Iron Curtain. A man full of energy, deep compassion, and piety, he was greatly respected in the Chabad community.

"What should I do?" Drizin asked the venerable Chassid. The man who stood up to the Soviets was being asked about standing up to the Jewish establishment. "If the shopping center doesn't work, will they keep their word and let you return to Union Square?" Reb Mendel asked. "Yes," Drizin replied. And then, using one of his famous parables, Reb Mendel said, "Before a bull charges he takes a step back, gathers his strength and roars forward. Take the compromise and if it doesn't work return to Union Square."

Drizin informed the Federation that he would move the menorah. As he suspected, the new location didn't draw much of a crowd the following year. So Drizin decided to move the menorah back to Union Square. As had been agreed upon, Rabbi Asher dropped his public opposition in the wake of the unsuccessful lighting in the shopping center. Since then, the menorah lighting has turned into an annual – and wildly successful – Chanukah Festival, drawing tens of thousands to Union Square[11] and becoming a part of San Francisco culture.

The Rebbe encouraged shluchim to put menorahs in public places. As with many other Chabad innovations, the idea caught on. Some were erected in shopping malls, others in front of government buildings, public parks, and city squares. As the menorahs grew in number, so did the opposition across the country, mostly from Liberal

Jewish organizations, including the American Jewish Congress (AJC) founded by Reform Rabbi Stephen S. Weiss,[12] the Anti-Defamation League, local Jewish Community Relations Councils, the Union of American Hebrew Congregations (now the Union for Reform Judaism), and some local chapters of the American Civil Liberties Union, influenced by its Jewish leaders.

When the Jewish organizations failed to convince the shluchim to remove the menorahs from the public square, they took varying strategies: lobbying government officials to deny Chabad permits, challenging the efforts in the media, taking Chabad to court, or supporting lawsuits that were launched in some communities by the ACLU.[13]

The Jewish organizations were confident Chabad would collapse from the communal pressure. It was unimaginable that a bunch of Chassidim from Brooklyn would defy the Jewish leadership. When Chabad did not bend to their will voluntarily, they were convinced that their position would be vindicated in court. These groups rarely sued over the Christian symbols; it was clear that the menorah troubled them. The American Jewish Congress and the ACLU brought the cases, and were, at times, supported by the Reform Movement and the ADL.[14] These lawsuits pushed the issue into the public arena; Jew vs. Jew was a great story.

In 1978, Rabbi Joseph Glaser, executive vice president of the Reform Rabbinical Association, wrote[15] to the Rebbe expressing concern about the menorahs on public property. He said that the menorah lightings were "undesirable," asserting they were a "violation of the constitutional principle of separation of church and state." Glaser was apprehensive that Jews would be put at risk in the US if the "wall of separation was weakened." He was also troubled by the "heated debates that had spilled over to the media." He warned the Rebbe that if these disputes continued, the matter could even end up in court. He requested the Rebbe direct a cessation of menorah lightings on public property.

The Rebbe responded: "Years earlier, I would have had a more difficult task defending it. Now my task is an easy one since the general acclaim and beneficial results have been observed for a number of years."

The Rebbe said the objections were isolated and motivated by other sentiments, arguing that the same groups[16] "thwart every effort to get state aid for Hebrew day schools and yeshivot to alleviate the burden of the secular department and other non-religious needs."

The Rebbe also believed that America is a country in which religion is respected, noting in his letter that "the US is a nation whose money carries the motto 'one nation under G-d' as does the pledge of allegiance," and that "Congress opens with an invocation."

To Chabad, the menorah was a freedom of expression issue. Jews had a right to put up menorahs on public property as long as they were paid for by private funds. At a time when Jews were drifting from tradition, the menorahs instilled pride and fostered Jewish identity.

With each year, Chabad's efforts garnered greater community support. In 1984, Rabbi Avrohom Shemtov of Philadelphia, in an address at the annual shluchim convention in New York, said that the various local Jewish groups that had urged him to relocate the menorah from the Liberty Bell Park to private property had ceased their protests.

"For years they have not said a word," he said, explaining that the Liberal Jewish groups realized that they were losing community support for their positions.

Even though Chabad was gaining grassroots approval for its religious displays in public settings, Jewish leaders weren't so quick to give their endorsements. In 1986, the Jewish Federation of Bergen County, New Jersey, voted to criticize the menorah lightings.[17] The vote carried with a majority, but there were many abstentions. Rabbi Yisroel Brod, the director of Chabad in Bergen County at the time, noted that significant progress was being made: "A few years ago the vote would have been unanimous against the idea."

Rabbi Brod decided not to take the Federation head-on. He organized a countywide grassroots campaign to expand the scope of the menorah lightings. He sent letters to Chabad supporters, many of them members of Reform or Conservative congregations, to form local committees to sponsor menorah lightings. That year, menorahs were lit in ten new towns in the county.

My own menorah skirmish occurred in 1986 in Orange County, California. A few rabbis were returning together to Los Angeles from the annual shluchim convention in New York, just a few weeks before Chanukah. On board, there was an intense discussion about the ongoing litigation by the American Jewish Congress[18] over a menorah in Beverly Hills. They had challenged in court the placement of a menorah in one of the city parks.

Rabbi Shlomo Cunin, the head shliach in California, said, "The best answer we can give them is to put up more menorahs." On the plane, he drafted each of us to put up menorahs in our communities.

For years, the County of Orange sponsored a Christmas tree in a small park in the Civic Center in Santa Ana. I called the parks department, took out a permit, and a few days before Chanukah, erected a menorah. A news story in *The Orange County Register* attracted the attention of the ACLU and the American Jewish Congress. They marched into court asking for an emergency temporary restraining order against the menorah. The ACLU lawyer was Jewish. The American Jewish Congress had no office in Orange County. It had never been active in the community. Suddenly they were riding the white horse of indignation down the freeway from Los Angeles to save the Jews of Orange County from the danger of a menorah in a public park. It was the end-of-the-year holiday doldrums, and the media latched onto the story. Jew vs. Jew moved into the courthouse. We were front-page news.

In the courtroom, the AJC attorney, who turned out to be an old childhood friend of my wife, argued, "The Christmas tree is not religious. It should stay, but the menorah is, and it must go." The Jewish attorney[19] from the ACLU told the *Los Angeles Times*, "A tree is decoration, while the menorah is a religious symbol." It was irrelevant to them that the Christmas tree was sponsored with government funds and the menorah erected with private donations. In a break in the proceedings, I turned to my wife's old friend and chastised him for his hypocrisy. "A Christmas tree is not a religious symbol and a menorah is? Fighting to take away our statement of pride and identity and arguing to retain the tree?" The judge ruled that the menorah must go.[20] However, in protest, I lit a small Chanukah menorah in the park under the glare of TV cameras.

The city of Pittsburgh permitted Chabad to place a menorah near city hall. There, the ACLU sued. Pittsburgh became the turning point in the court cases that were being waged across the US. The city sided with Chabad as the case moved through the court system. Finally, in 1989, the United States Supreme Court ruled to permit menorahs in public spaces, as long as they were paid for by private funds.

Chabad had stood up publicly to the liberal establishment and won. But the most important victory was not in the courthouse, but in the court of public opinion. Each year, tens of thousands of Jews came to menorah lightings in city halls, shopping centers, and other public venues.

Public menorah lightings have become part of the national culture. In Washington, the menorah is placed by American Friends of Lubavitch on the Ellipse opposite the White House, named the National Menorah by President Reagan. President Carter attended the lighting of the menorah the first year it was erected in 1979, emerging for the first time from a self-imposed seclusion in the White House begun at the onset of the Iranian hostage crisis. Since then, noteworthy public officials, including Secretary of Treasury Jack Lew, former White House Chief of Staff Rahm Emanuel, Attorney General Michael Mukasey, Senator Joe Lieberman, and others have joined the lighting. Chanukah has even spilled over to the White House with an annual Chanukah party. The director of Chabad's Washington arm, American Friends of Lubavitch, Rabbi Levi Shemtov, supervises the kosher catering in the White House for the festivities.

Across the country, menorahs are now commonplace in shopping malls and public squares. At my Chabad Center in Yorba Linda, we light our sixteen-foot permanent menorah every evening on Chanukah. Through the night, the menorah shines brightly along a six-lane boulevard. Down the block is the Nixon Presidential Library. One day I got a call: "Can't we have a menorah lighting in the Presidential Library?" It was something I had never even considered. Now, it's an annual community event. The Reagan Presidential

Library in Simi Valley followed suit a year or so later. Theme parks are even getting into the Chanukah spirit. Universal Studios started a menorah celebration in conjunction with Chabad on the famed City Walk in Universal City. A couple of years ago at Joe Robbie Stadium, a local Chabad Rabbi, Raphael Tennenhaus, lit a menorah at halftime of a Dolphins game.

Why had Liberal Jewish organizations taken such a strong stand against the menorahs? Why did they lobby against government support for Jewish day schools, the norm in other Western democracies? What did they really fear, government involvement in religion? Or was it an anxiety over religion? Did they want to stifle the empowerment of more traditional Jewish groups in order to protect their turf as the dominant voice in the Jewish community?

Shluchim were trying to reach out to Jews to connect them to celebrate their heritage. They were opposed by demands that Chabad toe a certain communal line. In some communities, Jewish Federations and other Jewish groups had worked to undermine Chabad influence. They didn't mind cute, harmless programs, but when Chabad developed greater influence, and started to attract communal support, many felt that it needed to be controlled. They were used to a docile and, at times, self-absorbed Orthodoxy: a synagogue down the block with maybe a day school that took care of the needs of the observant community. They were far from happy with a dynamic organization.

The Rebbe labeled America "a country of Chessed (kindness)," for the freedoms that Jews were afforded in the United States. With all the freedom, Jews in the mid-twentieth century were still uneasy about being seen as too Jewish. Memories of pre-war anti-Semitism and the Holocaust were still very fresh. As social scientist, Charles Silberman, says in his book, *A Certain People*, about growing up at that time, "Our Jewishness was a source of anxiety and discomfort."

The Rebbe wanted to shatter this assimilationist doctrine. In the early fifties, Crown Heights was the posh Jewish neighborhood in Brooklyn. The Chassidic community was still small. The Yeshiva at Chabad's headquarters had just a few dozen students. One of the dorms was a twenty-minute walk away. The Rebbe insisted that the students of the yeshiva walk there. He wanted the Jews who were beginning the process of assimilation to see young yeshiva students strolling down Eastern Parkway attired in hats, jackets, and with beards – unafraid to express their identity.

Historian and professor, Arthur Hertzberg,[21] served as president of the American Jewish Congress[22] between 1972 and 1978. It was a time when the AJC was engaged in an intense battle with Chabad. Decades later, Hertzberg had a change of heart, telling me in an interview, "We were trying to draw a line between the outside culture and Judaism.[23] We thought that by having Judaism stop at the door to the house we would preserve the Jewish identity inside. The Rebbe believed that being a Jew on the street would keep the home Jewish. He was right and we were wrong."

The menorahs were the public battle. Behind the scenes, the real conflict was just getting started. Chabad was looking for its place at the table. With its alternative vision of a return to traditional Judaism, Chabad was making inroads, slowly, Jew by Jew. To the established Jewish community, Chabad looked like a loose cannon. Could it be controlled? Its influence minimized? Underlying this was a deeper theological debate. For decades, American Jews had been drifting away from tradition. The foundation of Jewish identity in the post-World War II era had been supporting Israel, remembering the Holocaust, fighting for social justice, and the eradication of anti-Semitism. Chabad argued that Judaism must be tethered to the historic teachings of Torah, rooted in a deep spiritual mission of observing the commandments and studying Torah. Chabad was advocating a major shift in the modern Jewish life, a renaissance of classic Jewish values. The entrenched leadership in the Jewish community viewed traditional observance as irrelevant and, at best, nostalgic.

For me, all of these questions came to the forefront when I turned up as a young campus shliach at the University of Miami in 1974. College campuses became the next battleground for challenging the face of American Judaism. Rabbi Baruch Shlomo Cunin had purchased an old frat house on UCLA campus and opened the first college Chabad House in 1969. When Cunin presented to the Rebbe the key to the first Chabad House, the Rebbe asked, "Is this key symbolic or are you giving me ownership of the building?" Cunin answered, "We are giving the Rebbe the building." The Rebbe responded, "If so, I would like it open twenty-four hours a day. The building should have no lock. Chabad Houses will spread all over like Gimbels department stores."

The idea caught on and in the early 1970s, a network of Chabad Campus Centers began to expand around the country. Rabbi Avrohom Korf in Miami asked me to develop a full-time program at the University of Miami in Coral Gables. I arrived there in the fall of 1974 full of vigor and idealism and little experience. Rabbi Korf and his assistant, Rabbi Shalom Blank, had made regular visits to the campus and gave a weekly class at the Hillel Foundation.[24] I was supposed to broaden the scope of the activities.

My first stop was to the Reform rabbi who was the Hillel director. Hillel's policy was to be an umbrella for all Jewish groups. I thought they would be very happy with the new dimension that I would add. At that first meeting, however, he told me he had no choice. "I have to permit you access to the building since that is Hillel policy," he told me, but he was far from happy. Having a Chabad rabbi drop by once a week to give a class to a few traditional students was one thing. A full-time rabbi on campus was quite another. His boss, Hillel's regional director, was another Reform rabbi, and the founder of Breira,[25] a radical leftist group. He had just pulled off an organizational coup convincing the Jewish Federations across Florida to pool their money and give it to him to direct to Hillel programs. He was even more distraught to see me. Competition from a Chassid whom he could not control was the last thing he wanted.

Both Reform rabbis placed stumbling blocks wherever I went, attempting to undermine my credibility with the school administration and the students. Maybe 3 percent, a hundred of the three thousand Jewish students at the University of Miami, were involved weekly in Hillel activities. They had a beautiful building, tons of money, and the backing of the Jewish community. I was a young rabbi, wet behind the ears, no facility, little communal support, and my paycheck was usually a month late. But soon enough, the students started coming to my programs. I didn't wait for the students to find me. I set up a table in the Student Union, and organized classes, Shabbat programs and other activities on campus. After a year, I was pulling large numbers for Shabbat dinners. Hillel responded by investing tens of thousands of dollars to redo their social hall into a disco club, strobe lighting and all. My approach was to return to basics, connecting students with their heritage one by one, and taking a real interest in their lives. As it turned out, Hillel's nightclub could not compete with the fraternity parties. My success continued as they realized that thousands of dollars had been wasted on a nightclub.

I needed to develop a bit of independence on campus, so I formed a student organization called the Chabad Student Union. Rully Moskowitz, an Orthodox student from Bogota, was the first president. Ana Wasserman, who had connections with Chabad, was the vice president. These students and others were the nucleus of the organization that gave Chabad the right to use rooms on campus and sponsor programs independently of Hillel.

All other religious leaders were recognized as campus chaplains, and considered faculty members. So I decided to apply as a campus chaplain. I was one of the first Chabad rabbis in the US to request official recognition as a chaplain. My application brought the tension out into the open. The regional Hillel director attempted to thwart my recognition.[26] First, he claimed that Hillel was the sole official representative[27] of the Jewish community. I countered, saying that I represented the Orthodox community. In support of my position, I brought the endorsement of the Orthodox rabbinate, which consisted of twenty-five congregations. This argument undermined his position that Hillel was the center for all Jews.

"The Orthodox rabbinate is just a fringe group," the Hillel rabbi asserted, saying that only Hillel "represents the mainstream[28] of the community." His actions infuriated many of the students. When this tactic proved unsuccessful, the Reform rabbi switched tactics, saying that I was not considered a rabbi since I attended a yeshiva[29] rather than university. As a last-ditch effort to stymie my acceptance on campus, they claimed to the university administration that I was part of a cult.[30] This turned even more students against Hillel.[31] This battle continued for several years. Finally, exasperated, I called the chairman of the Chaplains Commission. He was a Catholic priest, bewildered by the Jewish infighting.

"In a few days, you are having a meeting," I told him. "If I am not approved as a chaplain, I will file a federal civil-rights lawsuit the day after the meeting." That finally got their attention, and I was approved.

In recent years, the New York-based Rohr Foundation has fueled that expansion by underwriting dozens of new Chabad Campus centers. Today there is hardly a major university in America without a permanent Chabad House and rabbi.

The scope of Chabad's inroads on American campuses became clear with a new program called Birthright Israel. The idea, the brainchild of philanthropists Michael Steinhardt and Edgar Bronfman, was designed to give college students a ten-day intense trip to Israel to strengthen their Jewish identity. Money was raised from Federations, the Jewish Agency, Hadassah, and private donations. Yearly, around twenty thousand students now visit Israel each winter and summer. Birthright Israel did not operate the tours. Instead, it recognized some forty diverse Jewish organizations – from the Israel Nature Society to the Reform Movement – to organize the trips. Mayanot, the Chabad Center for college students in Jerusalem, was recognized as a "Birthright Provider," though some Liberal Jewish groups attempted to block it as a trip provider.

Birthright's new strategy created competition between different trip providers; each had to market and run its own trips. Some organizations succeeded in filling a busload or two. Chabad's Mayanot emerged as a top trip provider with long waiting lists. According to Rabbi Shlomie Gestetner, Mayanot's director, "Over 95 percent of those on our trips are not Orthodox."

Chabad was finally playing on a level field and allowed to compete for funding based on its abilities to produce. It became clear that, if treated equitably, Chabad success was beyond expectation. Campus rabbis and rebbitzens escorted the trips, providing even more historical context and developing deeper relationships with the students, greatly enhancing the experience. The stronger relationships fostered on the trips were crucial in follow-up programs.

Change arrived in 2004 when Hillel came under the leadership of noted Jewish educator Avraham Infeld. At a meeting of Hillel directors, he asked them what is their biggest problem. They said, "The competition from Chabad." Next, he wanted to know what percentage of Jewish students came to Hillel's and Chabad's programs. They answered, "20 to 30 percent."

"If so," Infeld replied, "the real issue is the majority of students who don't attend anywhere."

Chabad leadership worked on mending the relationship. Rabbi Menachem Schmidt, president of the Chabad Campus Commission, began working with national Hillel staff, inviting them to conferences of Chabad campus shluchim, and they responded in kind. Hillel's national director, former congressman Eric Fingerhut, strives to partner with Chabad.

While Hillel and Chabad are cooperating on campus, most local Federations are just beginning to fund Chabad campus programs. At the University of California in Irvine, Jewish Federation and Family Services of Orange County partners with Chabad, funding Shabbat dinner programs. In other communities, the record is mixed. Hillel receives more than $100,000 annually from the Pittsburgh Federation. The Chabad Center, which has up to a hundred students attending its Friday-night Shabbat meals gets $7,700.[32] When a second Chabad Center opened at Carnegie Mellon University, the Pittsburgh Federation cut the allocations in two between the two campuses. The Los Angeles Federation changed its funding formula to one based on programs instead of the historic method of funding agencies. Still the Chabad programs are not getting a fair shake. The Federation allocated only 7 percent of its funding in 2014 to Chabad campus centers, which are a great success on southern California campuses. The LA Federation has repeatedly rejected requests for funds for capital improvements to campus Chabad Centers in the area.

In one major city, the Federation created a subcommittee to meet with the campus Chabad Center to consider funding. They

forgot to tell the Chabad rabbi that this committee was entirely composed of members of the Hillel board. The Chabad rabbi chuckled
to himself when he realized the level of objectivity he was dealing
with. Still, he managed to secure a small grant of $3,000, a pittance
when compared to the hundreds of thousands of dollars funded to
Hillel programs in that city.

In the late sixties and early seventies, Chabad began to expand
its community-based programs. In 1969, Rabbi Shlomo Cunin discovered the Long Beach Jewish Community Center had unused
classrooms that would be a perfect start for a Jewish day school. When
he asked the director, Gerry Bubis, to rent them, Bubis responded, "A
Chabad school in Long Beach? You must be kidding! If you succeed,
Cunin, I will eat your hat." In the first year, there were two classes
with a total of fourteen children. A year later, the enrollment doubled.
Cunin visited Long Beach and entered Bubis' office with a hat in one
hand, and bottles of ketchup and mustard in the other. "Bubis," he
asked, "what do you want on the hat?"

The Long Beach Jewish Community Center soon proved too
small for the day school, and an office building was purchased and
renovated on Atlantic Avenue. Down the block was the famed furniture store, Lloyds of Long Beach, which advertised itself as "the home
of truly snooty furniture." The Jewish owner, alarmed at the changing
demographics caused by Chassidic rabbis moving to his neighborhood, offered them $10,000 to leave the area.

The rabbi retorted, "We are not going anywhere, but you'll see
our school will outlive your store." A few years ago, Lloyds closed
its doors. Today the neighborhood is the center of a vibrant Chabad
community. In 1977, the school moved to a beautiful ten-acre, former
public-school site near Huntington Beach in Orange County.

Orange County was not as welcoming as Long Beach. The
Jewish leaders there decided to support another less religious school,
hoping to stifle the growth of the Chabad school. It would take
years before the local Federation would give any financial assistance
to the Chabad school. When it finally began, it was in a discrimina-
tory manner. The Chabad school received a subsidy of thirty-three

dollars per child; the less religious school, $543 for each student. When Chabad leaders protested, they were told, "You will do whatever is necessary to keep your school open and the other school will not."

When the school director had to mortgage his home to cover payroll, the Federation still didn't budge.

The Rebbe worked hard to change the agenda of communal groups. Still, many were unwilling to subscribe to his goal that placed the spiritual core of Judaism as the primary issue on the communal agenda. The Orthodox shared with him the goals, but they did not believe that they were attainable beyond their immediate communities. The Rebbe attempted to influence both groups. He met with many community leaders in the 1960s and 1970s, pushing them to see the importance of Jewish education. Time and again, he implored Orthodox leaders to look beyond their parochial needs. But this was uncharted territory, and they feared they could not succeed.

When local communities did not see the importance of tradition, Chabad had no choice but to build a new infrastructure. It would take decades of hard work and cost billions.

The Rebbe explained that most organizations sit down and have a meeting; afterward they plan a second meeting. Finally, they begin to analyze the problem and create a task force. The task force develops a plan and, finally, a year or so later, reveals its strategy that will solve the problem.

The Rebbe contrasted that with the Chabad approach that sends a rabbi to a community. "He meets one Jew and slowly draws him closer to Judaism, then another Jew. After a few years, he takes a look, and he has changed the whole community."

Slowly, by trial and error, Chabad created a system of programs: summer camps, adult education, youth programs, Hebrew schools, chaplaincy, and many other activities. The key difference with Chabad programs was that classical Jewish values were put center stage. Millions of Jews have become involved in Jewish life through Chabad programs.

In recent years, funding to Chabad schools has become the norm in many communities. Today, Federations around the country fund Chabad schools in most communities in an equitable fashion.

The Jewish Federation in Orange County has changed dramatically from decades ago. Today they are a full partner with the Hebrew Academy, treating the school equitably.

Still, much more has to be done. While the Jewish community invests great resources in Jewish Community Centers that promote a secular brand of Judaism, they hesitate to give money to more traditional outreach programs that Chabad operates, despite proven success. Nor does the Chabad network of day camps, the largest in the nation, receive direct funding in most communities. Programs like Friendship Circle that help special needs children and the Jewish Learning Institute have attracted support of some Federations. The Foundation for Jewish Camping created a grant program with Federations for children who had never attended Jewish summer camps, and Chabad camps were included.

The agendas of many Jewish organizations have slowly shifted, bringing them more in line with the goals of Chabad. In recent years, there has been a marked swing to concerns about Jewish identity and continuity. This buzzword moved to center stage after the 1990 Jewish Population Study proved that Jews are assimilating fast into American culture. The Pew Study of 2013 proved to be a second wake-up call for Jewish leaders.

As much as the surveys have moved the issues of Jewish education and outreach to center, so did the involvement of Chabad with the Federation leaders around the country. In almost every community, the local shluchim have created relationships with the local leaders. Many of those major givers now include Chabad in their support. While the population surveys focused the community on the importance of Jewish education and renaissance, it's clear that the personal contact of thousands of shluchim with untold numbers of community leaders moved the community's agenda in that direction.

In Cherry Hill, New Jersey, the Chabad shliach, Rabbi Mendy Mangel, opened up a Chabad Center in 1994. From the get-go, the Jewish Federation of Cherry Hill was welcoming. Mangel also made every effort to integrate himself into the community.

Joel Kaber, executive vice president of the Jewish Federation of Southern New Jersey, recalled, "When Rabbi Mangel arrived, a community leader told him to pack up and go home. Instead, he established positive relationships with community members. He was never going to compromise his principles but he took the approach of outreach, tolerance, and acceptance." In Columbus, the Federation awarded the Chabad House a major grant for an innovative new program of outreach to underprivileged children. Chabad rabbis are joining Federation missions to Israel, many times modifying the itineraries to include more Jewish content.

On a national level, Jerry Silverman, the president of the Jewish Federations of North America, has opened up the system to Chabad. His leadership is creating greater spheres of cooperation in the US and abroad.

In recent years, Chabad has been accepted as part of the fabric of Jewish life. Many Liberal rabbis learned to appreciate the contribution Chabad is making, and even their members who attend Chabad benefit greatly. As Dr. Jack Wertheimer, a leading scholar at the Jewish Theological Seminary, the flagship institution of the Conservative Movement, wrote in *Commentary* in 2013:[33] "Leading members of Conservative and Reform synagogues attend Chabad educational programs or community kolel study sessions and then return to their home congregations, probably as better informed Jews."

The willingness of Liberal Jews to consider voices of tradition became clear when, in 2013, the leader of the Reform Movement, Rabbi Rick Jacobs, stated in his keynote address at the Reform Biennial Convention: "We, too, must be open to hearing truths from those we meet, remembering that we hold no monopoly on wisdom." He told of his journey from Manhattan to Brooklyn to Chabad headquarters on Eastern Parkway. "That's why I met recently with Rabbi Yehuda Krinsky, a cherished member of the Lubavitcher Rebbe's inner circle, who now has the responsibility of overseeing Chabad's worldwide activities."[34]

That openness to learn from Chabad has reached down to the younger generation of non-Orthodox rabbis. Many times they have had strong personal involvement with Chabad. In 2013, Professor Ron Wolfson asked me to address the students studying to become

Conservative rabbis at the American Jewish University in Los Angeles. We began the session by asking each student to tell about his or her Chabad connection. All but one had been active in either a campus Chabad Center, or attended Chabad schools or summer camps. Many commented on how Chabad shluchim had had a significant influence on their lives.[35]

The formal opposition to Chabad on the national and local levels has dissipated. Partnerships, while not as strong as they could be, have been forming on both a local and national basis. The Jewish Federations of North America has been slowly building a stronger relationship with Chabad. In times of crises, the bond has been beneficial for the Jewish community. But this is still a work in progress. Overseas Federation funding to Chabad projects is still limited. While some communities are giving Chabad a seat at the table and a more equitable share of the communal funding, it is still a battle in some cities. The tensions that marked the relationships with Reform and Conservative rabbis in the past have dissipated in most communities.[36]

In my community of Orange County, the relations are better than most. Many of the lay leaders are heavily involved with Chabad and the Federation. The Federation has become more equitable in funding, treating Chabad with fairness. In larger cities, the record is mixed. But there are many positive developments. In Chicago, the Federation has been very generous to Chabad schools. In Pittsburgh in 2009, Zev Rudolph, a prominent businessman and Lubavitcher, was elected Federation president. In Ithaca, a small Jewish community, the Chabad Rebbitzen, Chana Silberstein, assumed the position of chairman of the local Federation. These appointments are the first steps, and time will tell if this is the beginning of a broader trend.

Some years ago, at a meeting of the Board of Governors of the American Jewish Committee in New York, Professor Jonathan Sarna was asked if Chabad was causing division in the Jewish community. Sarna responded, "Anyone writing the history of American Jewry in the twenty-first century would have to say that the most remarkable development of Jewish life here was the rise of the Chabad-Lubavitch

Movement. Lubavitch teaches all of us how to take care of our weak spots. They set up Chabad Houses on campuses for students and tend to the poor and elderly and those on the edge of the community, to those who can't be reached and must be reached. We must be grateful to Chabad for saving thousands of Jewish souls who would have been lost to the Jewish people forever if not for the late Lubavitcher Rebbe's efforts."

He then finished his remark staring at them straight in the eye: "And you must remember all this was accomplished without the support of UJA[37] Federation funds."

Kehot Publication Society

Sixth Rebbe, Rabbi Yosef Yitzchak Schneersohn, arrives in New York to a hero's welcome, 1929.

Jewish Educational Media

The Rebbe's farbrengen in the early fifties. Standing right is Rabbi Hodakov,
the Rebbe's chief secretary. January 22, 1952.

A farbrengen in the seventies. By then, Chabad had grown into a large, dynamic movement. January 12, 1976.

In 1956 the Rebbe sent a delegation of yeshiva students to Israel to console the community in Kfar Chabad after a devastating terror attack. Many became pioneering shluchim. Left to right: Yehuda Krinsky, Shlomo Kirsch, Berel Shemtov, Dovid Schochet, Rabbi Hodakov, Shalom Butman, Yosef Rosenfeld, Faivel Rimler, Avrohom Korf, Shmuel Fogelman. Not pictured: Zushe Posner and Shalom Edelman.

Federation leaders and Rabbi Chaim Drizen at the installation of the Menorah in Union Square, 1975. The public celebration would spark the Menorah Wars.

Rabbi Zushe Wolf

Reb Mendel Futerfas, center right, leads a farbrengen for his students. His generation of Russian Chassidim inspired many to become shluchim.

Cliff Lester

Hollywood stars and dancing rabbis brought Chabad into everyone's living room.
Rabbi Shlomo Cunin and Jon Voight.

Ronald Reagan Library

President Reagan meets with Chabad delegation led by Rabbi Avrohom Shemtov, on the President's right.
Far right, Rabbi Shmuel Dovid Raichek.

Chani and Shmulik Kaminetsky receive a blessing and dollars for charity from
the Rebbe before leaving for Dnepropetrovsk, Ukraine.

Jewish Educational Media, Chaim B. Halberstam

Kinus Hashluchim

Globetrotting Rabbi Moshe Kotlarsky at the International Conference of Shluchim.

Rabbi Yehuda Krinsky, left, Merkos Chairman, dedicating Chabad of Richmond, Virginia.

Russia's chief rabbi Berel Lazar welcoming Israeli president Shimon Peres to the Jewish Museum in Moscow.

Fifteen hundred CTeens gather in Times Square for Havdalah after a Shabbaton in Brooklyn.

Rabbi Chaim and Rivkie Lipskier at the University of Central Florida.

Thousands at the opening of the Chabad Synagogue in Novosibirsk, the capital of Siberia, 2013.

Philanthropist George Rohr carries the Torah scroll into the rebuilt Chabad Center in Mumbai, 2014.

164

Chapter Eight

Every Shliach Is an Entrepreneur

How did Chabad become a fundraising powerhouse? Why is Chabad expanding while other segments of the Jewish community are contracting, merging, and closing facilities? How is it creating viable organizations in smaller communities? How is its approach different from other Jewish groups?

With more than four thousand shluchim in over eighty countries,[1] the budgets for operations and capital projects is somewhere between $1.5 and $2 billion. (Due to the decentralization and the financial autonomy of the institutions, it is difficult to get an exact number.) The Chabad Center in the small Jewish community of Spokane, Washington, spends just under a $100,000 a year. The Yeshiva College, a sprawling network of schools in Melbourne, has an annual budget of $14 million. There is an urban myth that Chabad in Brooklyn dispenses unlimited funds to shluchim around the world. Nothing could be farther from the truth. Funds are raised and retained by the local shluchim. Success for each shliach is based on his own efforts; it is sink or swim.

George Rohr,[2] the New York investor, and his father, Sami, powered Chabad's expansion internationally with key gifts in the hundreds of millions over the past twenty-five years. According to Rohr, there is a difference between giving to Chabad and giving to other organizations. "Every shliach is an entrepreneur in his community. The Rebbe's organizational genius is that everyone has to make it on his own. It's an extremely local business; the shliach has to take ownership. He has both the responsibility and the autonomy to succeed."

Rohr feels there is a synergy. He provides the venture capital and the shliach provides the sweat equity. When investing in a business opportunity, Rohr wants to be assured of essential elements. "The first thing you look for is whether the entrepreneur has enough skin in the game. What do they have to lose if they fail? In Chabad society, the best and brightest go into shlichus; if you're driven and you're good, you become a shliach. The societal values support that concept."

Lev Leviev[3] and Rohr have underwritten much of the growth of Chabad in the former Soviet Union. Rohr has also provided funding for American college-campus centers and the Rohr Jewish Learning Institute, which has become the largest network of adult Jewish learning in the world. The substantial gifts from the mega-givers have fueled tremendous growth; still, over 98 percent of the Chabad worldwide budget is raised locally by shluchim and used in their communities. No dues are sent to New York,[4] unlike other national Jewish organizations,[5] who must send a portion of their income to headquarters.

Like many donors, Rohr considers philanthropy an investment. He says, "It's nine parts business judgment, and one part kishke (gut feeling)." He wants his Tzedakah, or charitable giving, to bring the maximum return. "With Chabad, you get the biggest bang for your buck."

Professor Jonathan Sarna[6] of Brandeis University concurs that the Chabad model is attractive to donors because it provides a great return on investment. "Chabad has lower operating costs," he says. For the shluchim, the commitment to mission comes first, so they are willing to pay themselves less and find creative ways to operate with less. As one Chabad rabbi joked with me, "You get two shluchim for each Conservative rabbi and three for each Reform." Younger rabbis starting out with new Chabad Centers will classically take a lower salary as part of the effort to launch a new center. Many smaller Chabad Centers begin in the rabbi's house, keeping costs down. As the support rises, the next move will be to a storefront, and from there to a property.

The lower costs also allow flexibility. Sarna claims that "Chabad's business model gives it the ability to survive difficult economic times. I think there is less debt and better use of space. A lot of Chabad rabbis live in their Chabad Centers." He observes that "around the country we are seeing synagogue mergers at the same time Chabad is growing." Traditional congregations have sizeable operating budgets that necessitate large memberships to cover costs. Chabad usually develops multiple smaller centers. Rabbi Zalman Marcus in Chabad of Mission Viejo says, "We operate more localized neighborhood centers servicing a smaller demographic." An important side benefit of the smaller centers is the creation of more intimate connections between the rabbi and the community.

The fact that shluchim see financial challenges as part of their mission causes them to be more willing to weather difficulties. As one shliach told me, "I feel that I am a shliach of the Rebbe with a sacred trust. I am willing to take a cut in pay or even, at times, not take a salary to ensure that the mission continues."

This sense of mission also prompts shluchim to be daring in the pursuit of their goals, motivating them to do more than they might think they are able to. As the Rebbe told a group of Jewish leaders, "What do you do if you have a good business investment and you don't have the cash? You go to the bank to seek a loan. If I don't make the investment today in a Jewish child, he may be lost forever." Rabbi Manis Friedman[7] says shluchim feel a sense of responsibility for Jewish destiny. "The state of Judaism becomes your concern; if that means getting into debt, and raising more money,[8] then you do it."

In Suffolk County, Long Island, Rabbi Tuvia Teldon's[9] courage was put to the test. The community day school's major donor reduced her annual funding from $750,000 to $375,000. "At that point I made some major cuts and tried to weather the storm." In 2009, when the economy tanked, she reduced the amount to zero. "There was no way the school could survive." Teldon faced a crisis of conscience. "I could not imagine, as a Chabad shliach, how I could close the only Jewish school in the region." Despite the odds, Teldon toughed it out, bringing in a new administrator whose experience and innovation turned the situation around. In retrospect, he says, "The decision to continue to keep the school open made no business sense at all. It was my L'chat'chila Ariber moment."

"L'chat'chila Ariber" is Yiddish for "at first you go over." It was the motto of the Fourth Rebbe, Rabbi Shmuel.[10] "When faced with an obstacle, you don't stop, or go around, you go over the top." It means reaching beyond your comfort level for a higher purpose. Many Jewish groups spend much time in planning and evaluating before embarking on a new project. Shluchim are not burdened by committees or creating a broad, communal consensus. They tend to act swiftly, seizing the initiative, at times taking financial risks as necessary.

Just before Passover in 1983, the Rebbe spoke of the Sixth Rebbe, Rabbi Yosef Yitzchak, as the model for these endeavors, saying he did not restrict his efforts based on financial limitations. "He had debt and he did not fear debt; when he paid off the earlier debts, he would incur new ones." The Rebbe argued that it's a mistaken approach to operate only within your comfort level. "The true sense of peace of mind is when you fulfill the mission." In the same talk, the Rebbe cautioned that one must weigh that financial risk. "While one may reach to the mountains, one must strike a balance based on what is realistic." It seemed to most observers the Rebbe was referring to the dramatic expansion of Chabad in California by Rabbi Shlomo Cunin. The Rebbe praised those who acted in this way. However, with the growth, Cunin had encumbered himself with large financial liabilities. The Rebbe said that the approach of "L'chat'chila Ariber[11] should be based on what is realistic.[12] Push the edge of the envelope, but be responsible and do not put the organization at financial risk.

Driven by mission, fearless and entrepreneurial in spirit, the shluchim become solely responsible for their success or failure. To succeed, the shliach must build his organization while finding local supporters who not only share the vision, but are willing to support the vision. Rabbi Shalom Moshe Paltiel[13] of Port Washington, New York, elaborated: "The Rebbe sent you to a community. If you are offering meaningful programs, the community will support you; if they don't find that what you are providing is something of value, you might as well pack your bags."

For most shluchim, fundraising is the toughest part of the job and creates the greatest angst. Rabbi Manis Friedman says, "Fundraising is the most difficult part of being a shliach, and we are not trained to do it. It's something completely out of our experience." The entrepreneurial model demands that a shliach push himself to uncover prospective donors[14] then convince them of the importance of the mission and earn their support. You have to overcome anxieties about rejection.

For most, there is never enough money; the constant grind for funds never ends.[15] The shliach knows that if he does not pick up the phone and ask for the gift, or get out and see his supporters, he will have trouble making payroll on Friday, and no paycheck for home. As one shliach told me, "There are days I dread lifting the phone, calling yet another person to ask again for money." There is a feeling of dependency on others. Another shliach explained, "People can be fickle, at times very insensitive. What they don't realize is that you are dependent upon them. When a donor says to you, 'Rabbi, call me in a few months,' you may not have someone else to call in the meanwhile." Rabbi Abba Perelmuter[16] says, "Many shluchim are just making it, in particular the younger ones in smaller communities. They struggle to cover the monthly expenses."

In the early seventies, Rabbi Moshe Kotlarsky[17] received his first fundraising lesson. He had just started working in Chabad headquarters. A trustee of a major foundation was impressed with Chabad. Kotlarsky was quietly told that if he submitted a proposal for a million dollars, "the money is already approved." Excited with this opportunity to score his first major gift, he prepared a detailed proposal. A week later, a letter arrived with a list of conditions that turned out to be quite arduous. He says, "The whole thing fell apart;

I was very brokenhearted." Crestfallen, he was invited into a meeting with the Rebbe, who gave him another perspective.

In a poetic, rabbinic Yiddish, the Rebbe described the basics of fundraising to the young Kotlarsky. "Some think we go into an affluent individual, you say good morning, and he answers, a good year. 'What do you want?' he says, and you reply, 'A million dollars.' He takes out the checkbook from the writing table and his pen and writes you a check and says, 'Thank you very much, thank you very much, thank you very, very much.'" The Rebbe then told him, "We can never forget what you must go through." He expanded in rabbinic lexicon, "Planting the fields and reaping the harvest, and all the thirty-nine melachot (work activities prohibited on the Sabbath) before you reap the harvest." Kotlarsky understood. This was his first lesson in fundraising: you need to cultivate people, you need to put in time and energy, and then you might be successful.

Dr. Steven Windmueller[18] of the Reform Movement's Hebrew Union College writes that the number one reason for Chabad's success is that they "begin with one Jew at a time; the quintessential organizing principle for Chabad is framed around this concept. Their outreach approach is about building personal connections as the basis of their work." That personal bond is the catalyst for greater giving. Community members feel a strong connection to the shliach; they value his work and they respond by supporting their community.

A major difference for Chabad in relationship building is that shluchim are building relationships that are meant to last a lifetime. According to Professor Sarna, this is one of the most critical factors in Chabad's billion-dollar success. "The Rebbe told people, 'you are going for life.'" Chabad shluchim are not on a career track. George Rohr sees this as crucial. "You can't fail. You're never leaving. Your posting is not a three-year resume-building tour of duty before you can qualify for some cushy pulpit in Scarsdale." Sarna claims that those years of hard work create positive attitudes toward Chabad and the shluchim. "This has built up a large amount of goodwill; few non-Chabad rabbis spend their entire career in the same community – making ties and helping people." That lifetime commitment changes attitudes. "In the long run, this approach creates a willingness to support the work of the shliach in that community." Professor Ron Wolfson of American Jewish University writes in his book *Relational Judaism*[19] about the shliach in his hometown of Omaha. "Rabbi Mendel Katzman has been there for twenty-six years. He knows every Jew in the community. His wife is a beloved teacher."

For many organizations, the entire reason for building these relationships is fundraising. Chabad goes beyond this simplistic relationship. The relationship is more than just a fundraising tool; it's about bringing traditional Torah values into other people's lives through personal connections. The real goal of the connection is to bring other Jews closer to G-d and Jewish values. Rabbi Shalom Lipskar[20] of the sprawling shul of Bal Harbour, Florida, says, "Our mission is to bring G-dliness to the world, and part of that mission is fundraising. If Chabad did not need money, we would still go out and give charity boxes to Jewish families to teach them the mitzvah of Tzedakah (charity)."

The Rebbe underscored this point in a 1975 letter to Zev Putterman, a TV producer in San Francisco. Putterman had written to the Rebbe with ideas to help Chabad establish a firmer financial base for its recently opened center in Berkeley. In his response,[21] the Rebbe used the opportunity to outline his view on fundraising. "One of the aims of Lubavitch is to involve the maximum number of Jews in its activities." Fundraising, the Rebbe argued, makes them "partners in such activities." The Rebbe compared the work of the shluchim to the ancient Biblical tribes of Zevulun and Yissachar. "The former were primarily businessmen, supporting the latter, who were primarily Torah scholars." The Rebbe noted that the Sages explain that "wherever the two are mentioned together in the Torah, Zevulun, the businessman, is – significantly – mentioned first."

There was a major communal philanthropist who rejected my calls for many years. When I reached him once, he said, "Look I am not interested in Chabad," and hung up. Finally, one of his close friends prodded him to meet with me. He had prepared a long list of insightful questions. Afterward, I made my pitch and he provided a major gift to our building project. A year later, I went to meet with him again. I'm sure he expected another solicitation, but I told him, "I appreciate your generosity, but it's time for you to learn some Torah," and I invited him to a luncheon class. Never in many years of community involvement had anyone asked him to study Torah.

Lipskar studies Torah with most members of his board of trustees weekly. "Other Jewish organizations don't do that. It's not part of their mission." Once a year, Rabbi Lipskar says, "we talk about making a gift. They are investing in something that is important to them. It's an ideological discussion on how to best spend his money; G-d gave him an opportunity." Rabbi Moshe Kotlarsky once told a major donor that the Jewish people have undergone many difficult tests starting from ancient times with Abraham. The test of modern times is the one of affluence. "G-d has bestowed on you great wealth to make a difference, to change the world, to bring Moshiach."

Rabbi Lipskar says shluchim view fundraising from a more spiritual perspective. "It's part of their mission to connect more Jews with Judaism." This attitude drives the effort to reach more people. I learned this firsthand when an elderly donor passed away. We had honored him at a fundraising banquet for his "legacy gift" after he put Chabad in his will. A few weeks later, I was at the shluchim conference when I checked in with the attorney handling the estate. It was devastating news. "You were in the will but it was changed." The caregiver had modified the will in the last months of the donor's life. I had hoped that his gift would put us on a firm financial footing after a period of financial challenge. Devastated, I walked into the lobby area of the conference. Sitting on a couch was my classmate from yeshiva days, Rabbi Yisroel Deren of Connecticut. I told him the story and expressed my great disappointment. Succinctly, he put it into perspective. "This means there is another Jew that you must reach out to." As Rabbi Yosef Loschak[22] of Santa Barbara would say, "When you need money, you reach out to more people, which in turn connects more Jews to Judaism."

Chabad itself represents something meaningful to many donors. Sarna asserts that for some, Chabad is a nostalgic sense of connection to the traditions of Judaism. Brian Chisick,[23] a major Chabad supporter in Orange County, California, explains what happened to him when a Chabad rabbi knocked on his door. "He brought me back to my childhood. I had an uncle who came from the camps; my grandparents were very observant. I was reawakened and taken back to my Yiddishkeit."

Sarna claims that they see the vibrant religious observance of Chabad rabbis and their families. "At times, the reason for supporting the shluchim can be vicarious. They want to share in the mitzvah of supporting the religious observance of the rabbis and their families." Others are driven by the esteem they have for the shliach. "They give out of respect," the donor possibly thinking, "I will give him money and some of his connections in the next world will help me." Dennis Prager,[24] who has visited Chabad Centers around the world, says, "People admire the devotion of the shluchim."

For many donors, the Chabad model is a welcome alternative. This may be the first Jewish organization they encounter that doesn't demand an upfront commitment. Most Chabad Centers do not require membership dues, which are customary in most congregations. Sarna says of Chabad, "You just provide and take no money." Wolfson writes that the Chabad strategy "is to lower the economic barriers of participation. Contrast this with the model for most membership-based institutions: pay up-front dues and then you engage." Wolfson contends it's not really fair saying Chabad rabbis are aggressive fundraisers. "When the rabbi asks for support, they willingly respond, sometimes at levels that exceed what a fair-share and other dues structures would collect." Many times, donors who gain an appreciation of this approach are moved to give even more.

Rabbi Shalom Lipskar says there is a deeper reason behind Chabad's business model. At the core of Chabad's philosophy is a sense of responsibility for all Jews, those who choose to be involved and those who do not. "Many congregations see their mandate to service their membership. Chabad's approach is radically different.[25] Just as cities are responsible for municipal services, we are responsible for the spirituality of the community."

For many American Jews, the catalyst for taking a synagogue membership is a child who will soon have a bar or bat mitzvah. The former president of the Reform Movement, Rabbi Eric Yoffie,[26] says Chabad is making it too easy for some. He argued in Israel's *Haaretz*[27] against the Chabad policy of accepting all without many conditions. "Celebrating a bar or bat mitzvah in a synagogue should require preparation and serious training, including membership[28] and involvement for more than a few months." Yoffie claims many Chabad rabbis are willing to take in a prospect for bar mitzvah without the preconditions that congregations have of several years of membership and Hebrew School. He claims Chabad is undercutting the local synagogues. "Chabad is a purveyor of Jewish minimalism, lowering educational standards for our children and community."[29] Moving away from the membership model is shaking up the classical economic model in the Jewish community. As *The Baltimore Sun*[30] reported, "Rabbis fear that more families will bypass synagogues and opt for a la carte Judaism. That's particularly worrisome as the number of American Jews unaffiliated with synagogues increases and temples struggle to maintain their membership numbers."[31]

I have been faced with this dilemma many times. A family you have never met turns up with a child a few months before bar mitzvah who has had no Jewish education. You wonder what's best: give the kid some Jewish education and try to inspire him toward a path of deeper connection and observance, or lose him and his family, possibly forever because of a long list of prerequisites. The right approach is to seize the opportunity and use this moment as a way to reconnect the family with Judaism.

Yoffie asserts that "they [the Reform and Conservative leaders] are not simply protecting their membership model." Baila Olidort, editor of Lubavitch International, writing in response,[32] argued: "Many Jews are less inclined to pay heavy membership dues as a prerequisite to spiritual engagement." She says it goes to the core ideas driving Chabad's outreach, arguing, "Enabling someone to perform a mitzvah was no more and no less the fulfillment of the ethical obligation of Hashavat Avedah (returning a lost item to its owner). And you do not negotiate or make demands of the owner before returning his belongings to him." Olidort acknowledges that Jewish institutions depend on the community for their support. "Tzedakah (giving) is an obligation established in the Torah, not in synagogue boardrooms. And no rabbi should be so presumptuous as to believe that Judaism may be gifted selectively by those who 'have' it to those who 'pay for' it."

There is another tremendous advantage to the Chabad business model. Most Chabad Centers do not have a board of directors that can dismiss the shliach-entrepreneur.[33] The shliach has the responsibility for creating and expanding the organization. He creates partnerships with supporters; at the same time he has the freedom to pursue his mission without being constrained by many bosses.

Rabbi Chaim Block had that entrepreneurial approach from the moment he arrived in San Antonio in 1987. Block[34] says, "Most congregations look for their rabbi, I was a rabbi looking for a congregation." Finding those supporters for Block was not easy. Some locals wondered if there was a need for Chabad, or felt it might be too religious for their community. Block created the typical Chabad organizational model; the shliach is the executive and the local supporters become his partners.

Typically, a Jewish organization evolved when a group decided to form a congregation, a school, or social agency. The boards hired and fired their rabbis and organizational professionals as they saw fit. Contrast that with the Chabad model in which rabbis go to communities as shluchim for life, using the principles of Torah to define priorities. Congregational rabbis and Jewish communal professionals have to tread softly, building consensus and political support for their agenda. Chabad rabbis are empowered to decide and move forward, limited only by the money they can raise.

Some shluchim have created boards of local supporters, who work in partnership with the shliach, setting policy, budgets, and goals. At the Hebrew Academy, the Chabad school in Huntington Beach, California, Rabbi Yitzchak Newman works hand-in-hand with his board. "They are very supportive of our mission; their primary purpose is to assure we are on a solid financial footing, and they assist in bringing the mission to the community." Still, this kind of board operates very differently from the boards of directors of other groups. In Chabad institutions, Halacha (Jewish Law) is the final authority over communal policies, and the director cannot be removed without the approval of the region's head shliach.

On Shefa,[35] a prominent blog of the Conservative Movement, one rabbi explained the dramatic difference in organizational culture. "Chabad rabbis answer to the regional Chabad structure, not to a local or congregational board of trustees. This means that the Chabad rabbi can execute the well-defined mission of Chabad as he sees fit without a local board of congregants complaining about all the things that we've all heard that synagogue boards complain about. Chabad rabbis are entrepreneurs. One of the reasons Conservative rabbis need multi-year contracts is to protect them from boards who might otherwise act arbitrarily or even vindictively. The Chabad rabbi has no such concern, nor is the Chabad rabbi held back in his ambitions by board members who don't want change, or who want certain kinds of change not in comportment with the central mission."

There are weaknesses also in this system. In some communities, shluchim have been in place for many years and have become complacent. Rabbi Yosef Loschak would put it this way: "The community votes for the shliach by the financial support it offers him. If he is not doing his job, they will withhold their money, forcing change."

At a community dialogue on the future of synagogues in Pittsburgh, Conservative rabbi Hayim Herring, who is director of Star, a national initiative to create a new vision for synagogues in the us, noted:[36] "To their credit, Chabad has created a different model and synagogues have not yet found that magic formula to sustain the work they do that Chabad has; I think we all have a little Chabad envy in that regard."

This understanding that values are constant and that the rabbi is not disposable, but is there for life, creates another dynamic. One shliach told me that "when there are problems, we tend to work them out; it's more like a marriage than a job."[37]

Shlomo Cunin arrived in California in 1962. As one of the pioneering shluchim, he reached out to the local community to build a financial base. He was fearless and talented. In just over a decade, he launched a statewide network of centers, schools, and campus Chabad Houses. As he added staff, he told them they would not have to raise money. Rabbi Yehoshua Gordon[38] recalls that when Cunin set him up in the San Fernando Valley in 1973, he told him,

"Gordon, you will come out to the valley; you will build Chabad, and you will never have to raise money." Gordon received a regular paycheck and expenses were paid. He says, "In those years money was not an issue."

Gordon didn't expect the ominous changes on the horizon. During those pioneering years, Cunin says, "We had miracles." One way or another, Cunin would pull the cat out of the bag every year, and the organization kept expanding rapidly. By 1975, the situation was slowly becoming untenable. Clearly, one person could not be solely responsible for fundraising. Change was needed. One Saturday evening, Cunin invited the California shluchim to his home for a Melaveh Malkah, the traditional post-Shabbat repast. Customarily, these gatherings enhance the Shabbat experience with the retelling of Chassidic stories, words of Torah, and inspiration. The upbeat tone of the evening was dampened, however, when Cunin surprised everyone with a startling announcement:

"Chevre-Boys," he said, "we can't go on like this any longer. As of today, you have to fend for yourselves and raise your own money." Gordon says, "Everyone was in shock. It came out of nowhere and was totally unexpected." Taking the cue from that era's Watergate crisis, the shluchim labeled that evening the Saturday Night Massacre.

Instead of depending on Cunin, each rabbi had to reach deeper into his community to seek support. It wasn't easy; a group of young rabbis suddenly had budgets thrust upon them. Gordon says, "We were not trained to raise money. It was painful and a slow process." Cunin's announcement forced the rabbis to take ownership. "That night was a turning point for Chabad in California. It was the greatest catalyst for growth." Across the state, Chabad took off, each shliach taking greater initiative. Chabad in the Valley grew from one rabbi to thirty-five, from one small storefront to twenty-five centers, from Studio City to Ventura.

Years later, Gordon called Rabbi Cunin one day asking for a short-term bridge loan. "I need your help. I must find $100,000 immediately." Cunin did not have the money to lend, but he offered him some advice. "Gordon, imagine if you would be still sitting in that small storefront in Encino, you would be all stressed out looking for $5,000. Today you are missing $100,000, and look at the amazing accomplishments you have in the Valley."

"Ultimately," Gordon says, "what Cunin did that night was the greatest gift we could have been given."

Even in cities with fewer Jews, shluchim are finding ways to succeed. Rabbi Yisroel Hahn[39] moved to Spokane, Washington, in 2007. He faced many challenges. It was a small community and the economy was not the most vibrant. Orthodoxy had disappeared half a century earlier. Hahn launched adult education, holiday programs, and religious services. Even though the beginning was rough, he earned local support. To help defray the operating budget, he created a program of monthly giving. Within the first few years, he was able to sign up over forty local community members whose monthly donations covered his basic budget; others supported with annual gifts. Old friends and visitors who appreciated his work in Spokane also helped out. He says, "In addition to the support from the residents of Spokane, others around the country who admire our activities stand behind them."

It's the campus shluchim who have the toughest challenge in fundraising. They do not have the natural base of supporters that community-based institutions have. While there are grants to get started on campus, sustaining the programs over the long haul can be daunting. Rabbi Heshy Novack[40] at Washington University explains: "There is no natural overlap between those who participate and those who fund the programs. We need to be both successful with our programs and telling our story to our donors, who rarely come to campus." Campus shluchim reach out to parents, alumni, and local donors to raise money. While other campus groups get major funding from Jewish Federations, campus centers have just begun to receive some grants from them. Colleges located in small communities where there are few local donors pose unique problems. Rabbi Mendel Loschak[41] at the University of California at Santa Barbara (UCSB) travels once a week to Los Angeles seeking donors. Some of the money comes from his alumni who were active in Chabad. He says, "This is great since it enables me to retain a strong connection with them." Still, it's not easy. "It's hard because, once people graduate and move on, they have other interests in their lives."

The first generation of shluchim, in the fifties and sixties, had it the roughest[42] because Chabad had yet to prove itself. Rabbi Moshe Feller[43] discovered firsthand the challenge of fundraising in 1962 when he returned to his hometown of Saint Paul, Minnesota, to open the fourth regional office for Chabad. Feller recalls that the community's reception was like the weather – very cold. The attitude of the shrinking Orthodox community was: "Hush hush, let's not rock the communal boat." He received a small stipend from New York, but he had to raise his own local funds for the programs he was dreaming about.

As many other shluchim would discover, help for young Feller came from an unexpected source in a moment of serendipity. The holiday of Sukkot,[44] when Jews traditionally build temporary dwellings, was a few days off. Feller headed to Plywood Minnesota for some lumber for a Sukkah. Rudy Boschwitz,[45] a young entrepreneur whose family had fled Nazi Germany three decades earlier, was surprised to see a rabbi in his store. He could not imagine, as he recalled years later, "that rabbis needed much lumber and were too adept with hammers." He stopped Feller on the way out. "Next time you need some lumber, give me a call in advance and I will have some ready for you." What he didn't know is that Feller had started a local campaign to encourage people to build Sukkahs. "Within a short time I became the Sukkah king of the upper Midwest."

Boschwitz was an active member of a Reform temple, but it was Chabad he encountered again and again as he opened stores around the state. A hundred miles south of Saint Paul, in the agricultural hub of Albert Lea, Boschwitz was surprised to discover a Chabad Hebrew school. In these smaller communities, Boschwitz says, "the only services they got were from Chabad." As time went on, Boschwitz also found out that "it wasn't just lumber Rabbi Feller needed, it was money." His donations, which reached into the millions, were decisive in Chabad's expansion in the upper Midwest. Eventually, Boschwitz switched to politics and was elected to the United States Senate.

It seems that almost every shliach can tell you the miracle story of finding the money needed at a crucial time. Rabbi Abba Perelmuter in Long Beach, California says, "There is no rhyme or reason for this. We live on miracles."

Rabbi Yoseph Denburg,[46] dean of the Hebrew Academy in Coral Springs, Florida, said 1994 was a tough year. He had fallen behind in his withholding payments to the IRS for his teachers. Finally, he reached a settlement with the IRS. He had to make two payments of $75,000, one in thirty days, and the second, two months later. He says, "The first money came easy," but when he started to work on the second payment, he ran into a rough time. "I could not put two nickels together," he says, and the money was due by Monday. It was late Thursday and there was no hope on the horizon. Finally in desperation, he decided to crash the bar mitzvah that Sunday of the richest Jew in Coral Springs. "In the past, he had thrown me out of his office," Denburg said, but this time, he was desperate and saw no other way. "I had this harebrained idea I would ask him at the reception to help me out."

On Friday, a social worker called. Months before, she had asked Rabbi Denburg to visit an elderly Jewish lady who was living in a remote government housing project. He says she was a lonely woman. "The conditions were terrible, and the apartment was infested with bugs." In an effort to raise her spirits, he showed her a short video of the school. "She asked me to leave the video." Now the social worker was on the line asking him to do the funeral on Sunday at 11:00 a.m. The bar mitzvah was beginning at noon. Denburg hoped he could finish quickly and make it on time to plead his case during the smorgasbord.

The funeral was forty minutes south in North Miami Beach, and the only other person attending was the social worker. Still, he felt that all deserve the final dignity of a proper funeral. He made a eulogy, and was surprised to be told that the burial was at another cemetery. They drove there, Denburg worrying that he would miss his chance at the bar mitzvah. Without any help, he concluded the service, filling the grave himself in the hot Florida sun. Now he needed to rush to the bar mitzvah. He called his wife, "Rivkie, meet me behind the hall with a fresh suit, shirt and tie; I will change there." As he left the funeral, the social worker handed him an envelope. He thought to himself, "It must be a hundred dollars for the funeral," but when he stopped the car at a traffic light, he decided to open the envelope, and inside was a cashier's check for $75,000 with a note. "Thank you for visiting me, you came and treated me nicely. You asked for nothing in return. Here is a gift for the school."

Feeling on top of a mountain, he still decided to crash the bar mitzvah. The father was surprised to see Rabbi Denburg. Denburg recalls, "He couldn't say anything since he was surrounded by a group of friends." Denburg told him, "I had to come by to give you a blessing on this most auspicious day." The short speech at the bar mitzvah became the turning point in their relationship. "Today we are good friends and he is a great help to the school."

In Shanghai, Rabbi Shalom Greenberg[47] had been leasing space for his Chabad Center. In 2004, a building came on the market that suited his requirements. He needed at least a million dollars. Greenberg's local fundraising efforts were not successful. In desperation, he flew to New York to pray at the Ohel, the resting place of the Rebbe, and seek support. Jewish tradition teaches that prayer at the graves of the righteous is of special merit and invokes a blessing from above.

After twenty-two hours of grueling travel, Greenberg went straight from the airport to pray. At that same time, back in Shanghai, Mr. Georges Bohbot, a Jewish clothing manufacturer from Hong Kong, was finishing a meeting with Maurice Ohana, a Moroccan-born Jew who was president of the Shanghai Jewish Community. "I need to close up and go lead the services; tonight I am the rabbi," Ohana told Bohbot. When Bohbot asked why, he told him the community needed to buy a building. Since Rabbi Greenberg could not find the money locally, he had gone to New York to pray and find a solution for the crisis. "What do you need?" Bohbot asked. Ohana told him that a million dollars would solve the problem. "Wait a minute, let me call my partner." Bohbot stepped out and called Max Azria, an LA-based Jew who was born in Tunisia. When Bohbot came back to Ohana's office, he told him that they would help. Ohana asked how much. Bohbot said, "My partner and I will take care of the million." This transpired at the exact same time Rabbi Greenberg finished praying at the Rebbe's grave in New York.

Another aspect of the business model that is unique to Chabad is the support the shluchim give to each other, no matter how stretched they may be at the time. They live the core Jewish principles they teach. Tzedakah and Chessed, charity and acts of loving-kindness, must be part of every Jewish life, even of the shluchim. When one of theirs is in need, they are obligated to take care of their own.

Rabbi Eli Rosenfeld, a shliach in Miami, runs the Shluchim Fund, distributing grants to some four hundred shluchim annually. Rosenfeld[48] says, "There are shluchim who struggle to put food on the table. Others have medical emergencies." According to Rosenfeld, some live in smaller communities with limited demographics and economic base. Large families with the burden of hefty tuition bills face the greatest challenge.[49] Grants vary from a few hundred dollars to a family whose refrigerator broke a week before Passover and there is little money in the house, to larger grants of even $30-40,000 in cases of medical emergencies. Rosenfeld raises just under half a million dollars a year. Fifty percent of it comes from the shluchim themselves, the balance from the Chabad community. Rosenfeld reviews the requests with three other shluchim. The fund works quickly, many times intervening within a day. "The most important thing," he says, "is that every shliach knows that he has someone to help him when he really needs it." The Shluchim Office also provides interest-free loans for personal needs of shluchim.

In California, there is a similar grassroots effort. Shluchim themselves set up a loan fund that can give shluchim up to $5,000, repayable in ten months. Rabbi Reuven Mintz[50] serves on the committee overseeing the fund. "Loans require a cosigner, typically another shliach. They are usually processed within twenty-four hours; annually the fund turns over about $300,000. We have never had a loan that was defaulted on."

In the wake of natural disasters like Hurricane Sandy, the crisis in the Ukraine, or other places, shluchim band together to help the affected area. They organize e-mail-based campaigns, and the funds go to alleviate the disaster.

In times of severe crisis, shluchim unite to be of assistance to families in need. That's what happened to Rabbi Yitzi Hurwitz, the shliach in Temecula, California. On his forty-first birthday, he received confirmation of the diagnosis of the dreaded disease, ALS.

That night, seventy shluchim from as far north as Bakersfield and Chula Vista on the Mexican border converged on the city of Temecula, perched between Orange County and San Diego, for a birthday far-brengen. The mood was both foreboding and uplifting. Hurwitz was deeply touched by the outpouring of friendship. There were words of Torah, and Chassidic stories and melodies. At midnight, Yitzi stepped out of the small storefront synagogue for a few minutes. Rabbi Simcha Backman of Chabad of Glendale put the issue on the table. "It's a terrible disease and we have to stand by the family. Take your phones and text me your credit-card numbers or bank routing information and how much you will contribute monthly to support his family." Within minutes, there were commitments totaling $40,000 for the year. By week's end, $120,000 were promised by fellow shluchim, enough to cover the family's expenses and help keep Chabad afloat in this small community. Backman says, "Many of those who gave were, themselves, struggling financially." Additional funds were raised to help with medical expenses, underwriting the cost of a bar mitzvah, sending the family to a hotel for Passover, and to Israel for medical trials.

Rabbi Moshe Kotlarsky at Lubavitch World headquarters helps many shluchim in challenging situations. Kotlarsky provides emergency loans to shluchim in need of assistance. At any one time, there are close to $3 million in outstanding loans. In addition, special grants are given in situations of personal and institutional crisis.

This mentality to help has prompted Chabad's new role as the "boots on the ground" of the Jewish community when disaster strikes. In Hurricane Katrina, one of the deadliest hurricanes in US history, that hit the Gulf Coast and New Orleans in August of 2005, Chabad organized search-and-rescue teams that combed the byways of New Orleans looking for survivors on boats, even though their own community was greatly disrupted. The Jewish community in New York was amazed at the dedication of the shluchim after Hurricane Sandy, which devastated New York City and surrounding areas in October of 2012.[51] Staying at their posts, many times with their own homes or centers destroyed, they were the frontline of assistance to others. As President Bush said in a speech[52] about Rabbi Rivkin of New

Orleans after Hurricane Katrina, "He didn't say, 'Head away from the storm'; he said, 'Let's take it right to the middle of the storm area to help people.'"

The climate for Chabad fundraising has dramatically changed over the years. Rabbi Avrohom Levitansky,[53] one of the pioneering shluchim in California, told me of the early days in the late sixties. "People were unwilling to support us. To move forward, we had to borrow." Rabbi Shalom Lipskar recalls, "There were times we could not pay salaries." Deficit funding may have spurred Chabad's early growth, but today shluchim are having an easier time.

Rabbi Tuvia Teldon remembers thirty-five years ago, in the late seventies, when he started off in Long Island. "Few would give me an appointment; even fewer were willing to support our work. They questioned our ability to play a meaningful role in the Jewish community." Rabbi Marcus in Mission Viejo says that since the early part of the twenty-first century, six new centers have opened in his area. "Even with the new locations nearby, the number of supporters we have in Mission Viejo has grown." But there is a potential downside also. As Chabad opens more centers, there is a danger of the Starbucks syndrome. The coffee giant discovered that new stores were not creating new business, but pulling existing customers from other locations. As one shliach told me, "We have to ensure that the new area can survive without undermining existing Chabad Centers, which might create unhealthy competition for supporters and breed tension."

Today Teldon says Chabad has evolved into a brand name. "People trust us; we have a long track record of accomplishments; they know they can count on Chabad." As Jewish philanthropist Michael Steinhardt[54] told reporter Jonathan Mark of *The Jewish Week*,[55] "Chabad is the most effective Jewish organization in the world."

Professor Jonathan Sarna explains, "Communities have tended to support winners, and people who look at the landscape of American Jewish life see Chabad growing." Dr. Steven Windmueller writes, "Whenever I am invited to speak about institutional transformation within the Jewish community, invariably among the first questions is one associated with Chabad-Lubavitch. There are a number of elements that reflect the success and impact of Chabad. They have built a billion-dollar international empire that includes their own news service, publishing house, and hundreds of Web sites. Today, more than four thousand Chabad shluchim serve communities across the United States and throughout the world."

Professor Ron Wolfson of the American Jewish University recalls that his non-Orthodox colleagues reacted with disdain and laughter when Chabad began growing in the mid-seventies. "These leaders scoffed at Chabad, which was regarded as an unsophisticated throwback to the nineteenth-century Eastern-European shtetl Judaism that would have no resonance with modern Jews." According to Wolfson, however, there has been a fundamental shift in attitude: "Who's laughing now? Chabad is the Starbucks of Jewish outreach. Chabad collects in excess of a billion dollars annually, ranking it among the most financially successful Jewish organizations on the planet."

Chapter Nine

Dancing with the KGB

The helicopter rumbled over the battlefield. It had been just a few hours since the Israeli Tank battalion, outnumbered and surprised, blocked the thrust of Syrian armor on the Golan Heights. The Syrian onslaught began on the holiest day of the year, Yom Kippur, of 1973. The Israelis had been caught unprepared as the Syrian tanks threatened Israel's heartland. The situation was grave, and Defense Minister, Moshe Dayan, and Chief of Staff, Dado Elazar, were apprehensive. Prime Minister Golda Meir had years of experience as a politician, but her command of military strategy was negligible. Dayan and Elazar felt it was essential that she see the battlefield firsthand, and the risks that still lay ahead.

Pillars of smoke rose as the helicopter found a spot to land. Yehuda Avner,[1] the Prime Minister's aide who accompanied her, described the moment. "The stench of death was in the air, and fires smoldered from the battle that finished just a few hours earlier." On the ground, Dayan and Elazar opened maps and began to brief Golda. A few dozen yards away, soldiers were gathered in a hastily jumbled-together Sukkah in honor of the weeklong joyous holiday that comes five days after Yom Kippur. Weary from battle, the soldiers were gathered inside, finishing the prayers. Golda Meir's grandparents were Orthodox, but she was far from observant. Golda's Judaism was her ardent Zionism.

Helicopters had been buzzing over the battlefield the whole day. The soldiers hadn't realized that the one landing nearby carried the prime minister, defense minister, and the chief of staff. Golda, spotting the soldiers, began to walk in their direction. Yehuda Avner, who was himself Orthodox, reminisced: "She was a bit uncomfortable around the religious," and, uneasily, she pushed down her skirt as she got closer. As the service ended, the soldiers turned, astonished to see the prime minister standing surrounded by the leaders of Israel's military.

She asked them about the battle and wished them well, and they asked if they could pose some questions. One of the soldiers, the strain of combat etched on his face, asked in the classic blunt Israeli fashion, "Tell me, Golda, is it worth it? My father was wounded in the War of Independence in 1948, my brother suffered in the Six-Day War in 1967, and now we have just finished this terrible battle." The soldiers all stood in silence, the smell of death lingering in the air, wondering: should the Jewish people continue to fight to control their destiny? Golda pondered his question. Finally she answered.

"If it's worth it today, I do not know, but let me tell you what happened to me in Moscow in 1948. I was appointed the first Israeli ambassador to the Soviet Union. I felt it my duty to attend the services for Rosh Hashanah in the main synagogue in Moscow. The first day, I was surprised. Close to a thousand seats, and just a few old men. Disappointed, I returned to my hotel, wondering if I should go again the next day. Finally, I decided that as the ambassador of Israel, it was my obligation, so the next day, again, I went to the synagogue. As I got close, I saw that the street was mobbed. Thousands were gathered outside yelling my name, "Golda, Golda." Every seat was taken inside. That day I learned the power of the Jewish people, the common bond that links all of us together. That day I learned we must sacrifice for one another."

Golda told the story to celebrated Italian reporter, Oriana Fallaci,[2] commenting that she was surprised to discover that it was

Chabad that brought out the crowd. Then she added a caveat: "Seeing thousands of Jews greeting me on Rosh Hashanah in Moscow was the only moment in my life that I considered becoming observant."

A few years after Golda Meir's arrival in Moscow, the Mossad, the Israeli intelligence service, decided to use the embassy as a base to build a connection with Russian Jews. Yitzchak Shamir, who would later become Israel's seventh prime minister, was an intelligence officer in the fifties and sixties. Speaking at a memorial gathering[3] for the Rebbe in Tel Aviv in 1994, he recalled the early exploits of the Mossad in Russia. "In the fifties, we decided to investigate the status of Soviet Jewry, and we discovered there was a clandestine Jewish network already in place, directed by the Rebbe in Brooklyn."

That underground network originated with the secret covenant that nine Chassidim had made with the Sixth Rebbe, Rabbi Yosef Yitzchak Schneersohn, in 1924. They took an oath as a minyan[4] to keep Judaism alive in Russia until their last breath. The Sixth Rebbe directed the network, first from Russia and eventually from Latvia, Poland, and then the US, funneling funds through surreptitious methods and the diplomatic pouches of friendly countries.

In the fifties, the new Rebbe intensified the efforts behind the Iron Curtain. Secrecy was paramount.[5] The Rebbe instructed his secretaries not to write down information or briefings, and directives were transmitted verbally, and at times in code. Rabbi Yehuda Krinsky says, "The Rebbe did almost everything in yechidus (private meetings)."

Rabbis David Hollander and Herschel Schacter[6] led a mission of rabbis on behalf of the Rabbinical Council of America to Russia in 1955. It was the first time in the postwar era that a formal delegation of American Jewish leaders visited Russian Jewry. Schacter said they had a long meeting with the Rebbe in advance of the trip. "We sat with the Rebbe and took notes, the Rebbe gave us names of people we should look for. It was remarkable; we looked and found many of them."

When they returned, they briefed the Rebbe about their historic trip. In the Grand Choral Synagogue in Saint Petersburg, they discovered a room filled with Torah scrolls. At that time, Communism was powerful, the cold war at its height; no one could envision a rebirth of Jewish life in Russia. They suggested to the Rebbe that the scrolls be removed from Russia and given to Jewish communities around the world. "No," the Rebbe said, "there will be a time when they will be used in Russia." In 2002, President Bush and his wife, Laura, visited the same synagogue[7] as part of a formal state visit to Russia. The Chief Rabbi of Saint Petersburg, Rabbi Mendel Pewzner and his wife, Sara,[8] hosted the Bushes. It was supposed to be a quick twenty-minute visit, but the president lingered over an hour. The Pewzners had restored the Choral Synagogue to its prior state of grandeur. During the tour, Rabbi Pewzner told the president the story about the Torah scrolls, and Bush responded, "That was a prophecy."

In Israel, the legendary spymaster, and first head of the Mossad, Isser Harel,[9] launched Israel's clandestine operations to help Soviet Jews. He appointed Shaul Avigur[10] to direct the Lishkat Hakesher (the Liaison Office) of the covert division of the Prime Minister's Office. Avigur embedded agents in the Israeli diplomatic mission in Moscow. In 1953 he dispatched Nechemia Levanon[11] to the Moscow Embassy as an agriculture officer, but his true mission was Russian Jewry.[12]

Years later, in interviews with Chassidic historian Rabbi Yosef Yitzchak Kamenetsky, Levanon described the era: "After the rule of Stalin that destroyed the network of Jewish institutions, the only remnants were the synagogues." Levanon attempted to connect to Jews via the two existing synagogues in Moscow. There was the Grand Choral Synagogue and the small, wooden Marina Roscha Synagogue, which was erected by Chassidim in 1925 in the rough Marina Roscha neighborhood on the outskirts of Moscow, where even police feared patrolling too aggressively.

In the Marina Roscha Synagogue, Levanon met a Chassidic Jew who invited him to a secret meeting in a bathhouse in central Moscow. "In the bathhouse, I was approached by a Chassid who told me of the difficulties of sending messages to the Rebbe in New York and asked if the Israeli government could help facilitate the communication." Levanon was from a secular kibbutz and quite wary of the Israeli government using its resources to connect Chassidim in Russia with their Rebbe in Brooklyn. "Shaul Avigur approved the arrangement." From then on, every Friday, they met in the bathhouse. Questions from Russian Chassidim were funneled by diplomatic mail to Tel Aviv and on to the Rebbe in New York. The Israelis also transported religious books and materials provided by Chabad via diplomatic pouch. Levanon was finally forced out of Russia in 1956 when he was discovered in the home of a Soviet Jew and was declared *persona non grata.*

Arieh Eliav[13] was sent to Russia by the Israelis in 1958 with the official title of First Secretary of the Russian Embassy in Moscow. It was a difficult time, Eliav said years later in an interview.[14] "The Iron Curtain was at its fullest strength, the Soviet Union viewed any religious expression as an act against the state. We discovered another underground, with activities similar to ours, operated by Chabad. Everywhere we went, we found them. We knew their network connected to thousands." Eliav says the risks were much greater for the Chabad network. "If our actions were discovered, we could be declared *persona non grata* and expelled. They risked imprisonment and even death."

After three years in Russia, Eliav returned to Israel, and Shaul Avigur told him, "First, you must go to New York to see the Rebbe." At 11 o'clock in the evening, Eliav entered the Rebbe's office in Brooklyn. For close to eight hours, he was debriefed. "We spoke in Yiddish with some occasional Hebrew. For the first two hours, he wanted to know the situation in Russia. The Rebbe was interested in the politics, Soviet economic policies, and the status of the Jewish communities." The Rebbe dug deeper, leading Eliav from city to city probing for information about each community. "A Jew went to Tashkent?" asked the Rebbe in poetic rabbinic tone. "Yes," said Eliav. "And in Tashkent, was a Jew called to the Torah?" "Yes," he replied. "The Torah reader, was he good, did he have a red beard?" asked the Rebbe. Eliav said, "He wanted to know if I had connected with his man on the ground, and without revealing to me who he was." The meeting lasted some eight hours, until the morning light. The Rebbe led Eliav from one community to another, extracting detail after detail. Years later, Eliav reflected on the Rebbe's debriefing. "He did not want me to leave his office and tell Shaul Avigur that the Rebbe's man in Tashkent was the red-bearded Torah reader. Who knows where that information could have mistakenly gone? The Rebbe took precautions as the head of the secret underground."

The Rebbe dispatched his own emissaries to Russia; most came as tourists, others as businessmen. There were official delegations of Jewish leaders that the Communists wanted to impress. These groups would invariably meet with the Rebbe in advance of their trips, and be secretly tasked with missions behind the Iron Curtain.

One of those secret missions took place in 1965. Binyomin Katz,[15] a yeshiva student with a photographic memory, was dispatched on a mission that took him on a three-month trip across the Soviet Union. It came about quite unexpectedly. Katz was slated to spend the summer months in Scandinavia on Merkos Shlichus[16] (summer outreach), helping Rabbi Azriel Chaikin, who was the Chief Rabbi of Denmark. Customarily, Chassidim met the Rebbe privately on their birthdays. Just prior to entering the Rebbe's office, Katz's classmate, Ben Zion Shafran, pulled out a map and said, "Don't you see how close Copenhagen and Leningrad are? This is a golden opportunity to help the Russian Jews." Moments later, Binyomin entered the Rebbe's office and asked if he should travel to Russia to meet Jews. The Rebbe responded, "First go to Scandinavia and write me every week what you accomplish. When you finish there, we will think about what you should do in Russia."

The summer in Denmark would be Katz's testing ground. Rabbi Chaikin[17] observed Katz during that summer to see if he had the wherewithal for such a demanding mission. Katz visited communities in the region, sending weekly reports back to Brooklyn. Chaikin and his wife, Sara, were born in Russia. They had fled during the Great Escape, married in Morocco,[18] and moved to Denmark. At the end of the summer, Katz stayed on for the High Holidays. Just after Rosh Hashanah, he sent a telegram to the Rebbe asking for further instructions; the answer came back in code. Deciphered, it was a message to prepare to travel to Russia. In the coming months, the training began in earnest. The Chaikins taught him basic Russian and filled him in on numerous details on Russian life, telling him not to sleep on the sheets since they would be inspected if he was anxious during the night. He was to travel under the guise of a non-threatening affluent eccentric tourist with time and money to burn. To play the part, he gained weight and purchased a fancy wardrobe. His mission was to connect with the Chassidic communities across Russia. He was given a list of contact people in each town. Travel for foreigners in Russia was arranged only by Intourist, the then-state-operated tourist agency. It was founded in 1929 by Stalin and staffed by the KGB,[19] the Committee for State Security, to monitor tourists and bring in much-needed foreign currency. Katz was charged $18,000 for ten weeks, including lodging, transportation, and food, paid in cash to Intourist before the trip started. In Moscow, he was placed on the thirtieth floor of the Ukraina Hotel,[20] four miles from the synagogue.

Katz's mission was twofold: give hope to those he met, and collect names and addresses in Russia. As a young American with a full beard, brimming with enthusiasm, he would inspire the Jews behind the Iron Curtain. Katz possessed a photographic memory. It was not revealed to him the reason for collecting the names; that was "on a need-to-know basis." Only after leaving Russia, was he informed of the second part of the mission – to facilitate immigration to Israel under a program of "Family Reunification."[21]

In Moscow, Katz became a fixture in the main synagogue, the same one that Golda Meir had visited in 1949. The grand-style Choral Synagogue was built in 1892, and despite Bolshevik demands to convert it to a workers' club, it remained open throughout the Communist years. The Russians used it as a symbol to the West that Jews were free to exercise their religious rights. A few old Jews and some Chabad followers frequented it. Its poorly lit, cavernous interior with towering ceilings, balconies, and pillars, as well as seating for eight hundred, provided secret niches for Katz to connect to local activists. Off to the side was a smaller sanctuary that could accommodate eighty people, and it was known as the gathering place for Chabad Chassidim.[22] Early every morning, an Intourist car would transport Katz from his hotel to the synagogue, and he would loiter there until around 1:00 p.m. In the afternoons, he would visit museums and other local sites, returning to the synagogue near sundown for evening services. He volunteered to be the Chazzan (prayer leader), and he joined the daily Talmud lessons. Sometimes when he was leading the services, someone would snatch the prayer book and he would continue by heart. The locals were testing whether he was another Communist plant. Katz says that among the small group of observant Jews, there seemed to be three kinds: "the ones who had been to prison, the ones in prison, and the ones going to be in prison." Fear lingered behind the dark pillars and empty pews in the vast sanctuary.

Slowly, the mistrust of Katz faded, and some of the regulars began to seek contact. A money changer fumbled with some money on the floor. Scrounging around for the coins, he whispered to Katz, "I am from Dochshitz," which was a well-known Chassidic town, "do you know my classmate Yochanan Gordon?"

Katz's first real break came when Yankel Elishevitz, who was one of the respected Chassidic elders, passed a few words to him in the stairwell leading toward the mikvah in the basement. Elishevitz was a schochet, who would slaughter kosher meat in the area behind the synagogue building. Time and again, he had tugged at Katz's beard to see if it was real. Observing him day after day, he saw that he knew how to pray, and exhibited proficiency in the daily Talmud class. Finally, he was convinced that Katz was not a KGB spy. Katz told him he was sent by the Rebbe to collect the names of Jews. Elishevitz slowly spread the word about his mission, and others approached him clandestinely. A prayer book would be placed on a windowsill. A few minutes later Katz picked it up, slipped out the paper with the list of names, memorized and destroyed the evidence. Chassidim would stand next to him in services and, in a singsong voice mimicking the prayers, they would ask about their relatives overseas.

Ephraim Kaploun, the synagogue president, who may have been a KGB front man, repeatedly demanded that Katz leave the synagogue. "Why should I go?" Katz retorted. "I am just a tourist." To Kaploun's consternation, Katz continued to come every day. After a month in Moscow, he had collected a large number of names. On the last day, he quietly moved to the front of the synagogue and approached a reclusive Chassid who had never shared his information.

Instantly he was seized and forced into a room in the back of the synagogue.

"My heart was pumping, but I tried to show no fear, as I had been instructed by Rabbi Chaikin. The room was filled with KGB agents, but luckily for me, the translator was Mordechai Chanzin, a brother of a prominent Chabad rabbi in Israel. During my time in the synagogue, we had spoken secretly about his family in Israel." They pelted Katz with questions in Russian and Chanzin translated to Yiddish, massaging the answers, saving Katz from danger. A day later, Katz left Moscow.

Katz visited nine cities in Russia; Intourist managed every step of his trip. They selected the hotels and sights he would see. They had to permit this eccentric rich American tourist his wish to visit synagogues in each town. He had one major challenge. Somehow he had to find a way to get to Tashkent. This city, two thousand miles from Moscow, was the capital of the remote Soviet-controlled Uzbekistan. A large group of Chassidim had migrated there during the Nazi invasion and had remained after the war. A formal request to visit Tashkent would have been a red flag to the KGB. He had been instructed that, once in Russia, he should find a way to visit Tashkent without raising Soviet suspicion.

He arrived in Tbilisi in Soviet Georgia. Deep in Russia, it was the city closest on the official itinerary to Tashkent, located 1,200 miles further east. The Georgian Jews were noted for their fierce independence, and the Soviet Union's rule was a touch more benevolent there than in the rest of the country. Katz discovered the only Jewish community in the Soviet Union that afforded Jews a degree of freedom. "It was the only relatively relaxed place in Russia." In Tbilisi, he heard about a championship soccer competition taking place in Tashkent. Finally he had the excuse he needed. Overnight, he became an ardent sports fan, demanding from his handlers at Intourist, "I want to go to Tashkent for the game." At first, the officials resisted, but Katz insisted, paying a premium for the ticket to Tashkent.

He arrived on a Thursday and attended the game. The next morning, he headed to his real destination. Playing tourist, he went to the old market and slowly found his way to the Bukharan[23] Synagogue nearby. Friday evening, he returned for services and discovered a small group. It had been a long time since Chabad emissaries from outside the USSR had penetrated so deep into Russia. The Chassidim in this isolated province were very suspicious of the American religious Jew. Katz volunteered to lead the services. "I acted like a cantor from America, everyone would see me; I knew if I led the services it would give them hope." After services, the regular Cantor, Levi Pressman, approached Katz. "Let's walk and talk," he said. The streets were dark, a street light every few blocks. Pressman walked with Katz telling him that the Chabad underground had communicated with them. "We heard you were coming, we received postcards telling us something good was coming." He told him that if anyone came near to them as they walked they should sing melodies like two cantors. The next day, Katz attended services again, but fear was still in the air and few approached him. Michael Veshedsky,[24] a young Chassid, came close to the synagogue around noon. Discovering a ring of KGB agents, he stayed away.

Saturday night after the conclusion of the Sabbath, Katz spied a couple on the street in front of his hotel. "Pressman had told me that someone might come to give me a message." He stepped out on the sidewalk, and the women whispered in Hebrew, "First to the right and then to the left." They began to walk parallel on different sides of the darkened streets meandering in the direction of the Old Market and the synagogue. They weaved along the streets verifying that they had lost the KGB surveillance in the dark. When they finally paused, the young couple questioned Katz about relatives in Brooklyn. He told them about their families. He had some printed material, teachings from the Rebbe. They told him, "Leave it on a bench and continue walking toward the marketplace."

After they disappeared into the shadows, another man emerged. "Follow me," he ordered, and they walked between the streets to the outskirts of the town to the Oldmark, an ancient marketplace. The older man instructed Katz to lie down in a dark area of grass, head to head, warning him, "If you hear footsteps, we will quietly roll away in opposite directions." Who are you, he asked. "Binyomin Katz, the Rebbe's shliach to find people like you and help them get visas to leave Russia." The man identified himself as Rabbi Lazer Nanes;[25] for twenty years he had been imprisoned by the Communists, never having transgressed a Sabbath during that time. Still he was skeptical. Katz finally calmed him, "I know your brother-in-law in Montreal, Rabbi Moshe Newmark. He has three daughters, Nechama, Nacha, and Batsheva. His wife's name is Luba. I was a student in the Yeshiva in Montreal and would eat at their Shabbat table."

Nanes had been trying to leave Russia for a while. When family members sent him needed information for visa requests, the Russian censor blotted out the page. Katz had been carrying a verbal message to Reb Lazer from Israel with instructions about how the visa documents should be prepared.

Nanes faded into the night, and suddenly two sets of hands grabbed Katz. Alone, in the dark, in the hands of others, he was terrified, fearing that this could be his final moment. He heard a voice in Yiddish telling him not to fear. Katz recognized the voice; it was similar to a person he knew in Montreal. Astonishing those holding him, he said, "Mochkin."

"How do you know my name?" came the voice in the night. "I know a Mochkin voice, I know your father Peretz and your brothers Laibel and Berel and even your mother Henya," Katz answered.

Yossel Mochkin and Michael Veshedsky[26] told Katz that they had been watching him since he arrived in Tashkent. Both were in their twenties and had served time in prison. They worried that he was a KGB plant. Veshedsky told him, "On Shabbat, I approached the synagogue but found the streets around it full of KGB agents. Your arrival seemed too good, a man flashing a lot of money, with an expensive camera, offering to help his fellow Jews." They had searched his hotel room, seen his religious observance, and kept him under constant surveillance. Yossel Mochkin told Katz, "We couldn't take a chance; what if you had been sent by the KGB to catch us?"

The next day Binyomin Katz returned to the synagogue. A group of Chassidim waited for him. They prayed together and he shared with them some of the Rebbe's teachings and taught them Chassidic melodies. A crowd gathered. Quietly, he was warned, "Informers are in the courtyard of the synagogue." Binyomin decided a ruse was crucial; he began to do somersaults, laughing as he jumped around the courtyard. The Russian spies turned away from the antics of this daffy American tourist.

From Russia, Katz traveled back to Scandinavia. There, he was told of the details of the second part of his mission, and he was dispatched to Israel. The Russian government was quietly permitting limited numbers of Jews to immigrate to Israel under a plan of Family Reunification. To qualify, a Russian citizen had to receive an invitation from a family member abroad. Chabad leaders in Israel arranged access to the population registry. In post offices across the country, Katz spent months poring over records looking for names of Jews in Israel that matched those in Russia. Each person who initiated a request to their newly found relatives in Russia had to be vetted. The Communist Party was still active in Israel,[27] and there was a fear that some of the Russians still had loyalties to the Soviet homeland. After the background check, they were approached and asked to help Russian Jews immigrate. Applications were submitted to the Russian embassy, then in Tel Aviv. Jews in Russian towns discovered they had new relatives in Israel with the same name and at times from the same region and city. Hundreds of Jews arrived in Israel in the next year, surreptitiously, without publicity or fanfare.

Time and again Binyomin Katz was instructed that his mission was to be considered an absolute secret. No one knew he had been in Russia. He never told his family the true reason for his trip to Israel that lasted almost a year. A few years after returning to the US, he accompanied Professor Velvel Greene[28] to a speaking engagement about Chabad. The Soviet Jewry Movement was gaining steam in the late sixties. An audience member pestered the Professor why Chabad was not involved in the demonstrations against Russia. The Rebbe had told his followers and other Jewish leaders that the public demonstrations in the US were counterproductive. Finally Katz stated, "The Rebbe does what he can." A few days later, Rabbi Hodakov summoned Binyomin to his office and chastised him for saying even that much. "You broke the code of secrecy."

While American Jewry was increasing its public activism against the Russian government's treatment of Soviet Jewry, Chabad's

secret efforts continued. Groups like Ezras Achim,[29] Chama, and, in
later years, Shamir – all Chabad-backed organizations – continued to
send packages to Soviet refuseniks with food and marketable goods
that could be sold in Russia to sustain families. Rabbis, scholars,
and activists masquerading as tourists continued to make the secret
trips to Russia. While other groups attempted to seize the headlines,
Chabad shipped tons of matza to Soviet Jews, never announcing its
success. In Russia, underground Jewish schools continued to operate
in secret. Religious leaders who could leave Russia stayed to perform
key tasks with remarkable dedication.

In 1973, Rabbi Mordechai Lifshitz, the only mohel (rabbi qualified to perform circumcisions) in Moscow, was granted a short travel
permit to attend his daughter's wedding in New York. In a message,
the Rebbe asked him, "Who will be the mohel in Moscow if you
leave?" He changed his travel plans and remained in Russia, missing
his daughter's wedding.

The public campaign for Soviet Jewry in Israel had been
orchestrated by the Lishkat Hakesher,[30] the Liaison Office in the
Prime Minister's Office that coordinated the clandestine efforts in
Russia. Nechemia Levanon had been tasked with this project after his
deportation from Russia. With time, this small undertaking would
evolve into a public campaign that included major demonstrations
on behalf of Soviet Jewry in the US and around the world. American
Jews were not aware that the Israeli government was behind these
events.[31] This policy of public confrontation put the Israelis in direct
conflict[32] with their partners in Russia, Chabad.

The Rebbe was adamant that the public demonstrations were
causing the Russian government to hunker down, limiting immigration and freedom for Jewish religious activity in Russia. It came to
a head in 1969. Yoram Dinstein,[33] the Lishkat Hakesher agent[34] in
the Israeli Consulate in New York, was invited to meet the Rebbe.
When he entered the office after 11:00 p.m., he said, "I was astonished."
The Rebbe had opened the conversation, saying, "I understand you
are responsible for the issues of Soviet Jewry; how is Shaul Avigur?"
Dinstein says, "No rabbi in the US knew who Shaul Avigur[35] was.
The people I dealt with in the American Jewish community thought

I worked for the Foreign Minister. No one imagined I was an agent of the intelligence services." Dinstein says the Rebbe knew about the small wave of immigration from the Soviet Union that had started. "This was kept secret not to antagonize the Russians." The Rebbe asked Dinstein to transmit a vital message to the Israeli government. "The Rebbe wanted us to suspend the demonstrations for a period of time. He believed that this would cause thousands of Jews to be permitted to leave." Dinstein said, "I told the Rebbe that this suggestion has merit but I did not imagine that Avigur would agree." He told me, "I am sure that Avigur will consult with the higher-ups in the government." Dinstein was convinced that Avigur would discuss the issue with Prime Minister Levi Eshkol.

Dinstein says that Israel's embassy in Moscow had been the hub of its intelligence work in Russia. "From there, our agents had contact with Russian Jews." After the Six-Day War in 1967, the Russians cut diplomatic relations with Israel, and the Mossad was handicapped. "Israel had very limited direct contact, other than news stories, reports from friendly diplomats and some messages from Jews in Russia." Dinstein says that Chabad did not have these restraints. "The Rebbe had a full network that reached deep into Russia." The Israelis thought the Rebbe's network had made a tentative deal with the Russians. "We came to the conclusion that the Rebbe, or his agents, already hinted to the Russians of the possibility that there was what to talk about."

Two weeks later, Dinstein was notified from Jerusalem that the demonstrations would not be halted. Due to the seriousness of the issue, he asked Nechemia Levanon, the Lishkat Hakesher agent in the embassy in Washington, to join him in the second trip to Brooklyn. This time, they entered the Rebbe's office after 1:00 a.m.

The meeting was tense.[36] Levanon describes the encounter: "The Rebbe told us that five thousand Jews will leave Russia soon, including families and children; he felt nothing should be done that could endanger this." Levanon says the Rebbe claimed that even Shaul Avigur was against continuing the demonstrations, but there were other political concerns of the Israeli government concerning East-West tension that were impacting their decisions. The Rebbe said,

"I can understand this desire, but at least hold off on the demonstrations for a few months to allow this group to immigrate." The Rebbe asked that his request be relayed to the government a second time. Ten days later, Prime Minister Eshkol, unfortunately, passed away.[37] The new prime minister, Golda Meir, was not as willing to acquiesce to the Rebbe's request, and the demonstration took place as planned.

Two years later, the Rebbe went public when the issues emerged again. In a searing talk in the winter of 1971,[38] he lamented the fact that "those who organize the demonstrations" had not halted them two years earlier. At the time, we who listened[39] to the talk thought that he was referring to the American Jewish groups that were leading the demonstrations. No one imagined that he was really talking about the Israeli government.[40] The Rebbe recalled that he had asked the organizers to defer the massive protest scheduled for just before Passover. "I asked them to push off the demonstration to after Shavuot, for two months." The Rebbe described the tragic results of their refusal: "Hundreds of families who had emigration permits in their hands are until today in the Soviet Union. The situation has deteriorated even more, some lost their jobs, some had to leave their homes, because the Russian government thought they were connected to the demonstrations." Bitterly, he said, "The organizers of the demonstrations are playing with the lives of three million Jews."

The policy disagreement between the Rebbe and the Israeli government did not dampen the Rebbe's personal connections with government officials. Levanon recalls that a few months after their contentious meeting, "a package of handmade shmura matza (matza whose production has been watched from the beginning) with the Rebbe's blessing arrived for me at the Embassy in Washington just before Passover." Yehoshua Porat,[41] an Israeli agent in Russia and later in New York, says, "Even if the Rebbe did not agree with our tactics and even fought against them, in numerous operations we received the Rebbe's support. We helped Chabad and we worked together many times."[42]

Some of Chabad's secret activity in Russia was being coordinated by Ezras Achim (literally, helping our brothers) in Brooklyn. The organization was inspired by Reb Mendel Futerfas. After escaping Russia in the early sixties, Futerfas asked the Rebbe if he should have remained in Russia to continue the struggle. In response, he was told he should help Russian Jewry from overseas. Reb Mendel encouraged a group of Russian refugees in Brooklyn led by Rabbi Moshe Levertov and Rabbi Gedalia Korf to create an organization to help Russian Jewry. They had operated in the Jewish underground in Russia and they transferred their tradecraft to the US. Initially they started sending packages. Levertov explained in an interview: "We couldn't send money, so we bought items that could be sold on the Russian black market, like cameras, tape recorders, and clothing." Refuseniks invariably lost their jobs when they applied for visas, so the money they received from selling the goods from overseas sustained them in the darkest of times.

Dozens of emissaries were dispatched to Russia – yeshiva students, rabbis, and just regular Americans masquerading as tourists. They visited Jews and brought religious items. They cast a wide net looking for people who would volunteer. Levertov describes the efforts: "We sent material with Peter Himmelman, the son-in-law of the famous singer, Bob Dylan. We once sent packages with some people from Hollywood who went to make a movie in Russia." They would smuggle in Jewish books, but that posed a special challenge. "New books always aroused suspicion. My wife would spill coffee on them to make them appear old and used and were just being carried by the passengers for their personal reading." He says that emissaries sent to Russia were not allowed to have lists of contacts; "they had to memorize them or write them in code."

There was a risk of arrest. "It was no simple matter to arrest a tourist who held a foreign passport, but there were a few instances in which the KGB dared to arrest shluchim. Rabbi Leibel Schapiro and his wife once went to Odessa, where they were constantly under surveillance and were questioned by the KGB. Professor Yitzchok Block was harassed by the KGB for making contact with Russian citizens in Kharkov."

The major American Jewish organizations[43] operated in a public confrontational approach that the Israeli government covertly orchestrated. Ezras Achim functioned in total secrecy. More than once, suspicions had been raised that the long arm of the KGB reached into Brooklyn. To preserve secrecy, Levertov would not meet with the Rebbe at 770. Instead, he waited at the entrance of the Crown Heights mikvah, where he would be able to speak with the Rebbe without any public attention, and relay messages to and from Russia.[44] Fundraising was done surreptitiously. Donors were told they could not disclose whom they were supporting.

In April 1985, just three weeks after Mikhail Gorbachev became the leader of Russia, the Rebbe asked to meet with Professor Herman Branover,[45] a prominent Soviet academic at Ben Gurion University in Israel who was a devoted Chassid of the Rebbe. He was also the leader of Shamir, a Chabad organization that assisted Russian Jews. Professor Branover was astonished by the message that the Rebbe asked him to transmit to Jews in Russia.

"The Rebbe asked me to inform Jews on the other side of the Iron Curtain that the Communist era would soon be over and the Soviet Union would cease to exist. A new period was beginning in which Jews would be free to immigrate to Israel – or, if they chose, to live in Russia, without any restrictions on religious freedom."

The Rebbe asked that the information should be withheld from the press, but be shared with Jews in Russia to give them hope. Branover started calling contacts in Russia, but "they were very skeptical; one Jew told me that his wife was brought in for questioning the day before by the KGB, and there was a car outside monitoring them while we spoke on the phone." Branover informed the Rebbe of the disbelief he had encountered. The Rebbe responded, "The process of change is not yet apparent, but there is no doubt."

After the breakup of the Soviet Union, Mikhail Gorbachev was honored,[46] in June 1992, by Ben Gurion University in Be'er Sheva, Israel. Branover, a prominent Russian faculty member, was asked to escort Gorbachev during his visit, and he told Gorbachev the story: "Seven years ago, the Lubavitcher Rebbe told me to inform Russian Jews that soon a new era of freedom was coming."[47] Gorbachev was surprised, saying, "This is not possible. When I took office, I had no intention to liberalize Russia. In fact my plans were the opposite. The idea of Glasnost was for outside consumption only, to remove pressure from the West." Gorbachev told Branover that he was not going to allow Jewish immigration. "Only later did I change my mind."

Later when Gorbachev visited Oxford, Peter Kalms,[48] a Chabad activist from London, told him the same story of the Rebbe's instructions to Branover. Gorbachev responded, "How did he know if I didn't know?"

What others could not have imagined, the Rebbe envisioned. As the wall came down and the Soviet Union dissolved, the next phase for Chabad would begin in Russia. After decades, the clandestine network that kept Judaism alive would come out of the cold. Into the mix, the Rebbe would send a team to create a Jewish Russian revolution, Jewish rebirth on a scale and timeline never witnessed in history.

Chapter Ten

Out of the Shadows

Berel Lazar[1] was a rabbinical student in Brooklyn who had grown up hearing the stories of Russian Chassidim and their encounters with the KGB. It was 1987 and there were whispers about senior students in the yeshiva who had been dispatched on secret missions to Russia. He had always harbored a hope of going, but you could not apply, you had to be selected.

Berel (Shlomo DovBer Pinchas is his full name) grew up in Italy. His parents, Rabbi Moshe and Henya, were Americans who moved there as shluchim in 1960. Before coming to Italy, Berel's father founded Chabad's first overnight camp, Gan Israel, in the Catskill Mountains in the late fifties. In Milano, he was principal of the local day school and Rabbi of the Persian Jewish community. It was a home deeply rooted in Chassidic values. Lazar was by nature studious and reserved. At sixteen, he left home to attend yeshiva in the US. By the late eighties, Lazar was excelling in his studies in Chabad's most advanced yeshiva at 770.

In 1987, when Berel Lazar was 23, an Ezras Achim activist stopped him on the streets of Crown Heights, and asked, "Would you like to go to Russia?" Lazar was excited by the request, and responded, "What do I have to do?" He was told, "You need permission from your parents, the yeshiva administration, and the Rebbe." Lazar called his parents in Milano, and they agreed. Years later, they told him, "We realized this was not just a one-time visit; in the end, you would go to Russia for life." After collecting all three approvals, Lazar headed for the address he had been given. It was a non-descript basement tucked under a house on Lefferts Avenue in Crown Heights. He was told, "Your trip will be on this day, bring your American passport to make a visa." Lazar says, "Everything was very clandestine."

When people were sent to Russia, they were always sent in pairs. Yona Shur, another New York yeshiva student, was coupled with Lazar. Members of Ezras Achim prepared them for their trip. They were told to memorize lists of addresses, and guided about how to approach customs in the Moscow airport. As they departed the American airliner, the two young men separated, acting as if there was no connection between them. Nevertheless, individually they were grilled. "I was questioned for two hours," Lazar says, "the intention was to scare us. They wanted to send the message that they know what we are here for and they are following us." The surveillance did not end at the airport. "It was clear they were listening to our conversations in the hotel room. When we said we needed toilet paper, shortly afterward, someone turned up at the door with a new supply."

The men's first meeting in Moscow was with the legendary Reb Getche Wilensky. Getche was the coordinator of the Chabad underground in Moscow. Rabbi Lazar described him as "a true tzadik, a righteous man." They sat together until 3:00 a.m., singing songs and telling stories. This was Lazar's first encounter with poverty in Russia. "Reb Getche's wife served some soup with a piece of chicken in it." She offered the soup several times, and finally, Lazar told her, "I'm not going to eat the soup." He thought the main course was still coming. Later, he learned this was the main course, and it was a rare occasion to serve meat of any kind. "It was really canned meat that they saved for a special occasion, for a shliach of the Rebbe." Years later, Berel told me, "I feel regret for not eating the soup that evening."

In Moscow, Lazar discovered the modest wooden Marina Roscha Shul. Two generations occupied the shul, Lazar said, "the old and the young." The old were tired after more than a half century of Communism, worn down by years of oppression and surveillance, desperately clinging to Judaism. The young wanted to learn about their heritage, long repressed by the Communists. "The thirst for knowledge was unquenchable." Lazar and Shur taught classes incessantly. "People would learn until 1:00 a.m." Despite the poverty, they said, "Don't give us food; we will manage without. Give us books instead." Danger still lurked since "the KGB had control of the shuls." And it was difficult to know whom the KGB had intimidated into turning informer.

The trip changed Lazar's life. "I fell in love with the Russian Jews. We were like brothers." In the next two years, Lazar would return to Russia two more times as a yeshiva student. Between trips, he would help them from abroad, sending packages and medicines. Lazar said, "People called me and begged me to return." By the time he reached age twenty-five, Lazar wanted to go to Russia for a fourth time. This time, the Rebbe was opposed. "He would not give me permission until I got married." His whole life was focused on the Russian Jews and, jokingly, he said, "If the Rebbe had not pushed, I would never have gotten married."

Lazar married Chani Deren from Pittsburgh in 1989. Her grandfather was Rabbi Shalom Posner, the pioneer shliach in Pittsburgh. Her parents were Rabbi Yechezkel and Keny[2] Deren, second-generation shluchim, also in Pittsburgh. Chani[3] says she realized Berel's dream when they were dating, and she confided to her mother, "He might really want to go to Russia." Her mother responded confidently, "Then that's where you're going to go." Chani says her mother's sense of duty to the Rebbe's mission was the central motif of her life. This allayed her trepidation.

A week after the wedding the young couple wrote to the Rebbe volunteering to go to Russia. Chani says the Rebbe's response seemed more directed to her: they should stay for a year in a community where there is a religious group of women. Berel says it was clear the Rebbe wanted them to have one year living in a more stable environment before they set out on what would be a difficult mission. They set up house in Brooklyn; Chani worked and Berel joined the kolel, the institute for advanced studies. It was the beginning of Glasnost, a Soviet policy permitting open discussion of political and social issues and freer dissemination of news and information, initiated by leader, Mikhail Gorbachev. A new era was dawning in Russia. "When the year was up, a lot of people wanted to go to Russia; six or seven couples wrote to the Rebbe, but only three of us got permission to go," said Berel.

The Lazars headed to Moscow, and for the first time in half a century, the Marina Roscha Synagogue would have a rabbi. A few months earlier, Rabbi Shmulik Kaminetsky and his wife Chani had been sent to Dnepropetrovsk, and Rabbi Moshe Meir Moscowitz shortly afterward to Kharkov.

Moving to Russia was a major change for Chani Lazar, born and bred in Pittsburgh. She says, "There was less than nothing in Russia at the time." It was the beginning of Perestroika, a political movement for reformation within the Communist Party of the Soviet Union during the 1980s, and the shops were empty. Everything had to be brought in from overseas. Before they left the US, they prepared a large container full with goods and food. As they landed in Moscow, she gazed down from the airplane. "My first thought was my grandmother, who would tell me many stories about how hard it was for her to get out of this place and now I am coming in." At first, living conditions were very bad: "bed bugs, apartments full of mice and cockroaches." Their apartment in Moscow was robbed. Even when her family sent clothes from overseas, she opened the package and found only one item. "There was a hole on the side, they had pulled everything out." Other than what they brought in the container, "we had no food." Meat and chicken were very rare. Sometimes we had shechitah (kosher meat slaughter). On Shabbos, I had one chicken and whatever vegetables we could find in the market."

Ezras Achim had guaranteed to cover the budget. Berel Lazar said, "When we first came to Russia, a dollar in America was a hundred rubles here. You could buy the world." However, the dollar lost its value, Lazar realized, and "we couldn't depend on the money from the outside anymore; we needed to raise our own money here, and take care of our people." It was clear that the limited resources of Ezras Achim in Brooklyn could not build Judaism in all of Russia. He reminisced, "When I got married, I said to my wife, 'We should go to Russia for two reasons: there is no need to raise money and there is no politics.'"

There had already been important grassroots efforts by local Russians. Rabbi Zev Kuravsky had founded a Chabad school in Moscow housed in the Choral Synagogue. The legendary Rabbi Itche Kogan had been instrumental in strengthening Jewish life.[4]

An immense task still lay ahead. For seventy years, Communism had been dominant. In most cities, synagogues were closed and Jewish schools were nonexistent, nor were there communal institutions or structure. The prime public expression of Jewish identity was the annual gathering of Jews outside synagogues for Simchat Torah.

As the walls of the Iron Curtain were falling, most Jews who felt a Jewish connection were immigrating to Israel, the US, and some to Germany. Those left behind didn't have the desire, ability, or the sense of connection to leave. Some were drawn by the business opportunities in the new Russia. Many were elderly and poor. To the younger generation, Judaism was just a distant memory.

Rabbi Lazar was not aware that the Rebbe was setting the stage for a coming revolution in Russia, moving the players on the board who would stand beside him in rebuilding Jewish life. Berel Lazar would be the general; his first lieutenants would, in time, become Russian-born Baruch Gorin and Alexander Sasha Barada. The venture capital that would be the catalyst for growth would come from the generosity of Lev Leviev and the Rohr family. With time, Lazar, Gorin, and Barada would build connections with political leaders, in particular Russian president, Vladimir Putin. Together, they would build a communal infrastructure that would reach from Saint Petersburg in Russia's western border to Vladivostok nestled on the Pacific Ocean.

As the Soviet Union broke apart, they would ensure that in each of the countries that emerged, from Uzbekistan to Latvia, synagogues, schools, and soup kitchens would be established. They would have to find the rabbis and rebbitzens to lead this renaissance. Never before in Jewish history had a community emerged from repression to vitality in such a short time. As Lev Leviev told the leader of the Reform Movement, Rabbi Rick Jacobs,[5] when Leviev was introduced as the person who built Judaism in Russia, "It was the Rebbe who did it."

Alexander Sasha Barada[6] grew up in a home with what he calls Jewish Pride. On Passover, they had matza, but not much else. The details of Jewish observance had been dulled by Communism. Serving on a Russian aircraft carrier, he told his shipmates he was Jewish, but he had no idea what that meant. After the military, he decided to study, and he attended classes in Marina Roscha, only to discover that his grandmother, who passed away when he was five, had frequented the synagogue. The learning brought a change in his life. "After two years, I was fully observant," he said. Jews were leaving the Soviet Union in great numbers in the early nineties, many to Israel, others to the US and Germany. In 1992, Barada traveled to New York for the Jewish holidays. He decided to ask the Rebbe's advice. He was surprised, he said, when "the Rebbe told me to return to Russia." With time, he would earn a rabbinical ordination and become rabbi of the flourishing synagogue located in the posh Zhukovka neighborhood of Moscow. Barada understood the local scene and the Russian mentality. He built bridges to the Russian business and political world that were essential in developing the local financial resources to rebuild Judaism. Barada accompanied Lazar on many of his visits to political leaders like President Vladimir Putin and Prime Minister Dmitry Medvedev.

Barada's partner would be Baruch Gorin, a classic Russian intellectual, a man of books and ideas. At the age of sixteen, he left home in Odessa to join the yeshiva in Marina Roscha. Thirty young Russians were enrolled. He[7] said, "They were students who came from the university, brilliant minds who studied twenty hours a day." There were no proper facilities. "I slept in the shul," he said. "And the food was kasha and more kasha." Yet, it was a magical time. The Iron Curtain was falling. The curiosity of the younger generation was unleashed.

Gorin's parents were planning to immigrate to the us. He, too, wanted to leave Russia, but the Rebbe saw the future differently. Just like Sasha Barada, Gorin was surprised when the Rebbe told him to return to Russia. In time, Gorin would launch Russia's first post-Communist Jewish publishing house, which translated the Jewish classics, like the Torah and Maimonides, into Russian. He would become the director of Russia's most important Jewish cultural institution, the world-class Jewish Museum in Moscow.

When Lazar moved permanently to Moscow in 1990, he discovered internal conflict in Marina Roscha. Baruch Gorin describes the mood. "Lazar found an old generation and a younger one. The older Chassidim were scared to speak; everything was a secret." Barada says they thought Communism would still prevail. They told us, "In two or three years, the KGB will be back." Gorin explains that the younger generation lacked direction. "They would quarrel over a piece of chocolate or ten dollars given by the Joint."[8]

Rabbi Lazar provided the desperately needed leadership. Gorin describes the change. "When Berel came, he was the Rebbe's man." In particular for the younger generation, "Berel Lazar became their general."

Sasha and Baruch were essential in helping the Italian-born American, Berel Lazar, to navigate the political, social, and financial challenges in Russia. He had the vision, drive, and mandate from the Rebbe. They had the local street smarts that were essential in building a Jewish community from the ground up in a country undergoing major political, social, and economic change.

Sasha and Baruch started their first project together, publishing a monthly Jewish magazine, *L'Chaim*, for Russian Jews. Barada sold subscriptions and raised the money for the project; Gorin was the writer and editor. That pattern of partnership would continue for decades.

Barada and Gorin, working with Lazar, began to rebuild from the bottom up. They organized Shabbat dinners. "Little by little, a community began to evolve." The first Passover Seder drew sixty people. Those who came were the upwardly mobile in the new Russian society. They did not want to leave. They were the young people who started to go into business, and they drew closer to Judaism. Dmitry Perkoviv,[9] a Russian journalist, who, for years, reported for the Israeli media, including *Kol Israel*, closely observed the vicissitudes in Russia. He explains, "Chabad returned to Jews their history and tradition." With time, this core evolved into a new community in post-Communist Russia.

In December of 1990, Jewish pride took a leap forward in Russia. For the first time, a menorah lighting was held in the Kremlin. Jewish communities around the world were linked by satellite as they watched on TV menorah lightings[10] in over ten cites in Russia, including Moscow. Around the world, thousands saw Rabbi Avrohom Genen,[11] the legendary Mohel of Moscow, light the menorah in the great patriotic hall of the Kremlin. The Rebbe's speech in his synagogue in Brooklyn was broadcast live inside the walls of the Kremlin.

It would take massive financial resources to quickly propel Judaism forward in Russia. Two crucial players would provide the venture capital: Lev Leviev, the billionaire diamond magnate from Israel, and the father-and-son-team of Sami and George Rohr.

Leviev had grown up in Soviet-controlled Uzbekistan. His family came from the Bukharan community, Sephardi Jews, steadfast with tradition, whose roots reached back thousands of years. Chabad had a century-old connection with the region. Shluchim had been dispatched to Uzbekistan by the Fifth Rebbe, Rabbi Sholom DovBer, in the beginning of the twentieth century. Leviev spoke of his family experience in a speech at the shluchim convention. "A hundred years ago, the Fifth Rebbe, Rabbi Sholom DovBer, sent a shliach to Samarkand in Uzbekistan." Leviev explained that the challenges then were not much different from those facing the shluchim today. The local community resisted the idea of enhancing Jewish education. That shliach persevered and set up a school in Samarkand. One of his students was Leviev's grandfather, and the education he received formed the foundation for his Jewish identity. "The Jewish community in Samarkand had its greatest challenge during Communism when many gave up their observance. Those who had studied with the shliach years earlier kept Judaism alive in Samarkand." The KGB persecuted them, but they did not capitulate. "They were all sent to

Siberia for twenty-five years. One of those who was imprisoned was my grandfather Zevulun." (Their sentences were commuted five years later when Stalin died.) For Leviev, the family history of Jewish leadership under adversity was his inspiration and led to his partnership with Chabad. "If the Rebbe had not sent a shliach to Samarkand a century ago, I would not be standing here today."

Leviev's father, Avner, was his role model. Despite the danger posed by the KGB, he was a prime financial supporter of the underground Jewish educational network in Uzbekistan. "Every month Rabbi Simcha Gorodetsky would come and my father would give him money for the schools." After Avner Leviev left Russia, he visited the Rebbe in New York; he wanted to pursue a career in Jewish education in Israel. The Rebbe told him to continue the family tradition. "Open a business and support the schools."

In 1971 when Lev was fifteen, the family immigrated to Kiryat Malachi in Israel's south. He attended yeshiva in nearby Lod, but academics were not his strength. He apprenticed as a diamond cutter. When Leviev finished his military service, he went into the diamond business. In time, he would shatter the monopoly of the South African company De Beers in the diamond industry. Today Leviev is one of the wealthiest Jews in Israel.

Leviev[12] would be propelled into a crucial leadership role in Russian Jewry after an encounter he had with the Rebbe on a Sunday morning in February of 1989. On Sundays, thousands[13] would file by the Rebbe who would dispense blessings, advice, and dollar bills to be given to charity. The Rebbe shared a mitzvah with each person. Lev Leviev stood in the dollar line with thousands of others hoping to be able to ask a quick question. The Soviet Union was opening up; there were many business opportunities. Should he take a risk in the new Russia? Leviev spoke to the Rebbe in Russian, the Rebbe answered in the same language, telling Leviev that he should use the profits to help Russian Jewry. "In the best way and with health according to the family tradition to help Jews in Bukhara, Georgia, and all the countries where there had been persecution." The Rebbe contrasted the freedoms of life in Israel and the plight of Jews under Communist rule. "You are in a country where there is no persecution and you can observe Torah and mitzvot. Those there [referring to Russia] were not permitted to observe them." The Rebbe concluded by telling him to follow his family practice of philanthropy. "It should be with great success and the primary thing is it should be magnanimous, your charitable giving."

A year later, Leviev returned on a Sunday morning. The Rebbe again encouraged Leviev to give, telling him about his family: "They had a tradition of giving in Russia large amounts of charity." Leviev promised the Rebbe, "I will continue," to which the Rebbe responded, prodding him to think even bigger, "to continue and to do even more."

Leviev began his business investments and looked for partners for rebuilding Jewish life in the former Soviet Union. The Rebbe had given no specific instructions, expecting Leviev to use his good business sense to find the best places to invest his charitable dollars. Leviev asked a rosh yeshiva – dean of a Lithuanian-style yeshiva in B'nai Brak that he supported – to send some of the kolel[14] couples to Russia. The dean told Leviev that the young couples in his yeshiva feared leaving their religious cocoon. The rejection by the rabbi in B'nai Brak left Leviev very disappointed. "No one wanted to come. It was like I found diamonds but I had no one to cut them." He was looking for a partner, and finally, he said, when in Moscow once, "I met Berel Lazar."

Their first encounter was in Moscow in 1994. Lazar didn't know much about Lev Leviev, only that he was a successful Israeli businessman with a Chabad background. Lazar invited Lev to a bris (a circumcision ceremony) at the Marina Roscha synagogue. Afterward, Lazar made his pitch. He wanted Leviev to help cover the monthly budget of $18,000. He was having a tough time finding the money. Leviev says he saw "a young naïve rabbi, just getting started." A few days later, he got back to Lazar. "You continue to cover the $18,000; I will take care of the rest." Their first joint project was a summer camp. Leviev committed $35,000 to cover the expenses.

He was diversifying his investments, carefully watching the returns. That summer, Leviev also sponsored a second, non-Chabad Orthodox camp in Moscow. It had the same number of kids as Lazar's camp, and double the budget. When Lazar's camp went over its tight budget, Lazar went to Leviev and said, "We made a deal. You took care of your part. I will find the money to cover the deficit." Leviev realized that with Rabbi Lazar he had a reliable partner, and from then on, the sky was the limit.

Leviev's prime concern was Jewish education. He knew that after seven decades of Communism, Judaism was just a distant memory. He says that at the time, "The taxi driver would tell you, 'I am Jewish,' the government bureaucrat would tell you, 'I am Jewish.' But after Communism, they knew nothing." Leviev believed that only by creating a system of Jewish schools would a new generation of Jews in Russia have a strong identity. If he didn't act, "yet another generation would be lost."

He started opening schools, naming them after his father, "Ohr Avner," "the Light of Avner." In 1995, Lazar brought in Rabbi Dovid Mondshine[15] to coordinate the growing system. Mondshine was an Israeli who came first to Russia in 1992. Lev encouraged the shluchim, telling them, "You start the school and I will underwrite the expense." In many ways it was much easier than the challenges facing shluchim in the US and other countries. In most cities in Russia, the Chabad rabbis were the only rabbinic leadership. Leviev had political connections that helped protect the rabbis from capricious government officials. Rabbi Mayer Stambler,[16] director of the Teachers Seminary in Dnepropetrovsk that trains educators for the Ohr Avner system, explains: "He pushed us to get more kids, and to expand the schools. Budget was not a consideration."

The other key supporters would become Sami Rohr and his son, George. Sami, Chabad's prime backer in Colombia, began investing in Latvia in the early nineties. He saw a business opportunity in the falling of Communism. In 1991, he wrote to the Rebbe with the suggestion of sending a shliach to Riga, the capital of Latvia. Rabbi Mordechai Glazman and his wife, Rivka, were dispatched with the underwriting of Sami. Rivka Glazman[17] wrote years later, "We did not realize that we were getting not only a one-time sponsor but a lifelong friend and partner in our shlichus." As the investments spread throughout Russia, spearheaded eventually by Sami's son, George, the

Rohrs undertook the sponsorship of rabbis across Russia, paying the salaries of over a hundred rabbis. With Leviev pushing the shluchim to build schools, and Rohr ensuring they had the means to live, there was no holding back the growth of Chabad in Russia.

As Lazar was starting out in Moscow, other shluchim were putting down roots in other cities. Shmulik Kaminetsky and his wife, Chani, became the first rabbi and rebbitzen in Dnepropetrovsk in Ukraine in half a century. He arrived in the summer of 1990, a few months before Lazar came to Moscow. Dnepropetrovsk had special historical significance to Chabad. The Rebbe grew up in the city. His father, Rabbi Levi Yitzchak Schneerson, had been the city's last chief rabbi, assuming the post in 1909.

Rabbi Levi Yitzchak Schneerson, a renowned scholar and kabbalist, was the great-grandson of Chabad's Third Rebbe, Rabbi Menachem Mendel.[18] His strident defense of Judaism prompted his arrest in March of 1939 by the Communist secret police. They turned up at 3:00 a.m. and ransacked his home. He endured a year of torture and interrogations. Finally, after a show trial in Moscow, he was exiled to the remote village of Chili in distant Kazakhstan. After a long period of uncertainty, his wife, Rebbitzen Chana,[19] discovered his whereabouts. She undertook the arduous trip to Kazakhstan to care for her husband. The conditions in the village were dreadful, and the exile had adversely affected his health.[20] When the sentence ended in 1944, the couple relocated further east to the city of Alma Ata, a few hundred miles from the Chinese border. He was already very weak, and he passed away that summer. Using false papers, the Schneerson name a red flag to authorities, Rebbitzen Chana Schneerson eventually made her way through Russia. In 1947, she was smuggled out of Russia during the Great Escape and finally reunited with her son in Paris. She spent the last seventeen years of her life in Brooklyn, near her son, the Rebbe.

Chani Kaminetsky[21] came from a family in which shlichus was a tradition. Her grandfather was Berel Baumgarten, the early shliach in Argentina, and her uncle Michoel Lipsker had been the first shliach in Morocco. She says, "I could not think of anything else other than going on shlichus." Her husband, Shmulik, was raised in Israel, and he wanted to go, too, but "his family did not have the same tradition." Ezras Achim suggested them as candidates for Dnepropetrovsk, but Shmulik[22] was anxious. They had been married over eighteen months and still his wife was not pregnant. He felt that by committing to such a challenging place, he would receive a special blessing. Kaminetsky wrote to the Rebbe[23] that "if he will guarantee that we will have children in the way of the talmudic statement – 'a tzadik decrees and G-d fulfills' – then we would be honored to go to Dnepropetrovsk." Immediately, the Rebbe answered him that they should go. Before they left, a few months later, Chani was already pregnant.

The Kaminetskys flew to Moscow and took a seventeen-hour train ride to Dnepropetrovsk. It was in July, no one spoke English, and they did not speak Russian. Chani says, "It was hot, and there was nothing to eat or drink on the train." Exhausted, they arrived on a Thursday.

When they arrived, the Kaminetskys were not aware of the political intrigue surrounding their arrival. Two American yeshiva students, Kasriel Shemtov and Yisroel Spalter, had been in town a few months, organizing events and programs. There were over a hundred thousand Jews in town at the time, most clustered in one area. Dnepropetrovsk had been a center of the defense industry, and foreigners had been banned for decades. The presence of two young American rabbinical students had excited the community. Shemtov[24] says, "You would walk down the street with a hat and beard and everyone would say to you in Yiddish, 'Vos macht a yid?' (How is the Jew doing?)."

All the synagogues had been closed except for one small one, where Rabbi Levi Yitzchak had prayed before being arrested. Its leader opposed every step the newcomers made. Initially they thought it was just local politics, but after a while, they understood that it was the hand of the KGB. Shemtov says, "We realized he was a plant of the secret police. One shul was still open in the city, and a KGB agent ran it." It was clear that unless the KGB agent was neutralized, it would be impossible for Rabbi Kaminetsky to succeed."

Shemtov says the news that a new rabbi and rebbitzen were coming from America had electrified the community. "Rabbi Levi

Yitzchak had been exiled fifty years earlier. Those sixty and above remembered him, and those younger had heard the story. There was an excitement that one of the students of the Rebbe was coming." We told community members that "he will follow in the footsteps of Rabbi Levi Yitzchak." What really impressed the local community was the fact that "they were all dreaming of leaving, and now a rabbi from America is coming to help them."

Shemtov says they decided to strike at the height of the excitement and engineer a coup. Just a few hours after the Kaminetskys arrived – on a grueling train ride from Moscow – they came to the synagogue. "We organized an election the first day Rabbi Kaminetsky arrived. Two hundred people gathered in the small synagogue. It was packed." Feeling politically empowered, the local community stood up to the KGB agent. "He didn't get more than a few votes." Rabbi Kaminetsky was elected the first rabbi in the community in half a century. "When the KGB agent saw he was losing, he became very rowdy and disruptive." Dr. Alexandar Friedkes, a well-respected physician who would, in time, become the community president, "stood up to him, and the KGB agent never came back."

The next night was Friday and Shemtov and Spalter arranged to use a hall in the largest hotel in the center of town. It was the early days of Perestroika; the Soviet Union was falling apart. There were no products, the stores were empty. Shemtov says, "We got the hall by giving the proprietor a bottle of Smirnoff, which at the time, you couldn't find in Russia. He was so happy, he took out new dishes." There were still food shortages, so they bartered lipstick for potatoes, electronic gadgets for fish. "We exchanged a case of American cigarettes for vegetables."

Chani and Shmulik were amazed when five hundred people turned up for Shabbat dinner. They didn't speak Russian, the crowd knew no English, and the yeshiva students' vocabulary was just a few words. Still, the spirit was remarkable. That night they discovered what Shmulik calls "the special warmth of the Ukrainian Jews."

The beginning was very tough. Chani says, "We had nothing, no food, no clothes, no nothing." They did not have proper facilities. "I cooked potatoes in my hotel room. After a few weeks, we got a chicken and I plucked the feathers," Chani explained. Even though they had removed the KGB agent from the synagogue, Shmulik says, "The KGB was everywhere, they monitored us, I was followed all the time. When we tried to rent an apartment, we discovered that someone had told the owner not to take us as tenants."

When Rabbi Kaminetsky visited a local Hebrew teacher, Alex Samanski, Alex blocked the door of his apartment, telling Kaminetsky, "Please get away." Kaminetsky was surprised by the hostile reception when so many others welcomed him. He pressed Samanski for a reason, and finally, he confessed. "I was pulled into KGB headquarters for questioning and warned about Chabad. They told me a Chassidic rabbi is coming to Dnepropetrovsk, and they offered me a deal. You are Zionist and a Hebrew teacher, you will probably be asked to be his translator. We will not touch you if you will not have anything to do with the rabbi." Kaminetsky asked Samanski if he had been given a reason. "They told me that Chassidim are very dangerous since they are not afraid of anything," replied Samanski.

A few months after her arrival in Dnepropetrovsk, Chani decided to go to New York to give birth to her first child. "At the train station, the new community's president, Dr. Friedkes, brought me flowers and said good-bye." He told her that he realized how primitive the living conditions were; he could not imagine she would want to raise a child in such a difficult place. "You are a smart young woman – you will never come back," he told her. "In New York," she said, "I cried for two weeks." It was hard to communicate with her husband, who was still in Dnepropetrovsk. You had to wait three days to get a phone call from Russia; by then you forgot what you were going to say."

Chani returned with her first child. Together with her husband, they forged ahead. They always felt Dnepropetrovsk was different from any other missions undertaken by shluchim. Shmulik says, "When we came, many people still remembered the Rebbe's father and his mother, the Rebbitzen Chana. This is the Rebbe's city; I felt this should be a Lubavitcher city."

The money from Ezras Achim was slow in coming. Shmulik says, "It was very difficult. I needed to build institutions, to build the shul, a school, a center for seniors." Within a few years, he said, "I had a deficit of a million dollars; I was in a crisis." In 1995, Kaminetsky met Gennadiy Bogolyubov, a young Russian oligarch. As Kaminetsky put it, "Bogolyubov changed everything."

Bogolyubov[25] grew up in eastern Ukraine. He described his two annual childhood memories of Jewish observance. One grand-mother who was sick and housebound "fasted once a year." The other grandmother had an annual tradition. She dressed him up, invited the whole family, and served matza. No one ever told him why these traditions were being followed. In post-Communist Dnepropetrovsk, he was a successful businessman. A mutual friend asked him to meet Rabbi Kaminetsky. "He invited me to the synagogue. I had never been there before. I thought I would see something spiritual, but what impressed me most was the soup kitchen behind the shul." Twenty people were eating in conditions that, he says, "were not the best." Bogolyubov asked Rabbi Kaminetsky, "How do you really know if they really need the help? Maybe they have enough food and just want to eat for free." Kaminetsky responded, "Can you come and ask for food? If someone comes to ask, he really needs." Bogolyubov says that conversation "changed my life." The next day, he returned to the synagogue. "I gave the first $10,000." Years later, he said, "After that, I gave out the millions. Everything I can explain except for that first $10,000."

Bogolyubov was not the only major giver. Local Jews were beginning to make money in business and at the same time rediscover their Jewish roots. Kaminetsky says, "In 1998, we formed an official community with a board. Ninety people gave at least a thousand dollars a month, many giving more." It has become prestigious, Kaminetsky says. "The dream of every young Jew is to be on the community board. Today, the general budget is six million dollars a year, all raised locally." The community has also undertaken many special projects: schools, a medical clinic, senior home. The Jewish agency is supportive of the school in the community. The JDC, says Kaminetsky, "is doing a wonderful job" providing a safety net for those in need. The Jewish Federation in Boston has also been a partner in the community.

The most ambitious project was the construction of the world's largest Jewish community center, the Menorah Project. The 220,000-square-foot facility includes a museum, theaters, halls, kosher restaurants, stores, and offices. Bogolyubov and his associates underwrote the full cost of $90 million. According to Kaminetsky, the wide variety of programs nurtures Jewish life for all. "We employ almost a thousand people." Alik Nadan,[26] head of the JDC in Russia, says, "Dnepropetrovsk is the strongest Jewish community in the Former Soviet Union outside of Moscow."

In the early nineties, as the Soviet Union weakened, a wide variety of organizations, big and small, flocked there to test the waters and attempt to help Soviet Jewry. Major players were the Joint Distribution Committee and the Jewish Agency. The Joint, or JDC, is the overseas arm of American Jewry and partner of the Jewish Federation system. For almost a century, the JDC had a proud record of assisting Jews around the world. The Jewish Agency's prime agenda was promoting immigration to Israel. It, too, is supported significantly by the Jewish Federation system in the US. These groups, with a dozen other smaller organizations, jostled for space in the evolving community in Russia.

The Jewish Agency's first priority was immigration. It facilitated the move of a million Jews to Israel. While Chabad supported immigration to Israel for those who wanted, it also felt that building Jewish life in Russia was vital. The policy of community building in Russia, for those Jews choosing not to leave, put Chabad at odds with Israeli government policy.

Mark Levin,[27] head of the National Coalition Supporting Eurasian Jewry in Washington, always felt the Jewish community had a responsibility to those Jews who decided not to leave. "We don't turn our back on one of the largest Jewish communities in the world." He expressed this view from the beginning of the mass immigration, earning harsh criticism from the Israeli government and other American Jewish groups. He describes the situation after the large numbers departed Russia during the nineties. "Those Jews who wanted to make aliyah left, in particular the activists." He explains that connecting Jews with their heritage is uniquely difficult in Russia.

"We always have to remember that we are almost starting from the beginning to create a Jewish identity."

The issue of exclusively promoting aliyah or building Jewish life in Russia came to a showdown between Prime Minister Sharon, Lev Leviev, and Rabbi Berel Lazar in 2001.[28] Sharon summoned them for a meeting at his office in Jerusalem. Leviev had a long, close relationship with Sharon, but this time, the conversation was tense. The prime minister said that by building schools and synagogues in Russia they were limiting immigration to Israel. Leviev told Sharon, "Why should the Jews come to Israel where there are economic challenges and a military threat? A Jew in Russia can choose to move where he wants, be it in Germany, the US, or Israel." Leviev explained to Sharon that only through education will Jewish identity be built. "When a child in Saint Petersburg learns about Jerusalem, he will want to come to Israel." Sharon did not agree; the meeting ended very acrimoniously.

Later that year, Sharon made a trip to Russia. A group of children had traveled from the Ohr Avner school in Yekaterinburg to perform for the prime minister in Marina Roscha Synagogue.[29] He was deeply touched. Rabbi Lazar recalls, "He cried when he saw the children singing."

In the end, the Israelis adopted the Chabad approach. Rabbi Shlomie Peles,[30] who helps coordinate Leviev's philanthropy in Russia, said, "At first, the Jewish Agency put all its efforts into immigration. With time, they realized this was not working and started to focus on Jewish education." Today, the Jewish Agency in Russia is dedicating most of its resources to Jewish education, summer camps, and cultural activities.

With time, many of the overseas groups that came to Russia in the nineties full of plans and ambitions faded from view. Others continue to make vital contributions to Russian Jewry. ORT opened a network of technical schools in some Russian cities. The OU, the American Orthodox Union, helped strengthen the community in Kharkov; Agudath Israel continues to sponsor a school in Baku. Kolels and yeshivas were opened, in particular in Moscow. There were partnerships established between Israeli and Russian universities.

Other organizations initiated projects in various cities. The liberal movements also tried to find support, but their success has been marginal.

Reform Rabbi Eric Yoffie lamented his movement's limited inroads and Chabad's success in Russia to Professor Arthur Hertzberg.[31] Hertzberg told me that he said to Yoffie, "When you will have rabbis willing to move for life and live on a limited salary, then you will have success in Russia." Hertzberg said Yoffie concurred.

In 1983, Rabbi Adolf Shayevich[32] assumed the position of assistant rabbi in the Choral Synagogue. A few years later, after the passing of Rabbi Jacob Fishman, he became the head rabbi, eventually becoming known as the chief rabbi of Russia (originally backed by the Soviets, who needed a public face for Judaism in Russia). Eventually, the Russian Jewish Congress would formally endorse him for this position. He had studied in Hungary.

As the Jewish community was emerging from Communist oppression, it became clear that there was a need to unite the disparate Jewish groups in the Former Soviet Union (FSU). In late 1989, the Vaad,[33] a committee of Jewish communities, was established. This grassroots group organized a series of conferences. Internal dissension and the lack of financial support handicapped the Vaad.

Rabbi Pinchas Goldschmidt was named Chief Rabbi of Moscow in 1993. Originally from Switzerland, he was a student of the Lithuanian-styled yeshivas – Ponovitch, Telz and Ner Yisroel – noted for their historic enmity to Chassidim. The same year, Rabbi Goldschmidt founded Keroor (Congress of the Jewish Religious Organizations and Associations in Russia). He had hoped it would unite religious groups. Initially, it had some success, but in the long term, it failed to earn broad-based communal support.

In late 1996, Vladimir Gusinsky, one of the newly minted Jewish oligarchs, organized the Russian Jewish Congress, with the support of Rabbis Pinchas Goldschmidt and Adolf Shayevich. Gusinsky was a media mogul in the post-Communist era. His company, Most Media, controlled TV stations and important newspapers. He was a political kingmaker in the emerging democracy. PBS *Frontline*[34] reported that Gusinsky was crucial in electing Boris Yeltsin to a second term as Russian President. "In 1996, when a Communist-Party presidential candidate presented a real threat to Yeltsin's reelection, the rising media magnate suspended all criticism of Yeltsin. After Yeltsin won the reelection, Gusinsky was awarded the country's first private television network."

Gusinsky became the founding chairman of the Russian Jewish Congress in 1996; his key business associates took other leadership positions. Gusinsky wanted Chabad to join the congress. Together with Rabbis Goldschmidt, Shayevich, and a delegation of oligarchs, he visited Lev Leviev[35] in his Moscow home. He proposed to Leviev and Rabbi Lazar that they unite their efforts. Leviev's priority was Jewish education. Gusinsky told Leviev: "Let us make a congress; we will give unlimited money to education. I will be the president, you will be the vice-chair."

Leviev and Lazar agreed to join the Russian Jewish Congress (RJC). Gusinsky pledged to give $2 million to education; others made pledges. Leviev committed half a million. The JDC also supported the RJC, as did the Jewish Agency and other major American Jewish organizations.

The RJC's organization ambitions were big. In its first years, it invested significant resources in the construction of Poklonnaya Gora Holocaust Memorial Synagogue. It was located on Moscow's highest point, adjacent to the Russian National War Memorial. Its prominent location instilled a sense of pride for Moscow Jewry, but it was remote and, even today, it is rarely used. Many observers felt that investing the money in education and crucial communal structure would have been a much wiser idea. Dr. Betsy Gidwitz reported[36] in 1998 that the RJC claimed the cost was $8.5 million, but "others estimate its cost at between $10-17 million."

The Russian Jewish Congress was controlled by Gusinsky and his friends. As Professor Theodore Friedgut of the Jerusalem Council for Foreign Affairs[37] wrote, "Sixty percent of the budget came from only two donors, Vladimir Gusinsky, and his close associate, insurance magnate, Boris Khait."

At first, Gusinsky said that the RJC would concern itself with the welfare of the Jewish community. That changed when he began to use his position as chairman of the Russian Jewish Congress to promote his own political agenda. He controlled major media outlets in the country, and he stridently opposed government policies. Dmitry Perokoiv, an Israeli media correspondent, says, "Gusinsky knew little about Judaism and used the Jewish community to advance his interests." The Russian Jewish Congress[38] had become for Gusinsky a tool to promote his own political ambitions.

Lazar realized Gusinsky's actions posed a grave danger to the Jewish community. He said, "The Jewish community and politics don't mix." Lazar said that if Gusinsky[39] wanted to oppose government policies, he should leave the presidency of the Russian Jewish Congress, as it was dangerous to make the welfare of Russian Jews serve the business agenda of an individual. When the majority of the Congress leadership, made up of Gusinsky's business partners, voted to support his policy of political confrontation, Lazar suspended his membership. He said, "The institutions of the community should not be the patrimony of a single individual but must stand above politics and work for the advancement of Judaism in Russia." Goldschmidt and Shayevich supported Gusinsky, who was funding many of their projects.

But the future of the Jewish community could not be left up to the whims of an oligarch. Gusinsky's promises of funding Jewish education proved empty. Leviev was disheartened. He said, "In the end, no money went to education, just a few hundred thousand. I told them they were like American Jewish organizations: all talk and no action." In 1998 only $199,000 went to Jewish education out of a budget of $9 million and in 1999, things were not much better. Leviev and Lazar realized there was no future in the Gusinsky-dominated RJC. Leviev said that when he told Gusinsky the honeymoon was over, Gusinsky "threatened me that the police would be looking for me, the tax authorities would come after me."

Chabad had championed a model of Jewish leadership that involved a partnership between rabbis, guided Jewish values, and donors who appreciated Jewish tradition. The conflict in Russia between the Russian Jewish Congress and Chabad was reflective of this philosophical split on governance and communal structure. Should the leadership of the Jewish community be entrusted to someone whose qualifications were based on his economic prowess? Or should rabbis and donors partner with Jewish tradition as the guiding principle?

This was also a struggle over which religious perspective in the Jewish spectrum would set the tone for the future: the narrow Lithuanian yeshiva approach, as supported by Goldschmidt, or the more broad, inclusive Chabad approach that Lazar represented.

Goldschmidt and his ally, Shayevich, claimed that the RJC and Keroor were the sole representatives of the Jewish community. Tensions escalated when they informed mayors and governors around the country that only they are the true representatives of Russian Jewry, demanding that control of local synagogues be returned to Keroor, the organization controlled by Goldschmidt and Shayevich. In most cities, the only rabbis were Chabad rabbis. In the few communities where there were rabbis affiliated with Goldschmidt's organization, they came for a short stint and then returned to Israel.

Goldschmidt was willing to ally himself with Gusinsky because of the financial support he was getting. Lazar felt that, while in the short term, Gusinsky's deep pockets might be helpful, in the end it would endanger a Jewish future in Russia, which would be subject to the idiosyncrasies and political goals of an oligarch with a political and business agenda.[40]

Rabbi Shayevich, who used the title Chief Rabbi of Russia, was a strident public supporter of Gusinsky's attacks on the government, and this worried many local Jewish leaders. Discontent spread among Jewish leaders throughout Russia.

In 1999, the Roshei Kahal, heads of the seven largest Jewish communities in Russia, traveled to Moscow to meet with Rabbi Lazar. They proposed that an election be held for chief rabbi. Shayevich had been selected by the Communists. Now the time had come for the Jewish community to make its own choice. They wanted Lazar to be a candidate. He rejected their suggestions, telling them, "I am happy in my position as a Chabad shliach." Baruch Gorin describes Lazar's attitude at the time: "He did not want to be chief rabbi; he did not want to be involved in all the politics." Lazar feared if he were elected, it would create more communal tensions. By nature, he was quiet and reserved and did not want to be thrust into the political limelight.

Gorin and Barada felt differently. They told Lazar it was crucial to have an election. Some years before, they had set up the Federation of Jewish Communities of the Former Soviet Union as an umbrella organization to strengthen Jewish life in Russia. Gorin and Barada wanted to make a conference to bring the issue to a head. If Lazar were to become chief rabbi, it would give them the needed political clout to ensure that the Federation could succeed in its mission in Russia. Still, they were having trouble convincing Lazar.

Jewish communal leaders traveled to Moscow a second time. This time they told Rabbi Lazar, "You say you are not qualified to be chief rabbi, but at the very least, you should ask someone else's opinion."

Lazar wondered whom to turn to. It was 1999; the Rebbe had passed away five years earlier. He decided to seek the advice of Israel's Sephardi chief rabbi, Mordechai Eliyahu, a universally respected scholar and spiritual leader. Lazar had heard that the Rebbe suggested to some that if they were perplexed by an issue, they should seek Rabbi Eliyahu's advice. Lazar flew to Israel with Rabbi Dovid Mondshine and expressed his concerns to Rabbi Eliyahu. "This position is not for me, and I don't want this job. I am happy in my role in Chabad. However, the community leaders say there is a danger for the Jews in Russia."

Rabbi Lazar recalls that with great emotion, Rabbi Eliyahu stood up. "It took twenty-two years for the prophecy to be fulfilled that Joseph would be the leader in Egypt," referring to the Biblical story of Joseph's dream that his brothers would bow down to him, that was fulfilled after he became viceroy of Egypt. "It took only twelve years for the Rebbe's vision that you should become chief rabbi." Lazar was astonished at the outburst of Rabbi Eliyahu. Israel's chief rabbi told Lazar that he had met twelve years earlier with the Rebbe. They had discussed the idea of Rabbi Lazar becoming chief rabbi of Russia. A few months later, Lazar says, the Rebbe called

Rabbi Eliyahu, asking him to make an effort to ensure that Rabbi Lazar becomes chief rabbi. This story was an absolute surprise to Lazar. Never in his wildest dreams had he thought that the Rebbe wanted him to accept this post. Within Chabad, there was hesitation in supporting the idea. When news of Rabbi Eliyahu's story became known, the resistance melted.

Major Jewish organizations in the US[41] opposed Lazar being elected, saying, "A Chabad rabbi cannot be chief rabbi." The JDC in Moscow and the Jewish Agency wanted to retain their influence on the emerging Russian community. A chief rabbi like Lazar, who was not dependent on their largess, could prove to be independent and difficult to manipulate. It was a strange hypocrisy: American Jewish groups, who prided themselves on transparency and democracy, allied themselves with an oligarch and a Communist-appointed rabbi[42] to protect their organizational turf against a Rabbi who was independent, young, and democratically elected.[43] Some American Jewish leaders even claimed the conflict between Gusinsky and Putin was due to anti-Semitism and that Lazar's election was being orchestrated by the Kremlin. These leaders ignored the sentiments of the emerging grassroots Jewish communities throughout Russia.

Jewish leaders and rabbis representing eighty communities converged on Moscow's Olympic Renaissance Hotel in June of 2000. As a gesture of goodwill, Rabbis Goldschmidt and Shayevich were also invited, although only Rabbi Shayevich attended. An election was held and Lazar was chosen as the first democratically[44] elected chief rabbi in Russian history.[45] This was a crucial turning point that set the stage for Jewish life to flourish in Russia.

The community was shocked the next day when Gusinsky was arrested by Russia's authorities, who claimed a long series of financial crimes. Rabbi Lazar promptly protested his arrest. Allies of Gusinsky in Russia claimed his arrest was due to anti-Semitism. This prompted American Jewish leaders to step up their criticism, irresponsibly echoing the same sentiments. According to Professor Friedgut, the conflict between Gusinsky, who controlled much of the media in Russia, and the new president, Putin, had become personal, a battle between the media mogul and a tough politician. "It was not only a policy question that set the two men apart, but a clash of power and personalities."

After a few days, Gusinsky was freed; later, he left Russia. He stopped supporting the RJC, pushing it into crisis. Dr. Betsy Gidwitz, who has been a close observer of Russian Jewish life for decades, reported,[46] "Following Mr. Gusinsky's departure from Russia, the RJC limped along under uncertain leadership and reduced revenues." With time under new leadership, however, it was reconstituted. Yuri Kanner was elected president in 2009. He told me in an interview at the Chabad Marina Roscha synagogue that the RJC is not involved in political issues and has an excellent relationship with the Federation of Jewish Communities and Rabbi Lazar.

While other Jewish leaders had great doubts about the Jewish future in Russia, Rabbi Lazar was buoyant with optimism. In the coming years, Chabad would emerge as the most influential factor in Russian Jewry. Dr. Betsy Gidwitz, who was a frequent critic of Rabbi Lazar and Chabad in Russia, admitted in a 2006 report that "Rabbi Lazar leads a movement that has become the most visible expression of Judaism throughout the post-Soviet states."

Lazar's success in building a stronger Jewish community was greatly enhanced by the relationship he built with Russian president Vladimir Putin. Jews in the West generally view Putin in a negative light; they are disturbed by his autocratic style of leadership and civil rights that do not reach Western standards. His strident foreign policy has not endeared him to Americans, in particular his actions in Ukraine. Jews are concerned about his alliances with Syria and other countries that are inimical to Israel's interests.

A professor of mathematics at the University of Novosibirsk summed it up when he told me, "Putin many not be good for Russia but he is definitely good for the Jews of Russia."

Putin's support of Jews in Russia started long before he met Rabbi Lazar and Sasha Barada. He started his political career in 1993 as vice-mayor of Saint Petersburg.[47] A request had been submitted to the municipality to open the first official Jewish school in Russia. Saint Petersburg's Jewish mayor feared being accused of favoritism if he permitted the school. It was Putin who stepped forward and approved the school, the very first in post-Communist Russia. This would be the first of many actions over the years to bolster Jewish life in Russia. Many were accomplished far from the public eye, without an agenda to gain favor from Western critics. When mayors in Russian cities opposed returning historic synagogues to local communities, he repeatedly intervened. In Sochi, Rabbi Edelkopf[48] ran into a series of roadblocks in acquiring land for a Jewish community center. Putin dispatched a senior Kremlin official to ensure that land be allocated for the Jewish community in the city center.

Putin attended the opening of the new Marina Roscha building in 2000 and participated in the Chanukah menorah-lighting ceremony there. He donated his personal salary toward the construction of the Jewish Museum and visited after it opened. The constant public support of Putin for the Jewish community in a country where he is the dominant force has had broad domestic political ramifications.[49]

Russian Jews who feared being too open about their Judaism have lost that anxiety. "Putin is very popular in Russia," Rabbi Dovid Mondshine[50] says." Putin's public stance has trickled down into the political culture in the country. Mondshine describes the change: "We have seen a shift in attitudes toward Jews throughout the country by political leaders, and this has changed the way Jews view their own identity." Mayors in Russian cities and governors have vast powers and are very influential. "If the president is supportive of Jews, so are they."

Lazar has been successful in working behind the scenes to advance Israel's cause with Russian political leaders. Dmitry Perkoviv explains that Russia is not like the West where politics are public. The key to success in Russia is quiet, behind-scenes diplomacy. According to Lev Leviev, Putin had a personal rapport with both former Prime Minister Ariel Sharon and Prime Minister Binyamin Netanyahu. Their first meeting was in Marina Roscha Synagogue in Moscow before Netanyahu was elected prime minister.

Lazar and Putin met the first time in 1999 when Putin was named prime minister in Yeltsin's government. Lazar presented him with a menorah and was surprised to hear, "I know what that is; I grew up surrounded by Jews."

Lev Leviev believes Putin's deep personal warmth for Jews started in his childhood. Putin was raised in a Soviet-styled apartment building in Saint Petersburg. His parents struggled to make a living and worked long hours. He would come home from elementary school to an empty apartment. According to Leviev, "his neighbor was a Chassidic Jew who took him in. The family would give him dinner and help him with his schoolwork." In a speech Lazar gave in the United States, he recalled that "Putin saw this family cared for him and this touched him deeply." Dmitry Perkoviv says Putin "was raised with Jewish friends, and his whole life, he was surrounded by Jews." He views the growth of the Jewish community as an asset to Russia. Perkoviv says Putin values the fact that rabbis have come from abroad to help the country. "He is a Russian, and he has great respect for someone who wants to come to Russia as a partner to help the country."

Some Western Jewish leaders have chastised Rabbi Lazar for his relationship with Putin, citing Putin's record on civil rights and other issues. Some of this criticism is driven by an honest concern for the issues; some of it, an expression of jealousy over Chabad's dominant role in Russian Jewish life. It also reflects the attitudes of Westerners who think public criticism is the best way to advance change, an approach that is not always successful in Russia.

The issue troubled Lazar deeply. At the World Economic Forum in Davos, Switzerland, he sought the advice of Elie Wiesel. Wiesel told him that when he won the Nobel Prize, he was bombarded from all sides with requests to help Jewish communities. "Wiesel told me," Lazar says, "that he decided to ask the Rebbe what to do." Wiesel and the Rebbe had a long personal relationship. Wiesel told Lazar, "The Rebbe told me that my guiding principle should be: what I am doing helping the Jewish people." It was clear to Lazar that his own relationship with Putin has brought great benefit to Russian Jewry. Once he heard the story from Elie Wiesel, Lazar says, "This resolved the issue for me."

Lazar is following the worldwide Chabad policy of not intervening in political affairs in any of the over eighty countries where Chabad is active. While many other Jewish organizations – particularly in the US – take positions on a variety of political issues, Chabad always abstains from any political involvement. Its sole agenda has always been the spiritual and physical welfare of the Jewish community.

In a private meeting, Israel's president, Shimon Peres, thanked Putin for his assistance to Israel and support of Jewish life in Russia. Putin responded, "Whenever Rabbi Lazar comes and asks me something, I can't refuse him because he is such a good person."

It was the army of young rabbis and rebbitzens that were willing to move to diverse regions of the Former Soviet Union that was crucial to the success of Chabad in Russia. Dmitry Perkoviv says other groups sent rabbis to Russia for a short time, usually up to three years. "They were foreigners who didn't know the language. When they finally began to understand the dynamics of the community, they left." The Chabad approach was vastly more successful. "The Rebbe sent shluchim for life." He explains that when they first come, "they learn the language, and then they begin to build an infrastructure for the community." He says that Chabad looked at the real problems affecting communities. "Chabad shluchim met community needs, they related to Jews as they were. They understood that Russian Jews are different from Jews of other countries." Mark Levin, of the National Coalition Supporting Eurasian Jewry, says the reason that Chabad succeeded is "because of its experience and dedication to go to places that other groups wouldn't or couldn't."

Sasha Barada says the emerging group of influential, affluent Jews was involved with Chabad from the beginning. "We started off together and the partnership grew." Today, that funding reaches into the tens of millions in Moscow alone, supporting a wide variety of institutions, schools, synagogues, yeshivas, and a college-level women's seminary. This is coupled with broad-based communal programs like Chessed[51] that provides thousands of meals a year, and the Jewish Museum. Today, there are over 310 shluchim in the Former Soviet

Union serving institutions in 115 communities. The Ohr Avner school system operates fifty-five schools from Siberia to Belorussia.

The global economic slowdown created a funding crisis for Chabad's network in the Former Soviet Union, as donors from abroad were forced to cut back. This, says Rabbi Dovid Mondshine, forced a shift in local strategy. "Shluchim in communities have worked harder to develop local sources of funding." That's what happened to Rabbi Zalman Deutch[52] in Perm in the Ural region of Russia. He arrived with his wife, Sara, from Jerusalem in 2001. He says that, at the onset, Chabad in Moscow arranged funding. "Our budget was fully covered from subsidies from Ohr Avner and the Rohr foundation." Today he raises 70 percent of his annual budget of $600,000 for the school, community center, and synagogue. "Fifty percent comes from the local community, 20 percent from Jews who have had a connection with Perm who now live in Moscow." The final 30 percent of the money comes from Leviev, Rohr, and other funders, whose donations are funneled through Chabad's main office in Moscow. Mondshine, who administers much of the allocation throughout the FSU, explains, "Local communities are maturing and raising a larger portion of their budgets. This new mode of self-sufficiency will ultimately create stronger communities."

As Chabad became the dominant force for Judaism in the Former Soviet Union, they faced a unique set of challenges not encountered in the US and other countries. How do you advocate to government authorities to protect Jewish interests while remaining nonpartisan?[53] How do you support Israel and fight anti-Semitism? How do you create a variety of entry points to Jewish life for a population that has been barred from Jewish connection for decades? How do you assist the large population of Jewish poor and elderly?

In Moscow, Lazar championed a new concept when he restructured the new Marina Roscha complex not just as a synagogue, but also as a Jewish community center. Along with the kosher restaurant, he built a gym and cultural activities. Nearby, they built the Chessed Center. The fifty thousand-square-foot facility provides food, social services, and medical assistance, with over seventy doctors on staff, for the poor and elderly. The JDC partnered in this project with Chabad. Adjacent to the Chessed Center is the audacious ninety thousand-square-foot Jewish Museum. Lazar says, "We needed to find a way to engage the Jew who was not interested in a synagogue." In 2012, with Baruch Gorin at the helm, the Jewish Museum[54] was opened in Moscow. Israeli president, Shimon Peres, flew in especially for the event. Designed by the same architects as the Holocaust Museum in Washington, DC, it was named the Museum of the Year in Russia. Jewish tradition, culture, and history are presented in the world's largest Jewish museum with cutting-edge multimedia. The *Los Angeles Times*[55] reported on the opening and said that many visitors left the museum Sunday saying they felt shaken and awed. "I didn't expect to see such a phenomenally grandiose thing as I saw here today," said Anna Goldman, a twenty-seven-year-old art manager. "There are many Jewish centers and synagogues in Russia, but there was not a place to bring people of other nationalities to tell them what it really is to be a Russian Jew."

There are many questions about the future of Russian Jewry. Strong Jewish communities are emerging in major cities. Alik Nadan, head of the JDC in Russia, feels that many Jews are moving to the larger cities, and, in the future, smaller cities may not have viable Jewish communities. Large numbers of Kavkazi Jews from Azerbaijan and Caucasus who historically had a greater connection to tradition have relocated to Moscow, lured by the business, education, and a vibrant Jewish community.

Russia, like the US, has high numbers of intermarriage. Seven decades of Communism have blurred many people's connection to Judaism. They tend to melt into the broader Russian culture.

There are positive trends also. More Jews are becoming active in community life throughout Russia. Jewish community centers, schools, and synagogues established in over a hundred cities have created multiple avenues for Jewish engagement. The first generation of students of the Ohr Avner school system is maturing and has a stronger connection to Jewish life. Rabbi Dovid Mondshine says, "Our alumni are now enrolling their own children." Some, he says, are even becoming teachers in the schools they once attended.

Groups other than Chabad are making important contributions to the Jewish future in Russia. Academic programs have been founded in universities. The Jewish Agency has created projects bolstering Jewish identity. The Avi Chai Foundation and the Keshet Fund have made important strategic investments in Russia. Local communities have started schools in major cities like Moscow and Saint Petersburg, which are providing a wider variety of educational choice. Moscow boasts a kolel and yeshiva programs. Campus programs like Hillel and others run by Chabad are providing gateways to Judaism for college students. Grassroots groups in communities, in particular the larger urban areas, are bubbling with Jewish innovation.

Since the fall of the Soviet Union, a million Jews have immigrated to Israel, the US, and Germany. A new trend has emerged; Jews are now returning to Russia, lured by economic opportunities. There are some fifty thousand Jews in Russia with Israeli passports. Some are splitting their time between Russia and Israel. There are fifty weekly nonstop flights between Moscow and Tel Aviv.

The true number of Jews in Russia is unknown. Accurate assessments are difficult, since there are no proper demographic surveys. Researchers at Hebrew University speculate that the number is just under 300,000. The JDC claims the number is 600,000. Rabbi Lazar believes the number is much higher, maybe upward of a million.

Rabbi Zalman Deutch in Perm says he has over a thousand families on his list of local Jews. He suspects "the true number of Jews may be three times that number. Some still fear identifying as Jews, others are disconnected from Jewish life."

What is not in dispute is that Jews are emerging from the shadows after decades of Communism. Rabbi Shmulik Kaminetsky tells of an incident in 1996 that proved to him there are many more Jews than we think. "A woman came to see me telling me her grandmother is dying and she wants to see a rabbi, please come now." He headed to the small town some sixty miles from Dnepropetrovsk. The grandmother was in her nineties, and, in Yiddish, she told her story: "Before World War I, I was a young girl. There was a pogrom in my community and my parents were killed." She had resolved never to suffer again and hid her Jewishness, never even telling her family. "I saw you on television and wanted to see a rabbi before I die." Kaminetsky recited the Shema, and a few hours later, she passed away. Her eighteen descendants discovered they were all Jews.

Judaism today is recognized as an official religion in Russia; laws ensure religious rights. Dr. Betsy Gidwitz writes: "Official anti-Semitism has almost completely disappeared in Russia and the Ukraine. But there are nationalistic groups that have anti-Semitic attitudes. Natan Sharansky, head of the Jewish Agency, says that Putin's attitude for Russian Jews has been "very consistent" in making sure that there is no official policy of government anti-Semitism, and that those Jews who want to both develop their own communities and connect with Jews in Israel and elsewhere abroad can freely do it."

Rabbi Dovid Mondshine is optimistic about the future of Russian Jewry. He told me that in the summer of 2013, his son, together with a few friends, all yeshiva students around twenty, traveled the two thousand miles from Moscow to Novosibirsk. Along the way, they visited Jewish communities large and small. "It was amazing. They met with mayors and provincial governors. They were afraid of nothing." He says these kids grew up in Russia, they are Russian, they understand the country. "Today the shluchim in Russia have over 1,500 children." He believes that this new generation born in Russia feels comfortable in the country. "They will be the next generation of Russian rabbis, community leaders, and teachers."

The future of Russian Jewry became clear to me on Simchat Torah in Moscow. It's the holiday when Jews mark the end of the annual Torah-reading cycle and celebrate its beginning again. In synagogues around the world, it's a festive night.

The celebration had started in the evening as the crowds converged on the Marina Roscha Jewish Community Center. Young people filled the synagogue sitting next to the Russian Babushkas and the nouveau riche. That night, over a dozen billionaires danced in the synagogue with a thousand others, as their bodyguards congregated on the street below waiting for their charges. Old Yiddish-speaking Russians mixed with oligarchs who swung in circles with Chassidim and college students. Jews from the remote regions of Azerbaijan who had migrated westward, danced with the attorneys and doctors from

Moscow. The Israeli ambassador greeted the congregation. I witnessed a dynamic new Jewish world alive and well in Moscow.

At 3:00 a.m., a hundred holdouts from the marathon celebration that had started eight hours earlier danced in the street in front of the Marina Roscha Synagogue. The dancing reached a feverish pitch. The circles whirled around and around, the Torah Scrolls perched on the shoulders of the dancers. Suddenly, a police car approached the deserted street that weaves between towering buildings. This wasn't Moscow of the Communist times when Jews were full of fear. As the crowd parted for a moment to allow the patrol car to snake through the dancers, the police burst into smiles and waved. They, too, were touched by the spirit of the holiday.

At 4:00 a.m., we walked home, chilled by the beginning of the Russian winter. Rabbi Berel Lazar told me of the great success of the evening. It wasn't the oligarchs or the politicians that captured his imagination. His excitement was about those he had succeeded in prodding toward more observance, telling me, "Tonight, three men agreed to a do a brit (circumcision) and four agreed to start putting on tefilin daily."

In Communist times, Russian Jews expressed themselves publicly once a year when they joined the Simchat Torah celebrations. Then they congregated outside the few remaining synagogues with a nostalgic connection to the traditions of the past, sending a message to the Communist government that they had not forgotten they were Jews.

In Russia today, Jews fill their own newly built or reclaimed synagogues. They are upbeat about their future. Their optimism about Jewish life in Russia is more reflective of the American experience than the European one. Unlike in Europe, anti-Semitism and hostility toward Israel has not taken hold. Russian Jews know the present government will not tolerate any anti-Semitism. While government policies are tilted toward the Arabs, hostility to Israel has not reached the public square.

Still, anxiety lingers as Jews wonder about the long-term future. They are troubled about Putin's friendship with the Arab world. They hope that human rights in Russia will reach Western standards.

They are concerned about the large numbers of elderly Jews who live far below the poverty line. Some still harbor the fear that there might be a return to the dark days of Communism. There is concern about whether governments of the future will be as favorable to Jewish interests as the present one. There are serious questions about the high numbers of intermarriage and whether it will diminish the hope of a vibrant Jewish future.

While acknowledging the challenges, Mark Levin of the National Coalition Supporting Eurasian Jewry has a positive attitude. "I have been an optimist about the future of Russian Jewry for over a quarter of a century. Hopefully, with the creation of different Jewish institutions that are spreading across the country, if the community faces another political challenge, they will be better prepared."

The Russian Jewish community is maturing and seizing its own destiny. It is detaching itself from the largess of its American brothers, taking control of itself, and charting its own unique course. Today, Simchat Torah in Russia is not about nostalgia; it's about Russian Jews claiming their own future. This is the Russia the Rebbe envisioned decades ago, by keeping Judaism alive in the darkest days of Communism, and rebuilding the foundation for its renaissance after the Curtain came down.

Chapter Eleven

Building Bridges

Two weeks before Passover in 2014, the Israeli media was full of speculation about the fate of the world's largest Seder, the annual Passover celebration, in Kathmandu, Nepal.[1] Israeli consulates and embassies around the world shut down as part of a job action by unionized foreign-ministry workers. In Kathmandu, the embassy staff had partnered with Chabad in arranging the Seder, facilitating the import of supplies and security. The strike made that impossible.

Strikes are almost a weekly occurrence in Israel where unions hold sway. It wasn't the first time the diplomatic corps had walked out. In a 2013 strike, a Foreign Ministry spokesperson made a statement on Galei Tzahal, Israel Army Radio.[2] "The Ministry was issuing instructions to embassies worldwide to encourage Israeli travelers abroad to seek help at Chabad Houses if the need arose." Rabbi Mordechai Levenhartz, from Chabad in Kiev, Ukraine, responded on the air. "We can't issue visas, unfortunately, but we can provide travelers with a nice warm meal, a comfortable place to rest, and other assistance."[3]

The fate of the Kathmandu Seder had captured the attention of Israelis. Radio talk shows, the TV news, and newspapers[4] gave daily updates on its status. The Seder had become a highlight for thousands of Israeli trekkers on their shnat chofesh (year off).

The container full of supplies for the Seder, including tons of matza, wine, and gefilte fish, was held up in the port of Calcutta, waiting for an Israeli Embassy representative to authorize its release and shipment across India to Nepal. With the strike coming close to Passover, that didn't seem possible. Yigal Palmor, Foreign Ministry spokesman, told the Israeli daily, *Haaretz*, "The Seder will not take place as a result of the strike."

Rabbi Chezki and Chani Lifshitz, the Nepal Chabad shluchim, refused to throw in the towel.[5] They launched a Facebook Page, "Save the Seder in Nepal," and organized "A Seder in a Suitcase." Israelis traveling to Nepal packed their bags with supplies. Rabbi Lifshitz's request for help spread rapidly by word of mouth and social media. Backpackers and tourists arrived with hundreds of pounds of matza and Hagadahs. The Thailand Chabad emissary sent supplies with anyone traveling from Bangkok to Nepal. The yeshiva students who were joining the Lifshitzes to help with Passover lugged huge suitcases filled with food.

The Israeli strike ended a week before Passover. It was a race against time to get the shipping container released from the port in India and trucked over the mountains to Nepal. Just hours before the holiday, it arrived in Kathmandu. Rabbi Lifshitz says, "The Israeli trekkers organized like an army, unloading the ton of matza, two thousand bottles of wine and three thousand pieces of gefilte fish, and setting up the Seder."

Chabad's first public Seder in Nepal was in 1989.[6] Israeli Ambassador to Nepal, Shmuel Moyal hung out a sign in a local restaurant advertising a Passover Seder. "I expected thirty or forty people," he said, "but with three weeks to go until the holiday, close to a hundred had signed up!" Moyal realized he needed help. "I sent a telegram to the Rebbe, whom I knew from when I was a consul in New York. The Rebbe said not to worry, and sent three rabbinical students, one from Australia, one from New York, and one from

Canada. The Rebbe also dispatched matza, wine, and kosher meat for the Seder."

Chabad continued to send rabbis to Kathmandu to help organize and lead the Passover Seders. In 2000, Chabad sent a permanent shliach to Nepal, Rabbi Chezki and his wife, Chani, Lifshitz, who grew up in Israel. Like other Chabad Chassidim, he had served in the Israeli army. The tradition of the Passover Seders at the top of the world continued to grow in popularity, especially for Israeli backpackers. Within a few years, the number of Seder guests grew from a few hundred to nearly two thousand.

Chabad in Nepal is one of the network of Chabad Centers in the Far East, India, and South America catering to traveling Israelis. Young Israelis who would be wary to venture into the religious enclaves of Jerusalem and B'nai Brak sit around the Shabbat table in Kathmandu, Cusco, and Bangkok.[7] Free of the political baggage of Israel, they get a taste of home, a welcoming culture, find their Israeli friends, and discover their Jewish roots far away from Israel.

Esther Vender was one of those Israelis wandering through Nepal during her tour of the Far East.[8] She found herself overcharged for a taxi ride. "We were missing a thousand Nepalese Rupee," she recalls. "As we were discussing how to get the money together, Rabbi Chezki passed by and, without thinking twice, pulls out the money and gives it to us. The amount wasn't much (eleven dollars), but he didn't know if he would ever meet us again. And, even so, you felt his lack of hesitation to help out."

This chance encounter had a profound effect upon Esther. A seed was planted that would later blossom into the creation of a series when she became an Israeli TV producer. In 2012, the weekly drama[9] *Kathmandu* appeared on prime time that told the story of a young Israeli couple sent as shluchim to Nepal. Though the popular drama was fiction, the actors and stories share many resemblances to the Lifshitzes' real life. It dug deep, unveiling their anxieties, challenges, and successes. Vender explained, "It's very hard for such people to live in such a weird place."

Israeli TV viewers were fascinated by the series that focused on one of the toughest issues in modern Israel. In Israel, secular and religious Jews exist in different spheres. They live in different neighborhoods, they read different newspapers, listen to different radio stations and support different political parties. The two societies live side by side in a love-hate relationship. The weekly drama, *Kathmandu*, told the story of how they discover common ground in remote Nepal.

Esther Vender and her team of writers and producers spent many hours interviewing Rabbi Lifshitz and Chani[10] in Kathmandu. They also spent time in Kfar Chabad, the Chabad town not far from Tel Aviv where the secular actors immersed themselves in Chassidic life. The series was filmed in Kathmandu.

It was the focus on the real life of shluchim that made the show a hit. As one reviewer wrote: "*Kathmandu* was a success because of its expert fusion of the zany situations in far-flung places, held together with genuine characters."[11] The reviewer said that the show peeled away the layers to show the internal struggles that shluchim encounter. In real life, Chabadniks are often stereotyped as plastic and perky. Beneath the cheerful facades, shluchim wrestle with the same questions of doubt that plague all of us.

At the same time, major political issues were dividing the secular and religious communities in Israel. Israelis were debating the reversal by the Israeli Supreme Court of the Tal Law, that created a mechanism for yeshiva students to slowly move into mainstream society.[12] In 2012, the Israeli Supreme Court[13] ruled that the law was unfair, demanding that the system of deferments and exemptions be scrapped and yeshiva students drafted. While Israeli politicians debated how to create a new law in the Knesset, on Wednesday nights, the country was mesmerized by the story of a Chassidic couple in a remote third-world country taking care of its secular youth, who had just finished their army service.

For two years, the debate raged on about military service for yeshiva students in Israel. In the days before Passover in 2014, as the Israeli press was speculating daily on the fate of the real Kathmandu shluchim and their Seder, major legislation passed in the Knesset. It created a new mechanism to draft yeshiva students. Close to a half a million religious Jews protested on the streets of Jerusalem. Tensions between the secular and religious populations escalated to new heights.

Prime Minister Binyamin Netanyahu realized he needed to bridge those political gaps. He visited Kfar Chabad[14] to bake shmura matza[15] for Passover. He rolled the dough and watched as the oven finished his matza in the required eighteen-minute period. At lunch afterward, Netanyahu remarked, "Every encounter I had with the Rebbe was an uplifting experience." He told Chabad leaders in Israel that he appreciated all of their work for the Jewish people, saying, "Every place I travel, I witness the most beautiful side of Judaism."

The visit created a backlash against Chabad from the Haredi (traditional Orthodox) media.[16] They lambasted Chabad, angered by the new draft law that would mandate military or community service for most yeshiva students. "How could they welcome Netanyahu when his government passed such a law?" they lamented. Chabad spokesman, Rabbi Menachem Brod, told the media, "The Rebbe taught us to welcome every Jew."[17]

The new draft law heightened societal tensions in Israel. Much of the Orthodox community argued that this was just another manifestation of Israel's secular left imposing its values on them. In response, the Haredi parties walked out during the Knesset vote. Chabad took a different approach. It looked for ways of compromise. Chabad leaders negotiated a special "Chabad Track"[18] in the legislation in February of 2014. Yeshiva students received deferments while studying and, afterward, would join the military.[19]

The effort to find a middle ground is reflective of the core Chabad philosophy that all Jews share a destiny and bond with each other and the ancient homeland of the Jewish people. Chabad seeks to find common ground while staying true to Torah principles.

That bond to Israel goes back to the very genesis of the Chabad Movement. In 1777, Chabad's founder, as biographer Dr. Nissan Mindel[20] describes the First Rebbe, Rabbi Schneur Zalman of Liadi, underwent a personal spiritual crisis. His mentor and confidant, Rabbi Menachem Mendel of Vitebsk,[21] and other Chassidic leaders, were planning to move to the Turkish-controlled Land of Israel. Rabbi Schneur Zalman was deeply conflicted between the responsibility of Jewish leadership in Russia and his desire to immigrate to the ancient Jewish homeland.

After Passover, he packed up his home and began the journey, with the plan of joining Rabbi Menachem Mendel, who was leading three hundred followers in the first Chassidic aliyah. The Alter Rebbe got as far as Mohyliv in southwestern Ukraine. After three weeks of long conversations with Rabbi Menachem Mendel, he decided to return. Rabbi Schneur Zalman poured his energy into fundraising to support the new settlement in the Land of Israel. In 1788, he established what today is the oldest charitable organization in Israel,[22] Colel Chabad. Today it is a network of institutions in sixty Israeli communities, with soup kitchens, nonprofit food pantries, wedding halls for young couples of limited means, and other social-service programs that uplift the lives of hundreds of thousands.[23]

In the decades to come, Chabad would continue to expand in Eretz Israel. Rabbi Schneur Zalman's son and successor, the Second Rebbe, Rabbi DovBer, encouraged his followers to immigrate to the mystical city of Tzefat in the north. In 1823, he urged them to move to Hebron,[24] traditionally Judaism's second most sacred city after Jerusalem. The Jewish population in Hebron consisted of Sephardi Jews living under Arab rule. Through the centuries, they had endured expulsions, pogroms, and interludes of peace, as Arab sheiks came and went. The Chassidic migration infused a new energy into the community and a direct connection to the vibrant Jewish life in Europe. The Second Rebbe sent funds from Russia to his followers to erect a synagogue[25] in Hebron. Two decades later, in 1844, the daughter of the Second Rebbe, the Rebbitzen Menucha Rochel Slonim[26] and her family immigrated to Hebron, bolstering the community.

In 1847, a group of Chabad families moved to Jerusalem,[27] led by the scholar Rabbi Eliyahu Yosef Rivlin. Three years later, in 1850, they purchased land in the Old City for a synagogue and finished construction six years later. The Chassidim named it the Tzemach Tzedek[28] synagogue in honor of the Third Rebbe, Rabbi Menachem Mendel, who lived at the time in Lubavitch. It was the only synagogue not destroyed in the Jewish quarter of old Jerusalem during the Jordanian occupation between 1948 and 1967. The construction was supported by Sir Moses Montefiore of London and the Sassoon family from Mumbai.[29]

Zionism evolved in the late nineteenth century as a response to the challenges of Jewish life in Europe. The idea of establishing a Jewish state evoked a wide series of reactions in the Jewish world. In Europe, some rabbis supported the new movement; others opposed it for a variety of reasons, including the fact that many of its early leaders demonstrated a virulent anti-religious stance.[30] Some felt that Jews must wait for the coming of the Messiah before they could seek political independence. Others feared that the Jewish state would create political conflict and anti-Semitism. In the US, the new Reform Movement declared in the Pittsburgh Platform in 1885 that America is its new Zion and said there was no need for a Jewish state.[31]

BILU, the pioneering Russian Zionist group, was established in the wake of the pogroms in 1881. Israel Belkind,[32] one of the founders, wrote that "Jewish life had become unbearable in Russia." The organization's name was inspired by a verse in Isaiah: "Beth Yaakov Lechu Venelcha," (the house of Jacob will go out).[33] The leaders intentionally omitted the last two words of the verse, "B'ohr Hashem," (in the light of G-d). The Zionist pioneers[34] wanted to create a new Jew, unshackled by the traditions of the past. They were influenced by the ideas of socialism and secularism that were rising at the time.

Chabad's Sixth Rebbe, Rabbi Yosef Yitzchak,[35] recalled that his grandfather, the Fourth Rebbe, Rabbi Shmuel[36] of Lubavitch, lamented about BILU: "If they had not omitted the words 'in the light of G-d,' I would have also gone," indicating he would have been supportive of their efforts and even considered immigrating to the Jewish homeland in light of the difficult challenges faced by Russian Jewry at the time. Rabbi Shmuel understood that the BILU leaders wanted to establish a new society in which the teachings of the Torah were not the determining values.

Rabbi Shmuel's son, the Fifth Rebbe, Rabbi Sholom DovBer,[37] feared, as his father had, that the revolutionary change advocated by Zionist leaders would create a Jewish identity based on secular nationalism[38] rather than one rooted in classical Jewish values of Torah. Rabbi Sholom DovBer, the Fifth Rebbe, continued the Chassidic tradition of supporting the Jewish settlement that predated the Zionist effort by a century. Colel Chabad continued to raise money throughout Russia for projects in Israel. Rabbi Sholom DovBer expanded the Chabad presence in Hebron by purchasing a large property, Bet Romano.[39] In 1912, he dispatched a group of his outstanding students, headed by renowned scholar Rabbi Zalman Havlin, to Hebron. Their mission was to establish a yeshiva[40] in the property he purchased and strengthen the Jewish community.

In 1929, the Sixth Rebbe, Rabbi Yosef Yitzchak Schneersohn, visited what was then Palestine for two weeks. During the historic trip, he met with leaders of the blossoming Jewish community, making a pilgrimage to holy sites located throughout the country.[41]

In 1947, the Zionist leaders convened in Lake Success, New York, to shepherd the vote in the United Nations for a new state. Zalman Shazar, who later would become Israel's first Minister of Education and third president, was one of the leaders of the effort. He had been a student at the yeshiva in Lubavitch and came from a prominent Chabad family. He had drifted from observance, but still had a strong connection with tradition. Concerned that the vote would falter, he visited the Sixth Rebbe, Rabbi Yosef Yitzchak, in Brooklyn, to request his blessing for success in the UN vote. The Rebbe assured him they would triumph. In later years, Shazar recalled that during the vote he was singing the Alter Rebbe's Nigun, a melody composed by Rabbi Schneur Zalman, Chabad's founder, that had esoteric kabbalistic teachings, sung only on very auspicious occasions.

After the Holocaust, the Sixth Rebbe, Rabbi Yosef Yitzchak Schneersohn, sent many of his Chassidim who had escaped Communist Russia, to Israel, establishing, in 1949, Kfar Chabad,[42] a town just outside Tel Aviv. He was not departing from his father's and grandfather's rejection of the secular elements of Zionism. He firmly believed that Jewish identity should be rooted in Torah and tradition, not nationalism. Still, he recognized the momentous transformation of Jewish life in its historical homeland and the miraculous nature of diplomatic and military victories, and supported Jewish immigration to what was becoming modern Israel. He and his successor, the Rebbe, believed that the final redemption promised by Jewish tradition would come with the arrival of Moshiach, which would usher in an era of peace and prosperity.

The establishment of the modern State of Israel created a new dilemma for religious Jews. Some, like the religious Zionists, led by Mizrachi (the Religious Zionist Movement), saw the new state as the first stages of redemption, and celebrated it with religious fervor. Much of the Haredi (traditional Orthodox) community was deeply wary of a secular Zionist state. In response, they withdrew, creating insular communities, and dealing with the government as needed.

Orthodox historian, Rabbi Berel Wein, says, "The country began as a socialist, atheistic, anti-religious country." Mistrust between the religious and secular was bolstered by battles over education, community leadership, and funding.[43] There were incidents like "the children of Teheran."[44] In the midst of war, a group of religious Polish refugee children made their way to Teheran. Zionist groups brought them to Israel where they were forcibly placed into secular educational programs in non-religious kibbutzim, sparking a worldwide protest. There was hardly a religious family in Jerusalem who did not have a non-observant sibling in Tel Aviv who had been lured away from the religious lifestyle. The traditional Orthodox strategy was to build vibrant independent inward-looking communities that reflected traditional values and put Jewish scholarship center stage. They resisted efforts to draft yeshiva students,[45] wanting to ensure their control over their children's destiny. To protect their interests, religious political parties such as Agudath Israel,[46] and later on Shas, Degel HaTorah, and Yahadut HaTorah were established. For years, these parties held the balance of power in Israel's coalition governments, trading their political backing for support for their agendas.

The Mizrachi, the Religious Zionist Movement, took a different approach. They argued that the new State was the first stage of the redemptive process and was infused with sanctity. The religious Zionists supported integration into Israeli society, and created a political party, the National Religious Party.[47] For many years, it was a partner in coalition governments, working at times with the Haredi parties.

Chabad rejected both the insularity of the Haredim and the full integration of Mizrachi's religious Zionism. Chabad staked out a middle ground, differing with both. It felt that stepping away from involvement in the new Israeli society was an attitude based on insecurity. Nor did it agree with the religious Zionist viewpoint that the redemption had started and the state was imbued with sanctity, which to some degree was an acceptance of the secular Zionist agenda. Rather, Chabad argued that redemption could come only with the classical Jewish promise of Moshiach, a redeemer who would usher in an era of peace and sanctity.[48] It did not create a political party or join one of the existing parties, even though it could have earned a few seats in the Knesset. Nor did Chabad endorse any party. Chassidim voted in elections as individuals. There were no branches of the parties in Chabad communities. Chabad refrained from any formal involvement in the political process, instead focusing on responsibility for the spiritual and physical welfare of all citizens.

Chabad took the approach of principled engagement. Chabad Chassidim became active members of the workforce. Still, Chabad believed that the Chassidic way of life should not be compromised or dominated by the broader secular Israeli culture. Chabad did not take a negative view of those who were pioneering the land, even though they were not religiously observant. Chabad took the position that it must contribute to society by creating a bridge between the secular and religious populations.

Chabad, unlike other Chassidic groups and the Haredi community, supported military service in Israel. It sent its sons[49] to the army, most after they completed their yeshiva studies.[50] My classmate, Dovid Mizrachi, who sat next to me in the yeshiva in Kfar Chabad,[51] was killed in a tank battle[52] on the Golan Heights in the Yom Kippur War. Rabbi Yosef Loschak, a shliach in Santa Barbara, California, recalled,[53] "I was surprised one day in yeshiva in Israel when one of the heads of yeshiva turned up in uniform." This willingness to serve, and the respect in Chabad for those who did go to the army, created a totally different community culture from other segments of the Haredi community in Israel.

Straddling the middle ground, keeping religious observance while engaging Israeli society, is not simple. Contributing to a society whose values may not be fully in consonance with the principles of Torah is a complex challenge. As Rabbi Mendel Gluckowsky,[54] a prominent member of Chabad's rabbinical court in Israel, says, "We are in the gray area, and that is the toughest."

That middle ground became clear to me in an Israeli army bunker on the Lebanese border in the early seventies. I was studying at the time at Chabad's central yeshiva in Kfar Chabad. The Rebbe had sent us to visit soldiers on the front lines for Jewish holidays like Purim, Chanukah, and Lag B'omer. We drove hours through the night, arriving early in the morning. The busload of yeshiva students was divided into small groups, and each visited the string of bunkers along the border.

Our group arrived at an outpost on the border. We walked down a deep row of steps into a bunker that was dug into the ground. Bunks lined the walls. The soldiers were overjoyed to see us. Few ever visited these remote bases in the far north. We broke out the refreshments, and started the celebration. Suddenly I noticed an amazing dichotomy. On one wall was a picture you would expect to find in any army base: a woman, whose attire was far from modest. On the other wall, there was a picture of the Rebbe. I stared for a moment in disbelief; the incongruence had stunned me. I asked the soldiers, "I understand the picture of the woman in an army base, but why the Rebbe on the opposite wall?" They replied, "He is one of the few who truly care about us; every Jewish holiday he sends you to visit and uplift us." Writer Yossi Klein Halevi says, "Israelis love Chabad. When Chabad speaks about Ahavat Yisrael (love and concern for your fellow Jew) there is nothing theoretical about it. When our kids go off after the army, it's Chabad who takes care of them."

As part of the policy of principled engagement, Chabad has deeply influenced many Israeli leaders. The Rebbe would meet with generals, politicians, academics, and members of the intelligence community. The meetings were not for trading favors. The Rebbe was interested in the welfare of the country and the policies that affect Jewish destiny. Rabbi Yehuda Krinsky[55] recalls that the first Israeli prime minister Moshe Sharett, who visited the Rebbe in the early fifties, remarked as he left, "His head is in the heavens and his feet are on the ground." Israeli Ambassador to the US, Yitzchak Rabin,[56] left a meeting with the Rebbe in 1972. He confided to diplomat Yehuda Avner,[57] "The Rebbe knows more about Israeli security than the 120 members of the Knesset."

Ambassador Avner also accompanied Israel's president, Zalman Shazar, on one of his visits to the Rebbe. In his early life, Shazar stepped away from the traditions of his parents, but as the years went by, he reconnected with Chabad. He viewed his periodic visits[58] to the Rebbe as spiritual milestones in his life, and the Rebbe's guidance, priceless for Israel. The Israeli press and some in the political leadership complained that protocol required that, since he was Israel's president, the Rebbe should come to him. Sitting in the limousine[59] surrounded by a police escort as it raced from Manhattan to the Chassidic bastion in Crown Heights, Shazar remarked to Avner, "Prime Minister Golda Meir called me today, chastising me for going to the Rebbe, telling me the Rebbe should visit the president, not the other way around." Shazar lamented to Avner in Yiddish, "Vos veis Golda[60] vegen a Rebbe?" (What does Golda understand about a Rebbe?)

President Shazar returned from a formal State visit to the US, which included a visit to the Rebbe. The cabinet led by Prime Minister Golda Meir gathered at the airport, as per protocol, to welcome him back to the country. Rabbi Shlomo Maidanchik,[61] mayor of Kfar Chabad, also came to the airport with a delegation of Chassidim.[62] When President Shazar saw the Chassidim, he joined them in a Chassidic dance. Golda, quite perturbed by being upstaged, remarked to Maidanchik, "We run this country, not you." When the reporters asked Maidanchik what the prime minister had said, ever the diplomat, he replied, "How much she appreciates Chabad's contribution to Israeli society."

Israeli leaders from all parties would come to Brooklyn and spend long hours in conversation with the Rebbe. In the years that he led the opposition party, Menachem Begin visited the Rebbe regularly. In 1977, after being elected prime minister, Begin[63] had a long private meeting with the Rebbe prior to his first visit to the White House. Begin told the press that the meeting was confidential and he had been visiting the Rebbe for many years. After his meeting with Carter, Begin[64] dispatched Yehuda Avner back to Brooklyn to brief the Rebbe. Avner says, "The depth of the Rebbe's grasp of our political and strategic situation was deeply impressive."

Prime Minister Netanyahu surprised the Jewish leadership[65] of the predominantly liberal American Jewish establishment in 2009 when he told of his own meeting with the Rebbe that had a profound impact on him as a young diplomat. They had gathered at the 92nd Street Y to welcome him after he gave a strident speech in the UN about the Iranian threat. A few hours earlier, the hardnosed Israeli press asked him why he had given such a tough talk. Netanyahu retorted, "The Rebbe told me to do it."[66] The press was bewildered; the Rebbe had passed away fifteen years earlier. A few hours later Netanyahu elaborated, filling in the details about his experience as the UN ambassador years earlier:

"I had been invited to Simchat Torah in the Rebbe's synagogue.[67] The room was filled with thousands of Chassidim. Suddenly the crowd split and the Rebbe walked through them." Netanyahu was told to approach the Rebbe. Tapping the Rebbe on the back, Netanyahu said, "I came to see the Rebbe." The Rebbe smiled and answered, "To see and not to speak?" It was after midnight and the Chassidim were waiting for the Simchat Torah celebration to begin, but the Rebbe spent close to an hour[68] talking to Netanyahu. The conversation touched Netanyahu. "That night, the Rebbe told me I would go into a place of darkness [referring to the UN] and I must bring light."

Two years later in 2011, Prime Minister Netanyahu quoted the Rebbe in his speech to the UN General Assembly,[69] saying, "The Rebbe told me, 'Remember that in a hall of perfect darkness, if you light one small candle, its precious light will be seen by everyone. Your mission is to light a candle for truth and for the Jewish people.' That's what I've tried to do ever since, and this is what we are all asked to do."

There had been some speculation in the media and political circles about why Netanyahu had quoted the Rebbe by name in his speech in the General Assembly. Yehuda Avner wanted to dig a bit deeper. A few days later, they attended the same synagogue for Yom Kippur services, and during the break, they spoke privately. Avner[70] said to Netanyahu, "You spoke about the Rebbe in the UN." Netanyahu confided to Avner, "Of course. The Rebbe gave me my mission in life."

The Rebbe took strong positions on crucial issues facing Israel. Time and again, the Rebbe stated that by relinquishing territory, Israeli security would be endangered, arguing that, according to Jewish Law, giving up strategic territory could create a risk to life. Sadly, we have seen how withdrawals from crucial strategic areas have proven the Rebbe's concerns valid. Israel evacuated southern Lebanon and Hezbollah stepped in; after the withdrawal from Gaza, Hamas seized control. In each case, these areas have becomes bases for terror and more conflict. The Rebbe questioned the long-term viability of the Camp David Accords by Prime Minister Begin and President Anwar Sadat. At the time of the signing, the Rebbe remarked, "Who knows what kind of government will be in Egypt one year from now or thirty years from now?" A year later, Sadat was assassinated. Three decades after the signing, Egypt was shaken by protests and a new era of government instability started raising serious questions about the Accords.

The Rebbe met with many Israeli leaders from all sides of the spectrum; still, Chabad maintained its policy of neutrality in Israeli politics. This was key in Chabad's broader mission of being a bridge in Israeli society. Coupled with the fact that young Chabad men joined the army, Chabad earned respect from a broad spectrum of Israelis. There have been only two exceptions to this policy. Both interventions proved decisive in determining who would be prime minister. Once it was driven by internal issues within the Orthodox community and was due to a direct request from the Rebbe; the second time, after the Rebbe's passing, prompted by grave concerns over Israeli security.

Two weeks before the Israeli election of 1988, the Rebbe issued a call to support the religious party Agudath Israel in the upcoming election as what he called "a one-time participation" in the Israeli electoral process. Few political observers understood the factors behind the Rebbe's exception from Chabad's historic position of non-partisanship. The Rebbe was responding to a request from Rabbi Simcha Bunim Alter,[71] the Gerer Rebbe, leader of the Gerer Chassidim, a large Chassidic group that had originated in Poland and now was centered in Israel. The Gerer Rebbe was distressed about the creation of a new religious party in Israel, Degel HaTorah, by Rabbi Menachem Shach,[72] leader of the Lithuanian yeshiva community. Historically, Agudath Israel had united the Haredi community, bringing most Chassidic groups and the Lithuanian yeshiva world together under one banner of Agudath Israel.[73]

The conflict between Chassidim and the Lithuanian yeshiva community, known as the Misnagdim,[74] dated back over two centuries. The growth of the Chassidic Movement in the late eighteenth century prompted the Vilna Gaon,[75] Rabbi Eliyahu of Vilna, to place a ban on Chassidim in 1777. The challenge of the Haskalah (the European Enlightenment) and Zionism in the late nineteenth and twentieth centuries prodded the Chassidim and Misnagdim to cooperate against shared external threats to their values and lifestyles. Cooperation between the Third Rebbe, Rabbi Menachem Mendel,[76] and Rabbi Yitzchak Volozhin sparked better relations between the two communities for many decades to come. In 1912, Agudath Israel was founded in Europe as a coalition of many Jewish groups, other than Chabad and the Misnagdim.[77]

Lithuanian leader Rabbi Eliezer Menachem Shach[78] shattered that unity. For many years he opposed initiatives started by the Rebbe as diverse as children's parades on Lag B'omer and the institution of the annual study of Maimonides. In 1988, he created a new political party called Degel HaTorah that excluded the Chassidic groups such as Ger. The Gerer Chassidim believed that the new party, dominated by the Misnagdim, would marginalize the influence of the Chassidic community in Israel. The Gerer Rebbe turned to the Rebbe for support. The historic schism of Orthodox Jewry entered a new phase. Instead of being argued in synagogues and study halls, it became a test of strength in the Israeli ballot box.

Centuries earlier, the rise of Chassidism was partly a result of the intellectual elitism and insularity of the religious community dominated by the scholars in Vilna. Chassidism valued, instead, the spirituality of each individual; the Misnagdim saw a higher calling in the pursuit of scholarship, spending their lives in Torah study. Chassidim were concerned with the spiritual path of the average man; the Misnagdim were more focused on the elite. The contest between Degel HaTorah, dominated by the Misnagdim, and Agudath Israel, influenced by the Chassidim, was a replay of a two-century-old dispute between two worldviews of Judaism.[79]

The Rebbe was concerned with all of Israeli society. At the election's very core was a debate[80] over what vision of Judaism would be dominant in Israeli society – the narrow, particularistic, insular vision of the Lithuanian yeshiva community or the broader, inclusive perspective propagated by Chabad.

Chabad followers hit the streets with a massive campaign. Overnight, Agudath Israel rose in popularity to become the fourth largest party, and the deciding factor in creating a coalition government electing Yitzchak Shamir as prime minister."[81]

When the left-wing Labor Party seized control in the next election, it struck back with vengeance. Angered by Chabad's support of Agudath Israel, it cut funding to Chabad schools and social-service institutions in retribution. While other religious groups had political parties to protect their interests, no matter who was in power, Chabad did not, and was deeply affected by these politically driven cuts.

In 1996, after the Rebbe's passing, Chabad in Israel decided to enter the political arena a second time. It was a tense time. The Oslo Accords had failed to usher in the era of peace that many yearned for. The tragic assassination of Prime Minister Yitzchak Rabin had divided the country. Suicide bombings were rampant; terrorism was a daily threat. A new election had been called. Shimon Peres stood at the helm of the Labor Party; Binyamin Netanyahu, the Likud; military hero, Ariel Sharon, was directing the Likud campaign. Many feared that, if elected, Peres would make more concessions, further endangering Israel.

Sharon, like many other Israeli political and military leaders, had a long history with Chabad. In the wake of the Six-Day War, he visited the newly liberated Western Wall in Jerusalem, donning tefilin at a Chabad booth. Later, his twelve-year-old son, Gur, suffered a heartbreaking accident that took his life. The Rebbe sent a letter to Sharon and a delegation of Chassidim to provide consolation. Ezer Weizman, at that time head of Israel's air force, and later its president, said, "The Rebbe's efforts pulled Sharon out of a depression."

In 1968, Sharon visited the Rebbe in New York and was strongly urged by the Rebbe to change his return flight.[82] Sharon complied, though he did not understanding why. His planned El Al flight was hijacked by terrorists on the last leg between Rome and Tel Aviv, and diverted to Algeria. General Sharon would have been a big prize. The Israeli daily, *She'arim*, wrote at the time, "It seems the whole purpose of the hijacking was to get Sharon."[83] The Rebbe's advice[84] had saved his life.

I encountered Sharon a year later in 1969.[85] He had just returned to Israel after another visit to the US that included a meeting with the Rebbe. He went straight from the airport to Kfar Chabad to fulfill the Rebbe's request to give regards to the Chassidic community. It was late at night – after 10:00 p.m. – the crowd consisted of just a few dozen. Sharon described his meeting with the Rebbe, including his request that Sharon begin laying tefilin daily.[86] "This morning, I put on tefilin in Paris in my uncle's house." Sharon described his uncle's surprise with his religious awakening, and Sharon gave his tefilin to his uncle so he could perform the mitzvah, too. Sharon then turned to the Kfar Chabad mayor, Rabbi Shlomo Maidanchik, and asked, "Can you can get me another pair?"

Rabbi Shlomo Maidanchik and Sharon had a deep personal relationship that spanned decades. As Gilad Sharon writes[87] in the biography of his father, Shlomo Maidanchik was Sharon's personal rabbi, conducting the annual private family memorial service for his son, Gur. The bar mitzvah of Sharon's son, Omri, was held in Kfar Chabad. They later became family when Sharon's nephew married Maidanchik's daughter. After Maidanchik passed away, Sharon, then prime minister, traveled to Kfar Chabad to personally console the family.

With the election just weeks away, Ariel Sharon made a late-night visit to Kfar Chabad asking for help for Netanyahu. The campaign lacked momentum; a dramatic move was needed to prevent Peres from becoming prime minister. The Chabad community was wary of political involvement. In 1988, the Rebbe had instructed Chabad followers to support Agudath Israel only due to unique circumstances, saying it was "a one-time exception." Now, after his passing, the community leadership was very uncertain if they should step in.

Chabad's rabbinical court in Israel, headed by distinguished scholars, is the authority for the movement in the country. Halacha (Jewish law) and the precedent of the Rebbe's instruction serve as the foundation of its decision-making. The internal debate was intense. Terror attacks were happening regularly. Peres was describing them as "sacrifices to peace." It would later emerge that Arafat, leader of the Palestine Liberation Organization (PLO) himself, while publicly claiming to want peace, was secretly orchestrating the bus bombings and other terror attacks that had taken hundreds of Israeli lives. After long deliberation, the rabbinical court ruled that the protection of human life was paramount; Chabad should get involved to ensure a government that would guarantee security first, and stop the terror campaign – clearly something Peres had not accomplished.

Chabad in Israel launched a campaign to support Binyamin Netanyahu, enlisting thousands of volunteers to blanket the country.[88] In New York, the Chabad leadership differed strongly with the Israelis. They felt that, despite the critical issues, it was not Chabad's role to get involved in the election process, issuing a critical public statement.[89] Others in Israel were also disturbed by Chabad's entry into politics. Rabbi Maidanchik, Sharon's close friend in Chabad, wrote a letter saying it was a mistake for Chabad to take part in the election.

Late election night, it became clear that the election had been a strong upset; Netanyahu had won. The new prime minister offered Chabad leaders cabinet positions, but they refused. While the election had been a major victory,[90] Chabad experienced a backlash.

Leftist groups attempted to ban Chabad rabbis from visiting army bases for the holidays because, they claimed, "Chabad was now a political movement."

The involvement cost Chabad support in the broader society. David Horvitz, editor of *The Times of Israel*, says that it changed his perception of Chabad as a non-political movement: "You lost me, when a group like Chabad, who is dedicated to outreach and non-coercion took a crucial role in a couple of elections." What Horvitz and others failed to understand was Chabad did not enter into the fray to gain politically. It was motivated by a grave concern over Israeli security, fearing that more concessions would endanger Jewish lives.

In the wake of the political victory, there was a vibrant internal debate if involvement in the political process was the Chabad mission. Chabad's purpose in Israel was to be a bridge to Judaism for all Jews. Being part of the political process endangered that mission. Many in Chabad felt it had been necessary to intervene in the election to pull the country from the abyss of more concessions that would only breed more terror. Others thought it was a mistake. In the wake of the election, a strong communal consensus emerged that this would be the last time Chabad would enter politics. Chabad's mission was and is the spiritual and physical welfare of world Jewry. It would leave the politics to others.

In 2005, Prime Minister Ariel Sharon implemented his plan for a unilateral withdrawal from Gaza, uprooting close to ten thousand Jews from their homes. Many argued that the Jews living in Gaza formed a critical security buffer, and that leaving Gaza would create a military nightmare for Israel. This would prove to be true. Today, Hamas rules Gaza. Israeli groups organizing the opposition to Sharon's plan turned to Chabad to take a role in the protests. Despite having grave misgivings about the policy, Chabad refrained, leaving it to others to lead the protests and fight the issue politically.[91]

Privately, Chabad leaders met with Sharon[92] to try to convince him to rescind his decision. It was a long, emotional meeting between old friends. Sharon told the rabbis that his wife Lily, who had passed away five years earlier, loved the Chassidic melodies. The meeting evolved into a Chassidic farbrengen with stories, melodies, and toasts over vodka. Staffers at the prime minister's office were astonished to see Sharon sitting for hours with a group of rabbis led by the Rebbe's secretary, Rabbi Leibel Groner. As the gathering came to an end, Groner turned to Sharon a final time, "Arik, don't do this," he lamented in a broken voice. Sharon told him, "You never give up." Groner retorted, "We never give up on a fellow Jew."

It is this philosophy of never giving up on other Jews that has created a special affection for Chabad in Israel. Time and again, I have heard Israelis who tend to harbor resentment against religious Jews express their admiration. "Ah, Chabad is different," they say.

What is that difference? According to author Yossi Klein Halevi, there are three things. He says that, for Chabad, "Ahavat Yisrael (love and concern for your fellow Jew) is real; it extends to everyone." He explains that average Israelis feel that Chabad is part of them.

Secondly, Halevi argues, "Chabad is the only Haredi group in Israel that reaches across the spectrum. The shoemaker in my neighborhood in Jerusalem, who comes from Bukhara,[93] has a picture of the Rebbe in his store."

Historically, Halevi says, Jews lived in different countries and had different traditions. "The great miracle of the return to Israel is that it brought together Jews from all backgrounds. Jews who lived in separate communities are now living together." Halevi says that those differences remain in the Haredi sector of Israeli society where "Sephardim and Ashkenazim attend different schools[94] and vote for different political parties."[95]

"In Chabad," he says, "there are Jews from all backgrounds." This was clear to me as a student in the yeshiva in Kfar Chabad.[96] It is one of the few major yeshivas with students from Yemen, Morocco, Russia, and European countries. Jews from diverse backgrounds and customs all found a home in Chabad.[97]

Finally, says Halevi, Chabad has earned the respect of Israelis for its willingness to engage in difficult modern questions. "Chabad has the courage to confront real issues." He says the Jewish world was transformed in the last century by four upheavals: the Holocaust, seventy years of Communism, Zionism, and the emergence of a self-confident American Jewish community.

According to Halevi, the traditional Orthodox community has not dealt with these challenges. "The Haredi world has acted like these revolutions never happened;[98] but the genius of Chabad was to respond to these most fundamental transformations."

Halevi does not agree with all the Chabad positions; he was supportive of the Soviet Jewry Movement,[99] and believes that the modern State of Israel is part of the redemptive process.[100] "Still, I respect the fact that, in Chabad, there is a struggle with these issues."

Today Chabad's network reaches into all aspects of Israeli society. There is hardly a community without a full-time Chabad Center. The Ministry of Education partners with Chabad in hundreds of schools and preschools. Beth Rivkah, in Kfar Chabad, is an accredited college for women. Summer camps and youth programs reach into hundreds of communities in Israel. There is a network of Yeshivas offering intense academic programs for young men in over ten cities. There are urban housing developments in major cities, and synagogues in almost every urban neighborhood in Israel. There are outreach programs for soldiers, and Chabad provides hundreds of thousands of holiday packages for soldiers on the front lines.

Colel Chabad[101] continues its two-century-old legacy of leadership in social services in Israel. It's the only recognized partner with the government in food security. Its network of soup kitchens delivers over one million meals annually. Colel Chabad operates medical clinics and absorption centers; it also has subsidized markets in cities across the country for low-income families. Annually, it sponsors a bar/bat mitzvah[102] celebration at the Western Wall for hundreds of children who have lost their parents. In 2014, the budget of Colel Chabad topped $27 million.

In the fifties and sixties, the focus was on building the core infrastructure of Chabad in Israel. Kfar Chabad became the movement's Israeli focus. The early residents were involved in agriculture; others worked in nearby Tel Aviv. With time, the community would evolve into a national educational center with a variety of schools. The community hosts tens of thousands of non-religious children annually in Jewish enrichment programs like matza bakeries. Almost every weekend, the community hosts groups from around the country that want to get a taste of traditional Jewish life. On the evening following Simchat Torah, thousands converge on Kfar Chabad to celebrate.

During this first period of growth, Rabbi Ephraim Wolf[103] headed the central institutions of Chabad and the yeshivas in Lod, Kfar Chabad, and Kiryat Malachi in the south. He took the lead in developing urban housing developments for Israelis and immigrants in Lod and Kiryat Malachi. Chabad moved Israeli Chassidic families into these developments,[104] creating a new dynamic community that was a catalyst for integration of the immigrants into mainstream society.

In the seventies, Chabad grew in Israel. The postwar generation began to move beyond the boundaries of Kfar Chabad to cities and towns across the country. These people had been imbued with the ideal of shlichus, and began the process of building a network of centers and educational institutions.

The Rebbe sparked the growth by sending Americans to Israel as shluchim. The first was Rabbi Laibel Kaplan to Tzefat in the North in 1973. His task was to rebuild the Chabad community in the ancient mystical city. Three years later, in 1976, the Rebbe began sending couples and yeshiva students to Israel. In total, thirty couples and twenty yeshiva students were dispatched. These young men and women had been nurtured in the Chassidic community in Brooklyn. The American brashness coupled by the Chassidic passion that was imbued from childhood by spending years in the unique spiritual environment of the Rebbe's synagogue in Brooklyn propelled Chabad forward in Israel.

In 1986, Rabbi Yosef Yitzchak Aharonov[105] assumed the leadership of the Chabad Youth Organization in Israel.[106] Today there are over 350 Chabad Centers in Israel. Rabbi Menachem Brod of Chabad in Israel says that Aharonov has a broad vision and great determination. "Aharonov would not let obstacles stop him to reach the goals with which the Rebbe had entrusted him." When the Chabad network of elementary schools, operated in conjunction with the Ministry of Education, had a crisis, Aharonov stepped in and assumed the responsibility. Brod says that in Israel, he is nicknamed a bulldozer. It wasn't just his determination that earned him such a nickname. Aharonov surrounded himself with an outstanding staff of capable, creative people.

Chabad's role in Israeli society is dramatically different from in the United States and other countries. Israeli Jews are far more traditional, some 60 percent keeping kosher,[107] while in the US, the number is a third of that. There are many avenues to express your Jewish identity.

Rabbi Menachem Kutner,[108] who directs Chabad's Victims of Terror Project, says, "They don't need you to say Kaddish (the memorial prayer)." Rabbi Zalman Gorelick,[109] who directs the network of twelve Chabad Centers scattered in the neighborhoods of the southern city of Be'er Sheva, explains that "within a few blocks of our Chabad House, there are over a dozen synagogues reflecting a wide variety of traditions. Israel, he says, is not like the US where they need you for basic religious services.

According to Gorelick, Chabad has a different role. "The Chabad Center in Be'er Sheva is the bridge between the more secular and religious segments of the population." Before Passover, thousands of children from non-religious Israeli schools visit Chabad to learn about the holiday and bake the hand-made shmura matza. The kids roll the dough, act out the Passover story, and see a movie specially made by Chabad in Israel that features cartoon characters.

Chabad in Israel has to overcome the stigma of the politicization of the religion. Rabbi Kutner recalls visiting a family whose child had been seriously injured in a terror attack. "When I finished with the family, they promised me, don't worry, next election we will vote for Shas," referring to the Sephardi religious party. Kutner says he had to explain to them that Chabad has no connection to Shas or any other religious party, and he was not seeking their vote.

Gorelick says by being non-political, he has earned the respect of many in Be'er Sheva. Municipal Government[110] support is vital in Israel for social services, and education and religious services. He says, "Politicians from the non-religious parties help us, since they know we have no political agenda." In Be'er Sheva, Chabad operates an educational network with over a thousand students. It includes early childhood, elementary, and high school. Rabbi Kalman Druk stands at the helm of the educational programs. Druk[111] says, "We have babies starting at three months old; this is essential to many working mothers."

In Kiryat Shemona, a northern city, just a mile from the Lebanese border, Chabad's shliach, Rabbi Yigal Tzipori, was voted the most popular citizen in a local poll seven years running. Tzipori,[112] who served in a crack commando unit, says, "In addition to educational programs, kindergartens, and youth centers, we have twelve facilities in Kiryat Shemona, a dental clinic, food pantry, and meals on wheels." During the Lebanon War when the city was being shelled, Tzipori stayed. "We provided thousands of meals to residents in the shelters with the help of Colel Chabad."

Even Yehuda is an upscale suburban community near Netanya with twelve thousand residents, the great majority non-observant. The religious and traditional attend one of the seventeen local synagogues. In 1990, Rabbi Menachem Noyman started a Chabad Center in the town's main shopping mall. Noyman[113] says that "on Shabbat, the only two things open in the mall are the movie theater and the Chabad Center. They have popcorn, and we serve herring and cake. Many times, people going to the movies walk into the Chabad Center. They are surprised to find a synagogue in the mall." As with other Chabad Centers in Israel, Noyman must raise his own budget. The great majority comes from the local community where "98 percent of donors are not religious." The local municipality also helps. Mayor Avi Harari[114] says, "Chabad in Even Yehuda has the largest and warmest heart for the residents of the community." Jokingly, he adds, "If [Noyman] would run against me for mayor, he would win."

On the High Holidays, Noyman converts the open space in the mall into a synagogue. It's part of a new national initiative created by Chabad in Israel called "The Open Synagogue." In over 350 locations in Israel, Chabad has created venues for High Holiday services for the public who do not attend services regularly. Rabbi Naftoli Lipsker,[115] who coordinates the network of Chabad Centers in Israel says, "In many cities we set up large tents, or use other venues such as malls that are closed on the holidays, to create a more welcoming and open environment for Jews to attend High Holiday services."

Rabbi Noyman says that in Even Yehuda, traditional Jews tend to go to one of the regular synagogues on the holidays. "The secular come to us. We have songs, stories and insights on the prayers." Over a thousand join the services for the High Holidays. One of the major innovations was to make the services child-friendly. "All the children stand near the shofar blowing; three hundred children congregate around the podium. They feel that it's for them."

Lined up in the entrance to the home of Rabbi Danny and Batsheva Cohen in Hebron every Friday night is a row of upward of seventy automatic weapons. They are deposited by soldiers who congregate weekly for Shabbat dinner sponsored by Chabad of Hebron. Four hundred Jews live in the historic city, the second most sacred in Jewish tradition. Close to nine thousand Jews live in nearby Kiryat Arba. Jews lived under Arab rule from the time when the Egyptian Sultan Saladin expelled the Crusaders in the late twelfth century. During the centuries of Arab rule,[116] there were moments of benevolence punctured by expulsions and pogroms. Jews were banned from entering the ancient holy site of the Tomb of the Patriarchs, the burial site of Abraham, Isaac, Jacob, Sara, Rivka, and Leah. In 1929, local Arabs massacred sixty-seven Jews. Afterward, the British army forcibly relocated local Jews, many of whose families had been living in Hebron for generations. In 1967, Israel liberated Hebron, and in the next year, Jews began to trickle back to the city where King David was crowned. The historical enmity of the Arabs, most of them highly religious, continued to create great tension in the city.

Rabbi Danny Cohen, who served in the crack combat unit, Golani, says the prime focus of Chabad in Hebron is the army. He says[117] that Hebron is unique. Every five to six months, there is a rotation of five hundred soldiers into the area. "There is no place in Israel where civilian life and military life are so intertwined." Chabad's mission is to support the soldiers, Cohen says. "They can have grueling patrols for up to twelve hours dealing with difficult situations. Our visits to the checkpoints uplift them and show someone cares." He says that it's important for the soldiers to gain an appreciation of the unique history of Hebron. "We want them to understand that they have a great privilege in protecting the historical legacy of the Jewish people."

Ben Kaye[118] of San Jose, California, volunteered for the IDF. His Nachal unit was rotated into Hebron for a six-month stint. He says that Danny Cohen is amazing. "He does everything for the soldiers and it's an open house with Danny. When Danny's volunteers turn up at all hours at your checkpoint, they call it Chabad on the Run. The hardest part of guarding is it's really boring and you're really tired, and they come give you company, they make your night."

Rafi,[119] who grew up in a town on the outskirts of Jerusalem, is a member of Sayeret Commandos. In 2013, his unit made a secret incursion beyond Israel's border to prevent a terror attack. Heading home silently through enemy territory, they were ambushed. "Shells hit us; I was seriously injured in the leg, making it impossible to walk." Evacuation by helicopter would compromise the mission. They had to get back to Israel on their own steam, negotiating the difficult terrain in the night. "I was carried on a stretcher for hours," Rafi says, and when they crossed the border, he was rushed to a hospital.

The mission was secret. In the hospital, he told other patients that he was in a motorcycle crash, only to be chastised by other patients as young and impetuous. "Military officers who came to check on my progress were told to dress in civilian clothes to maintain secrecy."

Bituach Leumi, Israel's National Insurance, which assists wounded soldiers and victims of terror, works with Rabbi Menachem Kutner of Chabad's Victim of Terror Project. Kutner says this time it was different. "Because of the secrecy of the mission, this time they did not tell me about Rafi." Months after the attack, when he finally discovered him, Rafi says, "Menachem was wonderful. He gave me a computer to help connect with others. When I finally left the hospital, he made me a celebration. Since then he is constantly in touch."

The greatest uplift was eight months later. Kutner brought Rafi with a group of ten soldiers for a two-week trip to New York. "It was the first time I truly relaxed since the attack," says Rafi. Kutner's partner was the Chabad Israel Center in Manhattan's East Side, headed by Rabbi Uriel Vigler. According to Vigler, "When our community sees people who are so happy, it gives inspiration. And the connections are for life."

Creating connections between Jews is the core of Chabad's mission in Israel, transcending the societal differences. A network of centers that reaches into every community, it is uniquely poised as the bridge between stratified parts of what is at times a divided community.

Former Israeli President Shimon Peres wrote:[120] "Chabad is the largest movement in Israel that tried, in essence, to tell the Jewish nation that the Torah is not just a matter in the head but also a matter of the heart. And therefore Chabad is working its whole existence to bring about the uniting of people."

Chapter Twelve
The Yeshiva

It was just two weeks after the assassination of President John F. Kennedy in November of 1963 when a short Russian Chassid, with a long, flowing beard, bushy eyebrows, a Russian-style cap and passionate determined eyes arrived at what was then called Idlewild[1] airport in New York. Reb (Yiddish for Rabbi) Mendel Futerfas had been allowed to emigrate two weeks earlier from the Soviet Union. During an official visit to Russia in summer of 1963, Harold Wilson,[2] then head of England's opposition Labor Party, questioned Russian Premier Nikita Khrushchev about the fate of Russian Jews. Khrushchev wanted to bolster the Labor party to be more amenable to Russia. He responded that if they wanted, they could leave. On the spot, Wilson produced a list that had been given to him by Jewish community leaders[3] in London. Three Jews were given exit permits due to Wilson's personal intervention, the group departing using their Russian passports with full status as Russian citizens. In November,[4] Reb Mendel arrived to see his family for the first time after seventeen years of separation.

Reb Mendel was imprisoned for almost nine years in the Soviet Gulag. He was released in May of 1955. He could walk the streets of Russia, but he still was a captive of a society that denied him basic rights of freedom of speech, religion, movement, and emigration. His discharge from prison was a green light to his family in London to secure permission for him to leave Russia on the basis of Family Reunification.[5] Twenty-eight times, they submitted applications at the Soviet Embassy in London. When that failed, Mendel's wife, Leah, traveled to Israel and applied to the Russian embassy in Tel Aviv. Each time, the Russians refused.

Reb Mendel had been a central figure in the Jewish underground that kept Judaism alive under the totalitarian Communist regime. He was one of the organizers of the Great Escape,[6] the audacious plan that succeeded in smuggling Chassidim out of Russia in the postwar era. His wife and two children had been on one of the last trains that crossed the border to freedom. After ensuring that over a thousand Chassidim had crossed the border, Mendel made his own escape attempt. Russian police arrested him and four others. At first, he was jailed for almost a year in the notorious Spalerka prison in Saint Petersburg. In a mock trial, he was sentenced to another eight years in Soviet labor camps in Siberia.[7]

Moshe Katzenelenbogen,[8] son of one of the Great Escape leaders, the Muma Sara, says Reb Mendel could not write or communicate with his family. Outside Russia, the Futerfas family found sanctuary in DP camps and eventually moved to London. Freed from prison, Reb Mendel could at last send a letter to London. During that long period of seventeen years, from the time he was arrested in 1947 until he left Russia in 1963, he could not speak to his wife and children. Following the family reunion in London, Reb Mendel wanted to travel to New York to visit the Rebbe. Reb Mendel's Russian passport made entry into the United States difficult during the post-Kennedy assassination scare. Through the effort of Chabad activists in the US, permission was secured. Two weeks after his arrival in London, the visa was granted, and within hours, Reb Mendel was headed to the US.

Reb Mendel's connection with the Rebbes of Lubavitch[9] was deep. As a child he was orphaned; his father passed away before his birth. Named after his father, he was always called to the Torah as Menachem Mendel, the son of Menachem Mendel.[10] At age five, he had yechidus[11] (a private audience) with the Fifth Rebbe, Rabbi Sholom DovBer, who blessed him with a long life. The Rebbe's wife, the Rebbitzen Shterna Sara, who was deeply touched by the young orphan, engineered the unprecedented personal audience. Mendel's mother often impressed upon him the unique quality of his audience with the Rebbe and the blessings[12] he received. He studied under the great scholars in Chabad yeshivas in Russia, most notably, the mashpiah (spiritual mentor) Reb Zalman Moshe Yitzchaki.

I first met Reb Mendel in 1972. The Rebbe had sent him as the mashpiah for Chabad's largest yeshiva (rabbinical college) in Israel, located in the Chassidic town of Kfar Chabad. At the time, some two thousand teenagers and young adults filled the classrooms of a variety of educational institutions, including the yeshiva, vocational schools, and teachers' seminaries. I was a student in the yeshiva.

After World War II, American and Israeli yeshivas were infused with exceptional scholars educated in the great yeshivas of pre-Holocaust Europe. These centers of learning carried the original names of their namesakes in Europe. In Israeli towns, institutions sprouted with Polish and Russian names like Pressburg, Ponovitch, Mir, Telz, or Slabodka, recapturing the grandeur of pre-war European Jewish learning. In the postwar era, the yeshivas underwent a renaissance, each reflecting educational philosophies that had been dominant in Europe before the war. The majority were rooted in the classic Lithuanian approach. Students in those yeshivas primarily studied Talmud. Some also included the study of Mussar (Jewish ethics),[13] even though some yeshiva scholars resisted that idea,[14] questioning whether it might de-emphasize the centrality of Talmud study.

The Fifth Lubavitcher Rebbe, Rabbi Sholom DovBer (1860-1920), took a striking new approach to higher Jewish education. In 1897 in the town of Lubavitch, he founded a new yeshiva, Tomchei Temimim (Pillars of Piety). The new yeshiva made significant innovations, while maintaining the highest standards of talmudic scholarship, instituting the study of Chassidic philosophy, avodah (prayer), and character development, as integral components of the curriculum.

One-third of seder[15] (study period) was focused on Chassidic philosophy. The radical shift propelled the mystical dimension of Torah to new prominence.

In some yeshivas, Pilpul (a method of studying Talmud through intense textual analysis) had risen to importance; students would build theoretical arguments on talmudic principles. At times, it was debated for the sake of debate. Rabbi Sholom DovBer advocated rigorous study, coupled with the practical. He argued that students should explore the legal arguments, underlying principles, and applications of these principles in the Code of Jewish Law.

The Enlightenment,[16] the effort to secularize the Jewish community, and many other forces, were eroding Jewish observance in Russia. Other trends were emerging, such as Zionism and Socialism, each offering its own unique solution to the Jewish question. In the coming years, Communism would take hold in Russia. Rabbi Sholom DovBer believed that the greater prominence of the mystical teachings would "create students imbued with a deep devotion to the love and awe of G-d," which would strengthen the students when facing the challenges brought about by societal changes.

Rabbi Moshe Tzvi Segal[17] was a student in a classical Lithuanian yeshiva when Communism began its persecution of Jewish tradition. Years later, he told me, "The oppression was too much for many yeshiva students, and they shed their observance. The students of Chabad's Yeshiva Tomchei Temimim were among the few who held strong. That unwavering spirit impressed me. That's why I became a Chassid." The new yeshiva in Lubavitch was designed to produce a student whose commitment to Judaism was not superficial, but embedded in the very core of the student's identity, at the same time instilling a sense of responsibility to the totality of the Jewish community.

To accomplish these goals, the Fifth Rebbe, Rabbi Sholom DovBer, not only revolutionized the standard curriculum, but also the basic structure of the yeshiva.[18] Historically, yeshivas were centered around a rosh yeshiva (head of the yeshiva). Typically, he would be an outstanding talmudic scholar who would be the driving force in determining the character of the yeshiva. Most yeshivas are small institutions with rarely more than a few hundred students.[19] The rosh yeshiva can have an intimate relationship with his students. Yeshivas have a much more rigorous academic schedule than modern university. In Chabad yeshivas, study of Chassidic philosophy begins as early as 7:00 a.m. The day is divided between lectures and seder (peer study in the Zal,[20] or study hall). The formal end of learning is at 9:30 p.m. During the day, there are breaks for meals and religious services and a short rest period in the afternoon. Lithuanian-styled yeshivas are similar, starting with prayer and then study; they also finish late in the evening.

The newly established Chabad yeshiva had two departments and faculties. One was Nigleh, the revealed part of the Torah, such as Talmud, Jewish law, and Bible, which was headed by a rosh yeshiva, a talmudic scholar. The second division was Chassidus, the esoteric teachings of Jewish mysticism as expounded by Chassidic philosophy. This was headed by a mashpiah, which means, literally, "one who influences." The innovation of adding the mashpiah, or spiritual mentor, to the yeshiva faculty had a profound change in the educational approach of the yeshivas. The expertise of the mashpiah was Chassidic philosophy. The mashpiah's priority was molding his students' characters and directing them in the service of G-d. He would develop a close personal relationship with the students. Using Chassidic philosophy, he would challenge students to examine their personal qualities, helping them transform themselves into better people. The Alter Rebbe, the founder of Chabad, in his magnum opus, the Tanya, writes that a person has the ability to "change the nature of his character traits." One mashpiah once told me that this means not just transforming the way we act, but, rather, altering our underlying nature.

One of the central ideas of the Chabad approach that differed from other Chassidic groups was personal empowerment and taking responsibility for one's own improvement. Some Chassidic groups taught that attaching yourself to a Rebbe, a great Chassidic leader,[21] who himself was saintly, would ensure your spiritual welfare. For Chabad, the Rebbe would provide direction, the mashpiah, the tools. The avodah – the personal effort and, at times, the heavy emotional lifting – in examining one's traits and correcting them, must be done by the individual himself.

At times, an intellectual tension simmers under the surface in some Chabad yeshivas between the two divisions of Nigleh and Chassidus, the revealed and mystical parts of Torah. It's not unusual for the rosh yeshiva and the mashpia to be at odds over educational priorities. The rosh yeshiva's main concern is academic achievement in Talmud. The mashpia seeks to instill values, raise spiritual awareness, help the students to realize their potential, and encourage them to modify personal qualities that are undesirable.

Chassidic philosophy delves into the deeper spiritual essence of Judaism. It focuses on the nature of the soul, spirituality, G-dliness, and human spiritual resources. In a Chabad yeshiva, students explore esoteric mystical concepts. Students may be debating the ten powers of the soul or how G-d could be finite and infinite, good, evil, and the purpose of life.

In classical Lithuanian-style yeshivas, the primary focus is on the analysis of Talmud, occasional forays into ethics, and a bit of philosophy. Theological discussion about Divine Providence or the dynamics of the soul are not part of the curriculum. A student's prime goal in the classical Lithuanian[22] yeshiva is to become a Gadol, a great scholar of Torah. In Chabad, the suggestion of learning to "become a Gadol" was considered imperfect. Rabbi Schneur Zalman, Chabad's founder, argued that Torah[23] was the gift of Divine wisdom to the world; there can be no greater human aspiration than to connect with the Divine. "Learning Torah creates a spiritual bond between G-d, the giver of Torah, and man." He argued that learning should be for the sake of acquiring Torah and not as a means to achieve personal greatness.

Rabbi Sholom DovBer's new yeshiva's educational philosophy encouraged a student to transform himself with prayer, meditation, and commitment to religious observance and, at the same time, to excel in Talmud study. He taught that students should internalize their beliefs. The most derogatory term there was in a Chabad yeshiva was "Chitzon" (an externalist, one who puts on a show, whose ideals are not part of the essence of his personality).

Those differences in educational philosophies still exist today. When a young man goes off to a classical Lithuanian-style yeshiva in Israel or the US, he will be told, as the student a century ago in Europe was told, that his greatest aspiration is to become a Gadol B'Torah (a great Torah scholar). In Chabad yeshivas, this attitude is frowned upon. The purpose of learning is to become closer to G-d by studying Torah. Aspiring to become great could be driven by ego. The educational philosophies and academic goals continue to be radically different. A student in a Chabad yeshiva is told to aspire to Bitul (humility and sincerity in his service of G-d). Learning is central; there is a great focus on enabling the student to learn how to transform himself, to become a Pnimi (one who has internalized Judaism, so that it is truly a part of oneself, not simply displayed outwardly).

Across the globe, in the post-World War II era, the Russian mashpi'im had a tremendous impact on the future of Chabad and the development of the first generation of shluchim. They were not only imbued with the essence of Chassidic philosophy, they were living role models of spiritual courage, having endured hardships few could imagine: Reb Shmuel Levitin and Rabbi Israel Jacobson in Brooklyn, Reb Nissan Nemanov in France, Reb Shlomo Chaim Kesselman, and later Reb Mendel Futerfas in Israel, Reb Peretz Mochkin in Montreal, and Reb Zalmen Serebryanski in Melbourne.[24] They were outstanding Torah scholars, men of great piety, Chassidic passion, and devotion to the Rebbe and his teachings. This group of Russian émigrés was the link to a world rich in Chassidic lore and legend. They had walked down the pathways of the town of Lubavitch, most students of the original Chabad yeshiva there. They had been Chassidim of both the Sixth Rebbe, Rabbi Yosef Yitzchak, and, in their younger years, his father, the Fifth Rebbe, Rabbi Sholom DovBer.[25] In their youth, some knew elder Chassidim of a century before.[26] They were the bridge between the rich spiritual life that existed in Europe in the nineteenth century and the modern era. They had faced down the Soviet juggernaut undaunted. Almost all had spent some time in prison under the Communists. Their protégés became the next generation of mashpi'im that slowly took the reins as the Russians began passing away in the seventies and eighties.

For close to a quarter of a century, the mashpiah in Kfar Chabad, Chabad's largest yeshiva in Israel, had been the legendary Rabbi Shlomo Chaim Kesselman.[27] He had been a mashpiah in the underground yeshivas in Russia. Fleeing Russia after the war, he found refuge in Israel, where he educated a generation of Chassidim.

His devotion to his students was legendary. In the early fifties, the Chabad yeshiva was located in an old ramshackle building in the midst of an orchard near the train station in Lod. Off in the distance, the rumble of trains could be heard. Reb Shlomo Chaim lived in one of the rooms of the yeshiva with his family. A few years later, when the yeshiva moved to a larger building, Reb Shlomo Chaim finally moved into a small house of his own adjacent to the yeshiva. He demanded much from his students, prodding them to spend hours in personal contemplation and prayer. He wanted his students to develop a deep knowledge of Chassidic philosophy and apply it to their own spiritual development. Rabbi Elimelech Zwiebel,[28] who later became the mashpiah in Morristown, New Jersey, and who studied with Reb Shlomo Chaim in his younger years, says, "His whole life was avodah – prayer and meditation – and his dedication to his students."

By the time I arrived at the yeshiva in early 1968, the ramshackle building was a memory. The yeshiva had moved down the tracks a few miles west to Kfar Chabad. There was a new building with a large study hall, library, classrooms, and dormitory. Nightly at 6:30 p.m., Reb Shlomo Chaim would briskly stride into the study hall or Zal, as it was known, with his shoulders bent a bit with the years, his gait still strong. Suddenly, the room would fill with the noise of students who would push tables and chairs together forming one large table. They would listen over a hundred at a time to his nightly classes in Tanya, the classic of Chassidic philosophy. On days of importance on the Chassidic calendar, Reb Shlomo Chaim would lead a farbrengen. He would inspire the students through the night with Chassidic insights, stories, and guidance. Students from other yeshivas would join these nocturnal gatherings. Many a time we would sit until the sun peeked over the horizon.

Reb Shlomo Chaim demanded avodah from his students. Avodah, in Hebrew, means work or labor. According the Talmud, it is arduous spiritual work, done through prayer, which is service of the heart. It would not be unusual on a Shabbat afternoon to see twenty or thirty students in contemplative prayer. Sitting separately, immersed in his thoughts, Reb Shlomo Chaim would be meditating on the teachings of Chassidic philosophy that expounded the concepts of Divinity and G-dliness. This came after a morning filled with preparation, rising early, immersing in the mikvah,[29] followed by an extensive study of Chassidus, and the regular prayer service. After the formal prayers were completed, the students would practice Hisbonenus (contemplation, evoking deep feelings of awe and love of G-d that would be channeled into the prayers), which could last for hours.

Reb Shlomo Chaim would spend long periods at prayer, arriving daily to study at 7:00 a.m., followed by services and his own private prayer meditation. Many a time he would not arrive home for breakfast until just before noon. On Shabbos he could easily sit until two or three in the afternoon before he would go home for the Shabbos meal with his family. Reb Shlomo Chaim used to say, "They have created machines to do all kinds of tasks: dishwashers to clean, planes to make travel easier, but no machine to pray for a person. That, you have to do yourself." Davening, which is intense prayer, is considered the key to spiritual development in the Chabad system.

The Sixth Rebbe, Rabbi Yosef Yitzchak, explained, "If we want a sense of the Divine, we must work for it." He argued that in the Chabad approach to spirituality, "Everything begins with the mind; emotions are volatile and less easily controlled, and only through the mind are they harnessed and matured." Chabad philosophy attempts to bridge mind and emotion: "Prayer, prepared for by meditation and accompanied by reflection, bridges the gap between our minds and our hearts, and thereby influences the way we live our lives."

Reb Shlomo Chaim attempted to infuse his students with a sense of purpose in everything we did, not just with prayer. He would stress the idea of Iskafia (restraint from overindulgence in physical pleasures). At a farbrengen,[30] he once remarked, "We need to have bread and we need to have butter, but who says the butter has to be spread on the bread?" Food is needed for sustenance, not just for enjoyment. By eating, we would have the energy to serve G-d to the fullest.

When Reb Shlomo Chaim passed away on a Friday in the spring of 1971, the yeshiva was left bereft. Thousands had passed under his tutelage. Ingrained in the souls of a generation were the values of spirituality, avodah, and self-sacrifice.

The Rebbe turned to Reb Mendel, who had rebuilt his life in London, to assume Shlomo Chaim's position. After leaving Russia, he had started a textile business in England. There, he became one of the Chassidic elders. Annually, he would make a trip the US to raise money to send food to Jews in Russia for the holidays.[31] Life had not been easy for him. As soon as he arrived from Russia, his only sister died; some years later, his daughter suffered a terrible accident, losing her life and leaving her children orphans. Ever the Rebbe's soldier, Reb Mendel took on the task, even though he had reservations about his ability to fit into the academic world of the yeshiva. He wondered how he could communicate with this younger generation. In a private meeting, the Rebbe told him, "You will find the correct words for the right person in the right time."[32]

Reb Mendel ushered in a new era. Reb Shlomo Chaim's life had been centered in an academic environment, removed from the trials and tribulations of ordinary life. Reb Mendel had been a community activist, a businessman, and had endured a long sentence in prison. He had a sharp wit, was very perceptive, and was renowned for his insightful stories pulsating with life lessons. He brought a fresh approach to molding the next generation of Chassidim. Daily, we were confronted with a mashpiah who was a living legend. As per the Rebbe's instructions, after he left Russia he continued to wear the Russian-style hat to remind the world of the plight of Russian Jewry.

When Reb Mendel was released from prison in Siberia in the late fifties, he was ordered by the Soviets to live in the town of Chernovitz in southern Ukraine. On the way to Chernovitz, he traveled through Moscow. There he met his old friend Moshe Katzenelenbogen,[33] son of the legendary Aunt Sara,[34] who had worked closely with Mendel in organizing the Great Escape. Moshe had finished his seven-year stint in the Gulag. He was living quietly in Moscow, attempting to stay under the radar of the Soviet police. Moshe helped Reb Mendel to get started again. "We got a few friends together to provide Mendel with a financial stake. All he had were his prison clothes."

After the basics were taken care of, money was left over. "It was a sizable amount, but Mendel told me to hold onto the cash and he would send for the money when he needed it." Reb Mendel discovered that the Communists had eradicated all Jewish education in Chernovitz. Mendel sent for the funds to open a secret underground school. Moshe explained, "He used the money to bring a teacher to Chernovitz." Discovery of Reb Mendel's new school would have been the ticket for another long prison term. But fear was not a word in his lexicon. If Jewish children needed education, he would provide it, even if it meant risking a return to Siberia.

Reb Mendel was an embodiment of Mesiras Nefesh, self-sacrifice for others. To the students of the yeshiva, Reb Mendel was a real live hero in their midst. Despite the hardship[35] he encountered in his life, he had an upbeat sense of optimism that was infectious. He saw himself as nothing more than a foot soldier for the Rebbe, doing whatever he was called upon to do.

In most yeshivas, students are given free time on Friday afternoons. Students in Chabad yeshivas were encouraged to dedicate their Friday afternoons to outreach projects. We would travel to Tel Aviv and other nearby towns to give Jews the opportunity to fulfill the mitzvah of laying tefilin.[36] This was part of the Tefilin Campaign the Rebbe had started with the advent of the Six-Day War.[37] Reb Mendel would join his students, since he felt that, as a Chassid, he must follow the directions of the Rebbe.[38]

One Friday, he accompanied the students a few miles down the road to the infamous Ramle Prison, where Israel kept its toughest criminals. At first, the inmates looked at the man with the long white beard and funny Russian hat with amusement. He told them, "You're prisoners. Let me tell you about a real Russian prison in Siberia." Instantly, the mocking tone of the inmates turned to one of great respect. This old Chassid was one of them; Reb Mendel had found a

commonality with the lowest element of society, and was using that
bond to raise them up and inspire them.

Reb Mendel modified the educational direction of the yeshiva.
I don't know if this was by design or just the reflection of a nature
that was very different from his predecessor.

He wanted us, first and foremost, to be Chassidim of the Rebbe,
to be willing to put ourselves on the line as his followers. While
retaining a focus on prayer, there was a striking difference from his
predecessor. Reb Shlomo Chaim required that his students go through
a long period of spiritual preparation before making the pilgrimage
to the Rebbe in Brooklyn. At Reb Mendel's first farbrengen[39] in Kfar
Chabad, he encouraged the students to make the trip to New York
immediately, and not wait a few years until after they had moved up
the ladder of scholarship and spiritual service. Reb Shlomo Chaim
advocated a more deliberative process, and Reb Mendel a more spon-
taneous approach.

The spiritual objectives in a Chabad yeshiva are daunting.
Students are urged to be completely immersed in a series of high-level
learning goals: absolute devotion in prayer, highest levels of personal
adherence to Jewish Law, and active responsibility for the spiritual
welfare of others. Each one of these is a full occupation unto itself. As
part of one's daily responsibility, it seems almost impossible – unless
an altogether higher goal is aspired to, at which point all the huge
areas of focus become spokes in the wheel of ultimate fulfillment and
no longer appear contradictory. That goal is described as "hanochas
atzmuso" – giving one's own self away completely to G-d and spreading G-dliness. Reb Mendel felt that spiritual humility could be best
achieved by observing and learning from the Rebbe's embodiment
of that lofty ideal.

Not all were enthralled with Reb Mendel's new path. Some of
the students felt that the subtle shift away from such intense attention to avodah as the prime focus undermined the foundational
principles of the yeshiva.

At the time, we did not realize that this change represented a
transition of Chabad from within.[40] Chabad was a movement whose
priority was personal internal, spiritual development. Chabad still

differed from other Orthodox groups that advocated insularity from the broader society. Instilling in the students a sense of responsibility for those beyond the Chassidic world was always a priority. Reb Mendel shifted the focus; he moved the idea of being a Chassid of the Rebbe from important to center stage.

By the early seventies, the Rebbe's revolution was still in its early stages; the number of shluchim was still small. Reb Mendel stressed the bond between Rebbe and Chassid. This prodded students to think more seriously about the idea of becoming a shliach of the Rebbe. This, said Reb Mendel, "was the highest calling we could aspire to; there could be no greater purpose than dedicating our lives in the service of others." In the eyes of Reb Shlomo Chaim, becoming a shliach was a noble goal, but what was most important was your own prayer and learning. To Reb Mendel, being a shliach and fulfilling the Rebbe's mission was the paramount purpose in life.

Learning to engage Jews distant from observance is an essential part of the educational process of Chabad yeshivas. In the forties and fifties, Chabad yeshiva students in New York would dedicate an hour of time on Wednesday afternoons to Released Time,[41] teaching Jewish children in public schools the basics of Judaism. Summer months, the older students of the main yeshiva at 770 in New York would fan out to Jewish communities around the US and abroad on the summer outreach project known as Merkos Shlichus.[42] This culture of outreach had not yet been fully ingrained into the Israeli yeshivas until Reb Mendel arrived.

On Jewish holidays such as Purim and Chanukah, the Rebbe would instruct the yeshiva students[43] and his Chassidim to visit the soldiers serving in the Israeli army. During those years between the Six-Day and Yom Kippur wars, we would board buses after midnight, arriving in the Golan Heights, the Lebanese border, or the Suez Canal as the sun rose. One visit remains embedded in my consciousness.

One Purim at 2:00 a.m., we got on the buses destined for the Golan Heights. The War of Attrition was at its height in the wake of the Six-Day War. The border would heat up when Syria routinely hit Israel with artillery barrages. As the sun rose, we climbed the narrow road to the Golan Heights. Not far from Syria, the yeshiva students and Chassidim were split up into small groups. Our goal was to bring the holiday spirit to every base along the front lines.

Near the border, at one of the larger encampments, we broke out the Purim hamantaschen, some vodka, and other refreshments. We read the Megillah of Esther, the traditional Purim story, and provided soldiers with a chance to do the mitzvah of tefilin. It was just ten in the morning, but the joy was infectious. In an army camp in a war zone, we danced and celebrated the holiday in its fullest sense. I was in the midst of putting on tefilin with one of the officers and suddenly an artillery barrage began. The Syrians had decided to liven up the festivities. Fearing civilian casualties, the officer hastily removed the tefilin and ordered us all in an army truck. As artillery shells rained down, we evacuated the position.

Sitting in back of the canvas-covered army truck as it was racing from the front line, an old Russian Chassid turned to us and, in Yiddish, announced to the young students, "Today you had a tremendous zechus (honor)." We looked up in amazement, failing to understand the honor in almost getting killed by a Syrian artillery barrage. Finally, he explained in Yiddish, "Today you had true self-sacrifice for your fellow Jew."

This sense of responsibility for others started in the early twentieth century when Rabbi Sholom DovBer dispatched some of his leading scholars, graduates of the yeshiva in Lubavitch, to remote Soviet Georgia to care for the spiritual and educational needs of Jews in this distant land. In the US, this had evolved into a more formal approach in the forties when the Sixth Rebbe would send his yeshiva students out in the summer to visit Jewish communities. In the early fifties, when a father complained that he did not want his son spending a few weeks in the summer gallivanting around the small towns of America, the Rebbe wrote him that this was an important component of the educational goals of the yeshiva. "The fact that your son did not participate in these programs causes a deficiency in his education."

In February of 1967, this concept of shlichus took a leap forward. Rabbi Hodakov, the Rebbe's chief of staff, invited a group of students to a meeting. Yossel Minkowitz[44] was eighteen and wondered, "Why would Rabbi Hodakov meet with me, a simple yeshiva student?

Did I do anything wrong?" He felt consoled when he saw six others jammed into Hodakov's tiny office at the end of the hall on the first floor of 770. Hodakov wanted to know if they were willing to travel to far-off Australia to invigorate the small yeshiva in Melbourne.[45]

Avraham Altein[46] was not aware that he was on the list of those invited to the meeting. He was off in the Bronx, where his parents had founded the Chabad yeshiva in the forties, giving a class. He arrived back in Crown Heights after a long subway ride around midnight. Walking into 770, he heard singing. From the lobby, he observed a group of students gathered around the table in a farbrengen.

At first, he thought it was just a regular late-night gathering that would take place from time to time on a Thursday evening. Before he could find out, however, he was told that Rabbi Hodakov was looking for him. He hurried to the office at the end of the hallway on the main floor of 770. From behind the desk, Rabbi Hodakov peered at him; he was a man who measured his words carefully. He told Altein what he had shared with the others earlier. "Would you be willing to be one of the group that would spend two years in Australia? The mission is to energize the new yeshiva in Melbourne." He outlined three conditions: "You must go with Simcha V'tuv Levav – with happiness and full heart, you must have your parents' consent, and finally, you must have authorization of a doctor that you are in good health."

When Minkowitz and his friends met earlier with Rabbi Hodakov, they had asked him who wants them to go. Hodakov evaded the question: "I can't answer that question. You must make your own decisions with a full heart." The Rebbe had made the choice of the students. Hodakov feared that if he revealed that fact, they might feel a sense of obligation to go, and not make their own independent decisions.

At the farbrengen in the study hall, the students were debating that very issue – who was asking them to undertake this journey? Their mashpiah, Rabbi Dovid Raskin, told the students, "There is no question in my mind. The initiative came from the Rebbe." At the same time, Altein was asking Rabbi Hodakov the identical question. Hodakov, ever cautious with his words, finally admitted to Altein that the Rebbe had chosen the students.

The Rebbe's initiative of sending the students was not the first time the idea had been suggested to create a yeshiva in Melbourne. In 1940, a group of yeshiva students,[47] escapees from Europe, had ended up in a refugee camp near Brisbane in the north. They connected up with the small religious community in Melbourne. Moshe Feiglin and Yisroel New decided to pool some of their money and purchased a house in Carlton, the working-class Jewish suburb, to open a yeshiva. When the official community leadership, dominated completely by proper English Jews,[48] got wind of the plan, they raised money to send the refugees to the United States, saying, "We don't need this old-fashioned Judaism here in Melbourne."

In the post-World War II years, more Chassidim moved to Australia, mostly Russian refugees who had escaped the clutches of Communism. They started a small yeshiva in the farming community of Shepparton with three students. Eventually it moved to Melbourne, evolving into a network of Jewish schools. The idea of a full-fledged college-level yeshiva continued to percolate for some years. In 1965, a delegation of local rabbis headed by Rabbi Chaim Gutnick[49] traveled to Israel to meet the heads (roshei yeshiva) of the prominent Lithuanian yeshivas to request that rabbinical students be sent to Australia. They rejected the proposal outright. "We cannot send outstanding students to a spiritual desert. The risk is too great;[50] we can't undertake such a responsibility."

Nevertheless, the idea began to gain steam in the Australian summer of 1966, when Rabbi Zalmen Serebryanski, a community elder, publicly called for a yeshiva to be established. That year, the first class was graduating high school from the Chabad school. With a yeshiva in Melbourne, they could continue their Jewish studies instead of going abroad to study. Serebryanski felt that only a yeshiva would bring the proper spirit of Judaism to the community. Shortly afterward, he wrote to the Rebbe, and Rabbi Chaim Gutnick went to New York to discuss the proposal with the Rebbe, who insisted that, first, local students must begin the program in Melbourne, then he would consider sending students from overseas. A small group began learning and setting the stage for the arrival of the American students.

Australia was a distant land. This was at the beginning of the jet age. Travel was costly. Communications were difficult; phone calls were prohibitively expensive. There was no e-mail or texting. The only real means of communication was by mail. The students would have to spend a full two years in Australia, far from family and friends. In Australia they would miss the richness of Torah and spirituality that they had experienced being near the Rebbe in New York.

Eight had been asked; two had some personal doubts. Apparently they informed the Rebbe of their concerns and were immediately excluded. One of those six who went recalls, "The true reason was their own hesitation. Both seemed to lack the 'full heart' that was required."

By Friday afternoon, three students informed the Rebbe that they were ready. Some of the others needed a bit more time to get their parents' consent. On Shabbos morning, the other three notified the Rebbe via his secretary, Rabbi Groner, that they, too, were prepared to go. The Rebbe clearly was delighted, and it was announced there would be a farbrengen after services. At the farbrengen, the Rebbe talked about the importance of the mission and asked all of them to stand up and say, "L'Chaim!" He said, "You cannot go as a shliach unless you can stand on your own feet." The Rebbe wanted them to think for themselves and apply their own individual creativity to the assignment that he was entrusting them with.

Three of the students were eighteen, and three nineteen. The unofficial leader of the group was Laibel Kaplan, not yet twenty. In two and a half weeks, they were leaving. Airline tickets, visas – much needed to be done, but the most important preparations were spiritual, not logistical. The night before their departure, the group had a private audience with the Rebbe. For half an hour, the Rebbe talked about their assignment. "You must brighten Melbourne and transform all of Australia." In detail, he outlined their responsibilities: "First, you must dedicate yourselves to the study of Nigleh and Chassidus (Talmud and Chassidic philosophy) with great dedication." The Rebbe demanded of them to be role models to the rest of the community.

The next afternoon was the day of departure. The Rebbe met briefly with them again, reminding them of their mandate. He also spoke to them about Rabbi Eliyahu Simpson[51] who was traveling to Australia. "He is from the elder Chassidim, one of the early founders of the Yeshiva Tomchei Temimim in Russia, and he will give you direction and guidance." Simpson had been one of the outstanding students in the town of Lubavitch at the turn of the century; now six and a half decades later, he would escort a new generation of students, connecting the old world with the new. The Rebbe added, "You will have to use your own abilities," again stressing that the key to success was for them to use their own initiative.

When the Americans arrived in Australia, Yosef Loschak was a teenager in the high school in Melbourne. "In those days, Melbourne was a small, close-knit community, primarily of Holocaust survivors. They hadn't seen yeshiva students since before the war; now, all of a sudden, young Americans turned up. They were bilingual, fluent in old-world Yiddish, at the same time they had an American brashness. The community appreciated the sacrifice they were making, traveling from so far for their benefit."

Yitzchak New, a Melbourne businessman, recalled decades later at an engagement party in Melbourne,[52] "The students became role models for us on what a yeshiva student is supposed to be." Looking around the reception hall, he pointed out one person after another who decided to become Chabad Chassidim due to the influence of the yeshiva students. New was inspired to attend yeshiva, and at eighteen, he traveled to Kol Torah, a Lithuanian yeshiva in Jerusalem. After a while, he became a bit disillusioned, discovering firsthand the differing philosophies of the Lithuanian style and the Chabad style. "When I began to compare the values of those students to ones I had met in Melbourne who had been sent from New York, I realized the vast contrast. At Kol Torah, I did not find such a great emphasis on personal spiritual growth; the prime focus was intellectual achievement." Seeking that balance between academics and spirituality, New eventually left Kol Torah and joined a Chabad yeshiva.

The model proved a great success. The first group returned to New York after two years, and a second one was selected. A new pattern was slowly emerging of sending groups of students away from

New York to serve as the nucleus of a yeshiva. Eventually this plan would expand, transforming the Lubavitch educational system.

In 1973, the Rebbe took a new step forward, launching a broad initiative to develop the network of Lubavitch yeshivas. The first of the new smaller community yeshivas was in Miami. Not long afterward, a long list of cities was added: Los Angeles, New Haven, Johannesburg, Sydney, London, as well as places in Morocco and Argentina. A total of some thirty-five cities around the globe would eventually boast college-level Lubavitch yeshivas. Many had the same challenge as in Melbourne. Senior students from outside were essential to create the atmosphere that mirrored the values of a Chabad yeshiva. A core of students, usually eleven, just one more than a minyan, brought the vitality of learning required.

At first the Rebbe was personally involved in sending the groups. As the years went by, a system evolved. Until the Rebbe's passing, the administration of the larger yeshivas in New York, New Jersey, and Montreal would recommend the students and the Rebbe would approve. Today, they make the choices.

Young men attend main college-level Chabad yeshivas in Brooklyn, Montreal, or Morristown, NJ, for three or four years. After their senior year, they are sent as shluchim to one of thirty communities. Their primary goal is learning. They are given crucial responsibilities. They mentor the younger local students. This system is particularly helpful to weaker students who receive much needed personal attention. This system instills idealism at a young age. While studying in main yeshivas, the students apply themselves to learning. There is competition among the students to be selected for a prestigious place to be sent. Rabbi Leibel Schapiro, rosh yeshiva (dean) of the yeshiva in Miami, explained: "It gives the students a sense of responsibility. Until then, the student is learning for himself; he is focused on his own personal growth. Later, he is expected to go out in life and help others. Now, within the context of the yeshiva, he is assisting others in learning." More important, Rabbi Schapiro says, "The students serve as role models for the younger ones."

Propelled to leadership positions, it changes their own behavior, causing them to mature. A young man from America may find himself traveling up the Amazon to visit a small Jewish community, or studying with a lawyer in Los Angeles. He might be filling in at a synagogue for the rabbi away for the weekend, or assisting a weak student with educational challenges. Some students spend a year or two, depending on the needs of the various yeshivas. Afterward, most begin focusing on the final stage of their studies leading to Smicha (rabbinical ordination).

After Smicha, most get married and then spend a year or so in kolel (post-rabbinical training). At that time comes the decision about their direction in life. A significant number follow the path of shlichus, looking for a position around the world. Others go into business or careers that provide them with a livelihood. A few outstanding scholars may spend additional years in Torah study.

Chabad always puts a strong importance on Torah study for women.[53] In tandem with the yeshiva system, there is an international network of women's seminaries for college-level study.[54] Some thirty schools in Israel,[55] Europe, the us, and Australia provide an intense Jewish educational experience for young women. These educational programs reflect the philosophy of the yeshivas established a century ago in Lubavitch. In addition to the study of classical texts of Torah, there is a strong focus on the mystical, the study of Chassidic philosophy. Young women are challenged to explore the central ideas of Jewish mysticism and grapple with great questions of spirituality and purpose in the world.

Young women are also strongly encouraged to follow the path similar to yeshiva students in outreach and community involvement. Almost all Chabad teens and college-age women serve as counselors in the network of Chabad day and overnight camps that exist in almost every Jewish community across the globe. Many spend a year teaching or assisting in Chabad Centers after they complete their studies. Students of Beth Rivkah,[56] Chabad's central campus in Kfar Chabad in Israel, teach in communities in the Former Soviet Union as part of their academic requirements.

Simchat Torah in the small town of Lubavitch in 1900 was a special celebration. Chassidim had traveled from all over Russia to join the holiday celebration. Three years had passed since the Fifth Rebbe, Rabbi Sholom DovBer, had established his yeshiva. He said that he pondered the project for some fifteen years. Finally after making a spiritual pilgrimage to pray at the grave of the founder of the Chassidic Movement, Rabbi Israel Baal Shem Tov, he launched the yeshiva in 1897. Students flocked to the new yeshiva. Clearly the project was a success.

Rabbi Sholom DovBer's motivation to create the yeshiva was the shifting societal winds that were pulling Jews away from their heritage. To offset that, he created a unique yeshiva to instill in students a deep spiritual commitment. On that Simchat Torah, the Fifth Rebbe addressed the students, reflecting on the early success and the goals of the new yeshiva.

"We are assured that the students of Tomchei Temimim – wherever they may be on the four corners of the world – will realize the quality of self-sacrifice for the higher purpose of creating a dwelling place for G-d in the physical world."[57] The Rebbe quoted the talmudic dictum that an antidote is created before the illness, explaining that the students of the yeshiva would be a vanguard against the elements of change that had been eroding the historical bond of Jews to their heritage.

Temimim[58] (literally, the pure ones) is a term of endearment used to describe the students of the yeshiva. The Rebbe exclaimed, "You are like the soldiers of King David,"[59] recalling the ancient soldiers who were renowned for their devotion to the Jewish people. Citing the talmudic teaching that, before battle, the soldiers of King David would write a bill of divorce to their wives[60] (if their fate in battle was unclear, this would permit wives to remarry), the Rebbe drew an analogy saying, "You should detach yourselves from worldly concerns and make a priority of scholarship and spiritual development. The learning of Chassidic philosophy would give you the passion to overwhelm the coldness of the world to spirituality." He told them the study of Chassidic philosophy would give them the spiritual fortitude to be Jewish leaders and to "stand strong" for principles and ideals of Judaism.

In the coming years, these students[61] would serve as Jewish leaders. They would be propelled into tumultuous times starting with

World War I and the Communist revolution. The students of the yeshiva became the core of those who led the secret Jewish network in Russia.

The yeshiva itself would have an arduous history. With the German invasion, it relocated to Kremenchug and then Rostov, going underground with the advent of Communism. The Sixth Rebbe reopened the yeshiva again in 1927 in Otvotsk near Warsaw, after escaping from Russia. In 1940, after fleeing the Nazis, and arriving in the US, he established the yeshiva in Brooklyn, to educate the new generation of leaders who would spearhead his American revolution.[62]

In the US, a new set of challenges would emerge. Creating leaders whose spiritual fortitude could lead modern Jewry toward a renaissance in a time when traditional Judaism was losing momentum would be a challenge. The synergy of classical Jewish learning with the mystical teachings of the Chassidic philosophy, coupled with a focus of spiritual self-reliance that the Fifth Rebbe envisioned over a century ago, inspired a new generation of Jewish leaders. The yeshiva,[63] founded in Lubavitch in 1897, became the incubator for the next generation of Jewish leaders that, in time, would spark a worldwide Jewish renaissance. Today thousands of its graduates serve in communities across the globe.

Chapter Thirteen

Balancing on the High Wire

Many Chabad rabbis and rebbitzens live in a strange dichotomous world. Walk into a shliach's home in Jacksonville or Bangkok and it won't be much different from a religious household in Jerusalem or Brooklyn. Western culture seems to have paused at the front door. The walls are lined with classic Jewish texts. Arrive near the onset of the Sabbath or a Jewish holiday, and you will sense the aromas arising from the kitchen. A long table stretches across a dining room, set with fine china waiting for Shabbat to arrive. Bedrooms seem to overflow with children. Most families have at least five or six; ten and twelve is not unusual, and a few even exceed that. A Jewish melody may be emanating from a sound system. The art on the walls will be portraits of rabbis and pictures of Israel. Homes ooze the richness of Judaism. When you step outside a religious home in Brooklyn or Jerusalem, the surrounding community overflows with tradition. For shluchim the society surrounding them is incongruous with their own.

As Rabbi Yosef Loschak[1] of Santa Barbara, who lived on a four-acre expanse including his home, a synagogue, mikvah, and school, explained, "We need to create our own environment, we need to create Crown Heights or Jerusalem in our home." Another shliach says, "Our home is like a fort on the prairie. I live life as a Chassid in a world that dances to a different drummer." Still, Loschak emphasizes, "We do not cut ourselves off from modern society; however, the values that guide our lives are rooted in Torah."

Rabbi Laibel Wolf,[2] a noted scholar who travels the world speaking on the Chabad circuit, observes: "The shluchim have to do everything; they are overwhelmed. They are the fundraisers, community organizers, rabbis, teachers, parents, and spouses. They are pulled in every direction." Balancing such a diverse life is a complicated task. There is the social isolation; and then there is a 24/7 job that keeps you always in the public eye, constantly being there for others, even for some who may fail to appreciate your commitment to them. There is the grinding pressure of fundraising, and the financial stress from living dependent on the generosity of others. Upholding your religious standards in communities that do not live according to the same ideals isn't easy. The availability of kosher food can be an issue. In some countries, security and threats of terror may pose a risk. All of this makes the life of shluchim both challenging and rewarding.

The most daunting task is raising children. Nothing is more important to religious families than their children carrying on their values. Modern open Western society is poles apart from the shtetl, the small European village of centuries ago where everyone lived in a homogenous community. Even parents living in urban areas surrounded by a rich, religious life of yeshivas, synagogues, and kosher restaurants can find this task difficult. Educating children in a community that may give little reinforcement to the values taught in the home, and at times, few friends for your kids, is more daunting. In many cases, the shliach's children may be the only observant or Chassidic kids in town.

There had been strident criticism from Orthodox Jewish leaders,[3] particularly in the early years, that Chabad – in the quest to help others – was putting its own children at risk. The Previous Rebbe, and later the Rebbe, gave blessings guaranteeing his followers that their children would not be lured away by the culture that would surround them. Despite living outside the Orthodox world, their children would remain Chassidim. There has not been any formal research, but it seems, from anecdotal observation, that Chabad rabbis and their wives are enjoying a remarkable degree of success in inspiring the next generation.[4]

A majority of children of shluchim continue on the same path in life as their parents. According to the *Los Angeles Times'*[5] a surprising 67 percent of the married children of shluchim in California also become shluchim, assuming posts in California and across the globe. Former *Times* religion writer, Bill Lobdell, says, "This is an astonishing number compared to other religious groups." Two, and even three generations may be shluchim in the same families.

Noted educator, Rabbi Yitzchak Newman, says the idealism is instilled in the kids from a young age. "When you are brought up on shlichus, your model is passionate Judaism." He says the children see the joy the parents have in helping another Jew and drawing him closer to observance. "That is a motivating factor in their own lives."

Rabbi Zalmen Leib Markowitz is an educational consultant for the Chabad community, and he helps families of shluchim with educational challenges across the globe. "When you live in a religious community, you pay tuition and you throw your child into the ocean of Yiddishkeit." Parents expect the school to instill the values. He says that shluchim who live in smaller communities are much more involved with the educational process of their children.

Being brought up in communities where the majority is not observant prompts children (and their parents) to question their values. Parents work harder to instill Judaism in their kids. This creates a Judaism that is rooted in a deeper understanding of its teachings and the surrounding society. Children in religious communities may take their observance for granted. They may never have to question their own values and beliefs and may be ill-equipped to deal with a broader society with a different value system. Markowitz also says the children of shluchim are involved in their parents' work. "Judaism is not something you happen to observe. When you are giving to others, you are more sheltered from outside forces."

Rabbi Yosef Bolton, who is a Chassidic life coach in Meron, Israel, specializes in helping families with children who drift from observance. He himself suffered a crisis of conscience as a teen, stepping away from the religious lifestyle for a few years. At a shluchim convention in New York, he led a workshop concerning children who have become less religious. He says the numbers of those "who become non-religious is very small." Just ten people attended this closed-door session that was designed to help families who are coping with this issue. While parts of the Orthodox world tend to shun those who drop observance, he says, "In Chabad, most families keep the connection." Kids who may not be religious are still welcomed at their homes. He also argues that among shluchim, the dropout rate is lower than the general Chabad community. He says, "The shluchim tend to have strong family relationships, the kids suffer less from peer pressure, and the parents have a strong influence upon their children."

As the scope of Chabad's work has expanded, the challenge has become more diversified. Today, there is hardly a community where shluchim cannot be found, from cities like Tucuman in Argentina, to Tomsk in Siberia. In a thousand locales, children grow up with no peers who are religious like they are. Children carry the responsibility, and at times for some of them, the burden, of being different. Families that live close enough to a Chabad community have the benefit of a Chabad-run yeshiva-style school.[6] Others may attend a Jewish day school where many of the students do not share their intensity of religious observance.

Shluchim in smaller towns and remote communities are faced with difficult choices. Public school[7] is not an option; the key to Jewish continuity is Jewish education. If there is no Jewish school at all, or maybe one whose educational philosophy is far from classical Jewish values, parents face a thorny conundrum. Should they send their kids away, or homeschool? The Internet has opened new vistas with an online school. Parents still anguish over the choices, weighing the welfare of staying home against the need for proper

Jewish education. As Rabbi Heshy Epstein of Columbia, South Carolina, recounted some years ago at the major address at Kinus Hashluchim, "The most painful moment is watching your kids walk down that Jetway."

The Internet has opened new vistas, allowing for the creation of an online school. Parents still anguish over the choices, weighing the benefits of staying home against the need for actual brick and mortar school education. When the children of Rabbi Yosef Loschak were young, he faced this dilemma, and at that time, there was no online school. "At the time, it was the hardest part of shlichus – having to send away your kids," he said. When his children reached the ages of eight to twelve, he started sending them to Los Angeles, a hundred miles down the crowded freeway.[8] They would board in homes during the week and come home every weekend. Still, he found that "as good as the homes of our friends were, there is no replacement for a mother and father."

Some shluchim send their children to family or grandparents, but this may not always be the perfect solution. One shliach discovered his parents had a difficult time caring for rambunctious young kids. He said, "Bubbees and Zaides are great to visit, but not to live with fulltime."

Things have changed dramatically in recent years. In 2006, the Shluchim Office[9] in New York established an online school. It started evolving, as so many other ideas in Chabad, from the ground up. The first class was started for three girls with a daily forty-five-minute conference call. Within a month, it evolved to three hours on the phone. Rabbi Moshe Shemtov, who coordinates the program, said, "Initially, we called it 'home-school phone-school,' and within a few months, over a dozen kids were enrolled."

It was the ingenuity of two curious nine-year-olds that changed everything. Two Mendels, one a Shmotkin from Milwaukee, the other a Levertov from Santa Fe, New Mexico,[10] started learning Talmud on the phone with a teacher. The two Mendels did some research and discovered Paltalk, an online chat room that allowed them to see each other. Rabbi Moshe Shemtov says, "The idea sparked a revolution; next year we changed the program to online, using the Internet."

Now, over 650 children worldwide, from four years old through eighth grade, are enrolled. Classes are kept small, around fifteen kids each. Teachers around the country teach the classes.

One of the most amazing stretches of technology happened when Rabbi Chaim Goldstein flew from Texas to New York after celebrating Passover with his family in 2010. "I taught my morning class in El Paso," explains Goldstein, "but as I was boarding the plane, I still couldn't find a substitute for my next class. So I logged on using American's Wi-Fi service." Throughout Goldstein's flight, his nine students – who hail from Salt Lake City, Utah; Orlando, Florida; San Diego, California; and other places – were transfixed by an image of their teacher leading lessons from an airline cabin. Mendy Konikov from Orlando, who was ten at the time, says, "I was so entertained that I called my parents over to watch." According to Konikov, the class continued unabated until a flight attendant passed by and asked Goldstein to straighten his seat back, stow his tray table, and turn off his computer. "So we got a twenty-minute recess."

For Rabbi Berel Levertov in Santa Fe, New Mexico, it's been a great help. "This is an incredibly innovative program that allows me to keep my children at home while giving them the quality of education they would receive at a proper yeshiva or traditional Jewish day school," says Levertov, who has four out of five children enrolled in the online school.

The school uses modern technology to teach ancient ideas. Giti Rosenfeld, the school principal, explains: "We are on a platform where the teacher can view up to six kids at a time." The challenge is keeping all of the students involved. "Teachers rotate the students in groups. The younger classes are placed into groups by color. At one time, the red group is on webcam, then the blue group. When the kids are off webcam, the teacher may ask the kids to write on chat box." There are other ways to keep them involved. "One of the kids can be the pointer for the text on the virtual blackboard so the teacher can know the child is still participating."

Rosenfeld says the biggest challenge is that "the child is not in our room. When a student has an issue in a regular school, the teacher can go over to him and talk to him. That can't be done in the online school." Discipline problems require active parent involvement. To keep her hand on the pulse of a school in multiple time zones and teachers in various states, she gets copies of all communications with the parents. "We are constantly working with our staff to improve the program and assist them." She does have one advantage over a regular principal, though: "I can enter any class at any time; everything is virtual."

The English-language school based in the us has classes for children both in Europe and North America. Schools operate in their time tracks starting at 9:00, 11:00 or 12:30 Eastern Time. The Hebrew-language school is based in Israel.[11]

Rosenfeld says one of the school's goals is to create social opportunities for students. "Teachers assign study partners, joint projects, and school-wide programs that require teamwork among groups of students. The kids use the phone, e-mail, and Skype to communicate." Before the online school, Chabad children in smaller communities did not see another Chassidic child except in the summer or at family gatherings. Giti explains that "now they know other Chabad kids their age; they meet every day during school. We have the annual day of celebration in New York, and more than half of the students attend. When kids hit the bar/bat mitzvah year, some will travel to their classmates' celebrations."

The online school has enabled more children to stay at home, although the lack of friends can be a serious issue. One shliach in a small community in California told me, "The online school did not work for my son; he needs the classroom environment with other children and a real teacher." Another shliach, whose kids have a long commute from their suburban neighborhood to a local Orthodox day school, lamented the social isolation. "They have no peers in the area. The toughest time is on the weekend. Shabbos, they don't have friends to play with. Most of their classmates are not observant and live miles away."

Rabbi Yehuda Krinsky understands the unique problems. His son is a shliach in the small Jewish community of Manchester, New Hampshire. In the midst of a farbrengen with shluchim in New York, he became very emotional as he drew a comparison from the ancient

Biblical story of Abraham sacrificing Isaac, to the modern children of shluchim. "Why is the story of Akedas Yitzchak (the binding of Isaac) so significant in the Torah? Many other Jews have sacrificed themselves throughout history; what is so unique about Abraham? Our forefather, Abraham," Krinsky went on to explain, "acted quickly and zealously." With tears in his eyes, Rabbi Krinsky said, "Today's Akedas Yitzchak is the shluchim who raise their children in an environment where there are no other religious kids. The couple decided to go on shlichus, but the children didn't; they need friends and they don't have them in these communities, that is the greatest sacrifice."

For some children, the idealism of the parents is not enough. Some children yearn to live in a community where they can have other Chassidic friends. Other children find the communal demands on their parents difficult.

The problems are dependent to a large degree on the kind of community. The early shluchim went to cities with larger Jewish populations, places like Miami, Chicago, Los Angeles, and Philadelphia. At that time, many of these cities did not have Lubavitch-run schools, but there were schools under Orthodox auspices that met the needs of families. Nowadays, these cities have large Chabad communities. Today, the greater challenge is in smaller cities. As Rabbi Yitzi Loewenthal[12] of Copenhagen says, "Shluchim are going to towns where they know that, due to limited Jewish population, there will not be a proper school for their kids."

Shani Katzman[13] moved to Omaha in 1987 with her husband Mendel, to inaugurate the Chabad regional office for Nebraska. They moved into an apartment in town provided by a local supporter of Chabad, who told Mendel, "Rabbi, you won't make it more than a few months." He wasn't the only one full of skepticism. Rabbi Isaac Nadoff, the Orthodox rabbi in the local traditional synagogue[14] was nearing the end of his career when the Katzmans arrived. He was just as pessimistic, telling him that "Omaha had its own special kind of Orthodoxy." Despite his skepticism, Nadoff was very supportive, paving their way into the community.

The Katzmans were faced by the same dilemma as many shluchim in smaller communities. The local Jewish day school was a "community school,"[15] the curriculum was all-inclusive, a little of everything for everybody. Most are not under Orthodox auspices. At times, the educational philosophy may be at odds with classical Jewish values. In some communities, compared to traditional day schools and yeshivas, the Jewish studies are far under par. The teachers tend to be secular Israelis who might have little personal commitment to religious observance. Chabad shluchim are placed into a difficult situation. Local community leaders may ask, "Why isn't our school good enough for you?"[16] When the Katzmans' kids were growing up in Omaha, there was no online school, so they opted to homeschool. Shani says, "Homeschooling was the new in-thing in the US; many younger families who wanted a better education for their kids were trying it."

The Katzmans' oldest, Estie, left Omaha when she was twelve to study in Beth Rivkah in the midst of the Chassidic community in Brooklyn. Shani says, "I waited for Estie to say she wanted to go to New York." Estie[17] says, "I didn't really want to, but I was not getting the kinds of friends and learning I was supposed to have." She found New York different. The warm atmosphere of her grandparents' home helped the adjustment. Still, it took a while to fit in with the New York kids who were a bit cliquish. "They all knew each other for a long time and I was new. In some ways, they were also much more naïve about life; I knew a lot more about the world outside of Brooklyn."

Children who grow up on shlichus encounter a world much more diverse than kids who grow up in Lubavitch communities such as Crown Heights. Religious communities tend to be more insular, while children of shluchim encounter people from all kinds of backgrounds. Their homes are filled every Shabbat with guests, the great majority not fully religious. Estie says if she had the choice to do it all over again, she would prefer to be brought up in Omaha than in Brooklyn. "I'm glad I was brought up on shlichus. For sure, I missed something, but I am able to deal with different things that they are not able to."

Mussia Kesselman and her sister, Fraide Kessler, grew up in Rancho Mirage, California, where their parents, Rabbi Shimon and

Chaya Posner, are shluchim.[18] "In nearby Palm Desert, we had a small school with a few kids in the class," Mussia says. When the sisters were eleven and twelve, they began a weekly commute to Los Angeles. Every Monday at 5:00 a.m., they packed into the car to arrive at school on time for classes. "We dreaded those early mornings." They would board with a family member, and then come home every Thursday night. Growing up surrounded by a diverse group of people affected them, Fraide recalled years later. "I found we were much more mature than other girls the same age." She says her parents were remarkably involved. "They never just sent us off.[19] They took us to school, and they never missed parent-teacher nights, even though they had to make the long drive in from the desert to attend."

There were many lonely moments in the youth of Devonye Korf, who grew up in Casablanca, Morocco. Her parents, Rabbi and Mrs. Leibel Raskin, were pioneering shluchim to Morocco in the late fifties.[20] The girls in her high school in Casablanca were not as religious as she was. Young girls could not walk the streets of the Arab city without an escort. After school, Devonye had little social interaction and spent much time in her teens reading and listening to Jewish music. "Once, when my parents were out of town, one of my classmates invited me out to an event that was not appropriate. 'Come,' she said, 'your parents are away and will never know.'" Devonye felt it was unsuitable and did not attend.

Years later, Devonye and her husband, Leibel, became shluchim and started the Chabad Center in Los Feliz, a hip area of Los Angeles, filled with members of the entertainment community. Devonye plans to be protective of her kids as they grow up. It will be somewhat easier than her childhood in Casablanca. Just a short commute away is a Chabad school full of Chassidic kids.

Rabbi Shimon Lazaroff and his wife, Chiena, came to Houston in 1972. The Rebbe had stipulated that he could go to Houston on two conditions: one, that there be proper education for their children, and, second, that there be a kosher mikvah in the city. When they arrived in Houston, they discovered that the local day school under Orthodox auspices had a level of learning far below the yeshivas that their children had attended in Detroit.

A shliach in another community faced the same situation. He told Lazaroff that the Rebbe advised him, "Children need a social outlet and should be around other kids. Place the kids in the school for the general studies and homeschool them for the Jewish curriculum." The Lazaroffs decided to try it, and the principal of the school in Houston was very understanding. Half a day, Rabbi and Mrs. Lazaroff homeschooled their kids in Torah, and their children attended the community school for secular studies. This arrangement worked for four years.

A new principal took over the school and insisted the kids attend the whole day. The Lazaroffs gave it a try. Nine-year-old Lazer, whose level of Jewish learning far exceeded the local kids, was placed in ninth grade with kids some five years older than he was. He was advanced in Talmud and very bored. Rabbi Lazaroff met with the principal and requested that the previous status quo be reinstated. The new principal rejected his proposal. Finally, Lazaroff told him, "I will give you ten days to agree or otherwise I will open my own school." The principal laughed in response. Lazaroff then called the school president to apprise him of the situation and his intentions. Everyone thought he was bluffing.

Ten days later, Rabbi Lazaroff called the principal and asked, "Nu, have you made a decision?" He answered, "No. We have not even had a meeting." The next day, Lazaroff opened Torah Academy in the newly built Lubavitch Center. He placed an ad in the *Houston Jewish Herald* announcing that Chabad had started a day school. Mrs. Lazaroff left her job at the Hebrew Academy to become the principal and teacher.

When the paper was published a few days later, the calls started coming. "Why can't you make a compromise?" complained one local rabbi. Lazaroff responded that he had tried and now it was too late. Besides, he said, "Chabad does not close institutions; it only opens them." "How many students do you have?" asked the rabbi. "Four, thank G-d. I have four kids of school age," responded Lazaroff. Once the local pressure failed, one of the local community leaders even contacted some officials in Chabad headquarters in New York, seeking force on Rabbi Lazaroff to close his new school. Today, Torah

Day School has over two hundred students, and a beautiful facility of three buildings of forty thousand square feet. It receives support from the local Jewish Federation and is well regarded in Houston.

One of the keys in educating kids on shlichus is to imbue them with the ideal that they, too, are shluchim. Children of shluchim are instilled with a sense of mission from a very young age. They understand that they are shluchim and representatives of the Rebbe.[21] Kids take on responsibility at a young age, helping with programs. My kids began working as teachers' aides in our local Hebrew school when they became teenagers.[22] When my daughter attended post-high school seminary, she discovered a common bond with other children of shluchim, saying, "We all spent our youth sticking the labels on the mailings." One Chabad Rebbitzen who brings college-age Chabad girls to teach in her community every year, told me, "Right away, I can identify the children of shluchim; they pitch in to help, clear the table from the meal, and are much more willing to be of assistance."

Chabad has been developing programs in recent years to give spiritual, educational, and emotional support to shluchim's children. There are special camps for the children of shluchim in the US, Europe, and Israel. At the shluchim conference and the women's conference, a concurrent conference is held every year for the kids.[23] The kids have a program filled with activities, speakers, and inspiration. They participate in the banquet, the highlight of which is the Kinus, marching in, singing, with flags from the over sixty countries and states they represent. There are years when a child is selected to address the close to five thousand guests at the banquet. My Shliach, a program of Lubavitch headquarters, has special programs for the children of shluchim.

Being in the public eye can be stressful for children. Some kids relish the attention; others do not enjoy being in the public light. Once my oldest daughter,[24] who was just around ten or eleven, had been involved in some kind of mischievous behavior. A community member berated her, saying, "You are the rabbi's daughter; how can you act like this?" She retorted, "I am just a kid."

Some children resent the constant public pressures. Their parents' responsibilities can be 24/7. One son of a shliach, who grew up in a small Midwestern town, said, "My parents made the choice to live such a life separated from the Orthodox community where I would have few friends like myself; it was not my decision." Community members may drop in at any time for advice and assistance. As Rabbi Yossi Serebryanski in Denver[25] says, "In most families, Shabbat is a special time for the family and kids; for shluchim it's their prime time." Children need proper attention. The demands of the job can easily create conflict. For that reason, Rabbi Yitzchak Sapochinsky of Westlake Village, California, says, "You should remember to use the decline button on your cell phone. Dinnertime, bedtime, and even driving with the kids in the car should be times of minimal interruption."

Campus shluchim have it tougher than most. Drawing lines between family and community can be daunting. Keren Blum, a shlucha in Columbia University, lives on the upper floor of her Chabad House. Students tend to drop by any time, even late at night, but she gives her guests clear guidelines. "While we welcome them at all hours, boundaries need to be set. At times I must be firm in order to protect the family's closeness." She says that scheduled time together with her husband is a priority, even just to take a walk around the block.

Research of the lives of rabbis of all stripes has shown that they suffer from a degree of isolation. A Conservative rabbi told me, "Congregants don't want you as a friend; they want you to be their rabbi. They don't understand that you also need a social life; they prefer to put you on a pedestal as something to admire from a distance."

On top of balancing the budget and his family, a shliach must maintain fidelity to the ideals of Chabad and Jewish tradition.[26] I discovered that challenge firsthand when we used our newly built Chabad Center in Yorba Linda for the first time. I was faced with an indignant Israeli woman. It was Shabbos; her purse was dangling by her side with her cell phone clipped to it. Her husband had donated toward the construction of the building and something was clearly bothering her. "The mechitza is too high," she complained, gesturing with her hand and speaking in Hebrew.

The mechitza[27] is the divider between the men and women in the congregation. It ran through the middle of the sanctuary. Both women and men could clearly see the front of the congregation and feel part of the services. It is one of the prime features of a traditional congregation and reaches back to ancient times. Solomon's Temple in Jerusalem had separate sections for men and women. The mechitza had been a battleground[28] in American Jewish communities in the mid-twentieth century when many Orthodox synagogues shifted their affiliation to the Liberal Movement. Halacha dictates that a synagogue must have a mechitza.[29]

In her mind, her husband's donation gave her the right to dictate the religious standards of the sanctuary. Quietly, I attempted to be both firm and understanding. "This is what Jewish tradition requires. We are not going to remove it." She continued to berate me, demanding that the mechitza be lowered, at least. She felt that her opinion must be considered the most important. After all, she told me, "My husband helped you build the building."

Finally in exasperation I turned to her and said, "If you make another donation, I will be able to make the mechitza higher." She left in a huff, but the message was clear. Judaism is not for sale.

Unlike Chabad Centers, many synagogues spend much time arguing over issues of religious observance. Professor Samuel Freedman of Columbia University explains in depth in his book, *Jew vs. Jew*,[30] about the long debates in a Conservative congregation over a change in ritual. For decades, American rabbis have been fighting off the instructions of lay people on what kind of Judaism should be practiced. Congregations created religious committees that subjected tradition to a democratic review. The committees were filled with people who cared deeply about Judaism, but may not necessarily have been very knowledgeable. Historian Dr. Jack Wertheimer writes that the spirit of individualism in America causes people to define their own style of Judaism. Instead of the people listening to the rabbis, it became the reverse.

The problem for many American rabbis is they could easily lose their jobs if they don't heed their congregations. At times, synagogue boards select rabbis based on their willingness to accommodate them.

In many instances, the rabbi's scholarship, beliefs, or ideals are not the defining factor, but, rather, the feelings of the board.

As Walter Bruckner, a former president of a Conservative congregation and an active member of our Chabad Center in Yorba Linda, often jokes, "The religious committee meets once every fifty years on the second floor." He then points out to the listener that "we have a one-story building."

The Rebbe's approach reinstated the rabbi to a position of communal authority. He was following the traditional model for thousands of years, in which rabbis were communal leaders. It is an authority based on Halacha, not on the latest whims of a religious committee. The Rebbe had instructed the early shluchim from the beginning that they must ensure that institutional policies follow the principles of Jewish Law. When questions arose, the Rebbe would instruct the shluchim to consult a Rav (rabbinical judge) to respond based on Halacha. On important issues, Rabbi Hodakov, the Rebbe's chief of staff, would convey the Rebbe's decision. These guiding principles remain policies for Chabad Centers.

It was not only in issues of law but also even minor traditions that the shliach was instructed to stand up for on principle. In 1979, for the first time ever, Chabad had erected a menorah in Lafayette Park opposite the White House. This was during the height of the Iranian hostage crisis. President Carter emerged from the White House for the first time in one hundred days to attend the menorah lighting. It was the fifth night, and in accordance with tradition, that number of candles was to be lit. The president turned to Rabbi Avrohom Shemtov, "Why not light all the candles? It will bring more light into the world." Shemtov was in a dilemma, should he break tradition and light additional candles or hold strong on principle? Torn, Rabbi Shemtov suggested that a child light all the candles on a small menorah that was also being lit. He reasoned that it was just a custom, and this was a minor holiday. The president was happy. Later, Shemtov wrote a report to the Rebbe, who responded, "I thought you would have Gaon Yaakov (hold strong to the traditions with a sense of confidence)."

Following principles can have major financial implications. That's what happened to the Hebrew Academy, the Chabad-run community day school in Huntington Beach, California. The school had instituted bingo as a fundraiser. Before starting the program, the school director had consulted with a Rav, an expert in Jewish Law, and had received a ruling that tradition did not prohibit bingo. It proved a great success, raising over half a million dollars a year. Another Chabad institution in California also launched bingo. This time the Rebbe was consulted; he expressed strong opposition to the idea.[31]

Chabad's head shliach in California, Rabbi Baruch Shlomo Cunin, was passionate that the school must adhere to the Rebbe's policy. In Huntington Beach, the community leaders who made up the school board were deeply opposed. The rabbis in the school were caught in the middle. They all wondered, as Rabbi Yitzchak Newman says, "How could the school survive with such a dramatic loss of income?" Cunin persevered, saying, "The Rebbe said no bingo, so we can't have bingo." It was a painful decision. "We had to totally recalibrate our finances," says Newman. Despite the turmoil the decision caused, the school continues today to meet its annual budget and operate without a deficit.

The Rebbe succeeded in creating a new kind of Jewish institution – one that refuses to compromise on issues of principle and, at the same time, is free from much of the politics that dominate Jewish life. As Rabbi Yitzchak Adlerstein,[32] who teaches Jewish Law at Loyola Law School, explained, "This was the uniqueness of Chabad, it did not compromise on issues of Halacha. This was also the secret to its success: earning respect with clear standards." Leonard Weiner, who was active in our local Conservative congregation for years, used to tell me, "You guys don't move the goalposts."

When shluchim need guidance, they seek the opinion of a Rav (a rabbinical judge,[33] an expert in Jewish Law.) Rabbi Leibel Schapiro, dean of the Rabbinical College of Miami, answers questions from shluchim around the US. Rabbinical judges, he says, have to apply the laws of the Torah to modern situations: "Each question and community has to be judged according to its unique conditions." He explains that the role of the rabbinical judge is to assess the situation and review the legal precedents. "We have to try to rise to a higher standard," he says. "There are times when it's important to explore sources that may be more permissive, for instance in a case when a more lenient ruling[34] might create an opportunity for more Jews to gain an appreciation of Judaism." Schapiro says that we cannot change the core values of Halacha, which, according to Jewish tradition, are part of the Oral Tradition[35] of the Torah that reaches back to Sinai.[36] Rabbi Schapiro is a member of Chabad's Central Rabbinical Court in New York. "Larger questions that may not have precedent or that affect many Chabad Houses are submitted to the whole committee for review and adjudication."

The key to keeping motivated is Torah study in the great classics such as the Talmud and the codes. The richness of the Rebbe's teachings continues to inspire. Shluchim study the Rebbe's teachings each day – from more than two hundred volumes of published works – providing them with the Rebbe's insight on their everyday activities. The approach to outreach, the value of the individual Jew no matter his or her level of observance, the importance of Jewish education and fulfillment of the mitzvoth, the connection of all mankind with G-d and His desire to transform this world into a better place – the relevance of the Rebbe's talks is such that a person reading them today feels that they were, indeed, taught just today.

Security has become a more important concern to shluchim, in particular in the wake of the terror attack in Mumbai. Chabad operates in over eighty countries, and security procedures are designed to meet the unique needs in each location. Still, there is a tension[37] between the philosophy of openness and welcoming and the concern for possible attacks, such as Mumbai. Shluchim, in consultation with Chabad's Security Commission at headquarters in New York and local police officials, craft distinctive protocols for each community.

In the US today, kosher food is available almost everywhere, or can be shipped in from larger cities. In some smaller, more remote countries, the matter of kashrut can be a real problem. Korea has a small Jewish population. Rabbi Osher and Mussy Litzman arrived there just before Passover in 2008. They are both from Israel where kosher food is never a problem. Things are not so easy for the Litzmans. Mussy[38] says, "Bread, we have to bake at home, and there are no local kosher dairy products." They have to go to a farm an hour and a half north of Seoul, near the DMZ,[39] to get kosher milk[40] and make cheese. Meat is a major challenge, since the importation of kosher meat is banned. "Once we did have a kosher slaughterer, but it is not economically viable to bring a schochet (ritual slaughterer) to Korea due to the small Jewish population. We are dependent on the kindness of visitors who happen to bring meat with them," says Mussy. There are close to a thousand Jews living in Korea. Some are in business; many are English teachers.

Mussy grew up in Kfar Chabad, Israel, where she had dozens of friends her age. Nowadays communications are easy. "We have an Israeli number and call home regularly. Our kids, who are still small, use Skype to talk with their grandparents.

In the remote countries, the loneliness can be very challenging. Holding onto your sense of mission is not simple, when you are far from friends and family. My wife loves to tell the story of the shliach who went off to a faraway community. Every year he would write the Rebbe about the challenges of his situation – the lack of education, community, and other hardships. Every year, the Rebbe would instruct him, "Stay." Finally, after some years, he wrote the Rebbe that he was becoming more comfortable in his situation. Then the Rebbe wrote him that maybe he should consider leaving. Apparently the shliach was losing his sense of mission.

Constantly remembering that you have a mission entrusted to you is difficult. Keeping that spark alive is a challenge. Burnout can happen to anyone. Rabbi Tzvi Grunblatt[41] learned this firsthand in 1982. The economic situation in Argentina was terrible. The impact on the network of Chabad institutions was disastrous. Military coups, corrupt governments, and a shaky economy had created a situation in which it was next to impossible to raise the funds needed to keep the schools, outreach programs, and community activities afloat.

The situation was so bleak that some of the shluchim were considering leaving. "What will happen in this country, what will be the future?" thought Tzvi Grunblatt, the head shliach. The country was teetering on the verge of disaster. People in the community were coming to him seeking advice, concerned about the future.

Tzvi decided to turn to the Rebbe for advice, but getting a call out of the country was not easy. Calls had to be booked hours, if not days, in advance. He decided to try, and, surprisingly, he reached Rabbi Hodakov, the Rebbe's chief of staff, instantly. He told Hodakov to ask the Rebbe what he should tell the people. "They want economic and political predictions from me, what should I do?"

After asking the question, he hung up. A minute later, the phone rang. It was Rabbi Hodakov with a reply.[42] Hodakov gave over the Rebbe's instructions: "We did not send you there to make a calculation of the economics of the country; you were sent to spread Judaism and the teachings of Chassidism. You do this with trust in G-d. Surely the community leaders will ask your opinions about the economic situation. You should answer that you are not a prophet and your mission is Judaism with faith in G-d."[43] To Grunblatt, the point was clear: teach Torah, stay on message, steer the course, and give the people the spiritual fortitude to overcome the present crisis.

Balancing on this high wire, while being true to the values that the Rebbe instilled, and at the same time reaching out to the community, is not always simple.[44] There are over a hundred e-mail forums where these issues are debated daily.[45] Shluchim discuss programs, policies, and ideas. There is a constant need for balance between creativity and preserving tradition, with a variety of ideas. At the regional, national, and international conferences of shluchim, the discussion continues in sessions. Shluchim constantly ask themselves, "Is this the Rebbe's intention? Am I remaining true to my mandate and mission?" As Rabbi Shlomo Cunin says, "We have to remember why we were sent here."

No person exemplified that sense of mission more than Rabbi Shmuel Dovid Raichek. He was sent in 1949 by the Previous Rebbe as a Shadar to Los Angeles. A Shadar (Shlucha Derabanan) is a personal ambassador-at-large of the Rebbe. Shadarim do not run institutions or serve specific communities. They have a double mandate of instilling spirituality and collecting funds for the Rebbe's use. Each Rebbe had one or two such special roving ambassadors. Raichek was a Shadar until he passed away in 1998.

Rabbi Raichek was a student of the Chabad yeshiva[46] in Otvotsk near Warsaw before World War II engulfed Europe. Escaping Poland, he headed east toward Japan. From Japan, he went to Shanghai[47] where he spent the war years as a student in the Lubavitch yeshiva. After the war, he immigrated to the US. In 1948, he married Leah Rapaport, who hid from the Nazis during the Holocaust in Poland. Rabbi Raichek spent months each year on the road, with a variety of missions from the Rebbe. Rabbi Raichek's deep passion was to encourage others to put on tefilin. The Tefilin Campaign had been initiated by the Rebbe just prior to the Six-Day War. Raichek carried it out to his last day.

The most remarkable example of his commitment to his mission was in the White House in 1983. A group of Chabad rabbis had been invited to meet President Reagan in honor of Education Day USA,[48] declared by Congress in honor of the Rebbe's birthday. The rabbis were in the West Wing waiting to enter the Oval Office and meet with the President. Rabbi Shmuel Kaplan[49] of Baltimore described the events:

One of the staffers was Jewish and Rabbi Raichek asked him to put on tefilin. He was open to the idea, but stressed. In a panicked voice, he said, "In the White House?" Raichek was not deterred. "We will find a place," he said. He took him by the hand and started opening doors in the West Wing, finally finding a large closet. Raichek maneuvered the staffer into the closet, closed the door halfway, and began putting on tefilin.

Clearly, Raichek was not awed by the White House. In his mind, there was only one thing: the mission the Rebbe had entrusted him with. In the White House, he had an opportunity to fulfill a mitzvah with another Jew. Moments after the staffer performed the mitzvah, the rabbis were ushered into their appointment with President Reagan in the Oval Office.[50]

Rabbi Raichek never lost his balance, never for a moment forgot his mission.

Chapter Fourteen

A Tale of Two Cities

Growing up in the Israeli town Kiryat Malachi, Zalman Zaklos had heard tales about Siberia from older Russian Chassidim. A large group had immigrated in the late sixties to Nachalat Har Chabad,[1] the city's Chabad neighborhood. They would sit around the synagogue at farbrengens on Shabbat afternoon or late into the night. At these Chassidic gatherings, there would be melodies, toasts of L'Chaim on Russian vodka, and stories of the incarceration in the harsh Soviet Gulag. The old-timers in Kiryat Malachi had been part of the Jewish underground that sustained Judaism in Communist times. They had lived through the terror of the KGB, and, in secret trials, had been banished to Siberia for failing to surrender Jewish observance. Young Israelis like Zalman were in awe of such courage and conviction in their midst.

In 1999, sitting in the posh lobby of the Renaissance Hotel in Jerusalem, Zalman[2] was hearing about Siberia again. With his wife, Miri, he was meeting Rabbi Berel Lazar, Russia's chief rabbi. Lazar was looking for a couple to move to Siberia's largest city, Novosibirsk. Zalman[3] and Miri had been married less than half a year. The conversation was brief and to the point, not lasting more than ten minutes. Lazar told them, "Novosibirsk is an important city, it's an academic center; the majority of the year, it's winter."

The idea seemed farfetched. Novosibirsk was remote and cold. Zalman said, "Who wants to live in Siberia?" Miri's father was a Russian Jew, a professor in Jerusalem. When they dated she told Zalman, "I'm ready for shlichus, but not to Russia." She knew Russian Jews from their visits to her home in Jerusalem. But Russia was her father's legacy; she felt more Israeli, like her mother.

Sensing their hesitancy, Rabbi Lazar suggested they go "to take a look at the community." He would underwrite the expense, no strings attached. They wavered, and then Zalman discovered that a Siberian airline[4] had a non-stop flight every two weeks between Tel Aviv and Novosibirsk. They were freshly married, without any money for travel. He told Miri, "We can go for the adventure, let's have a 'honeymoon' in Russia." Miri agreed, intrigued by her father's birthplace. "I was curious to see Russia," she said.

Novosibirsk was founded in 1893 as a crossing of the Ob River for the Trans-Siberian Railway. A large decorative train station stood in the center of town. In March 1999, when the Zaklos family arrived for the two-week visit, there were over a million and a half residents; the city had grown into the third largest in Russia.

Other cities in the far reaches of Siberia had a Jewish history that reached back to czarist times. In 1812,[5] the Russian government gave Jews who lived in Siberia greater freedoms and economic opportunity. The town of Kainsk,[6] 195 miles west of the future Novosibirsk, was four-fifths Jewish in the nineteenth century. In Omsk, Tomsk, and Irkutsk, beautiful synagogues had been built in the late nineteenth and early twentieth centuries. Jews who finished the czarist army[7] remained in the region. There were no beautiful Jewish edifices in Novosibirsk. The Jews came later, after the founding of the Soviet Union in 1922. When the barriers to leaving Russia were lifted in the 1990s, Jews with a sense of identity immigrated to Israel and other countries. Some twenty thousand Jews remained in the city. Barely ten regulars attended the weekly services in a rented apartment that served as a synagogue.

When the Zakloses landed, it was springtime. Nevertheless, Miri says, "It was cold – twenty below zero." During their Siberian "honeymoon," Zalman and Miri met the small group of local Jewish activists. Miri says the people were very warm. They decided to host a Purim party, but they needed food. They didn't have kosher meat or a kitchen. Miri cooked the fish in the hotel room. The smell alarmed the management, who started to yell at her, and they called the police. Quickly, she finished up. "When the police arrived, thank G-d, the fish was ready."

A record crowd of fifty turned up for the joyous Purim celebration. The locals hoped that the Zakloses would stay, but they were resolved to return to Israel a few days afterward. Miri says, "Everyone was old; I did not see one child. There weren't any children's clothes in the stores; I didn't think there was any future here." Novosibirsk had been a brief fling, a two-week holiday; they didn't see it as a place to spend their lives.

The day after Purim, Zalman entered the small apartment synagogue only to discover that during the night, vandals had struck. It looked like a pogrom. The Jewish news service, the *Jewish Telegraphic Agency* (*JTA*)[8] reported, "Vandals this week went on a rampage at a synagogue in the city of Novosibirsk, destroying much of the synagogue in the attack. They demolished the synagogue's furniture, tore up prayer books and scattered Torah scrolls and prayer shawls around the hall."

The community was in shock, though it wasn't the first time there had been an attack on the tiny synagogue. The local leaders feared publicity, telling Rabbi Zaklos, "Let's not tell anyone, it might create more anti-Semitism." Zalman called Rabbi Lazar in Moscow, who said that the story should not be buried. He issued a statement in Moscow condemning the attack. The media converged on the destroyed synagogue. The reporters asked Zaklos, "Who are you?" He responded, "I am Rabbi Zaklos." That night in his hotel room, he saw himself on the TV news, identified as the Chief Rabbi of Novosibirsk. Zalman didn't even realize the subconscious seed had been planted. Back in Israel, Novosibirsk gnawed at him. He could not forget the TV broadcast when he was identified as the rabbi of the city. He says,

"If there hadn't been a pogrom, I would never have returned." Finally, he and Miri decided it was Divine Providence, a spiritual sign from above. In the end of December, they headed back – with a baby – to what Miri calls, "unbelievable cold." Money would not be an initial concern. Lazar ensured support from the Rohr Foundation in New York to underwrite their salary.

Mendel and Tzippy Slavin[9] had married in May of 2002; like Miri and Zalman, they were also looking for a shlichus. They had followed the classic Chabad track. For the first year after marriage, Mendel studied in kolel[10] in Brooklyn and Tzippy worked. They also started looking for a position. Her parents were veteran teachers at the Chabad day school in Huntington Beach, California. She grew up in nearby Long Beach, as the child of shluchim. Mendel was a Brooklyn boy, his father a businessman in New York.

A year and a half had passed and they were still looking. First they thought of going to work in another Chabad Center. "We didn't want to raise money," says Tzippy. They heard about couples who had gone to communities where things didn't work out. Despite the anxiety of having to fundraise, they thought maybe they should find their own place and start from scratch.

The dramatic expansion since the Rebbe's passing in July of 1994 had gobbled up much of the prime real estate. In 1994, there were 1,242[11] shluchim couples in the world. It had taken just over half a century to reach that number. By the time the Slavins were looking in 2004, the number of shluchim had risen by 65 percent to 2,097. There were few US communities with a significant Jewish population that did not have a Chabad presence.

Some two hundred young couples congregated in New York looking for options. The competition for any town with a Jewish population that could sustain a shliach was intense. The young couples with a bit of extra initiative would spend their evenings in Brooklyn poring over maps, looking for opportunity. Then they would call the head shliach in the state or shluchim in a nearby community and ask, "Can we help you open up Chabad in…" At times, the rush for places created questions. Should the center be opened, and who should go?[12] Each country or state has a head shliach[13] who is mandated to make the decision. In states or countries without a permanent Chabad presence, the decision would be made by Chabad headquarters in New York.

Mendel had an advantage; it was Tzippy. Her parents had been shluchim for over three decades in California. In California, the head shliach, Rabbi Shlomo Cunin, worked with his son, Rabbi Yossi Cunin, to manage the expansion in the state. The Cunins were seeking new communities to place shluchim. Rabbi Yossi Cunin[14] explains that precedence is given to the children of shluchim for new positions. "We prefer to take young couples who grew up in California; they understand the landscape of the state." He adds that it's a reflection of the values instilled by their parents. "It's a testament to the commitment of the parents when their children want to follow in their footsteps."

Slavin called Yossi Cunin regularly, but he was non-committal, telling Slavin, "We will see, we need to look around." Getting hold of Rabbi Shlomo Cunin was more daunting. Cunin was a busy man and tough to reach. Finally, after weeks of trying, one Thursday, he got him on the phone. Cunin said to him, "Let's talk. When will you be in California?" Slavin realized that this was his break. "I'm coming for the weekend." He booked a flight and on Sunday, Cunin welcomed the young couple to his house in Los Angeles. Tea, coffee, and cakes greeted them on the table. After a few moments, Rabbi Cunin arrived. Usually animated and lively, he struck a different tone, realizing the nervousness of the young couple. Tzippy says, "He was very gracious." Cunin shared his admiration for her parents, Rabbi Peretz and Rishie Greenwald. The Slavins told him that they were willing to look into any options in California. After thirty minutes, Cunin pulled out his cell phone and called his son, Yossi, telling him to work with them to find a place.

Yossi Cunin suggested that the Slavins take a look at Ojai and Riverside.[15] Mendel Slavin says Yossi Cunin hadn't given them much guidance; he just told them, "Check out these places." Tzippy says, "We were kids, we didn't exactly know what we were doing." Ojai, nicknamed the Shangri-La of California, was an hour and a half north of Los Angeles. Jews had been attracted by the mountain air, ranches, and beauty. Mendel and Tzippy drove around and started asking questions. The population was around ten thousand. Local realtors told them, "There are restrictions on growth." Then they headed to Riverside, an hour east of Los Angeles. A century earlier, it had been the center of a California boom. It was a working-class town with a limited Jewish population in the far reaches of what is called the "Inland Empire." Neither place seemed to be the right match for them.

That night at Tzippy's parents' house in Long Beach, they were talking. Tzippy's mother, Rishie, remembered a teacher who would make the long drive from the town of San Clemente on the southern tip of Orange County to teach in the Hebrew Academy in Huntington Beach, suggesting it as an idea. Mendel called Yossi Cunin, who told him to go take a look. Tzippy headed back to New York for her teaching job. Mendel drove the hour south from Long Beach to San Clemente. Right away he was taken with the place. He followed the signs to the housing development. California-style houses were rising on the hills of San Clemente not far from the ocean. His spirits were bolstered when the sales agent was a Jewish woman. It seemed like a sign from above. She extolled the wonders of life in San Clemente: families were moving in; the town had a wonderful future. Mendel was inspired by her enthusiasm and optimism. He felt that this was the place for him and Tzippy to build Jewish life. In the sales office, Mendel turned to the Jewish sales agent and declared, "I'm going to open a Chabad Center. I hope you will come to the programs." He called Tzippy, telling her, "This is the place," and spent the day driving around the town. By the weekend, the deal was done. The Cunins agreed. The Slavins went to the Ohel, the resting place of the Rebbe, to say a prayer for their success on the Rebbe's shlichus, and started to plan the move.

Mendel and Tzippy had a position, but there was no money for salary or expenses. They felt lucky; many other young couples were still in New York looking for places. The Cunins gave them $1,800 to start off, but they needed money to live as they built an organization from the bottom up in a new community. Mendel started fundraising and put together about $30,000 from friends and family in New York. With enough money to sustain them for a few months, they packed up and headed west.

It wasn't just the freezing winter with temperatures reaching below forty degrees that greeted the Zaklos family when they arrived to live in Novosibirsk. The police hauled in Zalman for questioning two days later. They suspected that the attack on the synagogue had been an inside job and he was the culprit. Zalman says it was terrifying: "They fingerprinted me, and interrogated me." They pummeled him with questions. "Why did you vandalize the synagogue?" Zaklos says, "I was afraid; I couldn't understand what they wanted from me." What was strange in the incident was that the Torah scrolls were placed on the talit in what seemed an intentional way. Police wondered if maybe someone in the Jewish community had staged the event for some reason. Zaklos vigorously protested his innocence, and finally the police believed him.

The conflict over Jewish leadership that was at its height in Moscow between the Russian Jewish Congress (RJC) and the Federation of Jewish Communities (FJC) spilled over to Novosibirsk. RJC was backed by communications magnate Vladimir Gusinsky. Chabad had initially joined with Gusinsky, but had backed away from the partnership. Gusinsky was turning the Russian Jewish Congress into a platform to pursue his personal political goals. Rabbi Lazar feared that partisan politics[16] would endanger the Jewish community. The FJC, supported by Chabad, was building a network of institutions in post-Communist Russia. They had sent yeshiva students for short stints in Novosibirsk; the appointment of a permanent rabbi was a major stride forward. The local chairman of the Russian Jewish Congress, Michael Kamcha, was very distraught that Chabad had dispatched a rabbi to the Siberian city. He tried every way to undermine Zalman's success. But Kamcha's effort to sabotage Zalman's mission was not getting much traction. The community was impressed by the young couple. Their upbeat optimism and energy was gaining them local support.

Zaklos was not deterred by his experience with the police; instead of slowing down, he says, "I decided to open a school." Ohr Avner[17] was backing expansion of schools in Russia. Zaklos went to work convincing the city to give him a building, then launched an enrollment campaign. Within a year of his arrival, the first Jewish school in Siberia was a success.

The media storm after the attack in the synagogue prompted the local mayor to designate a plot of land for a proper synagogue.[18] It was in a prime location, just blocks from the city center. The announcement of land allocation exacerbated Jewish politics in Novosibirsk. Who should build, the Russian Jewish Congress or the Federation of Jewish Communities?

Zaklos proposed to RJC's Kamcha that the building be a joint effort between both organizations. They should both invest money, jointly own it, and let it be a center for all institutions of the community. Zaklos had lined up a quarter of a million dollars, more than enough in a time when the ruble had been devalued. Michael Kamcha agreed. Representatives from both sides signed the deed, and the property was transferred by the city. There was a burst of optimism in the Jewish community – a new era of cooperation had dawned.

Zaklos did not expect the Russian style of heavy handedness. One day he was shocked to discover construction on the site. Kamcha had begun building on his own. Zaklos began to investigate and discovered that the deed, originally in both the name of the Federation and the Russian Jewish Congress, had been doctored. Michael Kamcha had removed the name of the Federation of Jewish Communities, forging the signatures of local community leaders.

With the false deed in hand, the Russian Jewish Congress was moving full steam ahead. Zaklos conferred with local community leaders and decided they had no alternative but to sue in the local courts. As the case progressed, the pressure mounted for them to back off. Failing to get Zaklos to stop his legal battle, Kamcha escalated the conflict. Miri says Kamcha sent letters threatening us.[19] "We feared for our lives; I thought that someone might attack us." Miri says there was tremendous pressure. "There were nights we did not sleep." Miri wanted Zalman to hire guards and even suggested leaving. But Zalman was not giving in to the Russian-style intimidation. Miri says, "Zalman was stubborn, and he is very optimistic. He would say everything would be all right."

For five years, the litigation continued in the Russian courts. The local community leaders testified that their signatures had been forged. The court ruled that the Russian Jewish Congress did not have the right to control the property. With the loss in the case, Michael Kamcha and the Russian Jewish Congress[20] disappeared from public view. Zalman says, "We did not hear from them again."

Zaklos had won the court battle, but the protracted conflict had demoralized the community. Local Jews had grown weary of the promises of building a synagogue that never materialized. The ruble had regained much of its value, so building costs had risen dramatically. Zaklos finally had the legal right to build, but he lacked money, and community confidence was at an all-time low.

Still, Zaklos was thinking big. He planned an even bigger and more ambitious structure. The progress was slow; it took years, but he persevered. Finally, in August of 2013, the 47,000-square-foot synagogue and Jewish community center was dedicated. The magnificent structure had been supported by over five hundred local donations, a hundred of them over a thousand dollars. A Jewish businessman in Novosibirsk made a lead gift of a million dollars. A third of the funding came with the help of Chabad in Moscow. Rabbi Lazar was able to secure funding from the Rohr Foundation, Ohr Avner, and other donors. Two thousand people attended the dedication. Since the opening, a thousand local Jews have become members of the synagogue, each given their own electronic access card.[21]

A few months after the dedication, I spent a Shabbat in Novosibirsk. Zaklos was full of ambitious plans for the future. On Friday, we visited the school whose children were bursting with Jewish pride. On Friday night, a group of young professionals gathered for a traditional Shabbat dinner in the new synagogue. Enormous Siberian salmon draped the table. Words of Torah flowed along with Shabbat melodies. This was a new generation of young Russians, seizing the opportunities in the growing economy. Here, like Moscow, it's cool to be Jewish. At the dinner, a young staffer from the JDC,[22] who provides care for the Jewish elderly in Novosibirsk, described the local Jewish scene. "Once a year, some rabbinical students visit Novosibirsk from the Conservative-affiliated American Jewish University[23] in Los

Angeles. We have to tell them that they should be sensitive to the fact that this is a Chabad town."

Mendel Slavin was not hauled in for a police investigation when he moved to San Clemente with his wife, Tzippy, and a baby in September 2004. But he had a challenge that Zalman Zaklos did not have initially: money. The $30,000 he raised in New York was enough to get them through the first six months or so. But living expenses in a beach town were high. They had very few supporters and no building. They were also limited in the area they could fundraise. A string of Chabad Centers in Orange County reached south all the way to Mission Viejo inland and Laguna Beach on the coast. The Slavins had to find a way to build a local organization without reaching into the area covered by other Chabad Centers just a few exits north on the freeway. Mendel had to make it work in a small area with a narrow demographic base.

Slavin found his first donor on 15 Shevat, the Jewish holiday that recognizes the importance of trees and fruit. "Tzippy had prepared ten holiday baskets to be distributed to friends in the area." He had nine people he knew. He had the name of another family he had never met and decided to visit them. He stood at the doorway with a sense of trepidation wondering if they would be friendly.

When they answered the door it was all smiles. A few months later, the need for funding became acute. He visited them again and received his first major donation of $6,000. To supplement their income, Tzippy taught in the Hebrew Academy in Huntington Beach. Mendel also had a part time job in local kosher food supervision. Despite challenges, they were keeping afloat. After about two years, Rabbi Levi Zirkind from Fresno told Mendel about chaplaincy jobs at the state prisons. With his help, Mendel got a job at a state prison not far from San Clemente. "It came at the right time," he says. While he built a base of local support, he had the position at the prison where "I was doing very important work helping those who truly needed it."

Mendel and Tzippy started monthly services in a local hotel. At first the numbers were not strong, but as time went on, more people began to come. There were holiday celebrations for Purim and Chanukah; High Holiday services drew under a hundred. Slowly, Jew by Jew, a community was evolving in San Clemente. They were the only Jewish presence in the neighborhood, the closest congregations twenty minutes north on the freeway. Mendel made weekly rounds at the local senior homes to visit the Jews who lived there. Every Shabbat, they hosted families at their Shabbat table.

No question, it was much easier now than for shluchim of earlier generations who faced skepticism and even hostility. In 1969, the rabbis first came to Long Beach, California, to start the Hebrew Academy. By 2002, a string of successful Chabad Centers had blossomed from the Hebrew Academy. The success in other communities was proof that Chabad could do well in San Clemente.

As time went on, a group coalesced and a consensus emerged that San Clemente needed a Jewish center. The challenges were daunting; the cost would exceed easily over a million dollars, even for something small.

The key was finding major donors. Mendel and Tzippy became friends with a Holocaust survivor who lived in San Clemente. One day she surprised Mendel, "I would like to help in the purchase of a facility with a major lead gift." Mendel says, "I was astonished. I never imagined she had the resources to help in such a significant fashion." There wasn't enough money to close the deal, but the financial backing was enough to start actively looking. The next problem was finding a facility. One was too small, the other too expensive, and another in the wrong location. Finally a six thousand-square-foot building went up for sale in the middle of town. Mendel jumped at it. "I was amazed at the generosity. Ten families made significant gifts, three of them quite large. All told, over a hundred local Jews participated in the building campaign." With signature donations in place, they closed escrow in the summer of 2013.

At the end of August, just one day after the opening of the synagogue in Novosibirsk,[24] to a crowd of thousands, two hundred Jews gathered to dedicate the Chabad Center in San Clemente. In the same week, a new era of Judaism had begun in a beach town[25] in California and the capital of Siberia.

The story of the growth of San Clemente and Novosibirsk has been replicated in Jewish communities across the globe. In the twenty years since the Rebbe's passing, the number of shluchim has quadrupled to over four thousand.[26] In many communities, Chabad has evolved from small storefront operations to major community centers, setting the stage for a fundamental shift in Jewish life in the US and around the world. Few outside of Chabad envisioned that this would occur. The Jewish academicians, media, and experts[27] prognosticated that after the Rebbe's passing, Chabad would lose its momentum and cohesion. Rabbi Yehuda Krinsky remembers the skepticism at the time. "No one said it's going to be OK; many were saying that Chabad would self-destruct."

There were internal doubts also. A day after the Rebbe's funeral, a shliach from South America told his old friend, Rabbi Levi Klein[28] from Memphis, "I guess we won't be seeing each other anymore." He said he did not envision a reason to come to New York in the future. A few months later, plans were underway for the first shluchim convention after the Rebbe's passing. Rabbi Lipa Brennan, the convention coordinator since its inception in 1983, said to me, "I wonder if the shluchim will come."

Hardly anyone imagined that twenty years later, Chabad would become the largest Jewish organization in the world, and the fastest-growing in the United States.

How did Chabad thrive in the post-Gimmel Tammuz[29] era? (Gimmel Tammuz is the third day of the Jewish month of Tammuz, the day of the Rebbe's passing.) Few realized that the Rebbe began years earlier to prepare the Chabad community for a whole new set of challenges that it would encounter after his passing.

In February of 1988,[30] the Rebbe suffered a grave personal loss. His wife, the Rebbitzen Chaya Mushka Schneerson,[31] passed away. That morning, thousands lined the streets of Crown Heights to pay their last respects. Many traveled afterward to Montefiore Cemetery in Queens for the interment. The Rebbitzen had been the Rebbe's closest companion throughout his adult life. He once remarked to his physician, Dr. Ira Weiss, about the daily teatime he had with his wife, "Those moments are as precious to me as putting on tefilin every day." At this point in his life, says Rabbi Yehuda Krinsky, who began serving as a secretary to the Rebbe in 1957, "the Rebbe was totally alone."

After the funeral, the Rebbe led Mincha, the afternoon prayer, in his home. After the service, the Rebbe sat on a low chair, following the traditions of Shivah, the seven days of mourning. Long lines formed on the street in front of the house. The crowds entered the house and passed by the Rebbe, offering their condolences.

At four that afternoon, the doors to the house had been closed, the long lines had ended. The Rebbe asked Krinsky[32] to meet with him upstairs in his second-floor study. Krinsky says that every time he entered the Rebbe's office, "there was a flutter in my heart." As he walked up the stairs, he felt a great sense of trepidation and sorrow.

Rabbi Krinsky says the Rebbe gave him three assignments. "He told me that he wants to write a will," saying it should be completed, if possible, before the end of the weeklong Shivah.[33] Krinsky's[34] instinctive reaction was to repeat to the Rebbe the ancient Jewish teaching: "A will is a segula (a sign) for a long life." Still, in his heart, he felt the request was an ominous sign. The Rebbe had two more requests: that a charitable foundation be created in his wife's name, Keren Chomesh.[35] He also told Krinsky that he wanted to update the central institutions of Chabad: Agudas Chassidei Chabad,[36] Merkos L'inyonei Chinuch,[37] and Machne Israel.[38] Some of those who had been board members of these legal entities had passed away. Krinsky says the Rebbe told him, "Review all the corporations, and the vacancies should be filled."

A week later, the will was completed. The Rebbe designated Rabbi Krinsky to be executor. In the presence of attorney Nahum Gordon, the Rebbe signed the will; two of his secretaries, Rabbi Leibel Groner and Rabbi Binyomin Klein, were the witnesses. Krinsky says, "I never told anyone about the will since the Rebbe had not given me instructions to do so."

The will was a simple document. The Rebbe bequeathed all his possessions to Chabad's umbrella organization, Agudas Chassidei Chabad. Krinsky explains: "The Rebbe owned nothing. He did not own the house he lived in;[39] he did not own a car. He had a small personal checking account for his monthly bills and donations to charity." Krinsky recalls that once the Rebbitzen, the Rebbe's wife, described her father the Sixth Rebbe, Rabbi Yosef Yitzchak Schneersohn.

"My father belonged to Chassidim and everything he had belonged to Chassidim; all he owned was his talit and tefilin." So too, Krinsky says, "was true of the Rebbe."

In the coming months, there would be a marked change in the tone of the Rebbe's talks and farbrengens.[40] He was preparing the community for the future. At the time, few grasped the true meaning of these measures. In the years prior to the Rebbitzen's passing, he had urged the Chassidim toward greater spiritual independence. Now he called again for each person to choose a rabbi and a mashpiah – a rabbi to give guidance in the realm of Jewish law, and a mashpiah (a spiritual mentor) to give advice and direction in issues of spiritual growth and personal affairs. In the past, the Rebbe had advised many people in crucial questions of health. During this period, the Rebbe encouraged people to consult expert medical opinion, seeking second opinions in important questions, or to consult with a physician who was also a good friend. Issues of contention, should they arise, should be resolved by a rabbinical court[41] of Chabad rabbis. Using Halacha as a guide, they would be the final adjudicators.

Historically, Chassidim would ask the Rebbe for guidance and blessing at important junctures in their lives. According to the members of the Rebbe's secretariat, the Rebbe answered fewer personal questions from Chassidim, instead recommending that they consult with others for advice. The Rebbe had also instructed Rabbi Dov Ber Levin, the scholar who headed the Chabad Library, to continue to prepare for publication the Rebbe's letters. So far, thirty volumes[42] have been published. The letters touched on a wide variety of topics, both personal and communal. These volumes, along with two hundred other published works of the Rebbe, provide a reservoir of invaluable advice for Chassidim.

Nine months after the Rebbitzen's passing, at the end of the holiday season[43] in October in 1988, the Rebbe notified Rabbi Krinsky that he would like to have a meeting that day with the board members of Agudas Chassidei Chabad (Aguch). This was quite unprecedented. That afternoon, nine people convened in the Rebbe's office, including Rabbis Hodakov, Krinsky and Shemtov. No one was aware that the purpose of the meeting was to set the organizational structure of Chabad for the future.

The Rebbe began the meeting by remarking that he had been observing the guests, including the shluchim, who had come for the holiday season. He said he had great pride in seeing how they had developed a sense of independence, matured, and accomplished much. He quoted the talmudic teaching: "the kid goats have become rams,"[44] referring to an incident in the Talmud when the Rabbis based in Israel told Rabbi Chanina, who lived in Babylonia, that a new generation of scholars had developed who were intellectually and spiritually self-reliant. The inference was clear.

The Rebbe moved to the practical. The Rebbe instructed the members of Aguch to write to all Chabad institutions worldwide and tell them that if the shluchim have issues to resolve, they should turn to Aguch in New York for advice and direction. He said it was important to review the legal structure of the boards of the organizations of Chabad, and asked that attorneys ensure that all was done according to law. He instructed that in each country and state, Chabad institutions should be operated in accordance with the local laws. Following the meeting, the status of the boards of each organization was reviewed, and vacancies were filled with the Rebbe's approval.

Though the Rebbe had always taught his Chassidim, community, and organization the significance of self-reliance, clearly in the period surrounding the Rebbitzen's passing his efforts took a more urgent tone. He was encouraging Chassidim to find ways to resolve crucial issues in their lives if he was unable to personally assist them. At the same time, the Rebbe was ensuring that the institutional structure that had stood at the center of Chabad's worldwide operations be strengthened and bolstered. Few Chassidim realized that this process had begun,[45] but some close observers sensed change was underway.

During the same period, the Rebbe was calling for greater efforts toward effecting the coming of Moshiach. He encouraged the study of the concept of Moshiach. He pointed to world events – the peaceful fall of the Soviet Union, for example – as indicators that Moshiach's arrival was imminent. Just two weeks after Passover in

1991, the Rebbe exhorted the community "to do all you can to bring Moshiach."[46]

Since accepting the leadership of Chabad, the Rebbe regularly visited the Ohel, the resting place of the Sixth Rebbe, Rabbi Yosef Yitzchak, in Montefiore Cemetery in Queens. On those days, he would refrain from eating before departing. There, he would pray on behalf of world Jewry and mankind, reading petitions from those who had requested his blessing and returning to Brooklyn in the late afternoon or evening. Rabbi Krinsky drove the Rebbe close to two thousand times. As the Rebbe stood in prayer, Krinsky would do office work in the car.

On March 2, 1992, Krinsky drove the Rebbe to the Ohel. As the Rebbe stood at the graveside in prayer, he suffered a debilitating stroke. He would be unable to speak again. On June 4, 1994, Gimmel Tammuz, the third day of the Jewish month of Tammuz, after two years of severe illness, the Rebbe passed away.

Those twenty-seven months from the day of the stroke to Gimmel Tammuz would be a time of deep anguish and prayerful hope for Chassidim – yearning for a miracle, but deep down fearing the worst. The period after the Rebbe's passing would be confusing for some. Debates erupted about a host of issues. The central theological dispute was over the issue of Moshiach. As mandated by Jewish tradition and ruled upon by Maimonides, the Rebbe had repeatedly affirmed the belief that the coming of Moshiach was imminent. For millennia, Jews have hoped for redemption,[47] and Jewish tradition teaches that in every generation there is a potential candidate for Moshiach.[48] The Talmud states[49] that students hoped their teachers exemplified the ideal human being and could be a candidate for Moshiach. To many Jews, the Rebbe[50] seemed the best candidate. For years, some had quietly wondered if he could become the Moshiach, and during the period of the sickness, the speculation grew.

When this idea had emerged in prior years, the Rebbe had strongly rejected it, both publicly and privately. In 1984, at a farbrengen, he publicly chastised those who attempted to identify him as Moshiach, saying, "Let it be known that anyone who continues with such activities fights a war against Chabad Chassidism, against the Rebbe (referring to the Sixth Rebbe) and the Baal Shem Tov."[51] When a Chabad follower in Israel printed flyers identifying the Rebbe as Moshiach, the Rebbe ordered them collected and destroyed.[52] After the Rebbe's stroke, I wrote a detailed letter asking a series of yes/no questions on the issue.[53] The Rebbe rejected the idea of promoting an individual as a candidate for Moshiach.

This debate reflected deeper issues. With the Rebbe's grave sickness and his subsequent passing, many Chassidim were struggling with profound issues. They were wondering about their future, their relationship with the Rebbe, and the historic hopes and dreams of the Jewish people for redemption.

That spiritual attachment between Rebbe and Chassid is profound. Chabad philosophy speaks of something much more than an emotional bond. As the Sixth Rebbe, Rabbi Yosef Yitzchak, notes, "A Chassid's great thirst to be bound with his Rebbe can be satisfied only by studying the Maamarim (Chassidic discourses) that the Rebbe delivers and writes, for merely seeing his face is not enough,[54] stressing that the connection between Rebbe and Chassid be rooted in learning and scholarship.

After the Rebbe's passing, public attention turned to Chabad, fueled by media speculation over its future. This created a public controversy over the question of the identity of Moshiach.[55] The intrigue of the story and the public stance of those individuals promoting the idea garnered headlines. Most in Chabad and its leadership did not support this viewpoint. With time, it lost[56] backing among the great majority in the Chabad community.

In addition to the theological debates, politics rose to the surface. Some attempted to question the role of those the Rebbe had appointed. In the past, these appointees were seen as a direct line of authority that had come from the Rebbe; now they needed to create a more bureaucratic, consensus-driven organization. In the period leading up to Gimmel Tammuz, the Rebbe had encouraged greater organizational autonomy. This helped prepare for the transition that would occur.

Rabbi Yehuda Krinsky, together with the others appointed by the Rebbe to leadership positions, was in the fulcrum of these debates.

Krinsky, a quiet and determined man, did not sway. He told me that Rabbi Joseph B. Soloveitchik, the renowned scholar from Yeshiva University, had been a close friend of his father who had been the chief schochet (ritual slaughterer) in Boston. Rabbi Soloveitchik had provided the abattoir with his kosher endorsement. He had once told Krinsky, "Your father was a stubborn and resolute person. Your parents decided from the day of the wedding that if they have children, they will grow up to be observant Jews," and this at a time when there were no Jewish schools. Krinsky carried on this family trait of tenaciousness. Unwaveringly, he carried out with inner resolve the mission with which the Rebbe had entrusted him, ensuring that the central institutions of Chabad were not compromised.

Still, the transition in organizational culture[57] would be a challenge. The central institutions of Chabad, Agudas Chassidei Chabad, Merkos L'inyonei Chinuch, and Machne Israel, are guided by boards made up of senior shluchim and distinguished members of the Chabad community. Rabbi Krinsky serves as chairman of Merkos and Machne and Rabbi Avrohom Shemtov, chairman of Aguch. Both stood strong, deterring efforts to undermine the central organizational structure that the Rebbe had instituted.

In this period, Rabbi Moshe Kotlarsky, the vice-chair of Merkos, began marshaling the resources to propel Chabad to new heights. Decades earlier, the Rebbe had dispatched young Kotlarsky to Bogota with instructions relayed via Rabbi Hodakov, "You will meet who you need to meet and with time you will understand." It was due to that trip that Kotlarsky first met Sami Rohr. Kotlarsky says that he only realized the implications of those words: "in time you will understand," after the Rebbe's passing, "when Sami Rohr began to support the major expansion of Chabad."

Rohr's first major foray outside his country of Colombia had been the opening of Chabad in Latvia in 1990. In the coming twenty years, Sami, his son George – and his son-in-law, Moshe Tabacinic – would push Chabad to new horizons. Kotlarsky would meet Sami in Miami, suggest opening Chabad in a new country, and Sami would respond in Yiddish, "Gemacht (done)." In country after country, he provided the seed money for new shluchim. Chabad grew from forty countries when the Rebbe passed away to over eighty. Much of that expansion, in particular in smaller Jewish communities, was with the partnership of the Rohrs.

Kotlarsky realized that it was not enough just to push the boundaries outward; the infrastructure had to be strengthened.[58] He was instrumental in a series of initiatives, many of which rose to the surface at the annual shluchim conventions. CTeens, a national youth program, convened in 2015, brought over fifteen hundred high-school students in Brooklyn for a national conference that was highlighted by a live concert and Havdalah ceremony (a short ritual held at the conclusion of Shabbat and most holidays acknowledging the end of a holy day and the beginning of an ordinary day) in Times Square. JNET created a national network of peer learning on the phone. The Shluchim Exchange provides an Internet forum for shluchim to share ideas, training programs, and internal publications for shluchim. The ideas would usually evolve from the ground up, and Kotlarsky would invariably find the funding to move these projects to reality.

In 1998, Rabbi Efraim Mintz invited twenty-six shluchim to come to New York to re-envision adult Jewish learning. He had written some course materials for shluchim and received incredible feedback: "Everyone was reinventing the wheel; shluchim who were burdened with myriad responsibilities from fundraising to funerals were attempting to create courses; they were overjoyed to be provided material."

What emerged from the conversation was a plan that, in the years to come, would become the Rohr Jewish Learning Institute (JLI) that would revolutionize adult Jewish learning worldwide. Chabad had a cadre of rabbis who were scholars who had been providing advanced Jewish learning for decades. They needed a teaching curriculum, marketing, and textbooks to help bridge the gap between their classical yeshiva-style learning and the modern Jew with limited levels of Jewish literacy.

Mintz says the most important goal is to demonstrate Judaism's modern relevance. "You are not going to combat Jewish illiteracy by creating a university course. It's by bringing Torah to the minds and the hearts of the average Jew." JLI courses are rich in academic material; at the same time, they bring the loftiest concepts to real life.

Rabbi Kotlarsky became chairman and Rabbi Mintz the executive director of JLI. They focused on curriculum development, teacher training, and creating attractive marketing materials. It launched its flagship series, three annual courses offered by shluchim today in over 350 communities. It created curricula for specific target audiences: teens, Sinai Scholars for college students, the Torah portion, and women's courses. In addition, it crafted advanced materials focusing on text study and a website full of lectures. JLI also created the National Jewish Retreat, the largest annual Jewish learning conference in the US. JLI organized national trips to Israel and Poland designed to enhance the understanding of the Jewish homeland. JLI also branched out internationally offering courses in Hebrew, Russian, French, Spanish, Portuguese, German, and Greek.

The Rohr Jewish Learning Institute has become the largest network of adult Jewish learning in the world. In 2014, 137,950 people attended its wide variety of courses in 962 communities internationally.

Chabad had begun its first foray on campus starting in the late forties when the Sixth Rebbe, Rabbi Yosef Yitzchak, sent some of his students to do outreach at universities. That was followed with weekend retreat programs for college students started in the mid-sixties in Crown Heights. The opening of the first Chabad House at UCLA in the late sixties set the stage for the evolution of a small network of full-time campus centers in the following decades. My wife and I arrived at the University of Miami in 1974 to start Chabad programs. We were on our own, finding our way with limited resources. By 1992, there were thirty-two campus centers and many other campuses were served part-time.

Chabad on Campus took a leap forward with another initiative funded by the Rohr family, led by Rabbi Kotlarsky and a group of campus shluchim, spearheaded by Rabbi Menachem Schmidt of Philadelphia. Centers opened at over a hundred new universities in North America. The small network in the UK expanded to fourteen centers. Internationally, centers opened in France, Russia, Australia, Israel, and South America. Today, Chabad serves four hundred colleges with permanent centers on 233 campuses worldwide. New centers receive three-year grants toward operational expenses, and grants for facility acquisition. A national organization was developed to provide training, resources, and funding. National and regional programs were developed, including the national Shabbaton held every year in Brooklyn with a thousand students attending.

Rabbi Yossi Gordon, executive director of Chabad on Campus, says Jewish life on campus has been revolutionized. He explains that, in the past, the campus shluchim had the greatest challenge. "They were alone, with little support. Some moved on after a few years to community work." He explains that the paradigm has shifted. "It's created a surge of productivity. A professional organization stands behind the shliach, who is strategically connected." One of the new horizons is the development of programs for alumni. "The more experienced shliach will focus on that demographic and newer, younger shluchim, on the students."

Chabad.org began in the early days of the Web. Rabbi Yossi Kazen[59] started using bulletin board systems, discovering Jews in remote corners of the world, setting up Chabad.org formally in 1994. Sadly, in 1998, Kazen passed away, and Chabad.org became a division of the Chabad-Lubavitch Media Center under the direction of Lubavitch spokesman Rabbi Zalman Shmotkin. Shmotkin was running a world-class public relations operation with almost nothing but his cellphone and a part-time assistant, employing his uncanny ability to communicate the movement's most delicate and esoteric concepts to the media.[60] This helped catapult Chabad to entirely new levels of public awareness and appreciation. He broadened the public understanding of the Rebbe's philosophy and Weltanschauung, which he considered even more important than publicizing Chabad's good work. He understood better than most the potential the Web held to bring the Jewish message to the world.

Shmotkin assembled programmers, writers, and editors – self-taught, innovative, creative individuals who were filled with passion to serve their brethren worldwide, and who allowed their imaginations to soar.

Once again the Rohr family provided funding. George Rohr pulled in his brother-in-law Moshe Tabacinic, himself a world-class philanthropist.[61] Today, a team of fifty full-time and part-time editors and writers scattered around the globe create[62] a dizzying array of editorially stellar and engaging material in eight languages (English, Hebrew, Spanish, Russian, Portuguese, French, German, and Italian) for readers worldwide. Content ranges from advanced Talmud to crafts for the kids, from explorations of existential questions of philosophy to recipes. Special sections include: holidays,[63] kids, news,[64] Jewish recovery,[65] mammoth audio and video collections, content for the hearing impaired, and a specialty site by and for the Jewish woman.

The team's efforts have clearly yielded results. Google practically any Jewish topic and Chabad.org will come up as the first or second result. Scholars and academics regularly reference it in their papers, as do journalists in their reporting. In day schools across the United States, Chabad.org is an integral part of students' daily research. Rabbis of all persuasions confide in me, that they get many ideas for their speeches from the Rebbe's thoughts as explained on Chabad.org.

Rabbi Meir Simcha Kogan,[66] managing director of Chabad.org, says that the number of unique visitors is constantly rising. "In 2013, there were 37 million; in 2014 the number rose by 16 percent[67] to 43 million." They also have a very active social media team, and have released a whole bunch of Jewish apps for use on mobile devices.

Rabbi Motti Seligson says, "Chabad.org is arguably the largest Jewish education initiative in the world."

Tabacinic is particularly happy about the vast numbers of completely unaffiliated Jews who use their services. "Chabad.org has become the primary go-to source for Judaism for people without a Jewish upbringing," many of whom are "uncomfortable getting that information in a personal way from a local rabbi, or who are in far-away places with no Jewish communities," he says proudly. Tabacinic also loves the fact that despite their millions of visitors, the staff dedicates lots of time responding to individuals. Kogan says that some eighty thousand personal questions[68] were sent to Chabad.org last year, each requiring its own response, tailored to that person.

The New York Times notes that Chabad.org "served as a model for other Jewish organizations." And in 2014 eJewish Philanthropy devoted an article to what other organizations can learn from the site.[69]

One of Shmotkin's unique ideas was to create customizable websites for local Chabad institutions. The content from the main site is accessible on each local website. However, each Chabad center can also customize the site to make it uniquely local, adding information about their programs, photo galleries, and articles. At its core, jewishafrica.com,[70] the web site of Chabad in the Congo, or jewishnewport.com, the site for Newport Beach, California, provide the same Judaism content and are driven by the same engine, but each highlights its own local programs and services. Chabad.org also develops custom websites[71] for schools, campus programs, and other projects.

Shmotkin says, "I feel that we're really holding a sacred trust for the Jewish people. This is not our private website – these are the tools and resources of the Jewish people. We've simply been blessed and entrusted to make it the best it can possibly be."

The rapid rate of growth caught the attention of many. As some other Jewish groups in the community were losing momentum, Chabad was booming, and many started asking why. Historian Professor Jack Wertheimer addressed this subject in an article published on the twentieth anniversary of the Rebbe's passing: "Why the Lubavitch Movement thrives in the absence of a living Rebbe."[72]

Wertheimer writes: "The most striking and surprising aspect of Lubavitch is its resilience in overcoming the loss of the Rebbe." He dispels the notion that economic motives are a central factor. "That would be cynical and naïve. There are easier ways to make a living, entailing fewer hardships for observant families than a posting in the Congo, South Korea, or Siberia." Wertheimer discusses three critical factors that he thinks are vital. The first is the power of the Rebbe's teachings. He says, "Many claim to be moved by the depth of learning and the inspiration they offer. As one Lubavitch rabbi put it, 'To me, those ideas are very much what drive the movement today.'"[73] The second factor Wertheimer writes about is the organizational culture of Chabad that empowers shluchim. "Even as the movement strives to coordinate, it gives enormous latitude to shluchim. The freedom granted to individuals unlocks a good deal of creativity and a spirit of innovation." Finally, Wertheimer claims the Rebbe changed the strategy of Jewish life from defensive to offensive. "He encouraged what in American parlance would be called a 'can-do' spirit. As early as 1951, he sought to embolden his followers to abandon their timidity. The Rebbe exuded a spirit of optimism and confidence that continues to shape the outlook of Chabad to the present day and spurs its innovation and expansion."

What Professor Wertheimer and outside observers don't understand is that the success and growth are intertwined with the distinctive philosophical approach that Chabad has to Jewish observance and Avodat Hashem (the service of G-d).

Rabbi Naftoli Silberberg tackled the question of Chabad success in "Paradigm Shift," a course he edited for the Rohr Jewish Learning Institute. He says Chabad's complex philosophy of serving G-d is based on ideas rooted in Jewish mysticism. "People think the Rebbe was a scholar and an organizational genius. They don't understand that his approach to shlichus (Chabad's mission in the world) was an extension of the worldview of Chassidic philosophy."

A central concept is that each person must internalize Jewish values and serve G-d based on Avodah B'Koach Atzmo (one's own efforts). Silberberg notes that the Rebbe stressed this very concept on the day he accepted the leadership in 1951, when he stated, "Listen up, fellow Jews, the Rebbes of Chabad demand that their Chassidim take personal action and not rely on the Rebbe. After all, even G-d himself does not impress piety or proper conduct upon anyone. We must work, therefore, with the entirety of our bodies and souls. I will not withhold my assistance, G-d forbid. I will help to the best of my abilities, but I cannot do the work on your behalf."

The Rebbe added that his father-in-law, the Sixth Rebbe, said, "Each one of us must personally transform our foolish tendencies and material passions into holiness."

Silberberg contends that Avodah B'Koach Atzmo means that every individual must go through the process of heavy spiritual lifting to internalize Jewish values. Chassidic philosophy grapples with the central questions of spirituality and human purpose. What is G-d, good and evil, faith and reason, free choice, and Divine Providence? How can each one of us transform the world for good? Students in Chabad yeshivas and seminaries[74] grapple with these issues as part of the learning process.

In the sixties, Herbert Weiner,[75] a Reform rabbi, explored the great Jewish mystics, writing in depth of a series of encounters with the Rebbe. During one late-night meeting, he asked about the character of the relationship between Rebbe and Chassid. "Isn't it the fact that Chassidim turn to the Rebbe for almost every decision in their lives, isn't it a sign of weakness, a repudiation of the very thing that makes a man human, his "bechira" (freedom of will)?

Referring to how Chassidim have internalized their values, the Rebbe responded to Weiner without any hesitation. "A weak person is usually overcome by the environment in which he finds himself. But our Chassidim can be sent into any environment, no matter how strange and hostile, and they maintain themselves within it. So how can we say that it is weakness which characterizes a Chassid?"

Silberberg says being a shliach is different. "It's not a job, rather a crucial component of their service of G-d." As a result, Chabad Centers are diverse, each a reflection of the individual shluchim and how they have internalized the teachings of the Rebbe.

It was this vision of independence and self-reliance that the Rebbe emphasized to shluchim after his wife's passing. "My general response to shluchim who have doubts or questions as to which methods are appropriate or advisable in the course of implementing their shlichus of disseminating Judaism and the wellsprings of Chassidic teachings – my answer is that they should act upon their own understanding of the situation." Based on a talmudic dictum, the Rebbe added, "A judge must rule based on the evidence before him," adding, "in every location according to its unique needs and circumstances."

Rabbi Lord Jonathan Sacks, former chief rabbi of Britain, says, "Good leaders create followers. Great leaders create leaders. That was the Rebbe's greatness. Not only did he lead, he was a source of leadership in others." Rabbi Sacks met the Rebbe the first time in the late sixties when he was a young graduate student. "He was the only person among the dozens I encountered who performed a role reversal in the course of our conversation. Within minutes, I discovered that it was not me who was interviewing the Rebbe, but the Rebbe who was interviewing me. He wanted to know about the state of Jewish life in Cambridge, England; how many Jewish students there were; how many were engaged with Jewish life; and what I was doing to increase their number."

For Sacks, it was a life-changing experience. He was impressed "that a Jewish leader would take considerable time to listen to an unknown undergraduate student from thousands of miles away and speak to him as if he mattered, as if he could make a difference." The Rebbe prodded Sacks to take a leadership role in his campus community.

Rabbi Silberberg explains, "It's not that Chassidim are inspired by the greatness and holiness of the Rebbe and therefore act upon the Rebbe's agenda; rather, the Rebbe's agenda becomes the agenda of the Chassidim." Silberberg says Chassidim have so internalized the values of the Rebbe, that, intuitively, a shliach acts according to the Rebbe's teachings.

Silberberg's grandfather was a follower of the Radomsker Rebbe, the Rebbe of one of the great Chassidic Movements in pre-war Poland. The Radomsker Rebbe perished in the Holocaust, and the Chassidic group was severely weakened. Silberberg says that Radomsk was like other Chassidic groups.[76] "Historically, if they did not have a Rebbe, a Chassidic group did not survive."[77] Chabad was different. The Rebbe succeeded on the strength of his ideas "to get people to see things the way he saw things."

The teachings of the Rebbe, with an emphasis on the internalization of those ideals, and individual empowerment, was the catalyst for Chabad growth in recent decades. The richness of the legacy of learning[78] that the Rebbe left inspired Rabbi Zalman and Miri Zaklos in Novosibirsk and Rabbi Mendel and Tzippy Slavin in San Clemente to have the intellectual and emotional grit to thrive in the far reaches of Siberia and the coastline of California.

That success, being replicated globally, is setting the stage for a monumental shift in Jewish life in the US and around the world.

In the post-World War migration to the suburbs of America, Jews left the Orthodox synagogues[79] and observance behind. They flocked to the Reform and Conservative temples.[80] We are seeing now a trend in the opposite direction.[81] Many Jews who are not fully observant have become active in Chabad Centers. They see the rabbi and his rebbitzen as role models they can aspire to emulate. They are also fully aware that the rabbi and rebbitzen will encourage them to increase their observance step-by-step, mitzvah by mitzvah.

With a thousand Chabad Centers in the US and Canada, ever increasing numbers of American Jews see Chabad as their prime place of affiliation.[82] For many others, it's the other synagogue they also attend for classes and programs.[83] In a 2014 demographic[84] study by the Greater Miami Jewish Federation, 26 percent of Miami Jews said they were active in Chabad;[85] families with children, 42 percent; and among Jews age thirty-five and below, the number has skyrocketed to 47 percent.

We are witnessing the first stages of a reorientation of American Jewry toward tradition. This trend will continue to grow for two reasons. Chabad today is ubiquitous; there is hardly a neighborhood in North America with a Jewish population that does not have a Chabad Center. They may be small, storefront operations that slowly mature into communal institutions with proper facilities. Or they may be large centers offering a wide variety of programs. A family in suburban USA can send their children to a Chabad preschool, then on to Hebrew School and CTeens. When the children go off to college, there is a Chabad Campus Center waiting for them. The adults find a community in their local Chabad Center, expand their intellectual horizons with JLI classes, and participate in holiday celebrations and other programs. Even if they are not walking in the front door they are finding meaningful Jewish experiences with Chabad online.

The second element is a shift in attitudes of many Jews toward Chabad. For many older adults, Orthodoxy was the tradition that their ancestors abandoned. According to a Miami survey of those over sixty, only 20 percent are active in Chabad. The memory of their ancestors' rejection has molded their perspective, creating a prejudice toward tradition. For some of this generation, Chabad is "too religious."

It's very different for the children and grandchildren of this generation. Most do not have these apprehensions. Harvard's shliach, Rabbi Hirschy Zarchi, says, "Chabad is natural for them." Tens of thousands of young American Jews have been involved with Chabad, attending Chabad's Gan Israel camps and Hebrew schools, and they have been active in campus Chabad Houses or traveled to Israel on Birthright programs organized by Chabad. As the Miami survey clearly proves, 47 percent of Jews under thirty-five are involved with Chabad. The next generation is even more open to Chabad. As they get older and marry, many will continue to identify with Chabad, attracted by the culture of welcoming, quality programs, and the richness of tradition. The majority may not choose to be fully observant, yet the synagogue they will be active in, the place they will send their kids, will be Chabad;[86] their community and rabbi will be Chabad. This involvement will place them on a path toward tradition, increasing their personal observance of many mitzvahs. This is a marked difference from their parents and grandparents of a generation or two ago who were moving away from observance. With time, there is no question that this connection will deepen their commitment to Judaism and their adherence to tradition.

This development has the potential to bring about a fundamental realignment of American Jewish life. Tragically, some on the periphery will continue to slowly drift away from the Jewish community. The rising numbers of intermarriage and lack of Jewish education will continue, sadly, to be a catalyst for assimilation. For those engaged in Jewish community life, we are seeing the beginnings of realignment to three major groupings. However, a new trend is emerging amongst college-age students. According to Rabbi Hirschy Zarchi at Chabad Harvard, young Jews from very assimilated backgrounds are beginning to connect, and "many of those attending Chabad are having their first Jewish experience."

The Reform and Conservative Movements are facing shrinking numbers. Still, they will continue to be a place where many will choose to affiliate. If present trends continue, with Reform gravitating toward more tradition and Conservative away from it, the lines between these movements will become more blurred.[87]

On the other end is the Orthodox community, which has been steadily rising in size. This will continue due to high birthrates, a successful educational system, and influx of Baalei Teshuva (Jews from non-Orthodox backgrounds who choose to become observant).

In the center of the community will be a new paradigm. Significant numbers of Jews, who are either observant or traditional, will elect to affiliate with Chabad. In my community of Orange County, California, there is a network of fifteen Chabad Centers. On the High Holidays, the attendance at the Chabad Centers is three times that of the local Conservative congregations. There is little doubt, as Chabad Centers continue to grow from embryonic storefronts to proper facilities, Chabad affiliation will rise. Bottom line, in the next generation, a significant percentage, if not the majority of Jews engaged in Jewish life, will either belong to Orthodox synagogues or be on a trajectory toward fuller observance through their involvement with Chabad.

The change is already happening. In the US and Canada, the Conservative Movement has dropped to just 595 Temples, from once close to 900.[88] According to a survey by Synagogue 3000,[89] "attendance is down and there is a dearth of young people." Reform has 860[90] congregations. According to Professor Steven Cohen,[91] "All is not well in the Reform world," a significant percentage of its members is above fifty. "Reform may have the biggest denominational market share of American Jews, but it is a diminishing share of a diminishing small number." The percentage of American Jews who are actual members of the liberal congregations has plummeted. According to the 2013 Pew Study,[92] only 14 percent of American Jews belong to Reform Temples and just 11 percent are members of Conservative congregations.[93]

Chabad has a thousand centers in North America, and it is constantly opening new locations[94] and expanding existing ones. The numbers of Jews involved with Chabad is on the rise. Chabad is also developing new programs to target specific populations; one of the most recent initiatives has been the opening of centers focusing on young professionals. In urban settings like Los Angeles, Dallas, Miami, Detroit, and New York, these programs have met with great success. Millennials do not feel the need to join a synagogue as their parents or grandparents did. They want to be involved in the programs that interest them. Chabad's approach, according to Professor Ron Wolfson of the American Jewish University, "has lowered the barriers of engagement." In the Jewish community, many remain fixated on the old model of membership and large institutions. The doors to Chabad Centers are wide open and welcoming. Chabad's strategy of smaller neighborhood centers, unique programs that target specific demographics, and no prerequisite of membership has uniquely positioned it for even a greater role for the next generation of American Jews. Most important, Jews are looking for meaning in their lives. Chabad's prime focus on the timeless teachings of the Torah makes it relevant to growing numbers of American Jews.

This has already occurred in Australia, Russia, and South Africa[95] where the great majority of synagogues and many community institutions are led by Chabad rabbis. In Europe and South America, Chabad's influence is on the rise. In Berlin, Chabad has spawned a network of centers including a school, Israel Center, and a $10 million community center. This kind of activity is being duplicated throughout the continent. In Paris, there are thirty-five neighborhood Chabad Centers and more in the suburbs. In addition, many Parisian synagogues are led by Chabad rabbis. In European countries, 25 percent of the rabbis are Chabad.[96] Forty percent of the European rabbis under sixty are Chabad. Rabbi Yitzi Loewenthal, the shliach in Copenhagen, says Chabad has made a game-changing contribution to European Jewish life. "Twenty years ago, people were saying that there was no future for smaller Jewish communities in Europe. The success of Chabad programs has shown others that it's possible to have a vibrant Jewish life." According to Loewenthal, many communal groups have either emulated or supported Chabad.[97]

Chabad growth is beginning to change the dynamics of Jewish communal life in the US in the decades to come. Jewish tradition will have greater influence.[98] People deeply involved with Chabad are taking a stronger leadership role in central communal institutions like Jewish Federations.[99] In many cities, this process of change has already started. This will pose a challenge to existing groups, who will need to be more sensitive to Chabad's agenda rooted in tradition and spirituality.[100]

Many observers have prognosticated that American Jewry is at profound risk. The emerging role of Chabad has the potential to mitigate that trend. No question that significant numbers of Jews who have minimal Jewish education and engagement will continue on the trajectory away from tradition. However, at the same time, growing numbers will renew the covenant of their ancestors with the Torah and its traditions. Chabad will continue to be a prime gateway for Jewish renaissance in the US and abroad, creating Jewish communities more rooted in classical Jewish values and the teachings of Torah.

Since his arrival in the US in 1941, the Rebbe occupied an office on the first floor of 770. Bookshelves lined the walls. Piles of books the Rebbe was using in his studies stood in columns around the room; boxes were filled with letters and materials. In the earlier years, when the Rebbe received visitors for private appointments, the books would be covered or removed from the room. In the later years, when the private meetings ceased, the office became filled with more books and documents. As Rabbi Binyomin Klein, the Rebbe's secretary, describes:[101] "When the Rebbe was studying, he would open a book to a page, set it aside, and then open another book and pile one on top of another." Klein explains that just before Shabbos the Rebbe would cover the books with a paper, and on Sunday remove them and begin again, creating more piles. When the secretaries suggested expanding the office, the Rebbe responded, "My father-in-law, the Rebbe, gave me this room and that's where I want to be," rejecting any ideas to alter the office.

Just after Passover in 1991, the Rebbe spent six weeks organizing his office. Rabbi Krinsky says, "It was apparent that the Rebbe was creating a new order, to a point that the room was almost empty." Klein says, "During the period when the Rebbe was organizing the books and materials in his office, some were sent to the library, others to archives, and some burned." The Rebbe's secretaries had been troubled by change, Rabbi Groner says. "This was not business as usual." After the Rebbe completed the reorganization, he would no longer retain books he used in his studies for extended periods of time, returning each volume promptly to the Chabad library.[102]

Nine months after cleaning[103] his office, the Rebbe suffered a debilitating stroke, which robbed him of his speech and caused his left side to become paralyzed. On the Rebbe's desk, a calendar and a few other items were left. The most prominent space was taken up by the large oversized volumes of the Sefer Hashluchim (the Book of Shluchim). Each page featured a series of pictures[104] of the families of shluchim, husbands and wives with their children. The pictures were organized according to states and countries; interlaced with the family pictures were images of Chabad institutions around the world.

The Sefer Hashluchim was published on the Rebbe's initiative. At the shluchim convention in October of 1990[105] the Rebbe asked that an album be prepared of all the shluchim in the world, their children, and pictures of institutions, suggesting that it be ready in three weeks.[106] Rabbi Yosef Friedman,[107] the project editor, says, "The Rebbe was an aficionado of souvenir journals, starting with the journal he himself published in the forties, of the work of Merkos and Mesibos Shabbos.[108] Later, the Rebbe encouraged books in honor of the public menorah lightings."

The shluchim-book project was massive. Rabbi Friedman says, "This was at the very early stages of desktop publishing and there was no e-mail." Friedman explains, "We had to collect thousands of images from around the world. Making sure they were of print quality and listing thousands of names and getting it right was quite a challenge." The actual printing was done in China. One member of the editorial staff, Rabbi Shaya Gansburg, spent months in Hong Kong overseeing production. At first, three volumes were published, one for the US and Canada, the second for Israel, and the third for the rest of the world. A year later, a fourth volume was added. All told, it included shluchim in thirty-seven countries and thirty-nine states. In the fourth volume, there was an extensive index in Hebrew and English, listing over fourteen thousand[109] names of those who appeared in the books. My kids still remember the excitement of getting dressed up in their best Shabbat clothing and going to a photographer in the local mall to take the picture.

The Rebbe said it was essential to include pictures of all of the children, saying, "They will be inspired by seeing their pictures in the book, giving them the encouragement to go in the right path when they grow older, as well." It was these pictures that encouraged Rabbi Isser New,[110] whose parents are shluchim in Atlanta, to follow in their footsteps. He was just seven when the book was published. As a child, he would look at the pictures and feel that he was part of a lofty and noble endeavor. He says, "There was a tremendous sense of belonging and pride in that second generation of Chabad."

The editorial staff proposed that the book be dedicated in memory[111] of the Rebbitzen Chaya Mushka, the Rebbe's wife. A full-page dedication was prepared with her picture. Friedman says, "We were not sure if the Rebbe would agree to a dedication of such a personal nature, but when we received the Rebbe's approval, it was clear the album was being treated by the Rebbe as a family album."

I realized that the Rebbe considered the shluchim his family on the day his wife passed away. Upon being informed of her passing, the Rebbe asked that the shluchim be notified. I, as many others, hastily flew through the night to New York. Shortly after the funeral, the word went out that the shluchim were invited to join the Rebbe for Mincha, the afternoon prayer, in his home. Chassidim had always respected the Rebbe's privacy, and, for almost all of us on that sorrowful afternoon, it was the first time we were in the Rebbe's home. Outside on the street, a crowd of hundreds, and later thousands, gathered. Only the shluchim and a few distinguished elderly Chassidim were admitted into the house. We waited downstairs, standing on the simple wooden floor in the living room. Finally, the Rebbe came down the winding staircase. There were fifty, maybe sixty of us, from across the globe. We stood in a semicircle as the Rebbe walked to the amud (a simple wooden podium), where he rested his prayer book. I was just a foot or so away as he led the prayers. Never before had I felt so deeply connected. It was the shluchim that he wanted next to him at this moment of great loss. At that instant, I understood. We, the shluchim, are the Rebbe's family.[112]

Rabbi Krinsky says, "The Rebbe loved the Sefer Hashluchim." During the difficult period of illness after the Rebbe's stroke, Rabbi Krinsky would at times sit with the Rebbe late into the night reviewing the Sefer Hashluchim. He says he could see the nachas (enjoyment) the Rebbe received from seeing the pictures of the shluchim and their children.

On the day of the stroke, the Rebbe's office was unusually neat. The piles of books had been organized and returned to the library. Personal papers and years of correspondence had been archived or removed. On that fateful day, on the center of his desk was the Sefer Hashluchim, those large volumes filled with the images of his family, the thousands of men, women and children whom he inspired to dedicate their lives to the welfare of the Jewish People, and care of others. The desk remains that way till today,[113] in its center, the Book of Shluchim, the Rebbe's legacy and gift to the world.

Afterword

The Oath

It was after midnight on Saturday night; a sea of Chassidic rabbis with black suits, fedoras and beards engulfed the TWA counter at Los Angeles International Airport, each scrabbling to find a seat on a plane that would get them to New York well before sundown the next day. Tradition mandated that their beloved leader, Rabbi Menachem Mendel Schneerson, who had returned his soul to his Maker on Saturday night, must be buried on Sunday. The solemn intensity of the rabbis overwhelmed the attendant behind the counter. Clearly, some of us would miss the flight – and the most important funeral in the history of the two-century-old Chabad-Lubavitch Movement.

The rush to Brooklyn had started an hour earlier, when just before 11:00 p.m. California time, the rabbis got the dreaded news that their spiritual leader, master teacher of Torah, their *Rebbe*, the man who had defined their movement and much of modern Jewish life for the past forty-two years, had passed away. That night was nothing short of an 8.0 earthquake for Chabad followers and Jews around the world. It was June 12, 1994, the third day of the Jewish month of Tammuz.

For me, the sense of doom had started a few hours earlier, when a fellow Chabad rabbi had told me that his father, who was in the Rebbe's inner circle, reported from the hospital that things had turned bleak. The Rebbe had suffered a stroke twenty-seven months earlier. Since then, there had been ups and downs. For a while, the Rebbe appeared to be gaining some strength after the first stroke. In recent days, however, despite prayers from around the world, he had taken a turn for the worse. Minutes later, the tragic news came from New York; a message was sent out on beepers: Shema Yisroel Hashem Elokeinu Hashem Echad (the iconic Jewish prayer said daily and before death). And I, along with thousands of other rabbis in the Rebbe's Army across the globe, rushed to the closest airport in the scrabble to get to the headquarters of Chabad in Crown Heights, Brooklyn.

Finally, I boarded the plane. I looked down the aisle and saw nothing but rabbis sitting somberly in their seats. Through the night, the air phone brought rumors from New York that rippled through the cabin. The funeral would be at 11:00 a.m. in Brooklyn. No, we then heard, it was going to be in Israel. Finally, it was confirmed. The funeral would be at 4:00 p.m. in Queens. The late hour, I was to discover later, was to allow for the arrival of a hastily chartered 747 from Israel. On the flight was the Rebbe's only living immediate relative, his niece, as well as hundreds of Chassidim, and Israel's chief rabbi, Rabbi Yisrael Meir Lau, dispatched by Prime Minister Rabin to the funeral.

On our flight, there wasn't much conversation. In the past, when Chassidim traveled to the Rebbe, there was great joy on the flights. But this trip was much different. We all sat quietly attempting to make sense of the loss, not really believing the real purpose of the flight.

The Rebbe would be interred in Montefiore Cemetery next to his father-in-law, the Previous Rebbe. Around his grave, a stone structure opened to the heavens, with room for one more grave.

As we departed from the plane, we walked side by side, most of us looking disheveled and depressed. Jerry Seinfeld, the comedian and television star, happened to be in first class on the same flight. As we walked through the terminal at JFK, I decided to share with him the tragedy we rabbis were feeling. I was going to suggest to him to do a mitzvah (an act of kindness) in honor of the Rebbe's passing. Seinfeld looked perplexed by the entourage of grieving rabbis that surrounded him. It wasn't the paparazzi that he was used to. When I made a beeline in his direction, he scurried off to the side. Clearly, he was not interested in any message of spiritual encouragement. At first, I was troubled by his hasty escape, but in retrospect, I realized that the sight of dozens of distraught rabbis would have been a foreboding for anyone, much less a Jewish comedian.

In Brooklyn, I was drafted to help deal with the press. Outside 770, on Eastern Parkway, the media had encamped and occupied a significant part of the parkway. The three-story red brick building with a large basement-synagogue had been the epicenter of the Chabad Movement for the last half century. Our task was to help the press understand a world they had little comprehension of – all in thirty-second sound bites. Throughout the afternoon, despite my deep anguish, I attempted to be patient with the gaggle of reporters from around the globe.

The street had been cordoned off. Thousands mingled, waiting for the funeral to begin. There was a block-long line of people wanting to pay tribute and walk past the Rebbe for a final time. Each entered the Rebbe's office, and walked quickly by in mourning. I had been given a special identification that allowed me to bypass the lines. First I went, barely grasping the moment myself. Inside the office, the Rebbe's body was enveloped in burial shrouds, surrounded by Chassidim saying Psalms. Then I brought a few selected reporters to the head of the line so they, too, could walk by in somber silence.

At four o'clock, the casket emerged from the front door of 770. An anguished collective cry emanated from the crowd – the wail of tens of thousands reaching up to heaven. Overhead, ominous clouds covered the heavens. The coffin was decked by the Rebbe's kapote, the long Chassidic-style rabbinical coat. As the coffin moved through the crowd, the kapote remained perched on top, a black symbol on a black day. People reached out with their hands to touch the coffin as it was carried through the crowd. It was placed in a vehicle stationed down the street, and the procession began to the cemetery.

I turned to my two sons, Yoni, who was then nineteen, who had flown in from his yeshiva in Miami, and Yehoshua, just fifteen, who had taken a later flight than mine from Los Angeles. As the hearse pulled away from 770, we ran up Eastern Parkway. I spotted a taxi on a side street and jumped in. I told the driver to follow the procession. Our taxi became the last car in the formal funeral procession. Police cars surrounded the entourage, their sirens blaring. The crowds back in Crown Heights were still getting on buses and looking for other modes of transportation as we drove down Eastern Parkway headed for Montefiore Cemetery, just beyond Kennedy Airport. As we turned to enter the Belt Parkway, I caught sight of a roadblock. All traffic had been stopped on this main artery to allow for the funeral procession. The New York traffic stretched back as far as the eye could see.

Montefiore Cemetery was established in the early twentieth century. It is filled with various fellowship groups from Jewish communities in Europe and various Jewish organizations. Over a hundred acres of tombstones, encircled by an old wrought-iron fence, reside within a middle-class African-American neighborhood in Queens.

Instead of driving around the side to the closest access to the Chabad section, which is off 224th Avenue, I ordered the driver to stop at the main entrance on Springfield Avenue. At the main entrance, a group of policemen stood guard. "You can't enter," they told us. I was not the only one who had rushed from Crown Heights; a group of fifteen or twenty had gathered there, too, including Rabbi Shalom Mendel Simpson of the Rebbe's secretariat. I showed the officer the special white passes that had been issued to shluchim to allow them access into the cemetery during the funeral. "No, you cannot enter," the policeman said again. Finally, in exasperation, I informed the cops we were going in. "You can pull your guns, but nothing will stop us," I told him. We pushed the gate, and they attempted to hold us back, but we persevered. With my sons in tow, I started to run the distance to the back end of the cemetery, at least half a mile away. Suddenly a car appeared on the narrow road that slivered between the graves. Some of the elder Chassidim were being driven to the gravesite. I stood in the middle, forcing them to stop, and jumped on the hood. Slowly, we made our way to the Ohel.

Ohel means tent. The Ohel is a stone building. Its granite walls tower up without a roof, allowing the heavens to peer down. Inside is the grave of the Previous Rebbe. For decades, since his passing in 1950, Chassidim would flock to pray at his grave. The Rebbe would make the trek on a regular basis, standing for hours in summer heat or winter snow, reading the thousands of prayer requests from all over the world. The Rebbe would be laid to rest beside his father-in-law, predecessor, and mentor.

When I arrived at the Ohel, I found myself the first person at the door to the stone structure. I leaned against the wooden door in exhaustion from the marathon that had started just after midnight in California. The funeral had not yet started. Many of the senior rabbinical leaders of the movement had already gathered inside the Ohel. Others trickled in. Suddenly, the entourage with the coffin appeared, guiding it into the structure. The door closed behind and I strained to hear what was going on behind the stone walls.

Chabad funerals are simple; there are no eulogies. A few chapters of Psalms are said, the funeral is conducted, and Kaddish (the memorial prayer) is recited.

Suddenly, the collective stress I had experienced since the night before had its effect; the emotional, spiritual, and physical strain had reached a peak. There was a strong pain in my chest and I thought that I was having a heart attack. Just inside the doors, two EMTs were stationed in the small entrance hall to the Ohel, with oxygen in case of emergency. Pushing the door open, I told them, "I think I may be having a heart attack." Immediately, they pulled me inside and did a swift check. "You're OK," they told me, "it's just the stress." Now, finding myself on the inside of the door through Divine Providence, I was torn between the feeling of being where I did not belong, and knowing my soul was bonded with the Rebbe's. The funeral was coming to an end. I glanced around and saw the Rebbe's secretaries, distinguished rabbis and the senior shluchim. Seventy, eighty people in total, the preeminent leaders of the movement. They were covering the grave with earth so I, too, grabbed a shovel, in order to share in the mitzvah.

A few moments later, the task was complete. One of the members of the Chevra Kadisha (the burial society), as Jewish tradition mandates, asked mechila (forgiveness) in case they had inadvertently done anything disrespectful during the funeral. The Rebbe's secretaries recited the mourner's Kaddish. When they finished the prayer, there was absolute silence. No one moved. The towering stone walls framed the heavens above as we stood surrounding the fresh grave. No one wanted to move. What next? How could we continue? These were the unspoken questions. It was clear that, suddenly, we were orphans. How could we face the future?

The silence that lasted a few minutes was shattered by the booming voice of Rabbi Shlomo Cunin of Los Angeles, a large, boisterous man, known for his intense devotion to the Rebbe. In Yiddish, he made a pledge, an oath for all: "Rebbe, we promise, we give you an oath, to continue your mission that you have entrusted to us. We will preserve the institutions of the Rebbe; we will expand and develop them."

Slowly, we filed out of the Ohel. Thousands were waiting in lines that stretched outside the cemetery and down the block. Throughout the night, thousands passed by the fresh grave in mourning and disbelief.

The Jewish pundits filled newspaper columns with prophecies of doom and gloom. University professors, whose secular bent was never appreciative of the Rebbe's dramatic vision of Jewish renaissance, forecasted that Lubavitch would fall into oblivion. "Without a Rebbe they will not survive," was the relentless refrain. Ari Goldman, religious writer at *The New York Times*, told Charlie Rose on late-night TV a few days later that he was skeptical about Chabad's future.

In the coming days, we returned to our cities and communities in the United States and around the world. The Rebbe's shluchim, or rabbi-and-wife emissary teams, had set up life-long posts in some of the world's most unlikely places: Kathmandu, Bahia Blanca, Playa Del Carmen, and even the suburbs of American cities, in order to reach Jews and transform modern Jewish life. But the Rebbe believed in doing the hard work of Judaism, finding Jews who have become estranged from their Jewish heritage and helping them rediscover Judaism, one small step at a time. It wasn't glamorous work. It wasn't well-paid work. It wasn't work, frankly, that other parts of the Jewish community wanted to do. But the Rebbe made it clear that this was the most important work we could do in our lives. If a boat has one hole in it, everyone on board is affected. We Chabad rabbis were commissioned to plug the holes to keep Judaism from going under and guide the Jewish people to safe shores.

But with the Rebbe's passing, some of us wondered, deep in our souls, whether we had been trained well enough or were worthy enough to carry on the Rebbe's mission. In our deepest fears, some of us thought that perhaps our critics would be proven right – that our movement would crumble without the physical presence of the Rebbe, a singular leader who infused vitality, spirit, and even a sense of holiness into Chabad. Without his physical presence, maybe we would flounder, like orphans who couldn't fend for themselves. The future seemed quite uncertain just then.

Then Cunin made sense of it. The responsibility was ours to continue the Rebbe's mission, to change the world for the better, to create a spiritual momentum that would be a catalyst for the coming of Moshiach, and usher in a period of peace and sanctity.

In the twenty years that have passed, the shluchim have continued to fulfill that oath. On that day by the Rebbe's fresh grave, there were 1,100 shluchim in the world; today that number has more than quadrupled. Chabad has grown to a presence in forty-nine states and over eighty countries. Today, Chabad is the largest Jewish organization in the world.

Rabbi Adin Even-Yisrael Steinsaltz, the famed Israeli scholar and translator of the Talmud into English, put it into perspective in 1995 at the Living Legacy Conference in Washington.[1] Jewish leaders had convened from across the globe to celebrate the posthumous award of the Congressional Gold Medal[2] to the Rebbe. Rabbi Steinsaltz questioned the title of the event, Living Legacy. At a lecture in the Library of Congress, he told the audience that the mission the Rebbe entrusted to his Chassidim still had to be carried out. Succinctly, he explained: "The Rebbe did not leave a legacy, he left us marching orders."

In August of 2014, those orders were fulfilled in Mumbai. Six years after the terror attack that took the lives of Rabbi Gabi and Rivkie Holtzberg and four others, the Chabad House was rebuilt. Dozens of rabbis from throughout Asia came to Mumbai for the historic ceremony. Local community members paraded with philanthropist, George Rohr, as he carried the Torah scroll into the refurbished building that had been seriously damaged during the attack. *The New York Times*[3] reported Rabbi Kotlarsky's emotional remarks at the dedication: "We are not going to be intimidated by acts of terror. It will only spur us to spread more light and more kindness and goodness in the world."

Acknowledgments

The Torah teaches us the mitzvah of Hakarat Hatov, acknowledging the kindness of another. I am very grateful for the help of many. In particular: Rabbis Yehuda Krinsky, Moshe Kotlarsky, Berel Lazar, and Manis Friedman for their advice and support; the shluchim from around the world who shared their stories; Rabbis Zalman Shmotkin and Motti Seligson from Chabad.org, Rabbi Efraim Mintz of the Rohr Jewish Learning Institute, Rabbis Zushe Wolf, Shlomie Peles in Israel, and Dovid Mondshine in Russia; and Rabbis Elkanah Shmotkin and Yechiel Cagen of JEM's My Encounter with the Rebbe Oral History Project.

A special thanks to Carolyn Hessel of the Jewish Book Council for her guidance. Thank you to Professors Jonathan Sarna, Jack Wertheimer, and Ron Wolfson; authors Dennis Prager, Yossi Klein Halevi, and Yechiel Harari, who gave me a broader perspective on Chabad; Rabbis Lipa Brennan and Tuvia Teldon, and Candace Sneider who offered important insights into the manuscript; and Matthew Miller and Gila Fine of The Toby Press for believing in this book, and giving it their expert direction.

This book was made possible through the generosity of Brian Chisick and Patricia Vienna. It was nurtured by our dear friends who make up the warm Jewish community of Congregation Beth Meir HaCohen/Chabad of Yorba Linda, CA. Special thanks go to Tal HaCohen.

I am deeply appreciative to my wife Stella and family for supporting this endeavor, which has included much time and travel.

Finally, I would like to dedicate this book in memory of Rabbi Yosef Loschak, shliach extraordinaire to Santa Barbara, California, taken from this world in the prime of his life. His wisdom and insight fill these pages.

Cliff Lester

The four-volume Sefer Hashluchim (Book of Shluchim) remains on the Rebbe's desk to this day.

Notes

INTRODUCTION

1   The Yeshiva, the Rabbinical College of Canada, in Montreal, was established in 1941 by the Sixth Lubavitcher Rebbe, Rabbi Yosef Yitzchak Schneersohn.

2   Chabad and Lubavitch are interchangeable terms. Chabad is an acronym for three Hebrew words: Chochma, Bina, Daat – Wisdom, Understanding, and Knowledge. Lubavitch is the town in Belorussia where the movement was centered for over a century. The Rebbes of Chabad are called Lubavitcher Rebbes after that town.

3   Rabbi Chaim Mordechai Aizik Hodakov was born in Russia in 1902, and was the head of the secretariat of the Rebbe. He became acquainted with the Sixth Rebbe, Rabbi Yosef Yitzchak, and his successor, Rabbi Menachem Mendel Schneerson, in Riga in 1928. He had been inspector of Jewish schools for the Latvian government. When the Sixth Rebbe escaped from Nazi-controlled Europe in 1940, he invited Hodakov to come with him to start a Jewish school system in the United States. Rabbi Menachem Mendel Schneerson became the Seventh Rebbe in 1951 and appointed Rabbi Hodakov as his chief of staff, head of the secretariat, and administrator of Chabad institutions worldwide. Rabbi Hodakov passed away in 1993.

4   Chabad has institutions in over eighty-five countries and forty-nine states in the US. There is no other Jewish organization with the reach and scope of Chabad in the world. (Worldwide Chabad Directory, Chabad.org/centers).

5   In the last twenty years, Chabad has quadrupled the number of shluchim worldwide from 1,032 shluchim in 1994 to over four thousand couples. In addition, many Chabad Centers have evolved from small facilities to major community centers.

6   At the middle of the twentieth century, Jews were disengaging from Orthodoxy. Prominent sociologist, Marshall Sklare, wrote in 1955: "Orthodoxy is a case study in institutional decay." For more, see *A Study of Orthodoxy in Milwaukee*, which concludes, "If Milwaukee is any kind of indication of what is happening to Orthodox Jews in similar-sized communities, it appears that American Jewish Life will continue its unique development without a significant Orthodox Movement in its midst." (Howard Polsky, *The Jews, Social Patterns of an American Group*, ed. Marshall Sklare, (Glencoe: Free Press, 1958).

7   Historically, in Europe, South Africa, South America, and Australia, Orthodoxy is the dominant form of Jewish religious expression. Even if Jews are not fully observant, they attend Orthodox synagogues.

8   Interview with the author.

9   Although throughout history a number of rabbinical figures in various countries undertook localized efforts in their regions, never before had one Jewish leader sought to reach every single Jew. For instance, Rabbi Shimshon Rafael Hirsch defended Orthodoxy in nineteenth-century Germany. Rabbi Moshe Sofer emboldened Jewish observance in central Europe in the early nineteenth century. Rabbi Ovadia Yosef brought about a rebirth in the Sephardi communities, particularly in Israel. Rabbi Joseph Soloveitchik of Yeshiva University created a cadre of Orthodox rabbinic leaders that deeply affected American Jewish life. The Belzer Rebbe, Rabbi Yissachar Dov Rokeach, rebuilt the Chassidic community of Belz in the last decades.

CHAPTER ONE: GABI AND RIVKIE

1   Interview with the author.

2   Watch Chani's address to the International Conference of Shluchot in 2009, Chabad.org/1401395.

3   Chaim Noy and Erik Cohen, eds., *Israeli Backpackers: A View from Afar* (State University of New York Press: Suny Series in Israeli Studies, June 1, 2006).

4   Every year Chabad in Bangkok organizes a reunion for Israeli trekkers in Israel, Chabad.org/633983.

5   These include centers in Thailand, South America, India, Cambodia, and New Zealand.

6   Interview with the author.

7   The JDC (Joint Distribution Committee) was established in 1914 as a vehicle for American Jews to provide aid and assistance to Jews globally. It is a primary partner of the Jewish Federations of North America. More at jdc.org.

8 The Taj Mahal is a five-star luxury hotel built at the end of the nineteenth century in Mumbai, a city renowned for its poverty and overcrowding. It was one of the targets of the 2008 terrorist attack.

9 Interview with the author.

10 Chabad.org/774747.

11 video.pbs.org/video/1341327345/.

12 "Lashkar-e-Taiba," Council on Foreign Relations, January 2010, www.cfr.org/publication/17882.

13 His father was a Pakistani diplomat and broadcaster; his mother worked in the Pakistani embassy in Washington. As a young child, Headley moved with his family to Pakistan where he was attracted to Islamic extremism.

14 In January 2013, after pleading guilty to his involvement in the Mumbai attacks, Headley was sentenced to thirty-five years in Federal Prison.

15 Interview with the author.

16 In Israel, Chabad is among the few religious groups not connected to any political party. Internationally, too, Chabad's policy is to refrain from any political activity.

17 Headley's interrogation by the Indian authorities is very illuminating, info.publicintelligence.net/NIA-HeadleyInterrogation.pdf.

18 "Mumbai Terror Attacks: And Then They Came for the Jews," *The Sunday Times*, November 1, 2009, jpfo.org/articles-assd/bendory-mumbai.htm.

19 www.vosizneias.com/23540/2008/11/30/jerusalem-netanya-resident-survives-miraculous-ordeal-from-the-chabad-house-in-mumbai/.

20 Bialka tells his story, www.youtube.com/watch?v=LFlxaUid__g.

21 Chabad.org/775350.

22 Interview with the author.

23 Interview with the author.

24 Interview with the author.

25 Chabad maintains internal e-mail lists for Chabad rabbis and rebbitzens. The lists are called Shluchim Achdus – literally "Unity Among Shluchim." There are over a hundred lists, divided up by language, geography, and interest. The primary English list of shluchim has over two thousand subscribers. There are lists in Hebrew, Italian, Spanish, Russian, and French. There are lists for rabbis and rebbitzens. There are lists for campus rabbis, educators, programs like Friendship Circle, Hebrew School and chaplaincy programs.

26 P.V. Viswanath, "Talking With a Terrorist: An Endless Call to India," *Forward*, December 12, 2008, forward.com/articles/14676/talking-with-a-terrorist-an-endless-call-to-india-/.

27 Interview with the author.

28 Seligson set up a team to monitor twitter comments that were coming from the area around the Chabad House.

29   Each time I spoke to her, I was touched by her sensitivity, professionalism, and graciousness.

30   Interview with the author.

31   Shemtov is renowned for his close capitol contacts, Ron Kampeas, "Chabad's Man in DC," *Jewish Telegraphic Agency* (JTA), December 15, 2006. Shemtov had been in contact with the White House chief of staff, and Vice President Elect Biden called to express his concern.

32   Interview with the author.

33   Jeremy Kahn, "Mumbai Terrorists Relied on New Technology for Attacks," *New York Times*, December 8, 2008.

34   Sites like COL, Shturem, CrownHeights.info, and Shmais are independent news sites. They are not official mouthpieces for Chabad; rather, they are private for-profit websites.

35   Major media outlets, including *The New York Times,* used the information from Chabad.org for their stories since they knew it was reliable.

36   The team was in constant contact with Israeli security officials. A senior former government official called me to relay the information that the government had not been able to secure permission from the Indian government to send the Israeli commando unit.

37   It seems that during the calls, the terrorists were distracted and did not realize that Sandra had secretly entered the third floor and saved the baby.

38   "Sandra Samuel: A Heroine in Mumbai," Chabad.org/775350; "In Her Own Words, Nanny's Brave Escape in Mumbai," www.cnn.com/2008/WORLD/asiapcf/12/04/nanny.mumbai.interview/index.html?iref=24hours

39   For more on Sandra: www.openthemagazine.com/article/international/the-nanny-who-saved-baby-moishe. Sandra lives with Rivkie's parents in Afula, Israel, where she has been given citizenship and where she still cares for Moshie.

40   Interview with the author.

41   "Chilling Mumbai Terror Attack Tapes Released," *The Telegraph*, February 24, 2009. www.telegraph.co.uk/news/worldnews/asia/india/4799802/Chilling-Mumbai-terror-attack-tapes-released.html

42   The Indian attack came too late and went on for hours. TV broadcasts of the attack compromised the efficiency of the attack. If the Indians had permitted Israeli forces to enter the country, there is a chance there would have been some survivors in the Chabad House.

43   A non-Jew made the call since Shabbat had already started in Mumbai.

44   Interview with the author.

45   Because his conversion was not yet complete, he was not bound by the Jewish prohibition of driving on Shabbat (the Sabbath).

46 Jewish tradition permits an autopsy when it will have a direct benefit in saving another life or in capturing a killer. Still, the autopsy must be limited and minimally invasive.

47 Interview with the author.

48 "Press Conference on Mumbai Tragedy," Chabad.org/773773; CNN report, November 28, 2008, www.cnn.com/2008/WORLD/asiapcf/11/28/india.jewish.center.attack/index.html?iref=allsearch.

49 Rabbi Dov Goldberg, interview with the author.

50 Jeremy Kahn, "Jews of Mumbai, a Tiny and Eclectic Group, Suddenly Reconsider Their Serene Existence," *New York Times*, December 2, 2008.

51 www.youtube.com/watch?v=JXBzBaj2i1E.

52 Goldstein had arrived from Israel with a team from Zaka.

53 Rabbi Nachman Holtzberg, interview with the author.

54 Chabad operates a network of elementary schools, high schools, and college programs in conjunction with Israel's Ministry of Education.

55 Interview with the author.

56 Interview with the author.

57 Interview with the author.

58 Interview with the author.

59 Rabbi Nachman Holtzberg, interview with the author.

60 Interview with the author.

61 The Talmud is the foundation of Jewish scholarship. Composed in Hebrew and Aramaic, its pages are filled with complicated legal arguments, philosophical insights, and ethical teachings. There is a total of 5,894 pages. To complete this as a teenager is remarkable.

62 Chassidic marriages are far different from the stereotypes depicted in Fiddler on the Roof. A shadchan may be a friend, relative, or professional. When young people date, they do so on their own without chaperones. Matrimony is the intention. Unless the relationship develops into something serious, it's usually terminated quickly. Marriage must be based on an emotional attachment. There is no intimacy before marriage and engagements tend to be brief, just a few months. Young people wait to date until they are ready for a serious relationship. Vetting prospective candidates and dating with matrimony in mind produces stable, strong marriages. The divorce rate in Chassidic marriages is very low, in the single digits.

63 Interview with the author.

64 Interview with the author.

65 He had been trained in kosher slaughter.

66 Interview with the author.

67 "Mission of Love: the Story of Those Cruelly Murdered at the Mumbai Jewish Center," Video on Gabi and Rivkie by JEM (Jewish Educational Media), Chabad. org/779312.

68 Interview with the author.

69 Interview with the author.

70 Kfar Chabad was founded in 1949 by the Sixth Rebbe, Rabbi Yosef Yitzchak Schneersohn.

71 Interview with the author.

72 Interview with the author.

73 The Ohel (literally "tent") is a stone structure with four granite walls and an open roof. It was originally constructed to enclose the grave of the Sixth Rebbe, Rabbi Yosef Yitzchak Schneersohn, after his passing in 1950. In 1994, the Seventh Rebbe, Rabbi Menachem Mendel Schneerson was interred next to his father-in-law and predecessor. Jewish tradition teaches that in times of spiritual need, one should offer prayers at the grave of a tzadik. Tens of thousands of Jews and non-Jews visit the Ohel annually. The graves are located in Montefiore Cemetery in Queens, New York, founded in 1904.

74 Yossi Klein Halevi, "Why Israelis Love Chabad," *New Republic*, December 4, 2008, www.newrepublic.com/article/politics/why-israelis-love-chabad.

75 A Hebrew term that refers to Chabad followers.

76 Video of the funeral, Chabad.org/778892.

77 In Israel, many adhere to the tradition of burying in shrouds and a talit, others follow the custom of using a coffin.

78 Interview with the author.

79 Interview with the author.

CHAPTER TWO: "AMERICA IZ NISHT ANDERISH" – AMERICA IS NOT DIFFERENT

1 Based on notes of an interview conducted by Sue Fishkoff, author of *The Rebbe's Army* (New York: Schocken Books, 2003). I am grateful to Ms. Fishkoff for sharing her historic source material. More at Chabad.org/585088.

2 The leaders of Chassidic communities were historically known as "Rebbe," an honorific title given to great scholars and leaders renowned for their piety and commitment to the community.

3 Interview with the author.

4 Chassidim follow the custom of prayer, edited by Rabbi Schneur Zalman, established by Rabbi Isaac Luria, the Ari, the fifteenth-century kabbalist.

5 Many Russian Jews attended Chassidic congregations in their homeland. For more, see Y.L. Levin, *Toldos Chabad BeArtzos Habris* (History of Chabad in

the United States) (New York: Kehot). They created American congregations reflecting that tradition even though very few lived a full Chassidic lifestyle.

6   Originally founded in the Russian town of Lubavitch by the Fifth Rebbe, Rabbi Sholom DovBer in 1897.

7   Interview with the author.

8   Poland was the center of Jewish scholarship and spirituality in the pre-war era. The major Chassidic groups: Ger, Belz, Radomsk, and others were centered there. In Poland, the great yeshivas of Chachmei Lublin, Mir, Ponovitch, and others drew students from all over the world. Hecht had been part of a group of American students who studied with Rabbi Israel Jacobson and drew closer to Chabad. Jacobson sent the group to the Rebbe's yeshiva in Poland. Rabbi Israel Jacobson was instrumental in founding Chabad in the US. For background on Jacobson, see *Memoirs of Rabbi Israel Jacobson* (New York: Kehot, 1996).

9   Dubin was a representative of Agudath Israel. After the war, he was jailed by the Soviets. He passed away in a Siberian prison camp in 1956, www.jta.org/1956/09/13/archive/mordecai-dubin-orthodox-leader-reported-dead-in-siberian-camp.

10 For more on the arrest and liberation of the Rebbe, see Rabbi Alter Benzion Metzger, *Heroic Struggle* (New York: Kehot, 1998).

11 Rabbi Yosef Wineberg was born in Poland in 1917. He was a student of the Sixth Rebbe in Poland and escaped the war via Shanghai. Arriving in the US in 1944, he was among those who were instrumental in raising funds for the network of Chabad yeshivas. He passed away in 2012.

12 Rachel Altein, *Out of the Inferno,* ed. Eliezer Zaklikovsky, Appendix 3, "The Lubavitcher Rebbe in Warsaw," (New York: Kehot, 2002). There is a wealth of original documentation taken from the archives of Rabbi Israel Jacobson. For an interesting account of the Rebbe's escape from the hands of the Nazis.

13 In 1929, the Rebbe spent ten months in the United States. He visited Jewish communities in New York, Boston, Baltimore, Chicago, Detroit, and Saint Louis. For details, see Rabbi Shalom Ber Levin, *History of Chabad in the United States and Canada* (*Toldos Chabad BeArtzos HaBris,* Hebrew) (New York: Kehot, 1988).

14 See Altein, *Out of the Inferno.*

15 K.H. Abshagen, *Canaris,* 1949 (German); Altein, *Out of the Inferno*, Appendix 5 (English).

16 It was Canaris who vouched for Bloch to Hitler. In late 1939, Hitler signed a document stating: "I, Adolf Hitler, leader of the German Nation, approve Major Ernst Bloch to be of German blood." After the war, Bloch returned to live in Germany. See Rigg, *Rescued from the Reich: How One of Hitler's Soldiers Saved the Lubavitcher Rebbe.*

17 For a detailed biography, see Dr. Nissan Mindel, *Rabbi Schneur Zalman of Liadi* (New York: Kehot, 2002).

18 Rabbi Eliyahu, known as Gaon (brilliant scholar) of Vilna, was born in 1720 and passed away in 1797.

19 Rabbi Dov Ber was the leader of the fledgling Chassidic Movement after the passing of the founder Rabbi Israel Baal Shem Tov in 1760. He moved the center of the movement to Mezeritch and surrounded himself with a group of outstanding students. His date of birth is unknown, between 1700 and 1710. He passed away in 1772. See Jacob Immanuel Schochet, *The Great Maggid: The Life and Teachings of Rabbi DovBer of Mezhirech* (New York: Kehot, 1998).

20 Mezeritch was a small town located in the Ukraine.

21 He was born in Turkey and claimed, at age twenty-two, that he was the Messiah. Many rabbinical leaders questioned his claims. He was banished from the city of Salonika and was met with great skepticism by rabbinical leaders in Jerusalem. When given the choice by the Sultan of Turkey of death or conversion, he became a Muslim in 1666.

22 *The Light and Fire of the Baal Shem Tov* (New York: The Continuum International Publishing Group Inc., 2006).

23 Today it is a town with a population of around two thousand. The grave of the Baal Shem Tov has been refurbished. Jews from around the world make pilgrimages to pray at this holy site. The synagogue of Rabbi Israel Baal Shem Tov has been restored.

24 The first edition of the Code of Jewish Law, the Mishneh Torah, had been authored by Maimonides (Rabbi Moshe ben Maimon) between 1170 and 1180. In 1563, Rabbi Josef Karo in Tzefat wrote the Shulchan Aruch (literally "The Set Table") explaining the rulings of Jewish Law according to the traditions of Sephardi Jews. Rabbi Moshe Isserles, the Remah (1520-1572) of Krakow, notated Karo's Code with Ashkenazi traditions. Rabbi Dov Ber, the Maggid, tasked Rabbi Schneur Zalman with writing an updated version of the Code of Jewish Law. He approached it differently from his predecessors, who simply stated the ruling without the legal reasoning behind it. Rabbi Schneur Zalman outlined the varied legal approaches to an issue, providing a succinct overview of Jewish legal thought on it; then he made a ruling. It became known as Shulchan Aruch Harav – the Rabbi's Code of Jewish Law. It is considered one of the seminal Jewish legal works and used today by scholars around the world as a prime authority on Jewish Law. It was written in Hebrew. In recent years, Kehot, the Chabad publishing arm, has begun publishing sections of the Code in English.

25 First published in 1797, it has been translated into English, Russian, French, Italian, Spanish, Yiddish, and Braille.

26 It is the oldest Jewish charity in Israel. It supports soup kitchens, medical clinics, and immigrant assistance in Israel, www.colelchabad.org.

27 Literally "those who oppose" in Hebrew. These were the religious Jews who opposed the innovations of the Chassidim.

28 Today, as part of a tourist attraction in the ancient fortress, a wax model of the Alter Rebbe is displayed in the cell where it is believed he was imprisoned.

29 The Czar came incognito to investigate firsthand the cause of the controversy. The Alter Rebbe stood and welcomed the Czar, acknowledging his identity. During the imprisonment, the Rebbe underwent extensive interrogation about the philosophy of Chassidism. Historically, Chassidim viewed his release as a spiritual vindication of his teachings. After his release, the Rebbe changed his style of teaching. Before, his Chassidic discourses had been brief; afterward, he began delivering discourses with greater explanation.

30 The Alter Rebbe opposed Napoleon who, while promising Jews freedom, forced their integration into French society. His Chassidim supported the Czar's effort to repel the French invasion.

31 Today no Jews live in Lubavitch. It has suffered the same fate as another hundred towns of vibrant Jewish life, falling victim to the destruction of the Nazis. The Third and Fourth Rebbes are interred there. The Chatzer (courtyard) that once housed the Yeshiva Tomchei Temimim, the synagogue, and home of the Rebbes, stands almost empty. The land was acquired by Chabad, and a museum was erected to memorialize the Jewish history of Lubavitch.

32 Established in fall of 1918 with the consent of Lenin to carry Communist revolution to the Jewish masses. The stated mission of these sections was "destruction of traditional Jewish life, the Zionist Movement, and Hebrew culture." The sections were staffed mostly by Jewish ex-members of the Bund, which joined the Soviet Communist Party in 1921. According to historian Richard Pipes, "In time, every Jewish cultural and social organization came under assault." However, the main emphasis of Yevsektsia was the assault on Jewish religion. Acting together with local Soviet authorities, they organized seizures of synagogues in many cities. For more, see Bernard Maza, *With Fury Poured Out: The Power of the Powerless During the Holocaust* (Sure Sellers, 1989).

33 A department of the Communist government.

34 At times the campaign against Judaism by the Jewish Communists was more strident than the government policy.

35 These included Rabbi Yisrael Meir Kagan, the sainted Chofetz Chaim, who returned his yeshiva to Radin in Poland. The great scholar Rabbi Baruch Ber Leibowitz moved the Kaminetz Yeshiva from Kremenchug in Russia to Lithuania. Rabbi Aaron Kotler reopened the Yeshiva of Slutzk in Kletzk, Poland, after escaping Russia in 1921. Twenty years later, Rabbi Kotler would play a key role

in the development of yeshiva scholarship in the US, again taking a radically different approach from the Rebbe. He advocated creating havens of scholarship, while the Rebbe would argue for a strategy that took responsibility for all of the Jewish community.

36 Berel Wein, *Faith and Fate* (New York: Shaar Press, 2001).

37 The Joint Distribution Committee (JDC) or as it is known, "the Joint," was a prime partner in the Rebbe's effort in Russia. It was founded by Jewish philanthropists in 1914 to provide for the needs of Jews overseas. More at www.jdc.org.

38 I recall students leaving the Soviet Union in the early 1970s who joined our yeshiva in Israel. We expected that they would need personal attention to raise their level of learning to ours. Instead we were astonished to meet a group of young men around twenty years of age with a level of learning similar to those students who had studied in the yeshivas in Israel since childhood. They were products of the secret schools that continued to function for over half a century.

39 Sefer Hasichos 5684, p. 55, n. 20.

40 Decades later at a farbrengen, the Rebbe turned to one of his Chassidim, Rabbi Bentzion Shemtov, and asked if he was one of the ten. Shemtov did not answer. Clearly, he was in a moral dilemma, since the oath made with the Previous Rebbe was one of total secrecy. The Rebbe, sensing his predicament, pressed no further. Shemtov served four years in a Soviet prison and was married in the jail. His children would serve as the nucleus of the first shluchim to be sent out by the Rebbe in the late fifties.

41 Six of his children survived the Soviet oppression, and most of his family followed Chassidic traditions. His great-grandson returned to Russia, where he heads Chabad in Ulyanovsk, the birthplace of Lenin. Numerous grandchildren and great-grandchildren serve as shluchim of Chabad, from the Golan in Israel's north to California in the US.

42 The Haskalah was the movement to secularize Judaism in Russia. It originated in Germany and moved east. One of the most audacious efforts was of Max Lilienthal, a German Jew who masqueraded as religious in Russia. He befriended a senior Czarist official, Count Uvanov, and attempted to use government coercion to change the Jewish educational system in Russia. In 1843, Lilienthal and Uvanov orchestrated a conference in Saint Petersburg to set policy in the area of Jewish education. Representing the Jewish community were: the Third Rebbe, Rabbi Menachem Mendel; Rabbi Isaac; Rabbi Yitzchak of Volozhin; Israel Halperin, a noted Berditchev financier; and Bezalel Stern of Odessa. The Jewish leaders rejected the ideas of Lilienthal. Subsequently, an accusation against Lilienthal for financial irregularities in the use of government funding

forced him to flee Russia to the US. There, he took a major leadership role in the fledgling Reform Movement. For more, see "The Tzemach Tzedek and the Haskalah Movement," www.jewish-history.com/chabad/index.html. For background, see Rabbi Nathan Kamenetsky, *The Making of a Gadol* (Jerusalem: privately published, 2004).

43 For an intriguing account of the arrest, see Uri Kaploun, trans., *A Prince in Prison: The Previous Lubavitcher Rebbe's Account of Incarceration in Stalinist Russia in 1927* (New York: Sichos in English, 1997).

44 A talit is a prayer shawl. Tefilin are donned by Jews daily in prayer, on the head and arm. They are made of leather, contain the central prayer, the Shema, on parchment, and are bound with leather straps.

45 Peretz lived in Springfield, Massachusetts, his brother in Boston. The Chabad community in Springfield, until today, celebrates the Chassidic holiday of Yud Beis Tammuz (12 Tammuz) with great excitement, calling the anniversary of the Rebbe's release the "Miracle of Springfield."

46 Interview with the author.

47 Yiddish for "The Truth," edited by Semyon Dimanstein. Later he, too, suffered from Stalin. Arrested in 1938, he was sentenced to death.

48 *Chicago Tribune*, February 10, 1930. According to the *Detroit Free Press*, April 28, 1930, "ten thousand people escorted the Rebbe to the Emanuel Synagogue."

49 For generations, the Chabad Rebbes had appointed Shadarim, who would expound the teachings of Chassidism and seek support from the community for the Rebbe's work.

50 Referring to the Nazis' control of Poland.

51 Yiddish for Judaism.

52 Nine years later, when the Rebbe formally became an American citizen, he again wore his fur hat, called a "Spodik," as an expression of joy. At that ceremony, he said it was a privilege to become an American citizen. For a video, see Chabad.org/471239.

53 Chabad.org/363468.

54 Interview with the author.

55 His nephew, Dr. Immanuel Schochet, in an interview with the author.

56 With time Rabbi Hodakov would emerge as the most influential figure in Lubavitch other than the Rebbe. It was in Riga before the war that he formed a personal bond with the Rebbe that would last a lifetime. He became taken with the Rebbe's devotion when he saw him saying the prayer "Veyiten Lecha" on Saturday evening after the conclusion of Shabbos.

57 The Rebbe was asked why he did not move to pre-State Palestine. He answered that he did not fear the future of Judaism in Eretz Yisroel. "There is a serious concern for the millions of Jews in the US; that's why I am going there."

58 Today, this building is used by Chabad as a boys' elementary school and yeshiva.

59 Today, there are over twenty-five college-level yeshivas operated by Chabad in North America.

60 A network of Lithuanian-styled yeshivas was established during the war and afterward. This network includes Ner Yisroel in Baltimore, Telz in Cleveland, Mir in Brooklyn, and Beth Medrash Govoha in Lakewood. Existing yeshivas like Chaim Berlin in Brooklyn, Torah Vodaath, Mesivta Tiferet Yerushalayim, and others rose to new levels under the leadership of outstanding scholars who emigrated from Europe, like Rabbi Moshe Feinstein, Rabbi Yaakov Kamenetsky, and Rabbi Yitzchok Hutner.

61 In many ways, the approach of the roshei yeshiva (scholars) was a remarkable success in rebuilding the Orthodox Jewish core, though one can make a strong argument that the influence of the yeshivas in the broader Jewish community is marginal. The strategy developed a generation of Jews who are fully tethered to Jewish scholarship and tradition. The greatest success story is Beth Medrash Govoha in Lakewood, New Jersey. Today there are over seven thousand students at the yeshiva. The yeshiva has sparked the growth of kolels (advanced yeshivas for married men) in many American Jewish communities.

62 The Lithuanian scholars' rejection of the Lubavitch approach of taking responsibility for Jews worldwide despite levels of observance was one of the primary causes of tensions that simmered just below the surface for many years between the Previous Rebbe, the Rebbe and other rabbis on the one side, and these scholars on the other.

63 On a deeper level, this difference in strategy was a reflection of the varied philosophical approaches of the Chassidim and the Misnagdim. The Chassidim, while being equally committed to Torah scholarship, always valued the spirituality of the simple Jew and the welfare of the totality of the Jewish community. The Misnagdim saw the learning of the elite as the greatest aspiration and wanted to preserve that cadre of scholars. The yeshiva community has been deeply influenced by Chabad and, in recent years, has engaged in outreach activity (Adam S. Ferziger, "From Lubavitch to Lakewood: The Chabadization of Orthodoxy in America," www.academia.edu/8083985). The long-standing differences in worldview animate a divergent approach into outreach. Chabad nurtures Jews toward Jewish observance according to their unique personalities, maintaining long-term relationships despite the level of observance. Some college outreach rabbis funded by the Lithuanian yeshiva community see their primary goal as sending as many students to yeshiva as possible. College students report that if they are not willing to make a dramatic change in their lives, many times the yeshiva rabbis focus their efforts

on other candidates that they think they can influence to make a total transformation in their lifestyle to full observance. While some students do become more observant, many are turned off by this hard-sell approach. In "Klal Perspectives," an online publication of the yeshiva community, the question of investing more time and resources into outreach when many are not willing to make the full commitment to observance is addressed, klalperspectives. org/fall-2012/fall-2012-questions/.

64 Interview with the author. Rabbi Fogelman passed away at the age of ninety-one after more than seventy years as shliach.

65 Established in 1917, it is viewed by many as the mother yeshiva of the United States.

66 Some argue that Rabbi Yochanan Ben Zakai was the role model for this strategy. He ensured Jewish continuity by establishing Yavne, a small town in southern Israel, as a center of Jewish learning after the destruction of the Temple and the loss of Jewish independence in 70 CE.

67 His partner was Dr. Max Lilienthal, who had attempted to have the Czarist government forcibly change the Jewish educational system in Russia.

68 The 1980 National Jewish Population Survey showed the correlation between Jewish education, intermarriage, and assimilation. That survey became a wakeup call for American Jewry. The statistics proved what the Rebbe had asserted forty years earlier: the more years of Jewish education, the less chance there is of assimilation. How different would Jewish life be today if the secular Jewish establishment had dedicated resources to Jewish education, as the Rebbe wanted decades ago.

69 Charles Silberman, *A Certain People: American Jews and Their Lives Today* (New York: Summit Books, 1985).

70 I remember visiting the small town of Mount Carmel, Pennsylvania, some years ago. The Ark in the synagogue, built in the 1920s, had an American eagle on its top as a symbol of its loyalty to America.

71 Founded in 1898 to unify Orthodox synagogues, it spawned the successful NCSY youth movement and is well-known for its symbol OU that certifies many products as kosher.

72 Established in 1912 to create a movement for younger Orthodox Jews. It has a network of over two hundred synagogues in the US and Canada.

73 Agudath Israel was established in the US in the 1930s to unify the traditional non-Zionist Orthodox segment of the Jewish community. It is a branch of the movement founded in Europe.

74 Yeshiva University today is one of the top fifty colleges in the US. Its beginnings were rooted in the founding of Yeshiva Etz Chaim in 1886.

75 The Religious Zionist Organization.

76 Hecht told me this story over a half century later, recalling the exact details of his public speaking debut. He would become an acclaimed public speaker and the rabbi of one of the largest Sephardi congregations in the United States. He passed away in 2013.

77 Interview with the author.

78 The Chassidic holiday marks the liberation of Rabbi Schneur Zalman of Liadi, founder of Chabad, from a Czarist prison in 1798.

79 Shalom Posner, born in 1901, studied in the Lubavitch yeshiva in Russia and immigrated to the US in 1929.

80 Interview with the author.

81 Rabbi Leibel Groner, interview with the author.

82 Seventeen volumes of the Sixth Rebbe's correspondence have been published by Kehot Publication Society, Brooklyn, New York.

83 Interview with the author.

84 Interview with the author.

85 Interview with the author.

86 Eli Wolf, *Echad Haya Avraham* (Kfar Chabad, Ashel, 2001).

CHAPTER THREE: EVEN A NEEDLE COULD NOT FIT BETWEEN THE CROWDS

1 Rabbi Shemaryahu Gurary was also known by his Hebrew initials as the Rashag (1898-1989). He came from a distinguished Chabad family; he was an outstanding scholar, studying in the yeshiva in Lubavitch. After his marriage, he worked with his father-in-law in communal service in both Russia and Poland. He escorted him to the US and Israel in 1929-30. He escaped Europe with the Rebbe in 1940. In the years to come, the Rashag would prove to be one of the new Rebbe's staunchest Chassidim. www.torahcafe.com/jewishvideo.php?vid=e64d1532e.

2 Yosef Yitzchak Greenberg, *Yemei Bereishis: Historical Biography 1950-1951* (New York: Kehot, 1993). This volume is a historical overview of the transition year, with interviews, documentation, and detailed background.

3 Interview with the author.

4 For copies of the articles from the Yiddish press, see Greenberg, *Yemei Bereishis*, 348-350.

5 Heard by the author.

6 The Rebbe opened a booklet with a Maamar starting with the same words of his father-in-law; he then expanded the concepts in a new, original Maamar.

7   The blessing reads: "Blessed be the Lo-rd our G-d, king of the universe, who has granted us life, sustained us, and enabled us to reach this occasion." It is uttered when we reach auspicious occasions in life.

8   One of the central principles of Jewish belief is the impatiently-awaited arrival of the Moshiach, who will usher in a period of holiness and goodness, a time when all of mankind will experience the spirituality of Creation. Judaism teaches that by performing mitzvahs and fulfilling G-d's commandments by doing acts of kindness to one another and learning Torah, Jews can hasten the coming of the Messiah. The Rebbe's teachings about the transformative nature of this event and the holistic goodness it will bring are profound and riveting.

9   The Talmud states the spiritual weakness that caused the destruction of the Holy Temple in the year 70 of the Common Era and the dispersion of Jews around the world was their lack of care and compassion for one another.

10 He passed away in May of 1952 and was buried in Tzefat, Israel. The Rebbe feared the news would greatly distress his mother, then living in Brooklyn. She had lost her husband in remote Alma Ata, and her younger son to the Nazis. The Rebbe withheld the news of his brother's passing from his mother. In the coming years, he orchestrated a fictional correspondence from his brother to his mother to spare her the anguish that she had lost another son. The Chassidic community was careful to keep the secret. His widow moved to London, and the Rebbe supported her financially throughout her life.

11 Retold by Avrohom Pinter, who was in Berlin at the time, to Rabbi Lipa Brennan. See also Chabad.org/840617. For a fascinating symposium on the relationship between Rav Soloveitchik and the Rebbe, see www.yutorah.org/lectures/lecture.cfm/812374/Rabbi_Zevulun_Charlop-Rabbi_Dr-_Jacob_J_Schacter-Rabbi_Moshe_Weinberger-Dr-_Lawrence_Schiffman-Rabbi_Yosef_Y-_Jacobson-Rabbi_Yehuda_Krinsky/The_Rebbe_and_the_Rav#.

12 Rabbi Joseph Krupnick heard this story from Rabbi Shaya Shimonovitz, formerly a student of the Mir Yeshiva in Poland. He was present in Vilna and witnessed this event, Chabad.org/666130.

13 Such letters were usually a public proclamation about a crisis in the Jewish community. Rabbi Chaim Ozer was one of the leading rabbinical figures in the religious world in pre-war Europe.

14 This amazing offer by Rabbi Baruch Ber must be seen in light of the almost two-century-old tension that existed between Chassidim and Misnagdim, Jews based primarily in Lithuania.

15 The Rebbe's private diary from that period in Vichy is inscribed with a reminder to fast the "Bahab" fasts. Many Jewish mystics have the custom of fasting after the holidays as an act of repentance. The fasts were three days of Monday,

Thursday, and Monday. Rabbi Shalom Ber Levin of the Chabad library says, "The Rebbe was on the run from the Nazis, yet he wanted to remind himself not to miss these fasts even under such adverse conditions."

16 Jerome Carlin, "The American Rabbi: A Religious Specialist Responds to a Loss in Authority," in *The Jews: Social Patterns of An American Group,* ed. Marshall Sklare, (Glencoe: Free Press, 1958).

17 The Pittsburgh Platform, adopted in 1885 by the newly formed Reform Movement, repudiated classical Jewish ideals like the divinity of Torah, kosher observance, and the centrality of the Land of Israel, claiming America was the new Zion. This was a catalyst for the eventual emergence of the Conservative Movement that attempted to straddle the fence between tradition and modernity.

18 Howard Polsky, "A Study of Orthodoxy in Milwaukee," in *The Jews: Social Patterns of An American Group,* ed. Marshall Sklare (Glencoe: Free Press, 1958).

19 This great Jewish sociologist would eventually discover the renaissance of Jewish observance firsthand. In the late sixties, his son turned up in the yeshiva in Kfar Chabad, Israel. His father had received an English translation of the Chassidic classic, the Tanya, as a gift. His son read it and that sparked his return to Jewish observance.

20 Between 1945 and 1965 the Conservative Movement grew from 350 congregations to eight hundred.

21 Five decades later, at the movement's biennial convention in 2002 in Dallas, Dr. Rabbi Ismar Schorsch, chancellor of the Jewish Theological Seminary, questioned that decision. By sanctioning travel on the Sabbath, he said, the Conservative Movement "gave up on the desirability of living close to the synagogue and creating a Shabbos community."

CHAPTER FOUR: THE GREAT ESCAPE

1 Rabbi Michoel Lipsker, *Twenty Years of Service as a Shliach of the Lubavitcher Rebbe in Morocco* (New York: privately published, 1981).

2 He also noted in the letter: "In the days prior to his passing, the Rebbe spoke to me about the need to expand his educational efforts to the children of Northern Africa, to help them by establishing educational institutions, and to train teachers from that community. You should travel to Africa to investigate the situation, to organize the work there and administrate it. First you should travel to Africa yourself and only later your family should join you."

3 The Joint Distribution Committee, known as "the Joint" or JDC, supported the school system Chabad operated in Morocco and Tunisia.

4 Rabbi Binyomin Gorodetsky was one of the first Russian Chassidim to escape Russia via Poland on a false passport. He was a roving ambassador for the

Sixth Rebbe and the Rebbe, and a key figure in the development of Chabad in postwar Europe, Northern Africa, and Israel. See Rabbi Binyomin Gorodetsky, *Light in the Darkness* (New York: Shengold, 1986).

5   Interview with the author.

6   Yiddish for "someone who is a sniffer."

7   Interview with the author.

8   Sara Lipsker did not realize that her husband-to-be, Azriel Chaikin, was a student in Kutaisi when she arrived with her family just after the war. They were married in Morocco.

9   The Georgian Jews were traditional, but lacked Jewish education.

10   Rabbi Moshe Levertov, *The Man Who Mocked the KGB* (New York: privately published, 2002), Chabad.org/312429.

11   Interview with the author.

12   Jews who converted to Christianity during the Spanish Inquisition, which started in the fourteenth century, but secretly continued observing Jewish tradition, despite great persecution and even under the threat of death.

13   Yechezkel Brod, *Chassidic Light in the Soviet Darkness* (New York: privately published, 1999).

14   Some Chassidim attempted to communicate the question to the Rebbe in New York. The question was sent and received in code and proved difficult to decipher. One thing was clear from the communication. The Rebbe did not want the Chassidim to stay in Poland if they escaped, due to the extreme postwar anti-Semitism.

15   In ancient times, the Sanhedrin, the High Court of Justice, was composed of seventy-one judges. A Minor Sanhedrin, which had the authority over death-penalty cases, had twenty-three judges.

16   Personal memoir by Yocheved Zalmanov.

17   The Rebbitzen Chaya Mushka Schneerson once described the Bricha as "Tzadikim who do not put on Tefilin."

18   Ephraim Dekel, *B'riha: The Flight to the Homeland* (New York: Herzl Press, 1973).

19   Rabbi Mendel Futerfas was born in 1906 and was a student of the Great Yeshiva in Lubavitch. See chap 12, "The Yeshiva."

20   Interview with the author.

21   She had made her way to Moscow after her husband's passing in Alma Ata, not far from the Chinese border. The Communist Secret Police labeled Chabad followers "Schneersonists." Being a Schneerson put her in exceptional danger.

22   She moved around Russia, evading the national manhunt. The Communist police intercepted a telegram to her son that she was coming to Uzbekistan

from Moscow. She realized they were following her on the train. They arrested her at the station along with an elderly couple who went to meet her.

23   He served seven years in a Soviet prison. After his release, he lived in Russia, then immigrated to England in 1974. He was a respected scholar. He passed away in London in 2014.

24   Upon appeal, it was changed to twenty-five years in Siberia.

25   She was held in a cell reserved for those condemned to death, in the lower floors of the prison. She would communicate with her son by lifting messages by string from one level to another.

26   The Paris-based international Jewish organization was founded in 1860 by the French statesman, Adolphe Crémieux. Its goals were to help Jews in foreign countries; it opened its first school in Morocco in 1862. There is no question leaders of the Alliance had noble intentions in helping their Jewish brethren. But they also wanted to impose their "enlightened view" on the Jews of Morocco.

27   Pessia Matusof, interview with the author.

28   The sentencing document stated he was a yeshiva bachur (student) and a member of the Drizin Organization, referring to the Chassidic leader, Rabbi Avrohom Drizin.

29   Interview with the author.

30   *Igros Kodesh* (New York: Kehot, 1987), Vol. 3, p. 396.

31   Lipsker, *Twenty Years of Service as a Shliach of the Lubavitcher Rebbe in Morocco.*

32   Interview with the author.

33   Djerba is an island off the coast of Tunisia with a Jewish community that reaches back 2,500 years.

34   After the First Lebanon War in 1982, the Israeli government decided that the Jewish community in Tunisia was at risk, since the PLO (Palestine Liberation Organization) had relocated its headquarters there. Ephraim Halevy of the Mossad, Israel's intelligence agency, who would later become director of the agency, discovered that the local community was not willing to relocate to Israel, due to the advice of Rabbi Pinson. Pinson was following the instructions the Rebbe had given to him. Halevy flew to New York to meet with the Rebbe. Years later, he recalled it was a very interesting meeting, saying, "We did not agree." The Jews remained in Tunisia. The fact that they refused to abandon the country shows the depth of Chabad's influence. Halevy on the meeting: www.youtube.com/watch?v=VJqkQ9yFlBo.

35   Chabad.org/1163700.

CHAPTER FIVE: THE FRONT ROW

1   The Kinus, Hebrew for "conference," started as a small event with fifty attendees in 1983. Originally it was just for shluchim in North America. In 1988, it

became an international conference. Today, over 3,500 shluchim attend annually. The celebratory banquet that concludes the Kinus has over five thousand attendees. In 1990, the Rebbe suggested a second conference for the shluchos, female emissaries, be organized. Now, it is held every year in late January or early February on the weekend closest to the yartziet of the Rebbitzen Chaya Mushka. Thousands attend this event, which is planned and run by Chabad rebbitzens from around the world.

2   The Rebbe suggested that a parallel conference be organized for the children of shluchim, The Kinus Tze'irei Hashluchim, the Conference of Young shluchim. It builds a sense of pride among the children of shluchim that they, too, are considered shluchim. There are many children who live in communities that do not have local Jewish educational resources. They attend one of the two online schools operated by the Shluchim Office that are based in the US or Israel. At the annual conference, the children get to know their classmates.

3   The senior shluchim sit in the front row, as do the members of Chabad national organizations.

4   Even today, in the outreach programs sponsored by the yeshiva community, a group of couples is sent to a city to establish a kolel, a center of learning. On college campuses, almost always, more than one couple is sent, so when their children reach educational age, they are replaced by another, younger, set of couples.

5   In France, the Conseil Représentatif des Institutions Juives de France is an official body funded by the government. In other European countries, too, governments support central communal institutions.

6   Interview with the author.

7   Interview with the author.

8   A yechidus, a personal and private meeting with the Rebbe, was a moment of monumental spiritual importance for a Chassid. He would prepare for the appointment with learning and prayer. It would be an opportunity to discuss with the Rebbe one-on-one crucial questions of one's spiritual life or of a more personal matter. Most Chassidim would meet with the Rebbe once a year in conjunction with a birthday. Couples would meet with the Rebbe prior to marriage, childbirth, or other significant personal milestones. The Rebbe would also meet with the young couples before they left as shluchim.

9   The Rebbe never endorsed anyone for public office.

10 This interview appeared originally in *Orthodox Jewish Life* in 1951. See Chabad. org/66877.

11 *The Jewish Forum*, April 1951.

12 Interview with the author.

13 Interview with the author.

14 Many were the children of Polish refugees who had been students in the yeshiva in Otvotsk near Warsaw and had escaped via Japan during the war. Some came to the US and Canada before Pearl Harbor, others spent the war years in Shanghai, studying in the Chabad yeshiva during Japanese occupation.

15 Kosher slaughterer.

16 Merkos L'inyonei Chinuch (Central Organization for Jewish Education) is the educational arm of Chabad. Most Chabad institutions operate under its auspices. Officially, the early shluchim were opening regional offices of Merkos.

17 The attack took place at the vocational school in Kfar Chabad. Five children and a teacher were killed. They were attacked during the evening prayers. It was one of the factors that led up to the Sinai Campaign in 1956.

18 *Yediot Acharonot*, May 5, 1957. This article can be viewed in English at Chabad.org/1765.

19 Interview with Krinsky. Rabbi Yisroel Alter, also known as the Beis Yisroel after the works he authored, was the fourth Rebbe of the Chassidic dynasty of Ger, a position he held from 1948 until his passing in 1977.

20 Interview with the author.

21 Rabbi Gross was a graduate of Yeshiva Torah Vodaath. He pioneered Jewish education and the building of a religious community in the postwar era in Miami. He was very supportive of Rabbi Korf.

22 Interview with Feller.

23 Interview with the author.

24 The Jewish month that falls around July.

25 Rabbi Hodakov was the chief administrator of Chabad. He would work with potential shluchim and oversee their placement.

26 During this early period, the Rebbe repeatedly tested candidates for shluchim to ensure it was their choice. Those like Sudak and Raskin insisted on being sent as shluchim. They were willing to take up daunting and difficult tasks. In this genesis period, the Rebbe was cultivating community leaders to have initiative and self-reliance. The Rebbe did not impose the task on anyone. Many graduates of the yeshivas who expressed an interest in becoming shluchim were lured by easier jobs in New York. The Rebbe did not necessarily oppose those choices, even though he must have been disappointed with some. Sudak felt the Rebbe wanted him to push to become a shliach, to prove this was a task he truly wanted.

27 Anash literally means "our community"; it refers to the Chabad community.

28 Interview with the author.

29 He is interred in the remote city of Alma Ata.

30 Zalman Shazar was one of the early Zionist leaders. In 1948, he was in New York as a delegate to the UN vote for ratification of Israel as a state. He came

from a Chabad family and was named Schneur Zalman after the first Chabad Rebbe. Even though he had drifted somewhat from religious observance, he maintained a strong connection with Chabad that deepened as the years went by. Later, he became Israel's third president.

31 This was reflective of the Rebbe's approach to building Jewish leaders. It had to be a choice they made. What is intriguing from this episode is that only half the students were willing to make this commitment. Clearly it was a challenge to change the mindset of the Chassidic community to become shluchim.

32 During that same meeting, the Rebbe told Raskin that his bride was a Chassidishe Tochter, a fine young Chassidic woman, and he was sure she was willing to join him on the mission to Morocco.

33 The great scholar, Maimonides, lived in Fez, Morocco, for ten years after escaping Muslim fundamentalists in Spain. In Fez, he wrote his commentary on the Mishnah. In 1168, he immigrated, briefly, to the Land of Israel, before settling in Egypt. Rabbi Raskin visited as part of a celebration marking the completion of the study of the Mishneh Torah, Maimonides's Magnum Opus on Jewish Law.

34 Uri Kaploun, *The Avraham Avinu of Australia* (New York: AAA, 2002).

35 Those five families: Althaus, Gurevitch, Serebryanski, Kluvgant, and Pliskin created the nucleus that would blossom into a vibrant community.

36 Chassidic tradition tells the story that her father, Rabbi DovBer, the Second Chabad Rebbe, promised her when she was very ill that she would merit to move to Eretz Yisroel (the Land of Israel). In 1845, she moved to Hebron, in the land of Israel, after receiving a blessing from her brother-in-law, Rabbi Menachem Mendel, the Third Rebbe, that "she would walk between the raindrops," alluding to the fact she was sickly, yet would not suffer from adverse weather. Sitting with Rabbi Groner in 1989, before the beginning of a farbrengen in New York, he told me the story of his first visit to Australia in 1948. "I met an old woman who knew my great-great-grandmother, Menucha Rochel, in Hebron, decades earlier. She told me that Menucha Rochel would walk with her during a rainstorm and nothing fell on her, fulfilling the Rebbe's blessing." Shortly afterward, my wife told me that we were being blessed with another child, and we named her Menucha Rochel. Years later, she married a young man from Australia, Yossi Spigler. It was his father, Solly, who had sponsored Rabbi Groner's trip to New York. On that weekend in New York in 1989, Groner told me the story.

37 Interview with the author.

38 Groner's son, Rabbi Chaim Tzvi Groner, is one of the leaders of the Chabad community in Melbourne. His brother-in-law, Rabbi Tzvi Telsner, is the dayan

(rabbinical judge) of the community. Other descendants are rabbis and community leaders. Gutnick's children play a major role in Australian Jewry. Rabbi Moshe Gutnick heads the kashrut authority and rabbinical court in Sydney; Rabbi Mottel Gutnick heads kosher supervision in Melbourne. The most well-known is Rabbi Joseph Gutnick. He has become a major philanthropist in Australia and globally.

39 Interview with the author.

40 Chassidim customarily met with the Rebbe annually on their birthdays. It was a time to make an assessment of personal and spiritual accomplishments.

41 Today, with some fifty thousand Jews in Melbourne, 50 percent of Jewish children attend Jewish day schools. This is the highest percentage in major Jewish population centers in a democratic country. As a result, Melbourne has the lowest intermarriage rate for Diaspora Jewry. Over a thousand of those children attend Lubavitch-run schools.

42 Chabad.org/844001.

43 Interview with the author.

44 Rabbi Hecht played a key leadership role in the development of Chabad institutions in the US. He was a deeply devoted Chassid. He headed the National Committee for the Furtherance of Jewish Education and many other institutions. He passed away in 1991 at the age of 67.

45 Cunin mustered support from seventeen local Orthodox leaders and overcame the opposition. The Board of Rabbis even went so far as to pressure two local Orthodox rabbis who protested Cunin's membership in the Interfaith Committee (Minutes of the Meeting of the Interfaith Committee, October 1, 1965; private correspondence between Interfaith Committee and Rabbi Judah Glassner; Archives, Chabad of California).

46 In general, the Rebbe wanted shluchim to work with local communal leaders. At times, particularly in the early years, this was very difficult. Chabad shluchim had to overcome the insecurity of Orthodox leaders and be willing to stand up to the Jewish establishment. This battle would rise to its highest point during the conflict over the public menorah lightings, which is detailed in chapter seven, "The Menorah Wars."

47 American Jewish leaders had championed the idea of strong separation of church and state, driven by the memory of pogroms and anti-Semitism in Europe, which was orchestrated by religious leaders with government support. In the sixties, the small Orthodox community did not share this view, but it did not have the self-confidence or the political resources to challenge that mentality. The absurdity of this policy was clear in the case of Released Time. The LA School board was permitting children to have an hour of voluntary religious instruction provided by the religious group of the parents' choice. Government

was not involved in the teaching or operation of the program; it was just releasing the children for instruction. At the time, many children were receiving no religious education at all. Instead of seizing the opportunity, the local Liberal Jewish leaders wanted to be more careful of the separation of church and state than any other religious group. They put their own insecurities ahead of the needs of Jewish children who needed Jewish education.

48 Correspondence between the Jewish Federation and the Los Angeles School Board (Archives, Chabad of California).

49 The Federation did exactly what it claimed it was opposed to: it attempted to use the power of the state to stifle the free exercise of religion.

50 Federation leaders exerted undue influence over one of the public schools, claiming that Cunin had breached the Released Time procedures with some technical violations. The Federation's behind-the-scenes intervention caused the suspension of the program at Laurel Elementary School. Cunin fought back with threats of litigation and called for public investigation by state officials.

51 The State Board of Education intervened, issuing a report accusing the local school board of not acting properly, stating in its report: "The decision to drop Laurel School (the Released Time Program) was not in accordance with regulations. In essence, this appears to be an encounter with Jewish groups in Los Angeles in which the Los Angeles City School System is immersed." (Released Time Program, Laurel School, Los Angeles Schools, Eugene Gonzales, State of California, Department of Education, January 24, 1967; Archives, Chabad of California).

52 Before the Federation leadership gave up, it attempted to orchestrate false criminal charges against Rabbi Cunin. The alleged crime occurred at the very same moment he was in the hospital, as his wife was delivering their first child. The Federation leadership was forced to apologize publicly, repudiating the allegations they had made. The actions of the Jewish leaders in Los Angeles against Cunin reached a new low rarely seen in community life. Many shluchim faced similar obstacles from the Liberal Jewish establishment to undermine their efforts in establishing Chabad as a presence in Jewish communities. Some of those efforts to stifle Chabad were underhanded, but never to my knowledge, was there an attempt to orchestrate a false criminal charge other than in Los Angeles.

53 Shlomo Cunin, interview with the author.

CHAPTER SIX: THE BIRTHDAY PRESENT

1 Zalmon Jaffe was a charismatic businessman from Manchester. He and his wife, Rosalyn, enjoyed a special friendship with the Rebbitzen, who avoided

the limelight. It was clear to all that the Rebbe enjoyed Jaffe's regular visits to 770.

2   "Reb" is a Yiddish honorific title like "Rabbi" in English. Zushe Wilimovsky was renowned in the Chassidic community simply as "Reb Zushe, the Partisan." He had been a member of the Bielski Partisans against the Nazis, featured in the movie *Defiance*. For many years he played a major leadership role in Chabad in Israel.

3   Years later, Rabin reflected on the meeting, which clearly had a great impact on him. They started off with the question of whether the distinctiveness of the Jewish people is due to outside oppression or internal spiritual values. The Rebbe argued that Torah and tradition frame Jewish identity. The conversation then turned to clandestine efforts of Chabad in the Soviet Union and the issue of Israeli security.

4   He was a close confidant of many of Israel's generals. His most intimate relationship was with Arik Sharon. Their bond started after the Six-Day War and lasted to his final days. He organized the bar mitzvahs in Kfar Chabad for both of Sharon's sons, and was his personal rabbi. They became family when Maidanchik's daughter married Sharon's nephew.

5   Chabad's connection to the Sephardi Jews from Soviet Georgia started in the late nineteenth century. The Fifth Rebbe, Rabbi Sholom DovBer, sent rabbis to this remote area to serve as spiritual leaders and to train Georgian rabbis. When Georgian Jews started immigrating to Israel in the late sixties and early seventies, Chabad built housing developments for them in Lod and Kiryat Malachi, where Chassidim and Georgian Jews lived together. The Chabad policy was always to respect the unique traditions of the Sephardim, helping them establish institutions that would meet the needs of the community in Israel.

6   According to Chassidic historian Rabbi Zushe Wolf. Records of the expansion outside of Israel do not exist. It is safe to say that over another one hundred institutions, if not more, were established worldwide.

7   It had been some years since the Rebbe actually suggested where couples should live. They would usually ask and the Rebbe would give his blessing. In the coming years, Kotlarsky would travel the globe, first opening centers in the US and then in other countries.

8   Shortly after that convention, in the summer of 1984, the movement's leader, Rabbi Alexander Schindler, attended the Rebbe's farbrengen. He came as a guest of his longtime friend, Rabbi Hershel Fogelman, the shliach in his hometown of Worcester, Massachusetts.

9   The Jewish year follows the lunar calendar. The new Jewish year begins with the High Holidays, typically in September of each year.

CHAPTER SEVEN: THE MENORAH WARS

1   Temple Emanu-El was founded by German immigrants in 1850. By 1866, it had erected a magnificent gothic-style building on Sutter Street with twin towers of 175 feet. In the late 1920s, it built a large new facility on Lake Street. Today, it is one of the largest Reform temples in the world, with a membership of over two thousand. Many of the members are prominent community, business, and political leaders.

2   Fred Rosenbaum, *Visions of Reform: Congregation Emanu-El and the Jews of San Francisco 1849-1999* (Berkeley: Judah L. Magnes Museum, 2000).

3   San Francisco, historically, has been a community dominated by the Reform Movement, and it has one of the highest rates of assimilation. The opening of a string of Chabad Centers in recent years and the resurgence of some Orthodox synagogues is beginning to create a shift toward tradition in the Bay Area.

4   Graham was a Holocaust survivor. His mother had placed him in an orphanage in Germany to protect him. He was smuggled to France and eventually to the US during the war. His mother died in Auschwitz and his sister perished while being hidden. He did not publicly identify as a Jew and many were surprised to discover that he had a Jewish heritage.

5   This menorah was much smaller and did not provoke a public controversy at the time.

6   There are 153 Jewish Federations in North America and a network that links another four hundred smaller communities. They raise money for local and overseas needs of Israel and Jews worldwide. Their primary overseas partners are the JDC (Joint Distribution Committee) and the JAFI (Jewish Agency for Israel). They are communal bodies supported voluntarily by donations. The national organization is called the Jewish Federations of North America-JFNA. More at jfna.org.

7   For a historical overview, see Jonathan D. Sarna, "American Jews and Church-State Relations: The Search for Equal Footing,'" www.brandeis.edu/hornstein/sarna/christianjewishrelations/Archive/AmericanJewsandChurchStateRelationsEqual-Footing.pdf.

8   Today, both the Orthodox Union and Agudath Israel maintain permanent representation in Washington. They are both advocates for the Orthodox community. Chabad also has a major presence in the nation's capital: American Friends of Lubavitch. However, its activities are non-partisan and educational.

9   Tanenbaum was a Conservative rabbi who first directed the Synagogue Council of America. He spearheaded interfaith activities for the American Jewish Committee representing the AJC at conferences in the Vatican. He was well-known beyond the Jewish community and considered a national authority on

church-state issues. His public criticism of the menorah moved the issue to the public arena.

10   The American Jewish Committee was established in 1906 by a group of leading American Jewish businessmen. It was an advocate for Jewish interests in the US and around the globe. It argued for a strong separation of church and state. Even today, most of its members are not Orthodox. In recent years, it has taken strong positions inimical to the Orthodox community, in particular on issues of religious life in Israel.

11   After the passing of Bill Graham in 1991, the menorah erected annually in Union Square was dedicated in his memory. Today, it is known as the Bill Graham Menorah. More at www.billgrahammenorah.com.

12   Wise was troubled that the American Jewish Committee that had been founded some years earlier was dominated by elite Jews, many from German backgrounds. They were unwilling to support the fledgling Zionist enterprise and advocated a more quiet, behind-the-scenes style of diplomacy. Wise envisioned the American Jewish Congress as a more democratic, grassroots organization, and one that would advocate for Zionism. Wise, in time, became the most influential Jew in America, in part due to his close ties to President Roosevelt. The idea of a grassroots organization may have been true in its early stages, but it evolved, in time, to be dominated by a small group of Liberal Jewish leaders. In its later decades of activity, it moved more strongly to the left, at times taking more extreme positions than other major Jewish groups. The conflict over the menorah was an example. Other groups were willing to let the issue be, but the American Jewish Congress litigated the issue on numerous occasions.

13   The American Civil Liberties Union had many Liberal Jewish members who felt any breach of the separation of church and state would endanger Jews and other minorities in the US.

14   Seeing the strong public support for Chabad, the ADL soon chose to voice its objections outside the courtroom, Jonathan D. Sarna et al., *Religion and State in the American Jewish Experience* (Notre Dame University Press, 1997).

15   The letter was written in a harsh tone, challenging Chabad's right to pursue its program of menorah lightings, saying between the lines, "What gives you the right to change the Jewish community consensus on church-state issues?"

16   Liberal Jewish groups had opposed any kind of funding for Jewish schools, lobbying aggressively against government support of any kind. This opposition was not just rooted in the church-state issue; it was an outgrowth of their view that Jews should fully integrate into American culture. Immigrant Jews should aspire to be good citizens, and by attending public schools, this goal would be achieved. They understood that Jewish education would bring about a resurgence of traditional Judaism. Liberal Jewish leaders in the US

were opposed to this. Jewish communities in other countries did not take such an extreme view. The US is the only western democracy where there is such a strong view on separation. In England, Australia, France, and numerous other democracies there is government support for secular studies in Jewish schools.

17 The conflict had been simmering for a few years. In December of 1981, the Rebbe wrote a long letter to the Bergen County Jewish community, stating, among other points, that the President of the United States and the State Attorney General of New York, as well as numerous other government officials, had participated in menorah lightings. In the letter, the Rebbe asked, "Why is it so important for Jews to have the Chanukah menorah displayed publicly?" He answered, saying, "It instills a sense of pride in their Yiddishkeit and a realization that there is no reason, really, in this free country, for a person to hide his Jewishness."

18 The American Jewish Congress in Los Angeles litigated time and again against the menorah in Beverly Hills, creating a major public controversy. In most instances it did not challenge menorahs placed in less prestigious California municipalities. "Controversy Smolders Over Lighting of Menorah in Park," *Los Angeles Times*, December 2, 1992.

19 At the time, Chabad shluchim noted that in cities where all the city council members were gentiles, there was rarely opposition to menorahs. Ironically, resistance would come from Jewish city councilmen, who feared the public menorah was "too Jewish."

20 Three years later, after the Supreme Court ruling in the Pittsburgh case, Chabad was permitted to put up a menorah again.

21 Our friendship grew following an encounter in Fresno, California, where his grandson attended a Chabad Hebrew school. In the later years of his life, he became a strong Chabad supporter, and even attended the annual shluchim convention as the personal guest of Rabbi Yehuda Krinsky. In his will, he donated his personal library to Chabad's renowned research library. I will be forever grateful to him for providing my teenage daughter with a personal scholarship that allowed her to attend a Chabad summer program in Israel.

22 In July 2010, the American Jewish Congress ceased formal operations. Over time, it had lost momentum and membership, and it had financial losses due to the Madoff scandal. There was an effort in 2013 to reorganize, and half of its membership of 250 attended a conference in an initiative to resuscitate the moribund organization. See Gary Rosenblatt, "Is AJCongress Jack Rosen's Show?" *The Jewish Week*, May 8, 2013.

23 Hertzberg told the *New York Times*, "If almost all the branches of Judaism and even some Orthodox groups in Israel 'have got into outreach,' Lubavitch is

the reason – they are the ones who in a sense have shamed all the rest of us,"
www.nytimes.com/2000/01/22/nyregion/beliefs-469874.html.

24 The national Jewish student organization originally started by B'nai Brith that
became independent and has centers on most college campuses is supported
by Jewish Federations around the country.

25 Founded in 1973, it was a radical group of ultra-leftists who advocated recognition of the Palestine Liberation Organization at a time when it was hijacking
airliners and organizing terror attacks against Jews.

26 The story of Liberal rabbis and Jewish leaders attempting to block Chabad was
repeated in communities across the country. While espousing pluralism and
tolerance, they were opposed to a dynamic expression of traditional Judaism
that could change the communal status quo. Many times, they acted in a very
unprincipled fashion.

27 Jewish establishment groups have time and again attempted to dictate to Chabad
that it must operate in a way they deem proper and must accept the rules they
have set up.

28 This refrain that they are the community and Chabad is something fringe was
used time and again. It's a subjective put-down of more observant Jews.

29 They claimed that the yeshiva was not a recognized academic institution.

30 One of the students active with Chabad worked as an intern in the Hillel
office. He discovered a letter that had been prepared to be sent to school
administrators and professors with strident criticism of Chabad. To the student it was an escalation of the smear campaign to new heights. The student
was deeply troubled by his discovery and shared it with other students and
with me. The students challenged the Reform rabbi directing Hillel, who
first denied the letter existed and then, when confronted with a copy, was
profoundly embarrassed. The issue created a major controversy with the Jewish students active on the campus. They were very troubled at how the local
and regional Hillel directors were willing to act in an unethical manner to
undermine Chabad.

31 Jewish students were shocked at this Reform rabbi's support of dealing with the
PLO. This was just after the PLO-supported attack that killed Israeli athletes at
the Olympics, and numerous other terrorist actions. A number of students seized
his office in protest, locking him out and attracting much press attention.

32 Local Federation officials told the directors of Chabad that they could only
provide funding with the approval of Hillel, due to their historic relationship.
In other cities, Federations have begun to fund programs of various campus
organizations, looking at results as a measure of success. To its credit, the Pittsburgh Federation provides major funding to local Jewish schools, including
large allocations to the Chabad School.

33 "The Outreach Revolution," *Commentary* Magazine, April 2013.

34 While Liberal Jewish leaders like Jacobs have become more open to the agenda promoted by Chabad, there are still significant theological differences. In the same speech, Jacobs went on to say that there were many ways to observe Judaism other than the one rooted so deeply in Jewish tradition. He took an additional troubling stance, saying, "Intermarriage is a reality that should be accepted."

35 Clearly, when these students graduate and take positions in Conservative congregations, they will have different relationships with the local Chabad rabbis and hopefully a greater appreciation of classical Jewish values.

36 In the summer of 2014, Rabbi Stephen Pearce, rabbi emeritus of Temple Emanu-El of San Francisco (whose predecessor, Joseph Asher, stood at the forefront against the menorah in San Francisco in 1975) attended the bar mitzvah of my grandson. My son-in-law is the rabbi of Congregation Chevra T'hillim, San Francisco's oldest Orthodox synagogue, located near Golden Gate Park. Pearce spoke to me in great admiration of Chabad, and in particular his friends, my son-in-law and daughter, whose home he has visited for Shabbat dinners. Of course, he praised the remarkable job of the bar mitzvah boy.

37 For many years the Jewish Federations were known as UJA, United Jewish Appeal.

CHAPTER EIGHT: EVERY SHLIACH IS AN ENTREPRENEUR

1 For a listing, see Chabad.org/centers.

2 Interview with the author.

3 Many other donors across the globe have played key roles in Chabad growth. Just to mention a few: in Australia, Rabbi Joseph Gutnick's strategic giving helped launch many projects there, in Israel, and in the US. (I am eternally grateful for his lead gift to our original building project in Yorba Linda, California.) In South America, Eduardo Edelstein is a vital partner. Most interesting has been the evolution of new donors from the Former Soviet Union such as Gennadiy Bogolyubov, who sponsored the Simcha Fund, which provided $25 million in grants to shluchim on the occasion of weddings, bar/bat mitzvahs and births.

4 Shluchim who choose to use national programs pay fees to help defray some of the costs. Users of Chabad.org pay a monthly subscription fee, as do branches of the Rohr Jewish Learning Institute, CTeens, and other national programs. However, shluchim are not obligated to use these services; they pay only if they decide the program will enhance their local Chabad Center.

5 Much of the income of groups like the ADL, the Jewish Federations, and other national Jewish groups comes from their branches.

6   Interview with the author.

7   Interview with the author.

8   I realized the difference in worldview when our local Federation was allocating money for educational scholarships. The committee put a limit, saying they wanted to hold some money in reserve for next year. I argued, "Give the money now, the kids need education, and raise more for next year." Clearly this was reflective of the diverse philosophies of, on the one hand, the consensus-driven, deliberative approach of many Jewish groups and, on the other hand, Chabad, which is more action-oriented.

9   Interview with the author.

10 Rabbi Shmuel was the Fourth Lubavitcher Rebbe, born in Lubavitch in 1834; he passed away in 1882.

11 Many times, the Rebbe would refer to Rabbi Shmuel as the "L'chat'chila Ariber." It was customary at the farbrengens of the Rebbe to sing melodies connected to each of the leaders of Chabad and founders of the Chassidic Movement. The song for the Fourth Rebbe, Rabbi Shmuel, is known as the "L'chat'chila Ariber Niggun (melody)." Watch children singing the melody at a rally with the Rebbe at Chabad.org/60083.

12 The Rebbe used a kabbalistic term to define the balance between pushing the envelope and not entering into a situation that could create a financial crisis: "Oros Detohu BiKelim Detikun" (Chaotic Light in Structured Vessels), referring to the kabbalistic concept that in the process of creation, the intense flow of Divine Light has to contract itself into the structured physical world.

13 Interview with the author.

14 There is constant tension about looking for money. According to Harvard Business School professor, Howard Stevenson, it is the idea of entrepreneurship: the pursuit of opportunity without regard to resources currently controlled. "They see an opportunity and don't feel constrained from pursuing it because they lack resources. They're used to making do without resources."

15 The constant need to raise money takes an emotional toll.

16 Interview with the author.

17 Interview with the author.

18 ejewishphilanthropy.com/unpacking-chabad-their-ten-core-elements-for-success/.

19 Wolfson's popular book, *Relational Judaism* (Woodstock: Jewish Lights, 2013), argues that other segments of the Jewish community should emulate the model of building strong personal connections to people as the key strategy to Jewish renewal in the US. His book has sparked a major shift in thinking among Jewish communal leaders.

20 Interview with the author.

21 In the letter, the Rebbe also rejected Putterman's suggestion that Chabad open businesses to support its programs, writing, "It would be incongruous if both spiritual activities and business activities were carried on by the same organization under the same roof. It would surely not enhance the inspiration and total devotion, which one usually associates with the activities of Lubavitch for spreading Yiddishkeit."

22 Interview with the author.

23 Interview with the author.

24 Dennis Prager, "Lessons for the Rest of Us From the Success of Chabad," *Jewish Journal*, July 13, 2010.

25 Decades ago Jews felt a stronger connection to the community and tradition. Synagogue membership was considered a social and personal obligation. Today, many are further removed from observance. The system of mandatory membership can, according to Wolfson, create a "barrier of engagement." Chabad's approach of non-membership was not a product of a study or calculated strategy. It was an intuitive expression of a philosophy of responsibility for all Jews, regardless of their level of observance.

26 His successor, Rabbi Rick Jacobs, made a case for what he called "audacious welcoming" in his keynote address at the Biennial Conference of the Reform Movement in December of 2013. He did not suggest the end of the membership model, which has served as the primary business standard for Reform congregations. Still, he strongly argued the time had come to seek ways to welcome Jews in a more open and non-bureaucratic fashion, clearly taking a cue from the Chabad playbook.

27 Rabbi Eric H. Yoffie, "Chabad's dangerous message of love without commitment," *Haaretz*, April 21, 2013. I find his argument that Chabad does not demand commitment to be disingenuous. The Reform Movement sees Judaism as an issue of individual choice, not obligation. At the philosophical core of Reform is the idea that each person defines his own Judaism. Chabad sees Judaism in its classical context, that Jews have a Divine mandate to fulfill the mitzvot. The task of the shliach is to encourage that commitment by inspiring a Jew along that path of personal spiritual growth, one mitzvah at a time. That path is a personal, spiritual one, not necessarily that of paying a membership fee. Understandably, if a Jew's personal observance grows, it will be a bridge to communal affiliation.

28 Some non-Orthodox congregations in the us have begun to experiment with the non-membership model: "When Jews Choose Their Dues," *Reform Judaism*, Spring 2014; Debra Nussbaum Cohen, "Dues Blues: us Synagogues Are Dropping Dues in Favor of Voluntary Contributions – Congregations Shift Focus to Commitment, Rather Than Membership," *Haaretz*, May 11, 2014.

29 I find this accusation in particular quite troubling in light of the academic standards in Chabad Hebrew Schools, which tend to be much more rigorous than in the non-Orthodox community. Most teachers in Chabad are highly trained rabbis and rebbitzens whose level of Jewish learning is on a far higher standard than many teachers in the non-Orthodox community.

30 Liz F. Kay, "New path to Judaism: Hired Rabbis Worry Some, but Others Say They Bring Needed Flexibility to Events," *The Baltimore Sun*, February 20, 2007.

31 The economy of many congregations is based on the model of membership for families with a focus on those who want a bar/bat mitzvah for their children. Congregations demand a prerequisite of membership for a period of years, and the children must attend Hebrew school before bar/bat mitzvah. Many families tend to leave congregations afterward. In 2000, a study was done by Brandeis University that revealed a major drop-off of membership after bar mitzvah. "Synagogues Try to Reverse Trend of the Post-Bar Mitzvah Dropout," *Jewish Telegraphic Agency (JTA)*, May 26, 2004, www.jta.org/2004/05/26/jewish-holidays/shavuot/shavuot-feature-synagogues-try-to-reverse-trend-of-the-post-bar-mitzvah-dropout#ixzz3BRZrVaCd. It's not a new trend. Stories reaching back to the sixties document the post-bar mitzvah drop-off. "Jewish Families Tend to Quit Synagogue After Bar Mitzvah of Children," Jewish Telegraphic Agency, February 4, 1966, www.jta.org/1966/02/04/archive/jewish-families-tend-to-quit-synagogue-after-bar-mitzvah-of-children#ixzz3BRMQWjrj.

32 Baila Olidort, "Chabad Replies: Reform Judaism's Shallow Message of Payment Without Commitment," *Haaretz*, April 25, 2013.

33 Chabad shluchim can be fired by the local director or the head shliach of the state. However, it must be for cause. An employee has the right to request judicial review or mediation by the Rabbinical Court, (Vaad Rabbonei Lubavitch) in New York, Beit Din Rabbonei Chabad in Israel, or Aguch.

34 Interview with the author.

35 shefanetwork.blogspot.com/.

36 Lee Chottiner, "Herring: Synagogues Must Change to Survive; Here's How," *The Jewish Chronicle*, 2010, thejewishchronicle.net/view/full_story/4098727/article-Herring -- Synagogues-must-change-to-survive -- here-s-how-?instance=news_special_coverage_right_column.

37 Time and again, I have watched the political maneuvering, which at times can become abusive, between rabbis and their boards. One Reform rabbi in a congregation near me served his community faithfully for more than twenty-five years. He was getting ready to retire and slowly phase out of his temple when a new group of families joined. They had moved over from another temple, dissatisfied with affairs there. Within a year, the newcomers had seized leadership.

They lacked institutional memory of the years of the rabbi's dedication to the community. Promptly upon their election, they decided that the key to congregational growth was a new rabbi. They decided to accelerate the current rabbi's retirement. One morning, the rabbi came to the office only to be told by his secretary that the new president had instructed her not to take any orders from him. The rabbi could have easily mobilized the congregation to help him battle the new board, but he was tired of fighting and retired quickly. The synagogue then hired a new rabbi, who alienated most of the members. Within a few years, that rabbi left the congregation, as did most of the troublemakers, leaving the original rabbi to pick up the pieces. Another time, a president of a Conservative synagogue came to me for advice. The board was having a meeting to discuss punitive actions, since the rabbi took a day off. He was not sure how to handle the problem. "Remind them of the time he visited a sick person in the hospital at midnight, or the long evening meetings he constantly attends," I said.

38 Interview with the author.
39 Interview with the author.
40 Interview with the author.
41 Interview with the author.
42 The first generation of shluchim took financial risks to establish a beachhead in the Jewish community. If they had not taken this approach, Chabad would not have been successful. Today, the landscape is vastly different. Then, Chabad was the new kid on the block with an agenda that would radically change the focus of the Jewish community. Today, there is trust in Chabad's ability to succeed, even among its detractors.
43 Interview with the author.
44 The holiday is observed every year five days after Yom Kippur. It memorializes the time the Jews wandered in the desert after the Exodus from Egypt.
45 Interview with the author.
46 Interview with the author.
47 Interview with the author.
48 Interview with the author.
49 These can easily reach upward of $10,000 a child. When children have to leave home, the sums can be over $15,000 a year, including room and board. Many Chabad schools offer discounts to shluchim. They, too, are forced, due to budget considerations, to charge hefty tuition for children. In other countries, where there are government subsidies for non-public education, the tuition may be lower. In countries other than Israel, government funding does not cover the expense of Judaic studies, which must be paid by the parents.

50   Interview with the author.

51   Chabad.org/2044460.

52   Chabad.org/314591.

53   He was the first shliach that Rabbi Cunin brought to California to assist him in 1967. Originally, he directed the Released Time program, later he founded the Chabad House in Santa Monica. He was a scholar and role model to many. Unfortunately, he passed away in 2007.

54   Steinhardt had taken a leadership role in many Jewish communal initiatives, in particular Birthright, which provides trips to Israel for college-age Jews.

55   Jonathan Mark, "Chabad's Global Warming," *The Jewish Week*, December 2, 2005.

CHAPTER NINE: DANCING WITH THE KGB

1   Interview with Ambassador Yehuda Avner. For more, see Yehuda Avner, *The Prime Ministers* (Jerusalem: Toby Press, 2010). Avner passed away in April 2015.

2   According to Avner, Golda felt a special kinship to Fallaci, who conducted the interview, then lost the tapes. Golda granted her a second interview.

3   I was present and heard his speech. It was sponsored by Chabad of Tel Aviv.

4   Rabbi Yossi Jacobson, "Stalin vs. Schneerson," *Algemeiner*, June 29, 2007.

5   Even today, it is difficult to unveil the layers of secrecy concerning the activities of decades ago. Many of those involved have passed on and there are few written records. The Rebbe compartmentalized the work. It was all on a need-to-know basis. It seems that no one other than the Rebbe knew the broad scope of the secret efforts. Even the Rebbe's secretaries were not privy to the vast majority of the activities.

6   Interview of Schacter with JEM (Jewish Education Media), unpublished manuscript, My Encounter with the Rebbe Project. My research for this chapter was greatly assisted by JEM's My Encounter with the Rebbe Project. Their highly professional research was an impeccable first-person sourcing and is of great value to any scholar researching this topic.

7   Michael Wines, "Visiting Synagogue, Bush Praises Russian Religious Tolerance," *New York Times*, May 27, 2002.

8   They moved to Saint Petersburg in 1992. The Bushes were so impressed by the young American couple, they invited them to a private visit at the White House.

9   He was the spymaster of the intelligence and security services of Israel and the director of the Mossad (1952–1963). In his capacity as Mossad director, he oversaw the capture and covert transportation to Israel of Holocaust organizer, Adolf Eichmann.

10 Avigur was born in Dvinsk (now Daugavpils) in Latvia in 1899 under the name Saul Meyeroff, but when his son, Gur Meyeroff, was killed in the 1948 Arab-Israeli War, he changed it to Avigur, meaning "father of Gur." Along with Reuven Shiloah, Avigur was instrumental in forming SHAI, the intelligence wing of the Haganah, in 1934. From 1939, he was involved in the Mossad Le'aliyah Bet operations to smuggle Jews into the British Mandate of Palestine, and was named its commander. During Israel's War of Independence, he acted as David Ben Gurion's deputy defense minister. In 1953, he was appointed the founding head of Lishkat Hakesher, also known as "Nativ," and headed the organization until 1970. Avigur was the brother-in-law of former Prime Minister Moshe Sharett. He passed away in 1978.

11 For more on Levanon, see Murray Friedman and Albert D. Chernin, eds., *A Second Exodus: The American Movement to Free Soviet Jews* (Hanover: Brandeis University Press/University Press of New England, 1999). In Hebrew, see Levanon's memoirs, *Code Name Nativ* (Tel Aviv: Am Oved, 1995). There is a memorial website with some English material: www.nechemia.org/nechemia.html.

12 Rabbi Yosef Kamenetsky, *The Rebbe and the Mossad* (Hebrew) (Kfar Chabad: Hamayan Hachassidi, 1998).

13 Zushe Wolf, *Diedushka: The Lubavitcher Rebbe and Russian Jewry* (Hebrew) (Moscow: Vaad Hashluchim Shel Chaver Haamim, 2006). The title "Diedushka" is Russian for Grandfather. Many Jews in Russia would use that term as a code name to refer to the Rebbe in communications to the West. This volume provides a wealth of source material on Chabad's efforts for Soviet Jewry.

14 JEM, My Encounter with the Rebbe Project, unpublished interview.

15 Binyomin Katz, interview with the author. There is also an account of his mission to Russia in Mordechai Steinman's *Secrets of the Rebbe* (New York: Mendelson Press, 2001).

16 Chabad summer outreach project where yeshiva students visit Jewish communities worldwide.

17 Interview with the author.

18 Her father was the pioneer shliach in Morocco, Rabbi Michoel Lipsker. See chap. 4, "The Great Escape."

19 The KGB was a military-run organization that operated as secret police to impose Communist policy.

20 Katz feels this was intentional, since observant Jews do not drive or use the elevator on the Sabbath. Today this hotel is affiliated with Radisson, and has a regular room rate of about $400 a night. $180 in 1965 is equal to around $1,200 in 2014.

21 The Russians permitted a small number of Jews to leave Russia on what they considered humanitarian considerations in a program of Family Reunification.

Many times the Rebbe advised those in leadership positions in the Russian Jewish community to remain in the country.

22 Today, the smaller sanctuary is a synagogue for Jews from the mountain regions of Russia and Azerbaijan who follow Sephardi traditions.

23 The Bukharan Jews follow Sephardi Jewish custom. Some claim that they first migrated to Asia during the time of King David. Despite being distant from other Jewish communities, they remained loyal to tradition. Today, most live either in Israel or the US.

24 Interview with the author.

25 Nanes was a legendary figure who had been active in the Chassidic underground from the onset. He spent two decades in the Soviet Gulag, which earned him the title Subbota, "Sabbath Observer," from fellow inmates. He was released from prison in 1955, and ten years later he left the Soviet Union. His exit was probably a result of the late-night encounter with Katz, who provided him with the information to ask for Family Reunification. Nanes moved to Jerusalem. In 1979, he wrote a book under a pseudonym, Avrohom Netzach, of his experiences in a Russian prison. The names and locations were changed out of fear that details could endanger Jewish activists remaining in the Soviet Union. He passed away in Jerusalem at the age of 100 in 1997. The story of his life – with the details of his imprisonment – was eventually published in Hebrew: R. Fridman, *Reb Leizer Nanes: Ish HaShabbat – Subbota* (Jerusalem: Hechal Menachem, available at Kehot Publication Society in Brooklyn). The English version: *The Subbota: My Twenty Years in Soviet Prisons: Experiences of a Russian Jew, Who Survived Twenty Years of Captivity in the Prisons and Slave-Labor Camps of the Soviet Union* can be found in libraries. The municipality of Jerusalem named a street after him in 2007.

26 Veshedsky today lives in Kiryat Malachi in Israel, and Mochkin in Crown Heights, Brooklyn.

27 The Communist Party had a strong political presence in Israeli politics at the time. In the parliamentary elections of 1961, Maki, the Israeli Communist Party, earned five seats in the Knesset. It was a coalition of Arabs and Jews. Leftist Jews of Russian origin still had positive feelings for the Soviet Union because it gave Jews in Russia opportunities and had battled the Nazis. In the elections of 1965, the party split into two factions, one Jewish and one Arab. The Six-Day War proved to be a turning point for Jewish supporters of the Israeli Communist Party, when Russia became hostile to Israel, severing diplomatic relations and supporting Arab states.

28 Greene was a renowned scientist from Minnesota who had drawn closer to observance in Minnesota through Rabbi Moshe Feller. Later in his life, he moved to Israel and was a professor at Ben Gurion University.

29 For more on their activities, see Zushe Wolf, *Diedushka.*
30 The first efforts were not in the United States. In 1955, Lishkat Hakesher, or Nativ, began an initiative in Europe to build support for Soviet Jews. Liberal activists were engaged to speak and write about the plight of Soviet Jewry. They began activities in the US in 1958, dispatching Ur Ra'anan as the Lishkah agent in New York. He was followed by Binyomin Eliav in 1960, Meir Rosenne in 1961, Yoram Dinstein in 1966, Yehoshua Pratt in 1970, Yitzchak Rager in 1973, Haim Ber in 1975, and Sara Frankel in 1978. Emissaries to Washington started with Nechemia Levanon in 1965, Nir Baruch in 1969, and Jerry Shiran in 1973. The archives of the Lishkat Hakesher remain classified; this information is based on a research project of the Bulletin Du Centre Recherce Français à Jérusalem in 2004, English Translation, "The Action of Nativ's Emissaries in the United States, a Trigger for the American Movement to Aid Soviet Jews," by Pauline Peretz, bcrfj.revues.org/270.
31 One of the first Americans who worked directly for the Lishkah in the US was Moshe Decter. He was a left-wing academic with strong anti-Communist credentials. He created an organization called the Jewish Minority Project that was financed secretly by the Lishkah. He moved the Soviet Jewry issue into the public consciousness with a series of articles, including a piece in *Foreign Affairs* magazine in January of 1963. According to Glenn Richter, founder of the Student Struggle for Soviet Jewry, Decter was involved with the early meetings to establish the organization, an indication of the Lishkah's early surreptitious influence over the US Soviet Jewry Movement, www.angelfire.com/sc3/soviet_jews_exodus/English/Interview_s/InterviewRichter.shtml. Apparently, US officials were aware that Decter was working for the Israelis. In a letter to Senator Fulbright from Walter Pincus, a staffer of the Senate Foreign Relations Committee, from September 1963, Fulbright is warned that "it seems that Decter is employed by the American Jewish Congress." In fact, however, Mr. Decter's financial support came from two sources: $10,000 from the Jewish Agency-American Section, and $5,000 from the Israeli Government Office of Information (apparently the Lishkat Hakesher). Personal archive of the author.
32 Richter mentions time and again, in his long interview, the involvement of the Lishkah in the Soviet Jewry Movement. At times, the relations were good; at other times, frayed. Richter says the Lishkah funded the National Conference of Soviet Jewry and the New York Conference of Soviet Jewry. He says it also underwrote the expense of the International Conference of Soviet Jewry in Brussels in 1971.
33 Dinstein was an attorney and expert in international law who would later become the dean of the law school at Tel Aviv University. An interview with him conducted by Rabbi Zushe Wolf appears in *Diedushka.*

34 I mentioned Dinstein to Joseph Telushkin, who had been an activist for Soviet
Jewry. Telushkin was surprised to discover that Dinstein was an agent of the
Lishkah. He told me that when he and Dennis Prager returned from Russia in
1969, Dennis started to speak at synagogues about the plight of Soviet Jewry, but
he soon discovered his speeches were being canceled due to the intervention of
an Israeli Consulate official in New York named Dinstein, who told synagogues
that Prager may be an agent of the Soviet Union. Only after the intervention
of the Israeli ambassador, who vouched for Prager, did this stop. Prager says
the real reason for Dinstein's intervention was his own desire to control the
Soviet Jewry agenda in the us. In his book, *Rebbe* (New York: Harper Wave,
2014), Telushkin examines the Rebbe's view of the demonstrations for Soviet
Jewry.

35 Dinstein says he thinks there must have been meetings on earlier occasions
between Shaul Avigur and the Rebbe. However, due to the high levels of secrecy
followed by both, there are no known records of such meetings.

36 Dinstein says there were two reasons for the refusal. The Israelis were concerned
that if they delayed or canceled the demonstrations, it would be difficult to
build public support again. Second, they were doubtful that the Russians would
actually permit the large number – some five thousand – to leave. The Rebbe
argued that common sense would demand that they push back the planned
demonstrations by six months or at the least until after Passover.

37 Eshkol died of a heart attack on February 26, 1969. Golda Meir became prime
minister. Dinstein says she was not so inclined to listen to the Rebbe. According to Levanon, Golda had a more activist and confrontational policy on Soviet
Jewry than Eshkol.

38 The talk was given during the farbrengen marking the yartziet of the Sixth Rebbe,
Rabbi Yosef Yitzchak Schneersohn. It was one of the largest farbrengens of the
year and broadcast to Chabad communities around the world. I listened to the
farbrengen in Israel. The Rebbe's tone and anguish over the demonstrations
made a deep impression at the time on the listeners. Until then, the Rebbe's
opposition to demonstrations was known. After the farbrengen, it sparked a
larger public debate. Most activists in the us had noble intentions but had little actual knowledge of the internal dynamics of Soviet policy making. They
viewed the issue in an American context, that public pressure would create a
policy change.

39 We thought he was referring to the us groups that were organizing demonstrations. Only decades later did the Israeli agents reveal the truth of their role
in this issue. The Rebbe never revealed the secret that he was dealing with the
Israeli government, not American Jewish activists.

40 In general, the Rebbe was careful not to speak about individuals directly in public, rather referring to them more obliquely, with the intention that those to whom his words applied would understand what he was saying.

41 Kamenetsky interview with Porat. He was born in Poland; his father attended a Chabad synagogue in his hometown before the war. He even studied the Chabad classic, *Tanya*, while in high school.

42 Telushkin tells a remarkable story of that continuing cooperation in his book, *Rebbe*. Rabbi Shlomo Riskin, now chief rabbi of Efrat, Israel, was asked by the Rebbe if he was willing to undertake a mission in Russia. When Riskin agreed, the Rebbe called Levanon on the spot and told him that Riskin had agreed. It's clear that while they disagreed on tactics about the demonstrations in the US, they maintained a strong cooperation in areas of joint concern.

43 Chabad was involved in many covert efforts to lobby the US government for the freedom of Soviet Jewry. One of those who took the lead in many initiatives was Rabbi Avrohom Shemtov, www.torahcafe.com/rabbi-avrohom-shemtov/how-the-rebbe-influenced-the-release-of-soviet-jews-video_e28b95623.html. For more background on Chabad's efforts in the US behind the scenes with President Reagan, see David Luchins, Chabad.org/1041753.

44 Dr. Mindel, one of the Rebbe's secretaries, was fluent in Russian. He would hand-write letters with coded phrasing to Jews behind the Iron Curtain. The Rebbe would sign with endearing terms like "Zaide" (Grandfather).

45 Branover, interview with Rabbi Zushe Wolf, in *Diedushka*.

46 During the award ceremony at Ben Gurion University, Professor Branover can be seen standing to the immediate left of the podium, Gorbachev to the immediate right, www.youtube.com/watch?v=BIMyRnjl-7M.

47 In 2012, Russia's chief rabbi, Berel Lazar, met with Mikhail Gorbachev in Moscow privately. They discussed his decision to lift restrictions on Jewish immigration in 1989. Activists for the Soviet Jewry Movement in the US claim that the massive demonstration in Washington in 1987 prompted his decision to change Soviet policy. Gorbachev told Lazar that the demonstrations had nothing to do with his decision. Levanon writes in his memoir about a private meeting he had with Gorbachev in 1995. He asked him why he permitted Russian Jews to leave. According to Levanon, Gorbachev said the reason was the anti-Semitism they faced in Russia. It seems that Gorbachev made no mention of the demonstrations as a factor in his decision to change Soviet policy, www.nechemia.org/writings/nativ2.html.

48 Peter Kalms, interview with the author. Gorbachev spoke at the Chabad House on campus. Peter Kalms knew the story since he was a major supporter of Shamir. At the event, he was seated together with Gorbachev, and used the opportunity to tell him the story he had heard from Branover.

CHAPTER TEN: OUT OF THE SHADOWS

1 Interview with the author.
2 Her parents were Rabbi and Mrs. Posner, the pioneering shluchim who founded the yeshiva in Pittsburgh.
3 Interview with the author.
4 Kogan was raised in Soviet Leningrad.
5 I introduced them at the shluchim convention of 2013 when Jacobs came as my guest.
6 Interview with the author.
7 Interview with the author.
8 The Joint Distribution Committee supported Jewish life in Russia. In Communist times, they helped the efforts of the Sixth Rebbe, Rabbi Yosef Yitzchak. As Communism fell, they began again assisting Jews in Russia.
9 Interview with the author.
10 A project conceived and organized by Rabbi Avrohom Shemtov. The broadcast was coordinated by Rabbi Hillel Dovid Krinsky of JEM. The broadcast included menorah lightings in New York, Jerusalem, Paris, Melbourne, Hong Kong, and other cities.
11 Chabad.org/454539.
12 Interview with the author.
13 On an average Sunday, thousands of people would line up at 770 to meet the Rebbe. The Rebbe would stand outside his office for hours; men and women would file by the Rebbe. Each person was given a fresh crisp dollar bill by the Rebbe and a blessing. The dollar was intended to be given to charity. The Rebbe was making each person an emissary to do the mitzvah of giving charity.
14 A kolel is an institute of Jewish studies for married men. They receive subsidies for learning.
15 Interview with the author.
16 Interview with the author.
17 Chabad.org/2281728.
18 Rabbi Menachem Mendel, 1789-1866, was the Third Lubavitcher Rebbe. He was a renowned scholar who stood up for Jewish rights in Russia. He was known as the Tzemach Tzedek after a classic work on Jewish Law that he authored.
19 *A Mother in Israel: The Life and Memoirs of Rebbitzen Chana* (New York: Kehot, 2003-4). Her riveting diary is published at Chabad.org/1638270.
20 In the remote village, Rebbitzen Chana soaked herbs to create ink, which enabled Rabbi Levi Yitzchak to write a kabbalistic commentary. Later, it was smuggled out of Russia and published in the US.
21 Interview with the author.
22 Interview with the author.

23 Once, when the Rebbe was asked by a Chabad supporter why he does not give the shluchim more kudos, he became very serious and responded, "They have children?"

24 Interview with the author.

25 vimeo.com/16673429.

26 Interview with the author.

27 Formerly the National Council of Soviet Jewry. Interview with the author.

28 Interviews with both Lazar and Leviev.

29 "In Russia, Sharon Finds Sympathy – Both from Jews and President Putin," *Jewish Telegraphic Agency (JTA)*, September 10, 2001, www.jta.org/2001/09/10/archive/in-russia-sharon-finds-sympathy-both-from-jews-and-president-putin.

30 Interview with the author.

31 Hertzberg met me one evening in Manhattan and told me that he had just come from seeing Yoffie where they had this conversation.

32 Caryn Aviv et al., *New Jews: The End of the Jewish Diaspora* (NYU Press, 2005).

33 www.yivoencyclopedia.org/article.aspx/Federation_of_Jewish_Communities_and_Organizations_of_the_USSR.

34 www.pbs.org/frontlineworld/stories/moscow/gusinsky.html.

35 Interviews with Leviev and Lazar.

36 A Survey of Jewish Life in Moscow, reportsbetsygidwitz.com/survey_of_jewish_life_in_moscow_01.html.

37 Theodore Friedgut, "The Phoenix Revisited – The Jewish Community of Russia Since Perestroika: a View From Jerusalem," Jerusalem Council of Foreign Affairs, April 30, 2002. See more at: jcpa.org/article/he-phoenix-revisited-the-jewish-community-of-russia-since-perestroika-a-view-from-jerusalem/#sthash.5qgCOkFg.dpuf.

38 Gusinsky's strident use of the Russian Jewish Congress to promote his political agenda had a negative impact on American Jewish groups. In February of 2000, a delegation of the Conference of Presidents of Major Jewish Organizations came to Moscow, and Putin refused to meet with them due to their alliance with Gusinsky and the Russian Jewish Congress, www.jta.org/2000/02/22/archive/jewish-leaders-visit-russia-but-acting-president-a-no-show.

39 Friedgut notes in his research paper that Lazar and the Federation of Jewish Communities, unlike the Russian Jewish Congress and the Vaad that preceded it, did not involve themselves in domestic political affairs. There is no question that Lazar and the Federation have advocated for Jewish issues. They have not endorsed anyone for office, and remained neutral in elections. Gusinsky, on the other hand, was a kingmaker in Russian politics.

40 It would be as if in the US an individual controlled *The New York Times* and CBS News and was the head of the largest Jewish organization in the country.

Then he used that position as a Jewish leader to support a particular candidate for president, saying the Jewish community stands behind so-and-so.

41 Most of these groups, other than the JDC, had a limited, if any, presence in the FSU, nor did they have a long history of activity in the country reaching back two centuries like Chabad. The American groups were predominantly liberal and were prejudiced against Chabad.

42 Apparently some US Jewish leaders had some regrets in coming out so strongly and accusing the Russian government of intervening in Jewish affairs. According to a *Jewish Telegraphic Agency* (JTA) report at the time, Rabbi Shayevich had first accused the Kremlin of demanding he step down as chief rabbi, but he recanted his charge at a meeting with Jewish leaders in New York. Because of Shayevich's false original claim of Kremlin involvement, some Jewish leaders had approached President Clinton, asking him to intervene, www.jta.org/2000/06/07/life-religion/features/u-s-jews-misled-by-russian-rabbi-2.

43 None of these groups would have taken a partisan position in American politics the way Gusinsky did in Russia. Such actions by a Jewish organization in the US would be a direct violation of Federal tax code that prohibits political activity by nonprofit religious groups.

44 Shayevich had been appointed initially under a Communist government with the support of the KGB. Later, he had been endorsed by the Russian Jewish Congress; however there had been no formal election on behalf of communities' representatives from across the country.

45 Jewish communal tensions in Russia reached their nadir six months after Lazar's election, in December of 2000. Rabbi Avrohom Berkowitz, who served as the executive director of the Federation of Jewish Communities, was attacked. He almost lost his life in the Choral Synagogue on Shabbat after services when he was assaulted by three individuals. As the Jewish news service, the *Jewish Telegraphic Agency* (JTA), reported at the time:

> A Jewish leader may well have saved his life by doing the "dead man's float" in a local mikvah. In a bizarre incident possibly linked to rivalries within the local Jewish community, Avrohom Berkowitz had put on his winter coat and was about to leave Moscow's Choral Synagogue last Saturday when he was approached by three large men. The three, who he thought were wearing security badges, said something to Berkowitz in Russian, but he did not understand them. An American who serves as executive director of the Federation of Jewish Communities of the former Soviet Union, Berkowitz, 26, got his job in Moscow earlier this year after several years as a Lubavitch emissary in Brazil, and does not speak Russian.
>
> What followed, however, did not need any verbal explanation. Two of the men dragged Berkowitz downstairs while the third watched the stairs.

The two threw Berkowitz into the mikvah and held his head under the water. They left after Berkowitz went limp in the water, pretending he was dead. Synagogue guards were only a few feet away, but they later said they had noticed nothing unusual – although Berkowitz said he had screamed for help as he fought with his attackers.

Joel Golovensky, head of the Moscow office of the American Jewish Joint Distribution Committee, was among the first to meet Berkowitz when he climbed upstairs, shocked and wet. Golovensky said he, too, was deeply shocked, because "only an hour before that we sat together in the synagogue discussing setting up a committee to settle inter-Jewish controversies." He was referring to an ongoing rivalry between the Lubavitch-dominated Federation of Jewish Communities and the Russian Jewish Congress for control of the Jewish community.

www.jta.org/2000/12/26/life-religion/features/jewish-official-nearly-killed-in-moscow-mikvah#ixzz3AySe289C.

The questions of who was behind the attack and how it could have been carried out in the synagogue by individuals wearing security badges has never been resolved.

46 reportsbetsygidwitz.com/.
47 Rabbi Mendel Pewzner, chief rabbi of Saint Petersburg, interview with the author.
48 Interview with the author.
49 Rabbi Lazar, interview with the author.
50 Interview with the author.
51 Operated in partnership with the JDC.
52 Interview with the author.
53 Lazar was faced with such a dilemma when the Russian government scheduled high school matriculation exams on the holiday of Shavuot. One student told him he was going to give up his graduation since he was not going to take the test on the holiday, something prohibited by Jewish Law. Requests to the Ministry of Education to provide an alternative testing date for religious Jews failed. Lazar had a meeting scheduled with Soviet President Dmitry Medvedev. He explained the problem, and Medvedev promptly called the Minister of Education, telling him in Lazar's presence, "I have regards for you from Chief Rabbi Lazar." The education minister responded, "Why does the rabbi have to send regards through the President of Russia?" Shortly afterward, an arrangement was established for alternative testing.
54 www.jewish-museum.ru/en/main.
55 Sergei L. Loiko, "Russian Jewish Museum Opens in Moscow: The $50-Million Facility Would Have Been Unthinkable Even a Few Decades Ago in Russia, a

The Secret of Chabad

Nation Long Beset by Anti-Semitism," *Los Angeles Times*, November 11, 2012, articles.latimes.com/2012/nov/11/world/la-fg-russia-jewish-museum-20121112.

CHAPTER ELEVEN: BUILDING BRIDGES

1   www.theatlantic.com/international/archive/2012/04/1-100-pounds-of-matzo-in-kathmandu-welcome-to-the-worlds-largest-seder/255812/.

2   The statement by the Foreign Ministry that Israelis should turn to Chabad for assistance is indicative of the close working relationship, in many countries, between the Israeli government and Chabad.

3   www.israelnationalnews.com/News/News.aspx/169310#.U5cZLfldWxV.

4   www.haaretz.com/jewish-world/jewish-world-news/.premium-1.581717.

5   Chabad.org/2536285.

6   Chabad.org/1497338.

7   There are so many Israelis traveling through Bangkok that the Chabad Center there organizes reunions in Israel. More at Chabad.org/633983.

8   www.collive.com/show_news.rtx?id=20072.

9   Watch episodes at www.youtube.com/watch?v=WjFeqZDYVk8. This project was funded in part by a grant from the Avi Chai Foundation to broaden the understanding between religious and secular Jews in Israel.

10 One of the most touching episodes tells about the exasperation of Mushkie, the Rebbitzen in the series, when she can't get milk for her coffee. Many religious Jews drink only milk that is supervised from the time of milking to ensure it comes from a kosher animal. Her husband, Shmulik, buys her a cow so she can have milk regularly. The incident in the series is based on a true story of Rabbi Lifshitz getting his wife, Chani, a cow in Kathmandu.

11 For an English review, read israelity.com/2012/06/03/shmulik-and-mushkie-go-to-kathmandu/.

12 The Tal Law was crafted in 2002 as a compromise by Israeli Supreme Court justice Tzvi Tal. It created a mechanism by which religious Jews who studied in yeshivas could slowly move into employment and military service. In 2012, it was struck down by the ruling of Supreme Court President, Dorit Beinisch, who rejected her predecessor's compromise. Tal was a religious justice; Beinisch has been strongly identified with the secular left in Israel.

13 In the Israeli Supreme Court, justices are selected by a closed-committee of nine, including the Chief Justice and the three judges of the court. Seven votes are needed to select a judge. There is no public debate or legislative review by the Knesset as in the US and other countries. The result is a self-selection process. Jurists are appointed behind closed doors with their peers having a major influence in the selection. The court, whose judges wield immense power, tend to be

very secular, and politically attuned to the left side of the spectrum. The lack of balance on the court has created many tensions. Time and again, the court attempts to dictate by judicial fiat rulings that are hostile to traditional Jewish observance. Efforts to reform the court and create a system of judicial appointments with legislative review have been met with hostility by the judiciary and the political left in Israel.

14   Video on Chabad.org/2544375, and gpo.gov.il/English/PressRoom/Pages/PMmatza010414.aspx.

15   Handmade matza that is watched from the time of growing the grain through the final baking of the matza that many use at least for the Seder night.

16   *Kikar Shabbat*, the Haredi news site, as quoted by the *Jewish Telegraphic Agency* (*JTA*), www.jta.org/2014/04/03/news-opinion/the-telegraph/bibis-matzah-trashed.

17   Rabbi Menachem Brod, spokesman for Chabad in Israel, debated Beni Rabinovitz, from *Yated Ne'eman*, the newspaper of the Lithuanian yeshiva community in Israel, on Kol Beramah, a Haredi Radio station. Brod argued that the Chabad perspective is fundamentally different from that of some of the religious parties in Israel, saying its approach is to be a bridge to all segments of the society. Rabinovitz argued that Netanyahu's government had passed laws to undermine the religious status quo in Israel and should be treated with hostility. Hear the debate in Hebrew at www.col.org.il/show_news.rtx?artID=81920.

18   The present law includes a Chabad Track, which allows yeshiva students to study in New York at 770 prior to service or to intern in Chabad Centers overseas, www.jewishpress.com/news/breaking-news/rumor-draft-committee-to-launch-special-chabad-track/2014/02/10/. This arrangement had been made a few years earlier, but was enshrined in law in the legislation of 2014, www.israelnationalnews.com/News/News.aspx/146260. When their studies are completed, which for some is after marriage and a year of kolel (post-yeshiva graduate program), they join the army. Following military service, they enter the work force. A small number of outstanding students spend their lives dedicated to scholarship.

19   A separate law permitted a very small number of Chabad followers to fulfill the requirements of military service by volunteering for National Service, working in Chabad Centers around the globe, www.haaretz.com/news/diplomacy-defense/.premium-1.567338. Many of these centers serve the needs of young Israelis traveling the globe.

20   *Rabbi Schneur Zalman of Liadi* (Kehot, 1969), 59.

21   Rabbi Menachem Mendel of Vitebsk and Rabbi Schneur Zalman were both students of Rabbi Dov Ber, the Maggid (Preacher) of Mezeritch, the successor of Rabbi Israel Baal Shem Tov. Rabbi Menachem Mendel is buried in Tiberias, Israel.

22 *Challenge: an Encounter with Chabad in Israel* (Lubavitch Foundation: London, 1973). For a detailed history of Chabad in the Holy Land, see *Toldos Chabad B'Eretz HaKodesh* – History of Chabad in the Holy Land 1777–1950 (New York: Kehot, 1988). For more on the founding of Colel Chabad see chap. 7, p. 38. More at www.colelchabad.org/History_of_Colel_Chabad.bp. Video of the history of Colel Chabad at Chabad.org/2098354.

23 More at ColelChabad.org.

24 *Challenge*, p. 13. The Second Rebbe, Rabbi DovBer, urged his Chassidim to concentrate in Hebron. Apparently the tensions between Misnagdim and Chassidim that were prevalent in Europe spilled over to the small community in Tzefat where some of the followers of the Vilna Gaon had relocated from Europe. In Hebron, Chabad Chassidim were the first Ashkenazim. For more on Chabad history in Hebron, chabadhebron.com/hebron-history/and Sefer Hevron (Keter: Jerusalem, 1970).

25 Today, this is the oldest Chabad synagogue in the world. It was seriously damaged after the Arab riots of 1929, when many Chabad Chassidim lost their lives. It was refurbished by Rabbi Danny Cohen of Chabad, Hebron.

26 The Rebbitzen Menucha Rochel (1798-1888) was considered the matriarch of the Chabad community in Hebron. Prominent Jewish leaders would come to her for advice and blessings.

27 See *Challenge*, p. 23. The first synagogue was established by Rabbi Eliyahu Rivlin, a scholar who came with the blessing of the Tzemach Tzedek.

28 The Third Rebbe, Rabbi Menachem Mendel, known as the *Tzemach Tzedek,* due to his classic in Jewish Law called Tzemach Tzedek, "the Flowering of Justice."

29 See *Toldos Chabad B'Eretz HaKodesh,* Chap. 28.

30 *History of the Jews* (New York: Harper & Row, 1987), 404-405.

31 See the Pittsburgh Platform of 1885, the founding statement of basic beliefs of the Reform Movement. In the Columbus Platform of 1937, the Reform moderated their position, stating: "We affirm the obligation of all Jewry to aid in its upbuilding as a Jewish homeland."

32 "Our National Work in Palestine," reprinted by University of California Libraries, originally printed in *The American Hebrew*, January 1917.

33 Is. 2:5.

34 Some immigrants were also religious and established farming communities. For a deeper understanding of the secular-religious tensions in Palestine during the pioneering years, see *Rebels in the Holy Land,* Feldheim.com, 2012.

35 *Sefer Hasichos* (Kehot, 5705), 33.

36 Rabbi Shmuel, 1834-1882, was the Fourth Chabad Rebbe. He was the seventh son of the Third Rebbe, Rabbi Menachem Mendel.

37 Rabbi Sholom DovBer was the second son of the Fourth Rebbe, Rabbi Shmuel, and was the Fifth Rebbe. He was born in 1860 in the town of Lubavitch and passed away in 1920 in Rostov. When his father passed away in 1882, he was just twenty-one. Eleven years later, he formally became Rebbe. Known as the Maimonides of Chassidut, he was renowned for his profound Chassidic discourses, Chabad.org/272209. Rabbi Chanoch Glitzenstein, ed., *Sefer Hatoldos* (New York: Kehot, 1971).

38 Rabbi Sholom DovBer encountered the hostile activism of secular Zionist leaders in Russia, even in the town of Lubavitch.

39 This large building and its grounds in Hebron was an impetus for the growth of the community in Hebron. The Fifth Rebbe, Rabbi Sholom DovBer, raised the money in Russia and held title to the property. After the liberation of Hebron in 1967, permission was granted to Yeshiva Shavei Hebron to use the property.

40 The new yeshiva in Hebron, Toras Emes, was modeled on the innovative yeshiva, Tomchei Temimim, established in 1897 by the Fifth Rebbe, Rabbi Sholom DovBer, in the town of Lubavitch. During World War I, it moved to Jerusalem. Today, it continues to be a vibrant center of Jewish learning.

41 David Zev Rotenberg, *Massah HaRabi B'eretz Hakodesh* (Kfar Chabad, 1999).

42 Other areas farther from the center of the country were suggested by government officials for the location of Kfar Chabad. The Sixth Rebbe wanted it near the center so it could have a positive influence on society.

43 In Jerusalem in particular, there had been intense communal conflict between the historic religious community that was centuries old, and the newly arrived secular pioneers. For more on this subject, see *Guardian of Jerusalem: The Life and Times of Yosef Chaim Sonnenfeld* (New York: ArtScroll History Series, Mesorah, 1983).

44 This incident was part of a larger trend to take children of religious backgrounds and place them in secular educational programs. When immigrants began arriving from Yemen after 1948, and Morocco in the fifties and sixties, immigration authorities pressured families to place their children in non-religious schools. Most of these families were very observant and trusting of Israeli officials. They did not understand the agenda to secularize their children. These incidents, and many others, created a great sense of distrust between Orthodox Jews and Zionist leaders.

45 The army, particularly in the early years of the State, was a tool to integrate Jews from varied backgrounds and countries into one society. Haredim felt that this was yet another tactic to lure their children away from tradition. Yeshiva students received deferments for study, many spending much of their lives in scholarship. The system set up in the early years of the State made it impossible

to work unless you had served in the army, a legal strategy that many Haredim felt was designed to force them into the military. In the end, it pushed them farther away from integration into Israeli society. In recent years, the Israeli Army has taken a different approach, creating units where Jewish tradition is respected and Haredim can feel more comfortable serving. This is a reversal of the policies in the early years of the State that attempted to use the military to force integration into secular Israeli culture.

46　This political party in Israel was an outgrowth of Agudath Israel established in 1912 in Europe by the leading rabbis and scholars to stem the influence of secularism that was gaining momentum in the Jewish community. The party is guided by the "Council of Torah Sages."

47　In recent years, the National Religious Party has been recast as the Bayit Haye-hudi Party. It continues to play a major role in Israeli politics.

48　There continues to be a major debate in religious circles over the theological implications of a modern Jewish state. The religious Zionists argue that the modern State was the first step in the process of redemption leading to the coming of the Messiah. They believe the modern State is imbued with a quality of sanctity. The religious Zionists incorporated the term "first flowering of redemption" into the prayer service. Many Haredi Jews argued that the State is secular in nature and was created by people who were anti-religious and cannot be imbued with sanctity. The Rebbe took a different approach, arguing that it's an issue of Jewish Law and precedent. Maimonides writes in the Laws of Kings that the ingathering of the exiles happens after the coming of the Messiah. This ruling is a binding Jewish legal statement, since there is no historical view to the contrary. The Rebbe repeatedly recognized many events in modern Israeli history as miraculous, but still did not support the idea that the State itself is holy. In South Africa, some synagogues followed this practice of saying the prayer for the State of Israel that refers to it as the First Flowering of Redemption. Rabbi Norman Bernard, rabbi of the largest congregation in Johannesburg, was advised by the Rebbe to insert the words: "It should become the first flowering of redemption," alluding to the belief that the Messiah will come and usher in the process of redemption. The Rebbe feared raising a generation of Israelis who think their right to their homeland is based primarily on UN resolutions instead of the Divine Promise of the Land of Israel to the Jewish people. This could create a generation of Israelis fearful to advocate for their spiritual homeland.

49　Chabad firmly supported the position of much of the religious community in Israel against drafting women into the Israeli army. Under present law, religious women are exempt from service.

50　Chabad soldiers have also won awards for their service. See Chabad.org/1840348.

51 During my years in yeshiva in Kfar Chabad (1968-1972), just across from the yeshiva lived a Chassid named Mottel Rivkin who served in one of Israel's top commando units. The joke in the community was if Rivkin is not home, Israel must be involved in some secret military activity.

52 That ultimate sacrifice that some paid in the defense of Israel became deeply personal when Shimon Vorst, a student from Holland, joined our yeshiva in Kfar Chabad. His sister's husband, Dovid Morozov, lost his life on the Suez Canal in a skirmish just after the Six-Day War. Shimon would bring his young nephew to services every Shabbat. When he left for Holland, I undertook that responsibility, picking up the five-year-old Choni (the namesake of his great-grandfather, famed Chassid Rabbi Elchonon Morozov shot by the Communists in 1939), and taking him to services. His mother, Shifra, in the post-Six-Day and Yom Kippur War era, poured her energy, with the Rebbe's strong encouragement, into organizing bar/bat mitzvahs for the orphans whose fathers had died in battle. Those celebrations became national events attended regularly by the prime minister and military leaders.

53 Interview with the author.

54 Interview with the author.

55 Interview with the author.

56 Rabin on his visit to the Rebbe, Chabad.org/523714 (English); Chabad.org/524994 (Hebrew).

57 Interview with the author. Ambassador Yehuda Avner was the guest speaker at the Shluchim Conference, video at Chabad.org/770808. Some of his grand-nephews are shluchim. He accompanied many Israeli leaders to meetings with the Rebbe.

58 For videos of the visits, see Chabad.org/363473 and Chabad.org/394464.

59 Chabad.org/1351195.

60 Raised in Denver and Milwaukee in a traditional Jewish family, she had little exposure to the Chassidic world.

61 Shlomi Haski, *Maidanchik: The Locomotive of Chabad* (Israel: Yedidi Maidan-chik, 2013).

62 Golda had moved the reception into a side room to prevent Maidanchik from the stealing the show. He somehow got in and told Shazar the Chassidim were waiting for him. Overjoyed, Shazar headed out to them, much to Golda's dismay.

63 Chabad.org/132942.

64 Yehuda Avner, *The Prime Ministers* (Jerusalem: Toby Press, 2010), chap. 9, "To Ignite a Soul."

65 Video on his speech at the 92nd Street Y, www.youtube.com/watch?v=GvMIk_-CRjo.

66 Matthew Wagner, "Netanyahu Says UN Speech Was Inspired by Lubavitcher Rebbe," *The Jerusalem Post*, September 29, 2009,www.jpost.com/Israel/Netanyahu-says-UN-speech-was-inspired-by-Lubavitcher-Rebbe.

67 There was a long tradition of the Israeli diplomatic corps attending Simchat Torah, the second day of the holiday, in the Rebbe's synagogue. As Israelis they were only obligated to observe one day of the holiday.

68 This was unusual for the Rebbe to spend such an inordinate amount of time during this major public celebration with thousands waiting to begin the celebration. Netanyahu said that he felt that the Chassidim were getting antsy waiting for the Rebbe to complete his conversation.

69 Chabad.org/1632160. Video at www.youtube.com/watch?v=iTFtxoPGDog.

70 Retold to the author a few days after Yom Kippur 2011 by Ambassador Avner in a phone interview.

71 Rabbi Simcha Bunim Alter (1898-1992), also known as the Lev Simcha after the works he authored, was the fifth Rebbe of the Chassidic dynasty of Ger, a position he held from 1977 until 1992.

72 Rabbi Elazar Menachem Man Shach (1899-2001) was a leading Lithuanian-born Haredi rabbi in Israel. Not only did Rabbi Shach conflict with Chassidic leadership, starting in 1984, he endorsed the Sephardi Party, Shas, led by Rabbi Ovadia Yosef. Later, in 1988, Rabbi Shach sharply criticized Rabbi Ovadia Yosef and said that "Sephardim are not yet ready for leadership positions." Subsequently, he founded the Degel HaTorah political party representing Lithuanian non-Chassidic Ashkenazi Jews in the Israeli Knesset.

73 Chabad never joined Agudath Israel.

74 Literally, "those who are opposed." This name came about due to their opposition to the Chassidic Movement.

75 "Gaon" means "great scholar." Rabbi Eliyahu (1720-1797) of Vilna was renowned for his brilliance and scholarship. He strongly opposed the new Chassidic Movement. Rabbi Schneur Zalman, the founder of Chabad, also renowned for his scholarship, attempted to meet with Rabbi Eliyahu to diffuse the conflict. Rabbi Joseph Soloveitchik told Rabbi Leibel Schapiro, dean of the Rabbinical College of Miami, that there is a family tradition that the Vilna Gaon said, "If he would have opened the door and permitted Rabbi Schneur Zalman to enter, he would have given in to the Chassidim."

76 This began with a conference called by the Russian government in 1843 that they both attended, to examine the issue of Jewish education.

77 Even though the Fifth Rebbe, Rabbi Sholom DovBer, participated in the first conference of Agudah, he chose not to join Agudath Israel.

78 Rabbi Shach rekindled the ideological conflict between Chassidim and Misnagdim that had simmered for many years. He was harshly critical of the Rebbe on

many subjects. He rejected his policy of inclusiveness of all Jews, and he supported Israel relinquishing territory, a position the Rebbe felt would endanger Israeli security.

79 Rabbi Shach earned the enmity of many Israelis for his harsh criticism of its secular culture. He widened the social schisms in Israel by focusing, in a harsh way, on their shortfalls of observance. In 1990, he made a strident speech that was harshly critical of members of kibbutzim, questioning their links to their forbears. This prompted an unprecedented public response from the Rebbe, who stated at a farbrengen afterward, "Every Jew is part of G-d," and "anyone who berates any Jew is touching the apple of G-d's eye." See www.jta.org/1990/04/04/archive/lubavitcher-rebbe-speaks-out-against-rabbi-schachs-message.

80 The election was reflective of a deeper debate between the segments of the religious community about coming to terms with the modern State of Israel. Rabbi Shach was arguing that the best way to ensure survival of the religious community was to separate itself from that society, the approach of insularity. This concept had been championed by the Chazon Ish, Rabbi Avrohom Yeshaya Karelitz (1878-1953), the leader of the Lithuanian yeshiva community. He told Prime Minister David Ben Gurion in a famous meeting in 1952, using a talmudic parable of two wagons, one full and one empty, that the secular need to move to the side for the Orthodox. Still, the tone of Rabbi Karelitz was far less confrontational than that of Rabbi Shach, and he maintained respectful relations with Chassidim. The Rebbe's advocated approach was one of "engagement": maintain your lifestyle and values but contribute to the broader society.

81 Eliezer Mizrachi was one of two Knesset members who, at the last minute, switched their votes to ensure Shamir would be prime minister. He says it was their own decision. "We did not have specific instructions from the Rebbe in New York. Rabbi Yehuda Krinsky issued a statement that the Rebbe gave no instructions to the members of the Knesset to support one candidate or another.

82 Chabad.org/525272. Rabbi Zev Segal tells of his discussion with the Rebbe on his advice, Chabad.org/574972.

83 R.M. Rudeniski, "The General and the Rebbe," *She'arim*, August 29, 1968.

84 Chassidim have always believed that Rebbes have been endowed with special insight. There are hundreds of stories telling of advice and insight the Rebbe gave to countless individuals that are difficult to explain unless you accept the traditional Jewish belief that tzadikim (righteous individuals) are bestowed from above with Ruach Hakodesh, holy insight.

85 My second encounter with Sharon was in 1994. As head of the opposition Likud he came to Orange County to raise money for Jewish communities in Judea and

Samaria. A thousand came to hear him at an Irvine hotel. I was the MC. During the introduction I retold the story of Sharon visiting Kfar Chabad in 1969 and his commitment to put on tefilin. He turned to me and said in Hebrew, "It never happened." I held my ground and said it did. This drama played out in front of the massive crowd. The next day we met again and he told me, "I called Lily [his wife]; the story is true." My original intention in telling the story was to remind him of his promise from decades earlier. Clearly I had touched a chord.

86 Every Friday, yeshiva students would travel to Tel Aviv to conduct a Tefilin Campaign. Students would set up stands in public areas and ask Jews to don tefilin. When we heard that General Sharon was putting on tefilin, and encouraging his uncle, it inspired us to intensify our efforts.

87 Gilad Sharon, *Sharon: The Life of a Leader* (New York: Harper Collins, 2011).

88 The effort was underwritten by Australian diamond magnate, Joseph Gutnick. He had been instructed by the Rebbe years earlier to ensure that Israel did not make concessions and territorial withdrawals that would endanger Israeli security.

89 This itself is quite unprecedented; rarely does Chabad headquarters make public statements.

90 Netanyahu's first term as prime minister proved to be a disappointment in many ways. Clearly he lacked the experience necessary to govern effectively.

91 Chabad did organize a prayer service at the Western Wall, attended by over 700,000 Israelis, to beseech Heaven to avert the decree. However, the movement did not sponsor demonstrations.

92 israelforeignaffairs.com/pm-sharon-met-delegation-chabad-hassidic-leaders/.

93 Jews from Bukhara in central Asia are Sephardi.

94 Many yeshivas in Haredi communities in Israel tend to be either predominantly Sephardi or Ashkenazi. Part of the reason for this is differences in customs. There has been strong criticism of some Lithuanian yeshivas and seminaries for women who have discriminated against students of Sephardi background.

95 Shas is the religious party of Sephardi Jews. United Torah Judaism, historically Agudah, is Ashkenazi. Shas is led by the Moetzet Chachmei HaTorah (Council of Wise Torah Leaders) made up of exclusively Sephardi rabbis. United Torah Judaism is led by the Moetzet Gedolei HaTorah (Council of Great Torah Scholars), exclusively Ashkenazi rabbis. These councils guide the policies of each party.

96 The stationery of the yeshiva in Kfar Chabad stated on its header, "Olei Russia, and Olei Teiman" (immigrants from Russia and Yemen). For decades there has been an active effort in the Chabad community to enroll students from Sephardi backgrounds in Chabad schools and yeshivas.

97 There was a young woman from a prominent Chabad family who had been teaching in a Chabad school in Israel's south. She took an interest in a young

Chabad rabbinical student who came from Morocco, who was also teaching there. Instead of approaching him directly, she told her father, as per Chassidic custom, that she was interested in a shidduch (a matrimonial match) with this young man and asked her father to suggest the idea to the young man's family. Her father rejected the idea, saying he did not want a Sephardi son-in-law. She persisted, and finally he agreed with his daughter's suggestion that they ask the Rebbe for advice. The Rebbe responded, "In our community there is no difference between Ashkenazim and Sephardim." Following the Rebbe's answer, the father agreed and the match was proposed. The young man indicated that she is a fine young woman but he was not interested. He eventually married another Ashkenazi girl.

98 Orthodox historian Rabbi Berel Wein, whose views are reflective of the Haredi community, wrote an insightful article about the unwillingness of the Haredi community to come to terms with recent historical events:

> Dealing with the modern state of Israel is an even more vexing issue for much of Orthodoxy. The creation of the Jewish state, mainly by secular and nonobservant Jews and by political and military means, was not part of the traditional Jewish view of how the Land of Israel would again fall under Jewish rule.
>
> Since it occurred in the "wrong" way and was being led by the "wrong" people, this too shook the mindset of much of Orthodoxy. One of the great and holy leaders of Orthodox society in Israel stated in 1950 that the state could not last more than fifteen years. Well, it is obvious that in that assessment he was mistaken.
>
> But again, it is too painful to admit he was mistaken and therefore the whole attitude of much of the Orthodox world is one of denial of the fact that the state exists, prospers, and is in fact the world's largest supporter of Torah and the traditional Jewish religious lifestyle. It is too painful to admit that our past mindset regarding the state of Israel is no longer relevant. But as long as large sections of Orthodoxy continue to live in an imaginary past and deny the realities of the present, it will remain impossible to properly address such issues as army or national service, core curriculums of essential general knowledge for all religious schools, and entering the workforce and decreasing the debilitating poverty and dysfunction of so many families.
>
> The solutions are difficult and they cannot be dictated or legislated no matter how popular such steps may appear to be. But the change of mindset to the present must certainly and eventually occur. Jews have always been up to this task and I am confident we will be able to do so now as well.

The Jewish Press, May 1, 2014, www.jewishpress.com/indepth/opinions/why-many-orthodox-jews-cant-face-up-to-history.

99 The Rebbe, as outlined in chapter nine, felt in most cases the demonstrations for Soviet Jewry were counterproductive. Telushkin also examines this issue in his book *Rebbe*, Chap. 20.

100 Galut, the diasporic state of the Jewish people, is not just a physical removal of the Jews from their land, but a spiritual one. In ancient times, in particular during the First Temple prophetic era, there were unique revelations from above. While the present State of Israel may offer many benefits to the Jewish people, it is not the promise of redemption that is taught in Judaism. One can recognize the miracles that occurred in the wars, the spiritual and cultural richness of Jews living in their land, and at the same time yearn for a truer redemption through the Messiah, as promised in Judaism. The Haredi community says, "We see no signs of the redemption." Historically, Zionist leaders were hostile to Jewish tradition, so the Haredim reject involvement with the secular State. The religious Zionists view the State as the first stage of redemption. Chabad finds this perspective at odds with classic Jewish sources (Maimonides, Mishneh Torah, Laws of Kings) that outline the redemptive process. Still, Chabad struggles, as Halevi says, between the tension of a modern State that is not utopian, and the Jewish aspiration of a final redemption through the Messiah.

101 Colelchabad.org.

102 In 2014, Prime Minister Netanyahu welcomed a group of bar mitzvah boys to his office, www.youtube.com/watch?v=EoEhG1BdKJU.

103 Rabbi Wolf was an outstanding administrator. He came from a German Jewish family. As a teen, he met the famous Chassid, Reb Itche the Masmid, and began his path to Chabad. In 1939, he visited the Sixth Rebbe, Rabbi Yosef Yitzchak, in Otvotsk, Poland, for the holiday season, and extended his visit for two additional months. In yechidus (a private meeting), the Sixth Rebbe blessed his move to Eretz Israel that year. Wolf was instrumental in building up the central institutions of Chabad and was a scholar. The Rebbe praised him more than once publicly. For a history of the yeshivas and a biography of Wolf, see Zushe Wolf, *Neros Leha'ir* (Lod: Yeshiva Tomchei Temimim, 1996).

104 The Rebbe encouraged Chabad families to relocate and live together with the immigrants, many of them Sephardi Jews from Bukhara in central Asia. At the same time, Chabad helped create communal institutions that enshrined customs unique to these immigrants.

105 Yosef Yitzchak Aharonov grew up in Canada. He worked with Rabbi Yisroel Leibov, who headed the Chabad Youth Organization that operated the network

of community Chabad Centers in Israel. Upon Leibov's passing, he assumed
the leadership, pushing Chabad to new heights.

106 Known as Tzach, Tzeirei Agudat Chabad.

107 A comparison of beliefs and observance of American and Israeli Jews reveals
striking differences. Israelis are far more traditional, with over half believing
in the Divine revelation at Mount Sinai and the following of basic precepts of
kashrut, candle lighting, etc. In the US, the percentage of Jews keeping kosher at
home is just 22 percent. For more information, see the Guttman Institute Survey conducted by the Israel Democracy Institute (far from an Orthodox group),
avichai.org/wp-content/uploads/2012/01/A-Portrait-of-Israeli-Jews-Abstract.pdf,
and the 2013 Pew Study of American Jewry, www.pewforum.org/2013/10/01/
jewish-american-beliefs-attitudes-culture-survey/.

108 Interview with the author.

109 Interview with the author.

110 In Israel, there is no separation of religion and state. Municipalities, as well as
other government ministries, fund schools, synagogues, and cultural, religious,
and social programs.

111 Interview with the author.

112 Interview with the author.

113 Interview with the author

114 Interview with the author.

115 Interview with the author.

116 *Sefer Hevron* (Jerusalem: Keter, 1970).

117 Interview with the author.

118 Interview with the author.

119 Interview with the author.

120 In 2013, President Peres sent video greetings to Chabad shluchim (https://
vimeo.com/78279842). Mr. Peres met the Rebbe on a couple of occasions. See
Telushkin, *Rebbe*, 132 and http://myencounterblog.com/?p=1240.

CHAPTER TWELVE: THE YESHIVA

1 Now known as Kennedy Airport.

2 Wilson would be elected prime minister in October of 1964. For a video of
the visit to Moscow, www.britishpathe.com/video/harold-wilson-meets-mr-k/
query/harold+wilson.

3 Elchonon Lipsh, an activist with Agudath Israel in London, had succeeded in
placing the issue on Wilson's agenda.

4 Even though Khrushchev agreed in the summer, it would take months to
arrange the exit permits to leave Russia.

5   The Russian government allowed a limited number of exit permits for the purpose of family reunification. This proved a successful method of helping small groups leave Russia during Communist times.

6   See chap. 4, "The Great Escape."

7   Later in his life, Reb Mendel's farbrengens were replete with stories from Siberia that he would mold into powerful moral lessons in life. Two brief examples: One time, the inmates were planning an escape; the prison was lightly guarded, and getting out was not too difficult. The plan was aborted when the inmates realized they had no map of the region and would be lost in remote Siberia. This, said Reb Mendel, was a lesson to all of us. The Torah is the map for a Jew to live his life; without it, he would be lost. His most well-known story was that of the tight-rope walker. He had been imprisoned and promised the inmates that on the day of his release, he would celebrate by walking on the rope. When the day came, they strung a rope between two trees and he dazzled everyone with his feat. Mendel asked him what the trick was, and he said, "Never to look down." From that, Mendel told us that a Jew should always be looking above to G-d for help and direction, and if so, he will not falter.

8   Interview with the author.

9   That bond was rich in spiritual overtones. In 1948, during his imprisonment, Reb Mendel was at a point of deep personal despair, so he resolved, as Chassidic tradition teaches, to share his angst with the Rebbe, then Rabbi Yosef Yitzchak, who was in New York. In his mind, he imagined telling the Rebbe of his terrible situation. A week later, in Paris, a letter arrived from the Rebbe addressed to Reb Mendel. In the letter, the Rebbe said "he had received his message." When the letter was delivered, Reb Mendel's wife thought he had somehow escaped Russia, since the letter was addressed to Mendel as a response to his message. It was unimaginable that he had sent a letter from Russia to the Rebbe in New York. Fifteen years later, when Reb Mendel finally arrived in London, he was given the Rebbe's letter. See his grandson's description of this remarkable incident: Chabad.org/2243609.

10   In Jewish tradition, when a person receives the honor to read the Torah during services, he is called up by his name and that of his father. It is very rare that a person is named after his father. Traditionally, Jews of European descent do not name children after living relatives.

11   Literally it means to "be alone." Chassidim would prepare themselves spiritually for private meetings with the Rebbe. It would be a time to set life goals, and for spiritual reflection. A Chassid would write his questions on a paper and hand it to the Rebbe as he entered his office. The Rebbe would read it

and comment, and the Chassid would respond. For a five-year-old to have a personal yechidus was extraordinary.

12   Despite the difficulties of close to a decade in Soviet prison camps, Reb Mendel lived a long life. He was born in 1905 and passed away in 1992. He is interred in London near the graves of his mother, wife, and daughter.

13   The Mussar Movement was primarily centered in the Lithuanian-style yeshivas as a response to the growing secularization of many Jews. Rabbi Yisroel Salanter (1810-1883), an outstanding scholar, popularized the teaching of Mussar.

14   According to Orthodox historian, Berel Wein, there were three reasons for the opposition to the study of Mussar in yeshivas: 1. the focus on ethics was considered a distraction from the pure study of Torah, 2. it was considered divisive, and 3. it was considered modern. www.jewishhistory.org/dispute-dissemination/.

15   Hebrew for "order," this is a common Hebrew term used to refer to a time for study, like a period in an American High School.

16   The Jewish Enlightenment, or Haskalah, as it was known in Hebrew, originated in Germany in the eighteenth and nineteenth centuries, and afterward spread to Russia, advocating greater integration into European society and increasing education in secular studies, Hebrew language, and Jewish history. The Haskalah marked the beginning of the wider engagement of European Jews with the secular world. There was much conflict between the secular leaders of the Haskalah, who believed that Jews should lessen their observance, and the rabbinic leaders who advocated Torah study and tradition. Haskalah leaders tried to orchestrate government involvement to force change in the educational institutions in the Jewish community and to undermine the role of the rabbis as community leaders.

17   Moshe Tzvi Segal (1904-1985) moved to then-Palestine as a young man. In 1930, Segal blew the shofar at the end of Yom Kippur services at the Western Wall in defiance of the British police, and was arrested. The chief rabbi, Tzvi Yehuda Kook, told the British he would not break his Yom Kippur fast until Segal was freed. Late that night, Segal was released by the British police. Later he played an active role in the Irgun. He was a confidant of many of Israel's early leaders. He conducted the wedding for future Prime Minister Yitzchak Shamir. After the Six-Day War, he was the first Jew to move into the Jewish quarter in the Old City of Jerusalem. I encountered him for the first time in 1968, living on the second floor of the Chabad synagogue, the Tzemach Tzedek Shul. It was the only synagogue not destroyed by the Jordanians in their occupation between 1948 and 1967. The synagogue had been severely damaged and Segal lived amongst the rubble to encourage others to reclaim the old city after its liberation. Eventually, he moved to an apartment on the next street. After the Six-Day War, Israeli President Zalman Shazar offered Segal a ticket to visit the

Rebbe for the holiday season in New York. The Rebbe told Segal he had set a precedent of blowing the shofar at the Kotel (the Western Wall) and should not abdicate that responsibility. Segal remained in Israel for the holidays and did not take up Shazar's offer. I am eternally grateful for his personal kindness during the period I was a yeshiva student in Israel.

18   Until the establishment of the yeshiva in Lubavitch, most yeshiva students would eat their daily meals with various families in the local communities. The system was called *essen teg* (Yiddish for "eat a day") and was a way for the communities to help support Jewish learning. But in the new yeshiva in Lubavitch, students would eat in the Yeshiva. This innovation created less distraction from learning since students did not have to leave the yeshiva every day for meals.

19   There are a few larger yeshivas, such as Beth Medrash Govoha in Lakewood, NJ, Mir Yeshiva, and Brisk in Jerusalem, each with a few thousand students.

20   Zal is a Russian word for hall. The original study hall of the yeshiva in the town of Lubavitch was called the Zal. Even after the yeshiva was relocated in Israel and other countries, the custom of calling it a Zal continued.

21   This approach, of attaching yourself to a Rebbe whose sanctity and guidance would assist you in your service of G-d, was taught by many of the Chassidic groups in Poland. The Polish model was like riding in a wagon and the Rebbe was pulling you along. The Chabad model was that you drove your own wagon, the Rebbe as the signpost giving you direction.

22   The tradition of scholarship of the yeshivas of Lithuania is carried on today in the great centers of Jewish learning in Israel and the United States, the larger ones in the US being Beth Medrash Govoha in Lakewood, Ner Yisroel in Baltimore, Telz in Cleveland, Chofetz Chaim, Chaim Berlin, Mir, and Torah Vodaath in New York. In Israel, they include Ponovitch, Brisk, Mir, Slabodka, and others. These yeshivas are still referred to as Lithuanian or, in Yiddish, Litvish, according to the country where the educational philosophy originated.

23   Tanya, Chabad.org/1058319.

24   The seeding in diverse geographic areas of these great scholars was orchestrated by the Sixth Rebbe, Rabbi Yosef Yitzchak. He instructed them to settle in various countries, creating nuclei of leadership in the evolving Jewish communities in the postwar era.

25   Chassidim call the Fifth Rebbe, Rabbi Sholom DovBer, the Maimonides of Chassidic philosophy. He is renowned for his outstanding eloquent discourses that explain in depth the concepts of Chassidic philosophy. Till today, they are a central part of the curriculum in Chabad yeshivas.

26   Many of these mashpi'im, in their youth, met elderly Chassidim who had known the earlier Rebbes and had heard stories in *their* youth from Chassidim who had met the Alter Rebbe and other Chassidic giants.

27 For a detailed biography, see Shlomo Chaim Kesselman, *Mashpiah* (Israel: privately published, 2013, Hebrew).

28 Interview with the author.

29 A ritual bath. Many have the custom to immerse in the mikvah as a preparation for prayer or for Jewish holidays.

30 The farbrengens were spiritually rich experiences that would go on through the night. Not only did Chabad students attend – on Chassidic holidays students of Lithuanian yeshivas would come to get a taste of Chassidus.

31 See chap. 9, "Dancing with the KGB." Reb Mendel had inspired the establishment of Ezras Achim that sent food packages to Russian Jews.

32 The Rebbe also told him to get involved in the institutions of Chabad in Israel. Clearly, the Rebbe wanted Reb Mendel to shake up the Chabad establishment in Israel, which, at the time, had limited horizons. Understandably, Mendel's stirring of the pot disturbed some of those in leadership positions. They would have preferred that Reb Mendel stay in the yeshiva and not mix in other issues.

33 Interview with the author.

34 Known in Yiddish as the Muma Sara, she was one of the coordinators of the Great Escape. She died in a Soviet prison. See chap. 4, "The Great Escape."

35 He had six children; four passed away young in Russia, his daughter lost her life in a tragic accident in England. He has one surviving son, who lives today in Brooklyn.

36 Tefilin are leather boxes that contain the basic covenantal prayer, the Shema. One of the precepts of the Torah is to lay tefilin daily during the Morning Prayer service. Attached to the boxes are leather straps; one is placed on the head, the other on the hand opposite the heart. They represent the subjugation of heart and mind, intellect and emotion, to G-d. Jewish tradition teaches that tefilin create the spiritual merit of protecting the Jewish people in a time of conflict. Prior to the Six-Day War the Rebbe launched the Tefilin Campaign so Jews around the world could perform a mitzvah to invoke spiritual blessing on Israeli soldiers.

37 In the late sixties, as I was passing through the train on the way to Tel Aviv asking people to don tefilin, I encountered the famed Israeli archaeologist, Yigal Yadin. He showed me pictures of ancient tefilin thousands of years old uncovered in his digs and happily agreed to do the mitzvah.

38 This in contrast to Reb Shlomo Chaim who never joined the yeshiva students on Fridays. This was at a time when Reb Mendel was about seventy years of age.

39 The farbrengen in Yiddish with Reb Mendel: www.youtube.com/watch?v=xmcKvsEuuXk.

40 This transition had already begun in New York where the students in 770 were much more in sync with the change in direction the Rebbe had started in the fifties. Much of the Chassidic community was still focused on its own spiritual

pursuits, in particular in Israel, which was distant from New York at a time when travel was still more rare and expensive.

41 This program permitted children to be released from school for an hour a week for religious studies. In 1943, Chabad started the program in New York. Yeshiva students would leave their studies on Wednesday afternoons to teach the children. This program was started by the Rebbe as part of Merkos. It was he who encouraged the students to teach.

42 This project still continues today. Some six hundred students are sent annually to Jewish communities worldwide, www.chabad.org/blogs/rovingrabbis.htm.

43 In Israel, there is major tension about the drafting of yeshiva students. Chabad students receive deferments and serve after completing their studies, while other yeshivas shun any interaction with the army. The fact that Chabad students visit soldiers is a major difference and crucial in bridging the societal divide.

44 Interview with the author. Today Rabbi Minkowitz is the principle of Beth Rivkah of Montreal.

45 It was not the first time yeshiva students had been sent to other communities. In 1912, the Fifth Rebbe Rabbi Sholom DovBer sent eleven students and Rabbi Shlomo Zalman Havlin to Hebron in Turkish-controlled Palestine from Lubavitch in Russia to establish Yeshiva Torat Emet. With the onset of World War I, it moved to Jerusalem and continues to exist till today. For a more detailed history of this mission and Havlin, see Shlomo Zalman Havlin, *Hamashpiah, Toldot Hayeshuv Bechevron* (Jerusalem: privately published, Hebrew).

46 Interview with the author. Today Rabbi Altein is the head shliach in Winnipeg, Canada.

47 They were yeshiva students from a variety of backgrounds. One of them was Chaim Gutnick, who studied in Telz in Poland but came from a Chabad family. He wrote to the Sixth Rebbe, Rabbi Yosef Yitzchak, who replied that Divine Providence had brought them to Australia and they should remain to build Jewish life. Almost all the students left for the US other than Gutnick, who became one of Australia's leading rabbis.

48 After the war, there would be an influx of tens of thousands of immigrants who would bolster Australian Jewry. The more traditional from Poland tended to move to Melbourne, the less traditional from Germany and other countries, to Sydney.

49 Interview of Rabbi Chaim Gutnick with the author.

50 Years later, a Lithuanian-style kolel was established in Melbourne. Ironically, when it opened, its leaders announced that "finally Torah scholarship was coming to Melbourne."

51 He had spent fifteen years as a student at the yeshiva in Lubavitch. He immigrated to the United States, where he was the rabbi of a Chabad synagogue in Brooklyn. He served as a secretary for the Sixth Rebbe and was one of the Chassidic elders who strongly encouraged the Ramash (Rabbi Menachem M. Schneerson) to accept the position of Rebbe.

52 The party celebrated the engagement of my daughter to Yossi, the son of Soly and Beverly Spigler of Melbourne.

53 The Rebbe advocated Talmud study for women, something that historically was not practiced in the Orthodox Jewish community.

54 Schools exist in Brooklyn, Miami, Los Angeles, Montreal, Australia, France, England, South America, and Israel.

55 Many students from the US choose to spend a year in Israel where Chabad has seminaries that cater to English-speaking overseas students.

56 Beth Rivkah is recognized as a four-year college that grants degrees.

57 By learning Torah and fulfilling mitzvoth, Jewish mysticism teaches, we create a "dwelling place for G-d in the physical world." This is based on the Biblical verse, Ex. 25:8: "Make for me a sanctuary and I will dwell in them." The Talmud explains that "in them" means that each person can be a place where holiness is the dominant influence.

58 The name of the yeshiva is Tomchei Temimim – supporters of those who are pure or innocent. It is common to use the title "Hatamim" to refer to a person who is an alumnus of the Yeshiva Tomchei Temimim. It is customary to use it as part of a title, Harav Hatamim – the Rabbi, the Tamim. To be a student of the yeshiva is considered such a great honor, the term is also used as a title before a person's name on a tombstone.

59 The talk given on that Simchat Torah is considered until today the mission statement of the yeshiva.

60 According to Jewish Law, if a husband is missing in action, there must be proof of death before a wife can remarry. In the confusion of battle, the fate of a soldier could be unclear. To forestall this problem, the soldiers in the time of King David would write a bill of divorce that would come into effect after a period of time. If the husband would not return from battle, then the women would be free to remarry.

61 Those who learned in Lubavitch became role models for many in the postwar era.

62 He called a meeting on the day of his arrival to organize the opening of the yeshiva. Within a few days, it was functioning.

63 On Yud Shevat, the yartziet of the Sixth Rebbe, Rabbi Yosef Yitzchak, and the anniversary of the Rebbe assuming the position of leadership, there is an annual

conference of students of Tomchei Temimim. Over 2,500 students from around the world attend the event held in Brooklyn.

CHAPTER THIRTEEN: BALANCING ON THE HIGH WIRE

1   Interview with the author.

2   Interview with the author. Rabbi Wolf is the director of Spiritgrow in Melbourne, Australia.

3   For many years, prominent rabbinical scholars in the Lithuanian yeshiva community, and other Chassidic groups, criticized Chabad's outreach for a variety of reasons. One of the claims was that shluchim were putting their children at risk by raising them in communities with few religious Jewish children and with exposure to outside values. With time, it became clear that this accusation was baseless. Decades after Chabad, the Lithuanian yeshivas began to embrace outreach, though taking a different model from Chabad. Instead of sending a couple to a community for life, two or three couples are sent to a locale together. Those who go to smaller communities or universities tend to stay for a short stint and leave when their children require day school education. At times, they succeed in creating local schools. Others move to communities to establish a kolel, a center of Jewish learning. This approach creates a mini-yeshiva community that replicates the insular yeshiva communities that they originate from. Many kolels have uplifted communities with Jewish learning. Still, they tend not to engage the broader community and have limited influence beyond their immediate circle. This is a continuation of their approach of "fortress Judaism," outlined in chapter 2.

4   In certain segments of the US Orthodox Jewish community, there is a serious issue with what is called Dropout, or Off the Derech (the way), or children who cease to be Shomer Shabbat (Shabbat-observant). According to the Orthodox Union, the dropout rate in the Modern Orthodox community may reach as high as 25 percent. "Why are our teens going Off the Derech?" Rabbi Steve Pruzansky asks: www.ou.org/life/parenting/why-are-our-teens-going-off-derech-steven-pruzansky/. No studies have been done about the dropout rate among the Haredim (traditional Orthodox community). Apparently, however, it is far lower than among the Modern Orthodox. Among shluchim in California, the percentage of grown children who are not Shabbat-observant is less than 1 percent. If California is reflective of national trends, then it seems safe to say that the cohort of shluchim children have the lowest dropout rate in the Orthodox Jewish community in the United States.

5   Bill Lobdell, "Thriving sect sends emissaries abroad," *Los Angeles Times*, September 11, 2006, articles.latimes.com/2006/sep/11/local/me-chabad11.

6   There is a difference between the curriculum and education offered in yeshivas and in day schools. Yeshivas tend to have almost all religious children and put a greater emphasis on Jewish learning. Children as young as ten or eleven begin to study Talmud. Orthodox day schools usually serve a more diverse population and organize their programs with a great emphasis on secular education.

7   Study after study has proved the key to transmitting Jewish values to the next generation is Jewish education. For Chabad families, the first choice is a yeshiva-style program with an intense Jewish academic program.

8   Rabbi Mendel Loschak and his sister Sterna have both married and returned to Santa Barbara as shluchim. Their children are being spared the heartache of being sent away at a young age. They attend the online school.

9   The Shluchim Office was founded in 1987 to be a resource center for shluchim. It initiated many projects such as camp for children, publications, and services to help local Chabad Centers.

10   It was his great-grandfather, Berel, who laughed at the KGB, telling them, "My kids have left Russia." See chap. 9, "Dancing with the KGB."

11   The Hebrew-language online school serves the needs of children in Russia and the Far East.

12   Interview with the author.

13   Interview with the author.

14   At the middle of the twentieth century, there were many synagogues in the US, some formally affiliated with national Orthodox groups like the one in Omaha, that had mixed seating. Orthodox rabbis in such congregations waged valiant battles to keep them within tradition, at times succeeding and at times having the congregations move outside the Orthodox orbit and affiliate with the Conservative Movement. Rabbi Nadoff served the community nobly for over a quarter of a century. Rabbi Katzman was told by Rabbi Hodakov that an essential part of his responsibility in Omaha was to make every effort to strengthen the local Orthodox synagogue.

15   Rachel Wizenfeld, "Community Day Schools: Are They an Option?" *Jewish Action*, November 2013. Some community schools make an effort to be respectful of parents who have strong religious values. Others do not.

16   I faced this dilemma when I was in Miami. My daughter, Chani, was just three; it was a long commute to Miami Beach to the Chabad School for such a young child. The local community school's Judaic teachers were secular Israelis with different values from the ones we wanted to instill in our children. The Rebbe advised to "send my daughter there if the class had a religious teacher." Fortunately, Dror Zadok, the school's principal, worked hard to accommodate me. We arranged a young religious woman to come to the community to teach in

the school. My daughter stayed there until she was old enough to commute to Miami Beach.

17 Interview with the author.

18 They are the great-grandchildren of Rabbi Shalom Posner and Risia Kazarnovsky, who, as a young girl, waited for the Rebbe on the dock in 1940.

19 Mussia tells the story of when her great-great-grandmother escorted her great-grandfather, Aaron Kazarnovsky, to the yeshiva in Lubavitch a century ago. She accompanied her son, saying years later, "A child you don't drop off, you bring him to yeshiva."

20 See chap. 5, "The Front Row."

21 Even people outside of the Chabad community understand the concept that the children are also shluchim. When my youngest son was just eleven, he joined me for a meeting at the offices of Agudath Israel in Manhattan. Rabbi Moshe Sherer, the legendary leader of Agudah, came to greet us. He turned to my son, saying, "You are a shliach," clearly attempting to inspire him and to let him know that that he is special.

22 For community members, the children of shluchim provide remarkable inspiration. They are greatly intrigued by the Chassidic children whom they watch grow up in their communities, who retain the values of their parents. The kids growing up in these communities are comfortable with Jews of all backgrounds and levels of observance.

23 www.shluchim.org/main/inside_v2.asp?id=37853.

24 Today she is a Rebbitzen and second-generation shlucha in San Francisco, a mother of six and principal of the local Chabad school.

25 Interview with the author.

26 The Code of Jewish Law, Halacha, as defined in the *Shulchan Aruch*, touches on all aspects of human experience. Some of the laws focus on religious obligations, others on business affairs, and personal relationships. Religious Jews see Jewish Law as binding and a guideline for life.

27 Pinchas Stolper et al., *The Mechitza: Maintaining the Sanctity of the Synagogue* (New York: Union of Orthodox Jewish Congregations, 1988).

28 This was a contentious issue, dividing congregations between members who wanted to retain tradition and others who argued in support of "family seating," according to which men and women would sit together. Some thought this innovation would attract more members; others felt that separate seating was not equal. Some synagogues ended up in litigation between members. One case reached the Michigan Supreme Court, which ruled in favor of the mechitza. See Baruch Litvin, *The Sanctity of the Synagogue: The Case for Mechitzah – Separation Between Men and Women in the Synagogue – Based on Jewish Law, History and Philosophy* (New York: Ktav, 1987). In recent decades, we have witnessed a

reverse trend. Synagogues that removed mechitzas decades ago have reinstated them. Others that have had mechitzas that were very low have raised them to acceptable standards.

29 According to Rabbi Moshe Feinstein (the preeminent Jewish legal authority in the twentieth century in the US), a mechitza should be sixty-six inches high. Most communities follow this ruling. The European custom of balconies for women is not very popular in the US. In many Chabad Centers, the mechitza is down the middle of the sanctuary with the bimah (the stand for reading the Torah) in the middle of the men's section. This model upholds the Halachic standards and provides women with a sense of involvement in the service.

30 Samuel Freedman, *Jew vs. Jew: The Struggle for the Soul of American Jewry* (New York: Simon & Shuster, 2007).

31 The Rebbe gave no reason for his opposition to bingo at the time. It seems to me that there was a deeper moral issue. It is not befitting a Jewish institution to benefit from games of chance like bingo, particularly when those losing money tend to be people of limited economic means.

32 Interview with the author.

33 Smicha, Hebrew for "rabbinical ordination," is a certificate that attests to the completion of study of Talmud and testing on the core sections of the Code of Jewish Law in the areas of kashrut and Shabbat observance. A Rav does additional years of extensive study in broad areas of Jewish civil law, judicial practice, and rabbinical responsa. Candidates for rabbinical judges will intern with an existing rabbinical judge for at least a year to learn, firsthand, the application of law to real-life situations.

34 A rabbinical judge helps the local shliach navigate difficult issues in operating an institution within the parameters of Halacha. The challenge in Chabad Centers is that they serve a diverse community, many of whose members are not fully observant. They may have unique questions that demand much consideration. The role of the rabbinical judge is to examine the issue and apply the proper legal precedent with compassion. For instance, in my Chabad Center, it was suggested we do a roast as a community event. I felt this was inappropriate because Judaism has strong legal rulings against speaking disparagingly about another person, and such an event could be considered a form of Loshon Hara (speaking disparagingly about another person).

35 According to classical Jewish belief, both the Written Torah (the first five books of the Bible) and the Oral Torah (which was eventually embodied in the Talmud) were Divine gifts to the Jewish people at Mount Sinai. The Talmud explains in depth the detailed cases of Jewish Law and the Biblical source for each law. It differentiates between laws that were part of the Oral Tradition, that was

Divinely given at Sinai, and rabbinic legislation and decrees that evolved due to unique communal challenges.

36 The central pillar of Judaism is that in 1313 BCE, Jews received the Torah at Mount Sinai from G-d. This event was witnessed by 600,000 men between the ages of twenty and sixty, a total of over 2,500,000 people. The Kuzari, the classic of Jewish philosophy authored by Rabbi Yehuda Halevi in 1140, argues that it is not an issue of belief, but of historical fact. In this way, Judaism differs dramatically from other religious beliefs, in which one person convinced many others of the revelation he claimed to have had. Judaism is based on the eye-witness testimony of millions that the Torah was given at Sinai. They told their children, who told the next generation, who then transmitted this to the next generation. In modern times, a series of major devastating events: the Holocaust, Communist oppression, the rise of the Haskalah, created a doubt in this central narrative. Coupled with these factors was the breakdown in Jewish education. Today, most modern Jews cannot read a classic Jewish text, nor do they have a proficiency in Jewish theology and philosophy. This superficial understanding of Judaism causes many to doubt the veracity of the core historical narrative of Judaism, that the Torah was given to the Jewish people at Mount Sinai.

37 Security procedures in a Chabad Center in a suburban American city, Europe, and the Far East are vastly different. Security is taken seriously and not discussed publicly; that itself could be a breach and create danger.

38 Interview with the author.

39 Demilitarized zone.

40 Many observant Jews are careful to consume only milk that is supervised from the time of milking to ensure that milk from non-kosher animals is not used. This is called Chalav Yisroel.

41 Interview with the author.

42 Rabbi Grunblatt is under the impression that the Rebbe monitored the first call he made. As a rule, the Rebbe did not speak to individuals on the phone. He would relay messages via his secretaries.

43 Rabbi Hodakov also told Grunblatt, "The Rebbe is sending a loan to help you, that you will return when your own conditions improve."

44 As the Chabad role grows in Jewish communities, there is greater pressure to be involved in public-policy issues. Shluchim need to stay true to their mission of the spiritual and physical welfare of communities. As important as some of the political and public-policy issues are, it is not the role of Chabad to be engaged in them.

45 Shluchim Achdus (unity among shluchim) sponsors over a hundred forums for rabbis and rebbitzens. There are forums for different states, countries, languages, and areas of interest.

46   In 1974, Rabbi Raichek turned up in Florida where I was starting campus programs at the University of Miami. During the summer, he asked me to travel around the state to check up on the mikvahs. I discovered an old mikvah buried under the floor of a hundred-year-old synagogue in Saint Augustine, one that needed repair in Jacksonville, and in Tampa, a city with a large Jewish population, no mikvah at all. Raichek sprang to work arranging improvements to the Jacksonville mikvah, and prodding an effort to build one in Tampa. This style of behind-the-scenes quiet actions was his hallmark. His English was spoken with a strong accent, but you knew that here was a person who was real, and you listened.

47   Eighteen thousand Jewish refugees spent the war years in Shanghai under Japanese occupation, including yeshiva students who had escaped from Poland. They reopened their yeshivas in Shanghai. The larger was the Mirrer Yeshiva, the smaller, Chabad.

48   The Rebbe believed in strengthening education in the United States. He strongly advocated the establishment of the Federal Department of Education. Education Day USA was proclaimed first by President Jimmy Carter in conjunction with the Rebbe's birthday in 1978. Subsequent presidential proclamations in honor of Education Day USA were issued by Presidents Ronald Reagan, George H.W. Bush, Bill Clinton, George W. Bush, and Barack Obama.

49   Interview with the author.

50   Video of the delegation of rabbis with President Reagan in the Oval Office, Chabad.org/142889. Rabbi Raichek is seen as the second rabbi shaking the hand of President Reagan. During the presentation of the menorah, Rabbi Raichek is the second rabbi standing to the president's left as Rabbi Shemtov speaks.

CHAPTER FOURTEEN: A TALE OF TWO CITIES

1   Nachalat Har Chabad was founded in 1969 as a residential neighborhood in the city of Kiryat Malachi in Israel's south. Many of the immigrants were from the Sephardi communities of Bukhara in the Asian region of Southern Russia. Institutions were created that followed the unique traditions of Jews from that region.

2   As a yeshiva student, Zalman helped his sister, a shlucha in Kazan, the capital of the Russian republic of Tatarstan. He had also spent time in Milan helping Rabbi Lazar's father in his community.

3   Based on interviews with Zalman and Miri by the author in Novosibirsk conducted in October 2013.

4   I flew on the same airline, Siberian S7, from Moscow to Novosibirsk, and was amazed to discover the quality of the kosher meals, catered by a Moscow

company, far exceeded kosher meals on international flights between the US and Israel.

5   www.bh.org.il/database-article.aspx?48717.

6   Now called Kuybyshev.

7   Many of these retiring soldiers were Cantonistim, child soldiers drafted by the czar. Starting in 1827, the czar drafted Jewish boys as young as twelve for twenty-five years of military service. Children were forced into military schools where there was strong pressure to convert. The draft of new recruits was ended in 1856. After finishing their service the soldiers were permitted to live anywhere in Russia. Some remained in Siberia, creating Jewish communities.

8   *Jewish Telegraphic Agency* Report, March 9, 1999, www.jta.org/1999/03/09/life-religion/features/vandals-destroy-siberian-shul-as-anti-semitism-rises-in-region; *The Moscow Times*, March 10, 1999, www.themoscowtimes.com/news/article/vandals-wreck-synagogue-in-siberia/279579.html.

9   Interview with the author.

10 Most Chabad couples spend a year, sometimes two, in a kolel (an advanced yeshiva) after marriage. They focus on post-graduate rabbinical studies, while adjusting to life as a young married couple. Students are provided with a stipend. Many Americans attend the kolel in Crown Heights. There are kolels in Israel, Australia, and other countries. For more on kolels, see Herbert Bomzer, *The Kolel in America* (New York: Shengold, 1985).

11 Statistics provided by Chabad.org/Chabad Media Center, Brooklyn.

12 Young couples in New York with little understanding of local demographics can be very assertive in their suggestions that Chabad should open a center. The local shliach may feel it's untenable, or may not be overly impressed with the couple making the suggestion. At times, the head of state may feel that there is potential for an additional center and the local shliach feels that local demographics make it unsustainable. The success of Chabad growth has become one of the challenges of the future. There has been a series of initiatives to create new opportunities in shlichus. On a national level, funding has been made available for new programs for shluchim, such as youth programs, adult education, campus, and young professionals.

13 States and countries have a head shliach who is responsible for all Chabad Centers in his region. Even though most local Chabad Centers have a large degree of autonomy and financial independence, the head shliach sets policy for the state, has the final word in establishing new centers, appointing shluchim, and intervenes when there is a breach of Chabad policy.

14 Interview with the author.

15 Chabad did eventually open in Riverside. Rabbi Shmuel Fuss and his wife Tzippy have established a thriving center. More at Jewishriverside.com. In 2015, Chabad opened in Ojai.

16 See chap. 10, "Out of the Shadows."

17 Ohr Avner is the educational system with schools throughout the Former Soviet Union supported by Lev Leviev. It also has schools in Israel.

18 In other Siberian cities that had Jewish communities from the pre-Communist era, there were large synagogues. In many cities, they had been returned to the local Jewish community after the fall of the Soviet Union. In Novosibirsk, a proper synagogue had never been built. There was only a small building used for services that was sold in the seventies.

19 Miri says the letters included death threats.

20 In recent years, the Russian Jewish Congress has a new leadership and is strongly cooperative with the Federation of Jewish Communities in Russia.

21 For more on background and history of the Jewish community of Siberia and Novosibirsk see Betsy Gidwitz Reports, May 2009, www.betsygidwitzreports.com/pdfs/report30.pdf.

22 The JDC (Joint Distribution Committee) operates the Hessed, a center to assist Jewish families of limited financial means, in Novosibirsk.

23 Jewish Journal, August 23, 2011, www.jewishjournal.com/religion/article/rabbinic_students_bring_rite_of_passage_to_siberian_teens_20110823/.

24 forward.com/articles/182980/siberias-biggest-ever-jcc-set-to-open/, Chabad.org/2324888.

25 sanclemente.patch.com/groups/around-town/p/rabbi-slavin-thriving-sc-jewish-community-started-wit3f15e89d38.

26 There are four thousand couples, a total of over eight thousand rabbis and rebbitzens, plus their families.

27 *The New York Times* reporter, Ari Goldman, who reported for many years about Chabad, told Charlie Rose on Public Television the week the Rebbe passed away that he was skeptical about Chabad's future. See Sue Fishkoff, *The Rebbe's Army* (New York: Schocken Books, 2003). For one of the many articles that appeared at the time, see Beth Silver, "Hasidic Sect Fears For Future," *Chicago Tribune*, June 17, 1994, articles.chicagotribune.com/1994-06-17/news/9406170076_1_rebbe-rabbi-menachem-schneerson-worldwide-lubavitch-movement.

28 Interview with the author.

29 In the Chabad community, it is common to refer to the Hebrew date to mark a significant day on the calendar. To Chassidim, Gimmel Tammuz, the third day of the Jewish month of Tammuz (usually in early July or late June), is parlance for the Rebbe's passing. The day of the passing of the Sixth Rebbe, 10 Shevat, is commonly referred to as Yud Shevat. Other significant events are referred to in the same way. The anniversary of the freeing of the founder of Chabad from czarist prison is commonly known as Yud Tes Kislev, the nineteenth of Kislev, the day on the Hebrew month of Kislev that he was released.

30 The Rebbitzen passed away, according to the Jewish lunar calendar, on the twenty-second of the month of Shevat 5748, February 10, 1988. She is interred next to her mother and grandmother, adjacent to the graves of her father and, eventually, her husband, at Montefiore Cemetery in Queens. Two years later, the Kinus Hashluchos (Conference of Chabad Women Emissaries) was inaugurated in conjunction with the Rebbitzen's yartziet. It is held annually in New York with some three thousand women attending.

31 The Rebbitzen Chaya Mushka was the second of the three daughters of the Sixth Rebbe, Rabbi Yosef Yitzchak Schneersohn. She was born in Babinovitch, near the town of Lubavitch, in 1901 and named according to the suggestion of her grandfather, the Fifth Rebbe, Rabbi Sholom DovBer, after Chaya Mushka, the wife of the Third Rebbe. In the face of the German invasion of Russia in 1915, she fled the town of Lubavitch with her family, which had been home to the Lubavitcher Rebbes for over a century. Her grandfather relocated the family to Rostov-on-Don. She cared for her ailing grandfather, the Fifth Rebbe, who passed away in 1920 in Rostov. She assisted her father, Rabbi Yosef Yitzchak, who became Rebbe, in the operations of the Jewish underground network in Russia, in Rostov, and later in Leningrad, where they moved in 1924. She accompanied her father to exile in Kostroma after his death sentence was suspended in 1927. She left Russia later that year with her family. In 1928 she married in Warsaw her distant cousin Rabbi Menachem Mendel Schneerson. The young couple moved to Berlin and then to Paris in 1933. During this time, she took university courses. She fled Europe with her husband in 1941 via Vichy, France and Portugal, arriving in the US in July of 1941. In the US, she was reunited with her parents and older sister. Her younger sister, Shaina, was killed in Treblinka, together with her husband, Rabbi Menachem Horenstein. She prevailed on her husband to accept the position of Rebbe saying, otherwise, the work of her father would come to naught. During the years of his leadership she stood steadfastly at his side, not taking a major public role.

32 Interview with the author.

33 Jews traditionally "sit Shivah" (mourning) for a week after the passing of a relative.

34 Krinsky says that he realized the writing of the will and later actions of the Rebbe, such as cleaning out years of documents and books from his office, were ominous. He says, "It brought me a strong sense of melancholy." He also understood that the responsibility of becoming executor would place him in a situation that might not make him the most popular person in the community. He was acutely distressed when, in January of 1992, in a talk, the Rebbe referred to the medical challenges that the Sixth Rebbe faced, saying, "The Rebbe, my father-in-law, was paralyzed, and the doctors told the family that you have no

idea of the pain when a leader loses the power of speech." Krinsky says that moment "rang so many bells, it was a feeling of emptiness." Some six weeks later, the Rebbe suffered a stroke that made it impossible for him to speak.

35   Chabad.org/111019.

36   Agudas Chassidei Chabad (Association of Chabad Chassidim), known as Aguch, was established in 1924 in the US as the umbrella organization of the Chabad Movement. The Sixth Rebbe, Rabbi Yosef Yitzchak, assumed the presidency in 1940 upon his arrival in the US, and the Rebbe after his father-in-law's passing.

37   Established in 1943, it is the organizational entity that administrates the international network of Chabad institutions.

38   Established in 1941 in the US, it is the social-services arm of Chabad. It administrates the Machne Israel Development Fund.

39   The house the Rebbe lived in is owned by the educational arm of Chabad, Merkos L'inyonei Chinuch, and served as his home until his passing.

40   Binyamin Lipkin writes in great detail about this transition period. See Binyamin Lipkin, *Cheshbono Shel Olam* (Lod: Machon Ha-Sefer, 2000).

41   The Rebbe instructed Rabbi Krinsky to send a letter to all shluchim that in cases of institutional disputes they should turn to Aguch or Vaad Rabbonei Lubavitch to be resolved. There are two permanent rabbinical courts that resolve issues among shluchim and issues having to do with Chabad institutions: in New York, Vaad Rabbonei Lubavitch (Central Committee of Chabad Lubavitch Rabbis of the United States and Canada) and, in Israel, the Beit Din Rabbonei Chabad (the Chabad Rabbinical Court). The courts handle a wide variety of disagreements, according to Rabbi Nochem Kaplan, director of the New York-based court, ranging from employer-employee issues, to institutional ones. Cases can be initiated by either side. The New York court handles cases from many other countries besides the U.S. and Canada. Kaplan says the vast majority of cases are settled quietly and quickly. The Rebbe was always emphatic that Halacha (Jewish Law) must be the ultimate arbitrator in the policies and activities of Chabad. The court attempts to bring about compromise, otherwise the cases are decided by a tribunal of three rabbis. Many cases are settled before the actual trial date by efforts of mediation. There are also shluchim who specialize in mediation, helping to resolve conflicts in Chabad institutions and between shluchim.

42   The project had started nine months before the Rebbitzen's passing. There are thirty volumes of letters in Hebrew and Yiddish arranged according to years and indexed by name and topic. The volumes constitute remarkable historic source material about the public issues and private issues the Rebbe dealt with.

43   Many Chassidim would travel to be with the Rebbe for the holidays of Rosh Hashanah, Yom Kippur, Sukkot, and Simchat Torah. The holidays in 770 were deeply inspirational and spiritually uplifting.

44   Berakhot 63a.

45   There was one moment when the Rebbe was unusually direct on this issue. In March of 1988 the Rebbe related a story about the third Rebbe, Rabbi Menachem Mendel, who told his son and eventual successor, Rabbi Shmuel, about the talmudic passage: "Let us make an accounting of this world" (Bava Batra 78b). The third Rebbe explained to his son that the Talmud is alluding to the reward that awaits the righteous in the next world after their passing. Rabbi Shmuel cried after hearing his father make this statement.

The Rebbe noted that the reason we know the story is to provide us with a lesson for our lives. He went on to explain that "if there is such a consequence, Chassidim should seek the advice of a rabbi who is an expert in Jewish Law, in the areas of health, a caring physician, and that each community should have a committee of rabbis." For more on this see Lipkin, chap. 3, Hisvaadus 5748, vol. 4. The Rebbe's reference to the story caused great distress amongst the listeners.

46   The talk took place on 28 Nissan, 5751. The Rebbe stated, "Because of the unique emphasis on the Redemption during this time, an astonishing question arises: how is it possible that despite all these factors, Moshiach has not yet come? This is beyond all possible comprehension. It is also beyond comprehension that when ten (and many times ten) Jews gather together at a time that is appropriate for the Redemption to come, they do not raise a clamor great enough to cause Moshiach to come immediately. They are, Heaven forbid, able to accept the possibility that Moshiach will not arrive tonight, and even that he will not arrive tomorrow, or on the day after tomorrow, Heaven forbid. Even when people cry out, "Ad mosai (until when will we remain in exile)?" they do so only because they were told to. If they had sincere intent and earnest desire, and cried out in truth, Moshiach would surely have come already. What more can I do to motivate the entire Jewish people to clamor and cry out, and thus actually bring about the coming of Moshiach? All that has been done until now has been to no avail, for we are still in exile; moreover, we are in an inner exile in regard to our own service of G-d. All I can possibly do is to give the matter over to you. Now, do everything you can to bring Moshiach, here and now, immediately."

47   The requirements, according to Jewish Law, for identifying Moshiach are outlined by Maimonides in the Mishneh Torah/Code of Jewish Law, Laws of Kings, Chapter 11. This is the primary Jewish source for this issue. Maimonides lists the conditions for Moshiach and states that it's a two-step process. A person can be considered Moshiach if he: is a descendant of King David, is a scholar and righteous person, brings the Jewish people back to observance, and fights the "wars of Hashem." If he completes these tasks, according to Maimonides, he may be presumed to be Moshiach. Maimonides states, however, that he

is confirmed as Moshiach only after he fulfills additional tasks: he must then rebuild the Temple on its original site, gather the Jewish exiles from around the world, and return them to the Land of Israel. Once he accomplishes this, Maimonides says, "he is surely Moshiach."

48 See Hersh Goldwurm, ed., *ArtScroll Talmud*, Sanhedrin 98a-5, n. 57, (New York: Mesorah, 1995), citing classic sources such as the Chatam Sofer and Rabbi Chaim Vital. It states, "In every generation since the destruction of the Temple there has lived a person of outstanding piety, ready to be invested with the spirit of Messiah when the time for redemption comes."

The Rebbe was a direct descendant of the Maharal of Prague, Rabbi Judah Loew (1520-1609), who traced his lineage to King David. He had launched a worldwide effort to bring Jews back to tradition, and he was renowned for his scholarship and piety. All of these elements caused many to express the view, as was done by the students of the great sages in talmudic times, that their Rebbe was the prime candidate for Moshiach.

49 The Talmud, in Sanhedrin 98b, tells of the students of various rabbis who speculated that their teachers were Moshiach.

50 Critics outside of Chabad failed to note this crucial theological nuance. Chassidim, even those declaring the Rebbe as Moshiach, were not actually saying he was the definitive Moshiach, which would also indicate that the long-heralded era of Moshiach had actually arrived. After all, Moshiach cannot be identified until he has been revealed and built the Third Temple. Rather, they were saying that he had the qualities to be considered a candidate.

51 In the same talk, the Rebbe criticized those who "imagine they know what needs to be done." He ended the talk by saying, "May G-d spare me having to repeat this directive again." See *Toras Menachem 5745* Vol. 1, p. 465. The Rebbe was much more direct in a private response in May 1984 to Rabbi Shalom Wolpo, who publicly advocated this view in Israel. In an unprecedented harsh tone, the Rebbe wrote to Wolpo: "Now I warn him [Wolpo] that he must stop speaking, writing, and how much more so, publicizing, especially in print, anything pertaining to Moshiach, whether in his own name, under an assumed name, through an intermediary, or the like, with whatever kuntz (trick) he may concoct, and in whatever format or manner that may be. And if, chas v'sholom (G-d forbid), he goes ahead and does anything in this regard, he should know clearly that this is a specific and general war against me."

52 Retold to me by Rabbi Yehuda Yeruslavsky, secretary of the Chabad Rabbinical Court in Israel. The Rabbinical Court is the final authority over Chabad institutions in Israel. One late night, Yeruslavsky received a call from the Rebbe's chief of staff, Rabbi Hodakov, asking the Rabbinical Court to collect the flyers and

destroy them. Yeruslavsky had not been aware of these flyers and protested his innocence. Then he heard the voice of the Rebbe, who had been monitoring the call, expressing great anguish over their publication.

53   Due to the severity of the Rebbe's stroke, when he was only able to express himself in the affirmative or negative, it was important to ensure that nuanced questions were explored in detail in a yes/no fashion. Two months after the Rebbe had the stroke, I had a debate with a close friend in New York. He supported the idea of identifying the Rebbe as a candidate for Moshiach; I thought this was a distortion of the Rebbe's teachings. I decided to write the Rebbe a detailed letter outlining the issue. Due to the stroke, the Rebbe could not speak, so I decided to write the inquiry as a series of yes/no questions. The purpose was to focus on the issue in a very specific fashion. The Rebbe answered in the affirmative to a series of questions having to do with whether we, as shluchim, should see, as one of our prime missions, teaching about the concept of Moshiach to the public, as outlined in Maimonides and other classic sources. To the question about whether we should promote a specific person as a candidate for Moshiach – the argument that my New York friend and others had made – the Rebbe answered in the negative, clearly rejecting the philosophy being advocated by those who were claiming the Rebbe should be identified as a potential candidate for Moshiach. The next day, Rabbi Groner, the Rebbe's secretary, called me and asked if he could share the Rebbe's response with the public. I gave him permission, and he announced the Rebbe's responses to my questions publicly in the main sanctuary in 770. The answer was also published in the weekly magazine *Kfar Chabad*.

54   This quote appears in *Hayom Yom* (26 Sivan), a book of teachings for each day of the year, compiled by the Rebbe.

55   Those who argued that the Rebbe could be a candidate for Moshiach, posthumously, were basing their assertions on the Talmud. The Talmud (Sanhedrin 98b) discusses the identity of Moshiach and states: "If he is among the living, he is someone like Rabbeinu Hakodosh (referring to Rabbi Yehuda Hanassi, the compiler of the Mishnah). If he is among the dead, he is someone like Daniel the greatly beloved (referring to Daniel the prophet)." See Goldwurm, *ArtScroll Talmud*, Sanhedrin 98b-4, n. 42, that quotes many classic sources, including Abarbanel, Maharsha, and Maimonides, justifying the viewpoint that Moshiach can come from the dead. What is clear from this section of Talmud and the explanation of the classic commentaries is that Moshiach can either be a living person or one who has passed away. This is strikingly different from the Christian doctrine that Moshiach came and died. According to Jewish teachings, one of the tasks of Moshiach is the resurrection of the dead. In this scenario, a person who was resurrected would become Moshiach, not that he was the Messiah, failed his task, and then passed away.

56 Every year at the shluchim convention, a picture is taken in front of 770 of the convention participants. A year after the Rebbe's passing, a small group surprised everyone at the last minute by unfurling a banner promoting the Rebbe as a potential Moshiach. The committee overseeing the convention embargoed the picture. The next year, security staff stood by to ensure this would not recur. When the same small group of activists attempted to put up their sign, it was immediately taken down. The picture was then taken. Afterward, a small group stood for a second picture with the sign. The following year, their numbers had dwindled to just a few, when they took a second picture. By the third year, they did not even try to have a picture with the sign.

57 Prior to Gimmel Tammuz, there was a clear line of authority from the Rebbe to these organizations that was deeply respected by shluchim and Chassidim. Afterward, there would be a greater need to create communal consensus.

58 Prior to the Rebbe's passing, the Shluchim Office that helped with programming assistance had been established. It operates the English online school for children of shluchim, and other important projects. The new effort broadened those horizons considerably.

59 Chabad.org/782349.

60 Long time Haaretz editor Doron Rosenbloom paid him the ultimate compliment when he compared his powers of persuasion and linguistics to legendary Israeli Ambassador Abba Eban.

61 Tabacinic has since pulled in Israeli-Russian philanthropist Yitzchak Mirilashvili, Michigan donor Alan Zekelman, and others, in addition to his brother-in-law who remains involved, too.

62 They also partner with hundreds of large and small content creators outside of their own group.

63 In addition to the stellar holiday content, before each major Jewish holiday the AP directs travelers to browse the site's aggregated Chabad data to find Chabad programs worldwide.

64 *The New York Times*' "If it Involves Jews, Chabad's Tiny but Far-Flung News Organization Is on it," www.nytimes.com/2008/12/27/nyregion/27chabad.html is one of many news organizations lauding the site.

65 To assist those with challenges in the areas of drug, alcohol, or other addictions.

66 Interview with the author.

67 These statistics reflect only visitors to the eight flagship sites in English and other languages. They do not include visitors to the fifteen hundred affiliate sites.

68 These provide a fascinating window into the concerns of the Jewish people worldwide in the twenty-first century.

69 ejewishphilanthropy.com/why-do-we-love-chabad-org-let-us-count-613-ways.

70 Local centers pay fees to help defray the costs of their website.

71   Chabad.org also provides an e-mail with weekly e-mail newsletters and templates for many events. This is an invaluable tool for shluchim who send out weekly e-mails that include content from Chabad.org, linked to individual web pages, and can be customized with local news, events, and pictures.

72   *Jewish Action*, Summer 2014, published by the Orthodox Union.

73   Over two hundred volumes of the Rebbe's teachings remain a living legacy of knowledge.

74   The unsung heroes are the educators in the Chabad schools, the roshei yeshiva, and the mashpi'im who lead the network of yeshivas and seminaries. They infuse the next generation with true, meaningful Chassidic values.

75   Herbert Weiner, *Nine and a Half Mystics* (New York: Collier Books, 1969).

76   Today there are Radomsk congregations in Israel, the United States, and Montreal. The number of followers is tiny compared to the years in pre-war Poland.

77   There is one Chassidic group, Breslov, that exists primarily in Israel and a few cities in other countries. It has continued for two centuries since the passing in 1810 of its founder, Rabbi Nachman of Breslov, the grandson of Rabbi Israel Baal Shem Tov.

78   There is a constant stream of new material being published by Vaad Hanochos B'lahak and JEM.

79   Most Jews in the first half of the twentieth century who affiliated with Orthodox synagogues were traditional, but not fully Shabbat-observant. At the time, they self-identified as Orthodox even if they were not fully observant. Today, only Shabbat-observant Jews self-identify as Orthodox. Comparing the statistics of decades ago to today is like comparing apples to oranges. Researchers, who themselves tend not to be religious, fail to understand this nuance, that the very concept of who is Orthodox has changed. Often, they claim in studies that Orthodoxy has weakened in comparison to decades ago. Proper research would reveal two vital facts: First, the number of those who are members of Orthodox synagogues has dropped from the mid-twentieth century. Second, the number of Jews who are actually observant has risen significantly in recent decades. As Rabbi Yitzchak Adlerstein of Los Angeles says, "Studies lie but pizza shops don't lie," alluding to the fact that there far more kosher restaurants today than ever, which is a strong indicator of more observant Jews.

80   In the immediate postwar era there was a precipitous drop in Orthodox affiliation. At the same time, these were the boom years of the non-Orthodox movements.

81   In recent years we have seen a significant rise in religiously observant Jews. The Conservative Movement was once home to 40 percent of American Jews; today only 11 percent are actual members.

82 The Pew Study of Jewish Americans of 2013 made a major blunder in reporting affiliation to Chabad. It used a process of denominational self-identification to measure Jewish affiliation. This approach is outmoded in the new post-denominational environment in the modern Jewish community. Most Jews attending Chabad do not see themselves as Chabad Chassidim or Orthodox, since they are not Shabbat-observant. If asked, they do not self-identify as Chabad. The study should have asked specific questions to evaluate the number of Jews involved with Chabad. Clearly, if they would have crafted questions designed to ask about Chabad involvement – instead of the simplistic approach of denominational self-identification – they would have revealed a major new trend in modern Jewish life. At a meeting of leaders of major Jewish groups I heard the PEW study's author admit that in reference to Chabad the study could have been done differently. More at Times of Israel, blogs.timesofisrael.com/rescind-the-pew-r/and the Jewish Week, www.thejewishweek.com/editorial-opinion/opinion/pew-missed-newest-trend-jewish-life.

83 Writing in *Commentary* in April of 2013 ("The Outreach Revolution"), Dr. Jack Wertheimer asserts that the outreach efforts of Chabad and others is having an impact on non-orthodox congregations, noting: "Leading members of Conservative and Reform synagogues attend Chabad educational programs or community kolel study sessions and then return to their home congregations, probably as better-informed Jews."

84 jewishmiami.org/studyresults/. This survey took a different approach to the issue of Chabad from the flawed Pew Survey. Instead of just using the antiquated methodology of denominational self-identification, the survey asked questions about involvement with Chabad in the past year.

85 The majority of those active in Chabad were not Orthodox.

86 Jews becoming involved in Chabad are being prompted to increase their observance. Chabad does not change Jewish practice or ideology. People know that they cannot pressure Chabad rabbis to modify ritual; still they vote with their feet and checkbooks. Those attending are constantly encouraged to increase their observance. That choice of attending Chabad will eventually move them closer to Jewish tradition.

87 While there are theological divisions between Reform and Conservative, the liberal movements are growing closer on many levels. In smaller Jewish communities, Reform and Conservative congregations are merging as they have challenges of membership and finances. There are some congregations, like Temple Beth El in Aliso Viejo, California, that maintain affiliation with both movements and have both Reform and Conservative services. Their positions on many public-policy issues are narrowing. In areas of women's role in religious life, gay rights, and numerous political issues, their positions tend to be

identical or very close. Still, it's doubtful that these movements, each with a vast national infrastructure, will formally merge on a national level.

88   According to the directory of the Conservative Movement, www.uscj.org/Aboutus/FindaKehilla.aspx.

89   synagogue3000.org/files/factreport.pdf.

90   According to the directory of the Reform Movement, congregations.urj.org/display.cfm?state=ALL#US.

91   Steven M. Cohen, "The Shrinking Jewish Middle and What to Do about It," www.cajm.net/uploaded/file/fd.CAJM_2014_Cohen_Paper.pdf.

92   mosaicmagazine.com/essay/2014/11/the-pew-survey-reanalyzed/.

93   The numbers who self-identify – who feel an affinity but are not formal members – is higher, 33 percent saying they identify with Reform and 18 percent with Conservative.

94   Chabad.org/centers.

95   In these countries the vast majority of synagogues are Orthodox; Reform and Conservative are very small.

96   The number varies by country. In Hungary, Chabad rabbis are 85 percent; Holland, 80 percent; Austria, 50 percent; Italy, 50 percent; Britain, 25 percent; France, 25 percent.

97   There are two models of leadership in Europe. One is more open, transparent, and democratic; in those countries, such as France, Germany, and Holland, Chabad plays a larger communal role. In some other countries, in particular smaller ones like Poland, Lithuania, Norway, and the Czech Republic, there has been greater opposition to Chabad. As a rule these communities are in the hands of a small group, or at times one family, that controls most of the communal assets and government-provided restitution money. They are resisting a greater role of Chabad for two reasons: First, they are unwilling to provide for greater public accountability or transparency of communal assets. Second, they prefer to have rabbis who are not independent and are beholden to them.

98   We are already seeing this in many ways. Years ago, most major Jewish organizations had fundraising banquets that were not kosher; today this is a rarity.

99   At a recent General Assembly, the annual conference of the Jewish Federations of North America, I learned how true this was in a humorous fashion. I attended with my associate Rabbi Avrohom Berkowitz of Chabad headquarters in New York. At a reception, he approached person after person, looked at their name tags and then said, "Can you give regards to Rabbi so-and-so," identifying the name of the shliach in their city. In almost every case the person responded, "Of course, we are good friends."

100 At the same time, Chabad shluchim are going to have to learn to create stronger partnerships with local communal institutions. Some time ago, Dennis Prager

told a group of shluchim that their changing role in the Jewish communities is a new paradigm, saying, "It's easy being on the outside; when you become part of the establishment, it's more challenging in certain ways."

101 Lipkin, *Cheshbono Shel Olam.*

102 The library of Agudas Chassidei Chabad located in the building adjacent to 770 has over 300,000 books and thousands of precious manuscripts. It is one of the most significant Jewish collections in the world. It is open to the public as a research library. The library presents annual exhibits of its collection. More at chabadlibrary.org.

103 Posthumously, the Reshimos (Notations), a series of hand-written journals, was discovered in the Rebbe's desk. They were composed between 1928 and 1950. There are scholarly notations on Jewish philosophy, Talmud, mysticism, and practice. They include extensive notes of intimate conversations with his father-in-law, the Sixth Rebbe, Rabbi Yosef Yitzchak, in the thirties, about issues that were passed on from Rebbe to Rebbe. The Reshimos reveal the Rebbe's intimate involvement in many communal affairs in Europe during that period. Seven volumes of these Notations were eventually published by Kehot Publication Society, Brooklyn, New York.

104 In the years after the publication of the Sefer Hashluchim, there was an inside joke. Shluchim labeled the book "Sefer Hashidduchim" (the Book of Matches). When young Chabad men or women would be suggested for dating to marry, invariably the family would look at the Sefer Hashluchim to see who was being suggested, and their family.

105 A year earlier at the farbrengen of the shluchim convention in 1989, the Rebbe proposed that a memento album of that year's conference be published, including pictures of the conference participants and their families. At the next conference in 1990, the one-volume album was published. The new project was much more ambitious, including all shluchim from around the world and teachers in Chabad educational institutions in New York and Israel. It would consist of four volumes, with over 1,300 pages of pictures, with an index of those appearing in the volumes and a list of Chabad institutions.

106 This was a motif of the Rebbe to encourage action immediately. Joseph Telushkin writes about this at length in his book, *Rebbe.* See chap. 10.

107 Interview with the author. For more details see *Chassidisher Derher*, Issue 21, Tammuz (Summer) 5774/2014, published by Vaad Talmidei Hatmimim Haolami, Brooklyn.

108 Mesibos Shabbos were Shabbat clubs started by Chabad in the forties for children. It was one of the Rebbe's early initiatives.

109 Many pictures included extended families, even grandchildren. Every name was listed, even those of babies.

110 Isser New, who was so deeply inspired by the Sefer Hashluchim, married the daughter of Rabbi Yosef Friedman, the book's editor.

111 The Rebbe had not accepted earlier suggestions of publications in the Rebbitzen's memory by Chabad's official publishing arm, Kehot.

112 After the service was completed, the Rebbe sat on a low stool, as is the tradition for mourners. I was standing directly opposite him, just a few feet away. The large crowds that had gathered outside began to file past the Rebbe and offer the traditional words of condolence. Surprisingly, the Rebbe began to speak. His theme was that the mitzvah of consoling a mourner is part of the concept of Ahavat Yisrael, love and concern for another. He said we should return to our communities and turn the tragedy of the loss of the Rebbitzen into a stimulus to reach out to others. The Rebbe spoke for just a few minutes. Afterward, I remained standing directly opposite the Rebbe, watching as Chassidim and others filed by, each hastily uttering the traditional greeting said to a mourner, "May G-d console you among all the mourners of Zion and Jerusalem." For a half hour, I watched, standing opposite the Rebbe, then I, too, joined the line, offering my condolences, and headed back to California. I had been deeply touched by the intimacy we felt that day in the Rebbe's home. It was the shluchim whom he wanted with him at this time of great personal loss. The words of the Rebbe were profoundly inspiring. He had seized this moment of private bereavement to inspire us to reach out to others with care and compassion.

113 Publications of the Rebbe's work published posthumously, for instance, the Reshimos, have been added to the desk.

AFTERWORD: THE OATH

1 Organized by American Friends of Lubavitch in Washington.

2 The nation's highest civilian award given by Congress. Never before had a rabbi been honored, and this was the first time the award had been given posthumously.

3 Gardiner Harris, "Fulfilling a Promise, Jewish Center in India Reopens After Terror Attack in 2008," *The New York Times*, August 26, 2014.

The fonts used in this book are from the Garamond family.

The Toby Press publishes fine writing
on subjects of Israel and Jewish interest.
For more information, visit www.tobypress.com.